LISZT IN GERMANY

1840–1845

FRANZ LISZT STUDIES SERIES No. 2

Franz Liszt, Ritter des Ordens pour le mérite.

A portrait of Liszt from Leipzig's *Illustrirte Zeitung*
(27 September 1845)

LISZT IN GERMANY
1840–1845

A Study In Sources, Documents, And
The History Of Reception

by

MICHAEL SAFFLE

FRANZ LISZT STUDIES SERIES No. 2

PENDRAGON PRESS
STUYVESANT, NY

Other titles in the Franz Liszt Studies Series (formerly the **American Liszt Society Studies Series**)

No. 1 *Liszt, Carolyne, and the Vatican Documents: The Story of a Thwarted Marriage* by Alan Walker with Gabriele Erasmi (1991) ISBN 0-945193-09-2

No. 3 *The Symphonic Poems of Franz Liszt* by Keith T. Johns (1995) ISBN 0-945193-40-8

No. 4 *Living With Liszt: From the Diary of a Student, 1882–1884, by Carl Lachmund*, Introduced, edited and annotated by Alan Walker (1994) ISBN 0-945193-56-4

No. 5 *Analecta Lisztiana I: Proceedings of the International "Liszt and His World" Conference held at Virgina Polytechnic Institute and State University, 20–23 May 1993*, edited by Michael Saffle (1995)

No. 6 *Analecta Lisztiana II: New Perspectives on Liszt and His Music* edited by James Deaville and Michael Saffle

The author gratefully acknowledges permission to quote from Paul Theroux's essay "The Past Recaptured." Reprinted from *Sunrise with Seamonsters: Travels and Discoveries, 1964–1984.* Copyright 1985 by Cape Cod Scriveners Company. Reprinted by permission of Houghton Mifflin Company, Boston.

Library of Congress Cataloging-in-Publication Data

Saffle, Michael Benton, 1946
  Liszt in Germany, 1840–1845 / by Michael Saffle. p. cm. --
    (The Franz Liszt studies series ; no. 2)
  Includes bibliographical references and index.
  ISBN 0-945193-39-4
      1. Liszt, Franz, 1811–1886--Performances--Germany. 2.
  Liszt, Franz, 1811–1886--Journeys--Germany. 3. Germany--
  Description and travel. 4. Music--Germany--19th century--
  History and criticism.
  I. Title. II. Series.
  ML410.L7S24   1994
  780'.92--dc20
  [B]   4-29736
                                   CIP
                                    N

This book is dedicated to

LUDWIG FINSCHER & HELMUT HUCKE

scholars • colleagues • friends

without whose encouragement and help

it could never have been written

and

to the memory of

DORTE SCHWERDT SCHULTER

(1932-1965)

whose good-luck piece seems to have brought me

all the blessings I ever could have wished for.

CONTENTS

ILLUSTRATIONS

A portrait of Liszt from Leipzig's *Illustrirte Zeitung*
(27 September 1845)
is reproduced as the frontispiece

Maps

— *Both maps drawn by Patricia Mahoney* —

Plates (facsimile reproductions)

Tables

PREFACE

This book is a work both of history and of the history of reception. Its purpose, therefore, is two-fold: to elucidate Liszt's German performances and activities between 1840-1845 through the use of primary sources (especially sources published in the contemporary press), and to evaluate the influence of Liszt's reputation in Vormärz Germany on his reputation overall.

This book has been written neither to praise Liszt nor to condemn him; I hope the days of simple-minded Liszt deification and denigration are over. Instead, I have made every effort to present a complete and "objective" account of Liszt's German sojourns, and of some of their ramifications for his reputation and career. Like Paul Theroux, I am interested not merely in the foreground (i.e., in Liszt himself as a "Romantic hero"), but in the background: in details that invite us to look closer at the Liszt phenomenon and help us understand what can and cannot be understood today about it. I have to confess, though, that I have not been able to consult all surviving sources of information, and I am confident other scholars will turn up documents and performances I have overlooked.

Portions of this volume have been adapted from published studies of mine identified below. Other portions have been adapted from two additional studies: a paper about Liszt and national issues presented at the "Liszt und die Nationalitäten" conference held in Eisenstadt last March, and an article about little-known Liszt performances and tours scheduled to appear later this year in the *Liszt Society Journal* of Great Britain.

Nineteenth-century German newspapers and magazines were not always proofread carefully, and their authors and editors sometimes used words and phrases no longer fashionable today. Furthermore, a few Vormärz periodicals printed all proper names in italics or boldface type. Throughout this book, however, proper names in quotations appear in regular type unless italics were used originally to indicate emphasis. A few eccentricities and errors have been indicated by the word "sic" [in square brackets], but others have been left alone, and minor irregularities have simply been ignored. Furthermore, I have used German names for all cities and towns except "Cologne" (i.e., Köln), Munich (i.e., München), and Nuremberg (i.e., Nürnberg).

The assistance I have received from colleagues, friends, and family members during the writing of this history of Liszt's German concert tours deserves my acknowledgment. Ben Arnold, Kim and Robin Colvill, Geraldine Keeling, Charles Suttoni, and especially James Deaville read portions of what follows and helped me improve my work. James Deaville, Johan Lagerfelt, William Little, Günther Massenkeil, Pauline Pocknell, Michael Short, J. Rigbie Turner, Alan Walker, and David Witten supplied documentary information. Hans Krämer shared with me his knowledge of Liszt's visit to Ludwigsburg in 1843, while Steven Saunders provided me with photocopies of otherwise unknown documents pertaining to Liszt's Leipzig and Dresden performances of March 1840. Pauline Pocknell and Angelia Graf helped me decipher microform copies of the Liszt-Lefebvre letters described below in Chapter II. Stephanie Miya assisted with the preparation of the index, and my wife Sue helped me proofread several portions of the final draft.

The following libraries and archives—which, unless otherwise indicated, are located in Germany—also helped me with my researches: the Stadtarchiv of Aachen; the Rat des Kreises Altenburg; the Library of the University of Amsterdam (Netherlands); the Stadt- und Stiftsarchiv of Aschaffenburg; the Staats- und Stadtbibliothek of Augsburg; the Verbandsgemeindeverwaltung of Bad Ems; the Stadtarchiv of Baden-Baden; the Staatsbibliothek zu Berlin [formerly the Bibliothek Preussischer Kulturbesitz of West Berlin, and the Deutsche Staatsbibliothek of East Berlin], and the Staatsarchiv Preussischer Kulturbesitz, all of Berlin; the Stadtarchiv und Landesgeschichtliche Bibliothek of Bielefeld; the National Széchényi Library and the Liszt Ferenc Memorial Museum and Research Centre, both of Budapest (Hungary); the Staatsarchiv Coburg and the Kultur- und Schulamt der Stadt Coburg; the Royal Library of Copenhagen (Denmark); the Library of the Musicological Seminar and the Norddhrein-Westfälisches Staatsarchiv, both of Detmold; the Fürstlich Fürstenbergische Hofbibliothek of Donaueschingen; the Stadtarchiv and Stadtgymnasium, both of Dortmund; the Sächsische Landesbibliothek of Dresden, and the Staatsarchiv Dresden (Außenstelle Bautzen); the Universitätsbibliothek of Düsseldorf; the Wissenschaftliche Allgemeinbibliothek of Erfurt; the Universitäts-bibliothek of Erlangen-Nürnberg; the Stadtarchiv and the Stadt- und Universitätsbibliothek, both of Frankfurt am Main; the Universitäts-bibliothek of Freiburg im Breisgau; the Stadtarchiv of Fürth; the Universitäts- und Landesbibliothek Sachen-Anhalt of Halle-Wittenberg; the Staatsarchiv and the Staats- und Universitäts-bibliothek, both of Hamburg; the Niedersächsische Landesbibliothek, Hannover; the Library of the Musikwissenschaftliches Seminar, the Central University Library, and the Stadtarchiv, all of Heidelberg; the Gesamthochschul-Bibliothek of Kassel; the Badische Landesbibliothek of Karlsruhe; the Schleswig-Holsteinische Landesbibliothek of Kiel; the Stadtarchiv of Krefeld; the Musikbibliothek der Stadt Leipzig; the British Library and the Library of the Royal College of Music, both of London (England); the Archiv and the Bibliothek der Hansestadt Lübeck; the Staatsarchiv Ludwigsburg; the Staatsarchiv of Magdeburg; the Stadtbibliothek of Mainz; the Hessisches Staatsarchiv of Marburg a.d.L.; the Offices of the Rat des Kreises of Mühlhausen; the Offices of the City of Mulhouse (France); the Bayerische Staatsbibliothek of Munich; the Stadtarchiv and the Westfälisches Landesmuseum für Kunst und Kulturgeschichte, both of Münster; the Performing Arts Division of the New York Public Library, New York City (USA); the Niedersächsisches Staatsarchiv of Osnabrück; the Erzbischöfliche Akademische Bibliothek of Paderborn; the Bibliothèque Nationale and the Library of the Conservatory of Music, both of Paris (France); the Staatsarchiv of Rudolstadt; the Fürstlich Hohenzollernsche Hofbibliothek and the Staatsarchiv, both of Sigmaringen; the Archives of the *Stuttgarter Zeitung*, the Württembergische Landesbibliothek, and the Stadtarchiv, all of Stuttgart; the Library of the University of Toronto (Canada); the Universitätsbibliothek of Tübingen; the Stadtarchiv of Ulm; the Municipal Library of Versailles (France); the Music Division of the Nationalbibliothek, and the Library of the Gesellschaft für Musikfreunde, both of Vienna (Austria); the Library of Congress, Washington, D.C. (USA); the Deutsche Staatsbibliothek, the Nationale Forschungs- und Gedenkstätten der klassischen deutschen Literatur (especially the Goethe- und Schiller-Archiv), and the Stadtbibliothek, all of Weimar; the Hessisches Hauptstaatsarchiv of Wiesbaden; the Herzog August Bibliothek of Wolfenbüttel; the Biblioteka Uniwersytecka of Wroclaw (Poland); the Stadtarchiv of Wuppertal; and the Stadtarchiv and Universitätsbibliothek, both of Würzburg.

Finally, Ludwig Finscher and Helmut Hucke gave me invaluable encouragement and support during my visits to Heidelberg and Frankfurt a.M. in 1985-1986 and again in 1993. Those visits were supported in large part by the Alexander von Humboldt-Stiftung and, to a lesser extent, by Virginia Polytechnic Institute and State University. The latter organization also supported the preparation of this book for photo-ready publication. Marshall Fisher, Peggy Morgan, William Sanders, and especially Joseph VanDyke provided useful computer assistance and advice.

Blacksburg, Virginia
1 July 1994

LISZT IN GERMANY

1840–1845

Large are the treasures of oblivion, and heapes of things in a state next to nothing almost numberlesse; much more is buried in silence than is recorded, and the largest volumes are butt epitomes of what hath been. The account of time beganne with night, and darknesse still attendeth it.

Sir Thomas Browne
from a manuscript of the *Hydriotaphia*

It ought to have been apparent to us in reviewing the history of the past century that we were dealing with men and not gods, with dead soldiers and not casualty statistics. But to a large degree, we were cheated, given a foreground, or a full face, and denied the background, the periphery, the detail that tells more than the man at the focal point. . . . And it is details, particularities, that shock us, touch us, make us laugh, invite us to look closer—or, at any rate, make us understand what in the world we have lost.

Paul Theroux
from *The Past Recaptured*

CHAPTER I

Liszt's Germany: An Introduction

Wer den Dichter will verstehen
Muß ins Dichters Lande gehen.

Goethe

Between March 1840 and October 1845, Franz Liszt performed almost 300 times throughout the Germany of his day. These performances comprise approximately one-fourth of all those he is believed to have given between 1838 and 1847, his legendary "years of transcendental execution."[1] Liszt spent more time in Germany and performed there more often than in any other part of Europe, including France, Russia, Iberia, Italy, the British Isles, and Austro-Hungary.

Our knowledge of Liszt's musical career would be incomplete without an account of *all* his German performances, public and private. Yet none of Liszt's biographers has dealt with

---

[1] After Alan Walker, *Franz Liszt: The Virtuoso Years, 1811-1847*, rev. ed. (Cornell 1987; reprinted New York 1990). Hereafter "Walker." This estimate of more than 1,000 concerts for those years [Walker, p. 285] is based on one concert every three or four days, a figure very much in keeping with Liszt's documented activities during the 740-odd days he spent in Germany from 1840-1845. A similar estimate appeared in 1841 in *Das Rheinland, wie es ernst und heiter ist*, a contemporary magazine published at Mainz. According to this periodical, "Die Concert-Arrangements Liszts für die kommende Wintersaison sind so getroffen, daß er in jeder Woche *vier Concerte* in den bedeutendsten Städten Deutschlands geben wird. Die Bühnendirektionen von München, Stuttgart, Hamburg, Braunschweig, Hannover, [und] Berlin haben mit ihm bereits darüber abgeschlossen" [MzRh, "Album für Ernst und Scherz" No. 110 (14.9.1841), p. 439]. As we shall see, though, Liszt visited Munich and Stuttgart only in 1843, and Braunschweig and Hannover only in 1844.

Like several other sources of information about Liszt's German tours, *Das Rheinland* is discussed below in Chapter II. Sigla and abbreviations pertaining to periodical titles (e.g., MzRh) and to volumes like Walker's (i.e., volumes cited in several chapters below) may be found in Appendices A and B. A catalog of Liszt's individual German concerts may be found in Appendix C.

these performances in detail. Lina Ramann discussed some of them in her "authorized," three-volume monograph *Franz Liszt als Künstler und Mensch.*[2] But Ramann was not a professional historian, and her valuable biography is occasionally anecdotal rather than strictly factual.[3] Later biographers, including Peter Raabe and Alan Walker, borrowed heavily from Ramann (if only in terms of the performances and tours they chose to emphasize).[4] Consequently, a few of Liszt's public German concerts—especially those presented in Leipzig and Dresden during March 1840, and in Berlin between December 1841 and March 1842—have been described on many occasions. Others—among them the fabulously successful series of piano recitals and other events Liszt presented in Breslau and rural Silesia during January, February, and March 1843—have been almost completely ignored. This has not been the situation with Liszt's visits to other areas of Europe: detailed scholarly accounts of his performances in the British Isles, the south of France, the Iberian peninsula, Poland, Russia, and portions of Austro-Hungary began to be published during the 1960s, and new accounts continue to appear in print.[5] It is fair to say,

2   See Lina Ramann, *Franz Liszt als Künstler und Mensch*, 3 vols. (Leipzig 1880-1894). Hereafter "Ramann."

3   This is not to dismiss Ramann's work out of hand. See Eva Rieger, "So schlecht wie ihr Ruf? Die Liszt-Biographin Lina Ramann," NZfM 147/7-8 (July-August 1986), pp. 16-20. See also references to Ramann's work in Chapter II below.

4   See Peter Raabe, *Franz Liszt* 2 vols.; rev. Felix Raabe (Tutzing 1968). Hereafter "Raabe."

5   For example, in order of publication: Alexander Buchner, *Franz Liszt in Bohemia*, trans. Roberta Samsour (London 1962); A. Hoffmann and N. Missir, "Sur la tournée de concerts de Ferenc Liszt en 1846-47 dans le Banat, la Transylvania et les Pays Roumains," *Studia Musicologica* 5 (1963), pp. 107-124; A. Vander Linden, "Liszt et la Belgique," StMl 11 (1969), pp. 281-290; Adolf Donath, "Franz Liszt und Polen," *Liszt-Studien* 1 (1977), pp. 53-64; Marcel Carrières, *Franz Liszt en Provence et en Languedoc en 1844* (Beziers 1981); "'Fantastic Cavalcade': Liszt's British Tours of 1840 & 1841, from the Diaries of John Orlando Parry," LSJ 6 (1981), pp. 2-16; and 7 (1982), pp. 16-26; Robert Stevenson, "Liszt in the Iberian Peninsula, 1844-1845," *Inter-American Music Review* 7/2 (Spring-Summer 1986), pp. 3-22 [a conflation of articles published previously in JALS and MQ); Bohumil Plevka, *Liszt a Praha* (Prague: Supraphon, 1986); Geraldine Keeling, "Liszt's Appearances in Parisian Concerts, 1824-1844," LSJ 11 (1986), pp. 22-34; and 12 (1987), pp. 8-22; and Ben Arnold and Michael Saffle, "Liszt in Ireland (and Belgium): Reports from

therefore, that Liszt's visits to Germany between 1840 and 1845 represent "the least-explored tours" of his spectacular virtuoso career.[6]

The present study was written to correct this deficiency. It identifies and describes each of the 298 performances Liszt is known to have given in Germany during 1840-1845, and it evaluates the reactions to those performances recorded in a host of documents, especially contemporary press notices. The chapters that follow this one deal respectively with primary and secondary sources of information about Liszt's German tours; with the history of the tours themselves; with Liszt's German repertory as a pianist, composer, and conductor; and with the prejudices and perceptions that shaped the reception he received from the German critics of his day.

But what of the Germany Liszt encountered during the 1840s, the land of his travels and triumphs? Newspaper and magazine articles of those years present us with a multitude of facts (as well as a few fictions) about his activities in Germany, but they tell us almost nothing about the political, social, and cultural circumstances associated with those activities. Without some knowledge of the places Liszt visited and the things he saw and heard there, our knowledge of his tours would consist of little more than place names and dates, the titles of pieces performed, and isolated bits of critical chit-chat.

---

a Concert Tour," JALS 26 (1989), pp. 3-11. John Orlando Parry's diaries also served for much of the information found in David Ian Allsobrook, *Liszt: My Travelling Circus Life* (Edwardsville, Illinois 1991). Useful information about Liszt's international activities also appears in János Kárpáti, "Liszt the Traveller," NHQ 27/103 (1986), pp. 108-118. New studies dealing with Liszt's travels and international activities continue to appear regularly. Among the most recent is Luciano Chiappari, *La cinquecentesca Villa Abitata da Liszt a Monte S. Quirico di Lucca* (Ospedaletto 1991). See also Saffle, "Liszt's 'Unknown' German Tours," scheduled at the time the present volume went to press to be published in a forthcoming issue of LSJ.

Abbreviations for modern periodicals like the *Liszt Society Journal* (or LSJ), as used throughout the present volume, may also be found in Appendix B.

6   Quoted from Saffle, "Liszt Research Since 1936: A Bibliographic Survey," *Acta Musicologica* 58 (1986), p. 248.

Germany During the 1840s: Political and Geographical Realities

Liszt's Germany—the Germany of the early and middle 1840s—was quite different from Bismarck's Germany of the later nineteenth century, or from the reunified German nation of today. For one thing, there was no German *nation* during the 1840s; indeed, there never had been one, at least not in the sense that there had been a French nation at least since the days of Louis XIV. Instead of a single political entity, 1840s Germany consisted of a conglomeration of kingdoms, duchies, administrative districts, knights' holdings, and free cities that occupied much of the territory proclaimed by Charlemagne and his successors as the Holy Roman Empire. Technically, this salmagundi of states (some 1,500 of them, depending on how they are counted)[7] was known after 1815 as the German Confederation. Created by the Congress of Vienna and ruled from that city by the Habsburgs (aided and abetted by Prince Metternich and his cohorts), the Confederation officially included Austria as well as Prussia, Bavaria, Saxony, Hannover, and a host of smaller states and towns. Legally speaking, anyone born within the Confederation was "German." In this sense—and this should not be forgotten—Liszt was no German: he was born in Raiding which, prior to 1867, was part of the Kingdom of Hungary, not of the Confederation proper. In another sense, however, Liszt was "German," at least in the eyes of his many of his contemporaries: he grew up in a German-speaking household and was therefore sometimes considered a "cultural" citizen of the greater Germany discussed below.[8] (Austria has always been considered part of "German" musical

---

[7]   See George Bailey, *Germans: Biography of an Obsession* (New York 1972), pp. 335-336. Bailey identifies 1,789 German political units for the year 1789, more than existed in the 1840s but scarcely an exaggeration.

[8]   This was the argument German scholars of the Nazi era used to claim Liszt as a "German" composer. See, for example, Heinrich Frenzl, "Der deutsche Franz Liszt," *Zeitschrift für Musik* 101 (January 1934), pp. 23-27; and Magda von Hattingberg, *Franz Liszts deutsche Sendung* (Vienna and Leipzig 1938).
      Arguments about Liszt's "nationality" continue today, despite Liszt's own protestations of his Hungarian origins and loyalty. See, for example, Walker's review of Serge Gut's *Liszt* (Artigues-pré-Bordeaux 1989)—and Gut's spirited reply—in JALS 26 (1989), esp. pp. 37-39; and 30 (1991), esp. pp. 48-50.

history: Haydn may have been born in Rohrau, Mozart in Salzburg, and Schubert in Vienna, but they continue to be referred to as "German" composers.)

To a considerable extent the Confederation merely preserved the post-Napoleonic political status quo. Like the settlement of 1648, which concluded the Thirty Years War (a disaster from which Central Europe had not recovered even by Liszt's day), "the German settlement of 1815 was part of a European settlement: it was drawn up partly in the interests of the German princes, largely in the interests of the great powers, and not at all in the interests of the German people."[9] For Metternich and his allies, the Confederation helped the surviving members of central Europe's *ancien regime* cling to their aristocratic heritage. As historian Harold James put it, the Confederation "was yoked by the Habsburg Emperors to the international cause of political and social reaction."[10] Naturally enough, some people took the Confederation seriously: that is, they believed in its political and cultural viability. For these supernationalists, the post-1815 Confederation represented "Großdeutschland" (or "greater Germany"), heir to the empire of Charlemagne. Other nationalists, more concerned with the future than the past, anticipated the eventual political unification of "Kleindeutschland" (or "lesser Germany"): that is, Germany north of the Austrian border—roughly speaking, the Germany of Bismarck's day.[11] Still others clung to various forms of "Lokalpatriotismus" (or "local patriotism"): they believed that Bavaria or Baden or smaller states like the Grand Duchy of Sachsen-Weimar-Eisenach, where Goethe was Privy Counselor, should be independent not only from Vienna and Berlin, but from each other.[12]

---

[9] Geoffrey Barraclough, *The Origins of Modern Germany* (New York 1963), p. 410.

[10] Harold James, *A German Identity, 1770-1990* (New York 1989), p. 8.

[11] See Golo Mann, *The History of Germany Since 1789*, trans. Marian Jackson (New York 1968), p. 109.

[12] For a summary of attitudes about constitutional issues and the several states that comprised the German Confederation, see Frederick Hertz, *The German Public Mind in the Nineteenth Century* (Totowa, New Jersey 1975), esp. pp. 125-155.

The sheer geographical and cultural variety of the German Confederation was enormous. Encompassing the largest area of any European "nation," it stretched from Italy to the Baltic and from the borders of France in the west to those of Russia in the east. Even excluding Austria and her southern and eastern satellites, the Confederation was a world of its own. By 1848 its 200,000 square miles boasted a population of more than 25,000,000 people.[13] Yet this enormous region contained only one important city: Berlin. (It has been estimated that the combined population of Germany's university towns during the 1840s was less than the population of contemporary Paris.)[14] It was also a region of towering mountains and important rivers, broad expanses of marshlands and heath, and almost unbroken forests of birch and pine trees that covered areas as large as Switzerland. Thus throughout the 1840s "Germany" certainly seemed to be a great nation, even though it was actually no nation at all.

"Trying to fix the German geographically is like trying to fix him chronologically"—a difficult task, as George Bailey pointed out several decades ago.[15] Therefore, throughout the rest of the present volume, the term "Germany" shall refer somewhat (but only somewhat) arbitrarily to that part of Europe most often considered politically *and* culturally

---

[13] Statistics vary considerably from source to source. According to the ninth edition of the *Encyclopaedia Britannica*, Vol. X (Boston 1879), p. 455, the area covered by "Prussia" in 1844 was 171,900 square miles, while the total Prussian population was 28,498,136. In 1844, however, "Prussia" had not yet swallowed up Bavaria, Baden, Württemberg, Hannover, Hesse, and other substantial and populous parts of what eventually became Bismarck's empire.

[14] See Barraclough, p. 414. Other historians go even farther: A. J. P. Taylor, for example, maintains that "the entire town population of Germany [in and after 1815] was only half as much again as the population of Paris" [Taylor, *The Course of German History* (New York 1946), p. 54]. Claims like these seem to be reasonable ones. According to the ninth edition of the *Britannica*, for example, Berlin in 1840 had a population of 331,894 [Vol. III (1875), p. 593], while Paris in the same year had a population of some 935,261 [Vol. XVIII (1885), p. 277]. By comparison, university towns like Mainz and Heidelberg during the 1830s had populations of no more than 29,000 and 12,000 respectively. See the eighth edition of the *Allgemeine deutsche Real-Encyklopaedie* (Leipzig 1833-1837), as quoted by James Deaville in *The Music Criticisms of Peter Cornelius* (Northwestern University 1986), Vol. I, p. 38n.

[15] See Bailey, p. 342.

"German" by nineteenth-century authorities: viz., the German Confederation north of the Austrian border, excluding Luxembourg (originally part of the Confederation, although predominently French-speaking), but including East Prussia and other eastern territories. The boundaries of these areas (the Confederation, Luxembourg, and "Germany" per se), and of Alsace-Lorraine (which belonged to Bismarck's Germany only from 1871 to 1918) are identified on Map 1.[16] Considered in terms of contemporary political divisions, Liszt may be said to have visited every part of "Germany" except the regions east of Kiel and west of Cuxhaven (i.e., the Duchies of Oldenburg, Mecklenburg-Schwerin, and Mecklenburg-Strelitz),[17] a few of the smaller central German states (e.g., the Principality of Schwarzburg), and "Rhenish Bavaria" (roughly speaking, the area known today as the Saarland). Put it another way: German political geography since the seventeenth century can be described in terms of twenty-one regions, excluding Alsace-Lorraine and the Free Cities of Bremen, Hamburg, Lübeck, and Frankfurt a.M.[18] Of these twenty-one regions, Liszt visited nineteen: Prussia (including the Prussian Rhineland and East Prussia), Posen, Silesia, Pomerania, Brandenburg, Bavaria, Sachsen (or "Saxony"), Sachsen-Anhalt, Niedersachsen, Westphalia, Hechingen, Lippe-Detmold, Baden, Württenberg, Hesse, Thuringia, and Schleswig-Holstein. He also visited Hamburg, Lübeck, and Frankfurt a.M.

During 1840-1841 Liszt's tours of the British Isles took him to dozens of places in England and Ireland, and his 1846-1847 tour of the Balkans was remarkable for its length

---

[16] A more detailed political map of nineteenth-century Germany appears in the *Rand McNally Historical Atlas of the World* (Chicago 1981), p. 119. An even more detailed map of the same region appears in the *Sprunger-Menke Hand-Atlas für die Geschichte des Mittelalters und der neueren Zeit*, 3rd ed. (Gotha 1880).

[17] In 1842 Liszt was invited to visit Mecklenburg-Strelitz by Friedrich Wilhelm, son of the reigning Grand Duke, but the invitation was withdrawn at the last minute because of a death in the royal family. See *Briefe hervorrangender Zeitgenossen an Franz Liszt*, 3 vols.; ed. "La Mara" [pseud. Marie Lipsius] (Leipzig 1895-1904), Vol. I, pp. 42-43. Hereafter "BriefeHZ."

[18] For example, see *Geschichte der deutschen Länder* ["Territorien Ploetz"], Vol. II: "Die deutschen Länder vom Wiener Kongreß bis zur Gegenwart," ed. Georg Wilhelm Sante (Würzburg 1971).

and geographic thoroughness. But Liszt explored Germany
more thoroughly than any other part of Europe. Furthermore,
his German tours were so successful and so widely publicized
that they may have helped "unite" the various German
states—culturally, that is, if not politically. At the very least
they gave many Germans something to think and talk about for
years on end.

Vormärz Germany: Economic and Cultural Realities

Culturally and economically, Liszt's Germany was the
Germany of the "Vormärz" era: historically, the era that separated the Congress of Vienna from the beginning of the
"March" revolutions of 1848 and 1849. During these decades,
Germany remained an agricultural rather than an industrial
society, provincial rather than cosmopolitan, impoverished
rather than financially powerful. Yet the economic and political
unification of modern Germany, it has often been said, began
during the Vormärz years with the establishment of trade and
transportation agreements that made Prussia and her allies an
efficient economic organization. The most important of these
agreements, the "Zollverein" (or "Customs Union"), transformed
much of what eventually became Bismarck's nation into an
economic engine of considerable power. A second agreement,
the "Handelsverein" (or "Trade Union"), regulated trade between Prussia's hegemony and several southern German
kingdoms, Bavaria and Württemberg among them. Smaller
trade organizations competed for a few years with the
Zollverein and Handelsverein, but by 1842 most of modern
Germany had already been defined economically, if not politically or culturally.

The Vormärz era, especially the decade preceding 1848,
was unique in German history. Never before had the German
people enjoyed such peace and quiet or led such unassuming,
uneventful lives. Changes lay on the horizon, but for a generation Germany was "almost entirely devoid of significant political events."[19] There were no wars or rebellions, and even
strikes and demonstrations were rare and quickly put down.

---

[19] Robert-Hermann Tenbrock, *A History of Germany*, trans. Paul Dine
(Munich and Paderborn 1968), p. 177.

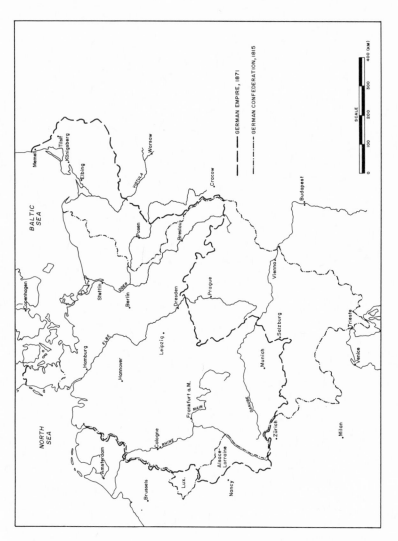

Map 1: Germany in the Nineteenth Century
(Towns in East Prussia appear on this map instead of on Map 2)

This does not mean that everyone was content: radical sentiments were common among university students, some of whom
organized secret "underground" discussion groups (or
"Burschenschaften") and spoke of democratic reforms. But local
authorities kept a death-grip on the reins of power. Throughout
the 1840s "censorship was tightened up" and "the number of
daily newspapers was cut down. Matriculations at the univer-
sities were supervised; secret societies were . . . prohibited;
[and] lecturers were to exercise their profession subject to
ministerial approval and recall."[20]

In short, Vormärz Germany was politically anxious as well
as placid, restless as well as reactionary. Consider, for example,
the social classes or "Stände." In some respects, German class
divisions were more rigid even than those of England; in others
they were almost as flexible as those of the United States. According to the Rev. George Gleig, who visited Europe in the
1830s, "There is throughout Germany . . . a line of distinction
drawn between the different orders in society, which, though
it appears to incommode no human being where crowds
congregate,—as in public places,—is never, in the private
amenities of life, overstepped."[21] Generally speaking, the titles
and privileges of nobility were reserved for hereditary aristocrats. Occasionally a commoner like Liszt would be received,
albeit on a lower level, into one of the aristocratic enclaves like
the Order of Vigilance (popularly known as the Order of the
White Falcon), but that was extraordinary.[22] True, public education (especially in Prussia) prepared many lower-class children for careers in civil service or one of the professions.[23]

---

20 Veit Valentin, *The German People* (New York 1946), p. 393.

21 George Robert Gleig, *Germany, Bohemia, and Hungary, Visited in 1837*
(London 1839), Vol. I, p. 199. NB: The quotations that follow from
nineteenth-century travel books contain original spelling and punctuation.
Titles of these and other works are abbreviated in footnote citations;
complete titles and publication information appear only in the bibliography.

22 The Order of the White Falcon, for example, could be held by no more than
87 individuals at any one time, 12 of whom were members of Weimar's
aristocracy. See Václav Mericka, *Orders and Decorations* (London 1967),
p. 71.

23 This did not mean, however, that middle-class Vormärz Germans were
necessarily prosperous or "modern" in outlook. On the contrary: most

Unfortunately, there were too many lower-class families and too few opportunities. Farmers, day-laborers, and even a few educated "gentlemen" were trapped in a quiet kind of poverty from which it was virtually impossible to escape. For most Germans, therefore, economic improvement was only a dream. The peasant families of the Vormärz years raised peasant children, just as middle-class families raised children who became the physicians, lawyers, clergymen, and professional musicians of the post-1848 generation.

It is difficult for us today to realize how poor most Germans were during the 1840s. Many people owned nothing but the clothes on their backs, and even merchants were often able only to rent (rather than buy) inadequate housing, much of it without access to plumbing or heating of any kind. Goods like carpeting, ceramic dishes, and even shoes were luxuries to members of the working classes. The Industrial Revolution had begun to ameliorate these conditions,[24] but almost everyone (including members of the bourgeoisie) lived more comfortably in England and France than they did in the states of the German Confederation.

Almost insuperable problems confront anyone who wants to explain the past in present-day terms. This is especially true of money and incomes: currencies change, and what individuals can buy with them changes too. Furthermore, it was difficult even during the Vormärz era for foreigners to grapple with dozens of German currencies and their values. George Atkinson, for example, writes that:

> But for the simplicity of our monetary transactions we should be sorely puzzled with the variety and multitude of the coins which are perpetually being introduced to our notice. What with rix-dollars, khron dollars, silver groschen, good groschen,

---

members of the emerging "middle strata . . . lived in a preindustrial world of state service, artisanal production, and small enterprise"; and, "despite some impressive signs of economic development, [the facts available today] portray a predominately rural, relatively backward economy" [James J. Sheehan, *German Liberalism in the Nineteenth Century* (Chicago 1978), pp. 24-25].

24 Information about industry and industrial production in Vormärz Germany appears in Helmut Böhme, *An Introduction to the Social and Economic History of Germany*, trans. W. R. Lee (New York 1978), esp. pp. 25-31. See also Sheehan, *German History, 1770-1866* (Oxford 1989), esp. pp. 496-500.

thalers, kreutzers, ducats, stivers, guilders, marcs, cents, liras, batz, *cum multis aliis*, to say nothing of the fractions of each, halves, quarters, thirds, and the like, one needs to be a perambulating compendium, or itinerant reckoner, in order to discover promptly the relative values of each. The oft-talked-of universal German currency would indeed be an acceptable boon; and though it might not be effected at once, yet it might eventually be carried out, by a gradual adoption of coins applicable to every state.[25]

It is possible, though, to obtain some idea of economic realities by comparing the incomes of Germany's working classes with those of their wealthier contemporaries. For those who lived in abject poverty, "long hours (12 per day was a minimum and 14 or even 16 quite usual) and low wages were a common and constant complaint." Historian P. H. Noyes explains that in Berlin, at least prior to March 1848:

> wages ranged from less than 1 thaler per week (approximately 84 cents at the contemporary exchange rates) to 5 or 6 thaler in the most skilled and exclusive trades. Printers, who were considered to be well off among the handicraft workers, received 3 thaler, 15 silbergroschen per week, and this at a time when the barest minimum upon which it was possible to live for a single worker with neither wife nor family was estimated at upward of 2 thaler per week. Many [workers] were attempting to exist below this minimum.[26]

Even six thalers a week was little more than 300 thalers a year, a paltry sum compared with the 2,000 thalers received by composer Ludwig Spohr at the height of his career.[27] Yet Liszt often earned 1,000 thalers in a single week, sometimes in a single evening! He may have been born in poverty, but by March 1840 he was poor no longer; the contemporary European press, as we shall see, marvelled over his money-making

25 George Francklin Atkinson, *Pictures from the North in Pen and Pencil* (London 1848), pp. 44-45.

26 P. N. Noyes, *Organization and Revolution* (Princeton, New Jersey 1966), p. 31.

27 See Ernest Newman, *The Life of Richard Wagner*, Vol. I (London 1934), p. 152. Hereafter "Newman." In 1841 Liszt turned down an offer of at least 1,000 thalers for three months' service each year as Weimar's "Kapellmeister im außerordentlichen Dienst," choosing instead to volunteer his services to the Grand-ducal court.

proclivities, and only his frequent, heartfelt donations to charitable causes prevented bolder public attacks on the prices that he and (sometimes) members of his entourage charged for reservations and concert tickets.

Conditions like those described by Noyes contributed directly to the revolutions of 1848-1849 and, indirectly, to the subsequent economic growth that transformed Germany several decades later into a world power. But long hours and low wages were not the only burdens Vormärz Germans had to bear. Universal censorship, imposed upon everyone who wrote for daily and weekly newspapers, made it difficult even for members of the middle classes to learn what was happening at home and abroad. Adolf Glassbrenner, a popular Berlin satirist of the 1840s who published under the pseudonym "Brennglass" (or "magnifying glass," because his words were intended to magnify the social ills he perceived around him), turned out a series of satiric social sketches that made him "one of the greatest literary forces of the time."[28] Born into the middle class but contemptuous of court flunkies and cultural philistines, Glassbrenner turned his attention to every-day affairs and even wrote a little play about Liszt's 1842 Berlin triumphs.[29]

Because his work appeared in "bound volumes" and thus was not considered journalism (at least in the eyes of the law), Glassbrenner was able to avoid the censorship imposed on newspaper and magazine writers of every kind. In "Berlin at Night," one of his many sketches, he acknowledges that fact when he observes that "the small fry, the newspapers and pamphlets are strictly dealt with: books of twenty sheets are exempt. Only the populace is under surveillance, the upper classes can do what they like." In another sketch, entitled "Berlin at Dawn," Glassbrenner depicts the beginning of a working-class day: the silent washerwomen who carries a "little lantern that lights her way to ever renewed and never ending toil"; the peasant women who, "with tired faces stream

---

[28] J. G. Legge, *Rhyme and Revolution in Germany* (London 1919), p. 220.

[29] See A. Brennglass, *Franz Liszt in Berlin: eine Komödie.* Published as a pamphlet as well as in FKB No. 199 (21.7.1842), pp. 794-795. See also Georg Münzer, "Eine Liszt-Karikatur," *Die Musik* 5/3 (1905-1906), pp. 53-55.

in from the neighbouring villages in their wooden carts"; and the bootblacks, "clad like writers for the press in the rags they have begged, run[ning] with blacking and cane from one gentleman's lodgings to another, freeing, alas, only their boots from filth."[30] As John Rodes has pointed out, these were people oblivious of the intellectuals who "regarded tradition and authority as stultifying," and who "gathered in 'reading circles' to discuss democratic concepts and search for some alleviation of their political frustratiors."[31] For Glassbrenner, aristocrats and members of the middle classes—the "arrogant 'Herr Councillor,' distant relation to some flunkey in the employ of 'His Excellency the Minister'," and the "gentleman of means" who gazes "on the crowd below, wondering what can be the aim in life of those who do not serve society" in his own capacity—were poseurs, as were the foolish Berliners who swooned in 1842 to Liszt's virtuosity. The poor were trapped by their circumstances, but for Glassbrenner and a few others (Karl Marx and Friedrich Engels among them) the poor represented Germany's hope for a better future, drinking their last gulps of morning coffee "without a thought" about adding "another day to the history of the world."[32]

Transportation and Travel in Vormärz Germany

By the 1840s it had become possible for increasing numbers of people to travel throughout Germany without extraordinary hardship or expense.[33] This was due in large part first to an improved network of roads, then to the construction of a

---

30 Quoted in Legge, p. 224. It is informative to compare these scenes with those of Liszt's Berlin triumphs.

31 John Rodes, *Germany: A History* (New York 1964), pp. 302-303.

32 Legge, pp. 224-225.

33 Even after the middle of the century, "leisure travel remained difficult and expensive enough to be out of most people's reach." Yet "a growing minority could travel, if not to some elegant spa or scenic landscape, at least to a nearby village or seaside town" [Sheehan, *German History, 1770-1866*, p. 464]. In 1835 the Koblenz publisher Karl Baedeker had already revised and republished a popular book about Rhineland travel, and during the 1840s other volumes in the famous "Baedeker" series began to appear in print. Competing German-language travel books also appeared, including Eduard Reis, *Mainz wie es ist, oder neues und vollständiges Panorama von Mainz* (Mainz 1844).

railroad system that by 1845 boasted more than 5,000 kilometers of track connecting cities and towns north of the Austrian border.[34] Several times during the early 1840s Liszt travelled on German trains; indeed, his quick trips back and forth between Leipzig and Dresden in 1840 and some of his excursions from Breslau into the Silesian countryside in 1843 would have been impossible without railways. Liszt, however, was no travel writer (at least during his German sojourns),[35] and we know only a little about his day-by-day travel experiences of the 1840s. Fortunately, others described what he must have experienced. The Danish storyteller Hans Christian Andersen, for example, left a picturesque account of a train trip he took from Magdeburg to Leipzig in the fall of 1840—the same trip Liszt took four years later, in March 1844. "The first sensation" of the voyage, according to Andersen,

> is that of a very gentle motion in the carriages, and then the chains are attached which bind them together; the steam

---

[34] An informative contemporary account of the German railway system prior to 1844 appeared in Leipzig's *Illustrirte Zeitung*. See LIZ Nos. 33 and 36 (10.2 and 2.3.1844). According to statistics provided by this periodical, almost 7,000,000 travellers made use of German trains in 1842 [LIZ No. 36 (2.3.1844), pp. 150-151]. Lines operating in March 1844 included the "Taunuseisenbahn" linking Mainz with the neighboring city of Frankfurt a.M. as well as lines connecting Berlin with Potsdam, Fürstenwalde, and Dessau, and with Brieg in farthest Silesia; Düsseldorf with Elberfeld; and Mannheim with Heidelberg—all places Liszt visited prior to October 1845 [LIZ No. 33 (10.2.1844), p. 104].

Additional information about early German railroad history may be found in several volumes, among them Elfriede Rehbein et al., *Deutsche Eisenbahnen, 1835-1985* (Berlin 1985).

[35] A few of Liszt's literary works contain descriptions of the journeys he took during the late 1830s and early 1840s, but these works were probably rewritten (or even written complete) by the Comtesse d'Agoult. In his splendid translation of Liszt's own *Lettres d'un bachelier ès musique*, published as *An Artist's Journey* (Chicago and London 1989; hereafter "Liszt/Suttoni"), Charles Suttoni has pointed out that, while "the basic underlying substance of [these] articles . . . can only be attributed to Liszt," the published articles themselves consist of "Liszt's ideas as expressed in d'Agoult's words." D'Agoult, in fact, "was probably the 'writer' responsible for the final, published [essay] texts" [Liszt/Suttoni, p. 244].

In any event, only one of the "Bachelor" letters touches on Liszt's German tours: No. 11, addressed to Léon Kreutzer, published originally in the *Revue et Gazette Musicale de Paris*, and reprinted in German in Kreutzer's own *Blätter für Musik und Literatur*. As we shall see in Chapter II, even this letter contains little information that cannot be found in other sources.

whistle sounds again, and we move on; at first but slowly, as
if a child's hand drew a little carriage. The speed increases
imperceptibly, but you read your book, look at your map, and
as yet do not rightly know at what speed you are going, for the
train glides on like a sledge over the level snow-field. You look
out of the window and discover that you are careering away as
with horses at full gallop; it goes still quicker; you seem to fly,
but here is no shaking, no suffocation, nothing of what you
anticipated would be unpleasant.

Andersen believed this was "just the way to travel through flat
countries! . . . Those who drive in carriages, on the by-roads,
seem to stand still; the horses lift their feet, but to put them
down again in the same place — and so we pass them."[36]

Mary Shelley, though, was somewhat less enthusiastic. In
1845 she recalled a railway journey she made to Berlin several
years earlier, the same journey Liszt made several times during his German tours:

The pace we went, when going, was very great, so that I heard
passengers call out from the windows imploring that the speed
might be lessened. Much time was lost, however, at every one
of the numerous stations, where the carriage-doors were
thrown open with the announcement of stopping for *funfzehn
minuten*, or *funf minuten*, or even *drei minuten*, (fifteen, five,
and three minutes,) when the passengers poured out and com-
forted themselves with all sorts of slight refreshments — light
wine, light beer, light cakes and cherries, nothing much in
themselves, but a good deal of it — offered by a whole crowd
of dealers in such wares.[37]

Hector Berlioz, that incomparable authority on European
"musical" travel, was likewise irritated by the delays he encountered on a train trip from Mainz to Frankfurt,[38] a route

[36] Hans Christian Andersen, *A Poet's Bazaar* (New York 1871), p. 15. Here-
after "Andersen." A somewhat more fanciful translation may be found in
Andersen, *A Visit to Germany, Italy, and Malta, 1840-1841*, trans. Grace
Thornton (New York 1985), pp. 41-42.

[37] Mary Shelley, *Rambles in Germany and Italy in 1840, 1842, and 1843*
(London 1844), Vol. I, p. 217.

[38] See the *Memoirs of Hector Berlioz*, trans. Rachel and Eleanor Holmes; rev.
Ernest Newman (New York 1932), p. 250. Hereafter "Berlioz." The
"Taunuseisenbahn" Berlioz and Liszt used was the busiest in Germany;
information about it, including fares for four classes of passengers and a

Liszt must have followed in 1840 and 1841. Shelley, however, notes that some trains were more comfortable than others; she also observes of the Prussian railways that there were "three classes of carriages, and the price is not dear:—1st class, five and a half thalers (a thaler is three shillings); 2d class, three and a half thalers; 3d class, two and a half."[39] Even for members of the middle classes, though, five thalers would have been a great deal to pay for a trip many of them would have considered unnecessary as well as much too exciting.

In any event, most Vormärz travellers were forced to rely on horse-drawn carriages and on steam-powered ships and boats. Germany's rivers were cleaner in the 1840s than they are today, and they were less thoroughly outfitted with locks, quays, and other improvements. Nevertheless, river travel then was very much like it is now. George Putnam observed of an 1847 steamship journey down the Rhine gorge that "competition [between the Cologne and Düsseldorf lines] does not seem to make the boats so splendid, nor the prices so cheap as on the Hudson—but still decent boats, and the fare is very reasonable."[40] Not so travel by road, which was always more tiresome, generally more expensive, and occasionally even treacherous. Journeying toward Schwalbach in July 1826, John Beattie found himself in some danger when he and his party encountered bad summer weather:

> [A] tremendous storm of thunder, lightning, and rain [came] . . . . on us as we cleared the heights of Nassau, in such hearty good earnest, that in five minutes the road was flooded, and the postilions so blinded with the lightning and slanting drift, that it was with difficulty they kept their seats. . . . The horizon

---

schedule of arrival and departure times, may be found in Reis, pp. 172-178.

[39] Shelley I, p. 217.

[40] George Palmer Putnam, *A Pocket Memorandum Book During a Ten Weeks's Trip to Italy and Germany in 1847* (privately printed), p. 124. Detailed information about schedules and fares for Rhine, Main, and Mosel river transportation may be found in Reis, pp. 178-186.

A few adventurers brought their own boats to Germany; among them was Robert Mansfield, whose *Cruise of the Water Lily* (London 1854) describes two trips up and down the Rhine, Main, Neckar, and other important German waterways. But trips on the rivers of nineteenth-century Europe were not always so pleasant; Andersen [pp. 321-323], for one, recalled an exhausting journey on the Danube from Vienna to Pest.

was so circumscribed, that we could discern nothing beyond the
dark ravines by which the road was flanked, and felt not a little
apprehension lest the carriages should capsize under the increasing violence of the blast.[41]

Fortunately, the weather was usually less threatening, and
throughout the Prussian Rhineland, Beattie found reason to
gloat over "the excellent state of the *roads*." Of Bavaria he observes that the public highways were "level, spacious, and kept
up with great care," while

> In [Württemberg] the government has taken especial pains to
> render the post roads inviting to travellers of every trade —
> from the bürschen with their haversack and God's providence,
> to him who visits the banks of the Neckar *à six chevaux*. The
> great road from Stuttgardt to Schaffhausen, through the Black
> Forest, is necessarily rugged and uneven, from the undulating,
> often mountainous surface . . . but kept with great and un-
> remitting attention. . . . The roads encircling the Lake of
> Constance, particularly on the Wurtemberg [i.e., the German]
> side, are excellent; that leading from Lindau to Ulm, on the
> Danube, and that again from Ulm through Geisslingen to
> Stuttgardt, are equal to the best in England.[42]

And Henry Chorley, who also encountered difficulties
during a cross-country trip from Cologne to Berlin by way of
Magdeburg in 1839, nevertheless compared his own experiences favorably with those of eighteenth-century British musical wanderers:

> Modes of conveyance and usages had changed with a vengeance
> since the year 1772, when Dr. Burney made the capital of
> Brandenburg a principal station in his musical pilgrimage. The
> night before he reached Berlin, he remained, as his own
> agreeable journal tells us, for seven cold, dark, wet hours, stuck
> fast in a bog, on a bleak and barren heath, between the last
> post-house and the city. . . . Thanks to the activity of Herr von
> Nagler, roads [for Chorley's journey] in 1839 were smooth, and
> conveyances punctual and commodious. . . . [T]here was, then,
> no excuse for bad humour—call it even by the convenient name

---

[41] John Beattie, *Journal of a Residence in Germany* (London 1831), Vol. II,
pp. 176-177.

[42] Beattie II, pp. 328-330.

of low spirits—on the part of the traveller entering the Prussian metropolis [today].[43]

But good roads were no guarantee of comfortable, dependable, and inexpensive land travel. Beattie also praised the quality of German horse-drawn coaches, especially their "durable materials and superior construction."[44] In 1842, though, John Aiton observed in his guidebook for English tourists in Germany that "the schnell posten or eilwagen, that is quick posts . . . ought rather to be denominated snail posts than snell posts, for after all, they travel generally only at a rate of five or six [miles per hour]." Furthermore, the "post wagons, called fahr posts . . . are of a still heavier mould, and much slower in their movements; and generally filled to suffocation by an inferior class of people." Only the "railroads with travelling trains, luggage waggons, and steam apparatus; and 'vapour' boats on the principal rivers" provided less demanding and expensive transportation.[45]

Coaches, especially smaller horse-drawn carriages, were unpleasant means of making longer journeys. "Eilwagen" (or express coaches) linked most of the larger German cities and towns; they often ran on schedule, but they were expensive and overbooked, and more than a few of them—especially the post coaches (which carried mail as well as passengers)—departed in the middle of the night, only to arrive around dawn at their destinations. Aiton used such coaches on several occasions and explains in detail how to arrange a more or less comfortable trip:

As the seats are numbered, and passengers obtain them in the order in which they apply, whenever your arrangements are fixed for leaving a place, let not one moment be lost in having the passport revised and properly indorsed [sic] for the place where you are going. Then forthwith repair to the office, and secure a seat in the corner, which every body knows is better,

[43] Henry Chorley, *Modern German Music*, 2 vols. (London: Smith, Elder, 1854), Vol. I, pp. 140-141. Hereafter "Chorley." "Von Nagler" is probably the General Postmaster Nagler who, beginning in 1823, standardized and improved Prussia's post roads and delivery services.

[44] Beattie, II, p. 329.

[45] John Aiton, *Eight Weeks in Germany* (Edinburgh 1842), p. 49.

especially in the night time, than those in the middle. You take
the luggage along with you, see it weighed, and notice where
it is put, that you may know where to find it at the end of the
journey; you pay the fare beforehand, taking a receipt for the
money and the luggage. This receipt bears the number which
points out your position. But in addition to this, you must be
forward at the place in plenty of time before starting, lest some
bull-horned fellow sit down on your number and refuse to give
it up.[46]

Smaller carriages had several advantages over post
coaches. They were more comfortable, and they could be hired
on short notice by small groups of travellers. Furthermore, they
departed at more reasonable hours, but travellers had to make
their own arrangements with their drivers, and the law of
supply and demand subjected unwary foreigners to constant
negotiations:

In the main streets of the great towns a foreigner is constantly
accosted by coachmen (Lohn Kutschers) offering you
conveyance for whatever destination you may be bound for; and
in the courts of the hotels there are always to be found carriages ready to start; and they have generally boards hung
upon them bearing the names of places to which they are willing to go. These are capable of being shut in with leather cur-
tains and glass windows; and when four or five individuals join
in hiring one of them, they afford a cheaper mode of conveyance
than the schnell post. They admit also of a tourist stopping at
night, or during the day, to see a place for an hour or two. But
to a single individual, or two, this mode is unattainable; it is
more tedious and inconvenient; it is dreadful for dust in warm
weather, and dirt in wet. It generally stops at inferior inns on
the road, where a person always fares worst and pays
most. . . . If he compares notes with his fellow-travellers, if
these be natives, it is ten to one but the Englishman has to pay
on his own account as much as all the others united.[47]

Trains, boats, or horse-drawn coaches alone were useful
only for shorter journeys. To cover a great deal of distance, as
Liszt often did, it was necessary to rely on a combination of
conveyances. In recalling her own tour the Continent, Mrs.

---

[46] Aiton, pp. 50-51. Detailed information about coach travel in and around
Mainz may be found in Reis, pp. 169-172.

[47] Aiton, p. 51.

Frances Trollope describes a trip she took with her son from Baden-Baden to Wiesbaden in 1833, a trip similar to one Liszt must have taken in July 1840: "I . . . hired a carriage to take us [to Mannheim] in one day; a distance that I should have thought too long for one pair of horses, being seventy miles, had not the driver assured us that he had repeatedly done it without distressing them." Yet Mrs. Trollope and her son had time to stop in Heidelberg and see the sights; leaving Baden-Baden at 6 a.m., they seem to have reached Mannheim about sixteen hours later. "Our first care, on the following morning," she goes on, "was to learn the time at which the steam-boat should start for Mayence. This being three o'clock, we ordered dinner at two, and amused ourselves in the interval by walking about the town and its superb gardens, and in taking a warm bath." Reaching Mainz, however, she was discouraged to discover that

> having greatly disliked the hotel *Des Trois Couronnes*, at our first visit . . . we now went to the *Cheval Blanc*; where, however, we fared still worse. Dark, dirty, comfortless, and most full of villanous smells, did we find it; and our first business was to secure an open carriage for the morrow, to take us, before breakfast, to Wiesbaden.[48]

Vormärz hostelries, it should be noted, were often disappointing. Putnam mentions "semi-barbarous inns" he visited in southern Bavaria, as well as a hotel he visited in Ulm, where repeated requests for private accommodations were "always met by a stare of astonishment."[49] Sir George Smart found the room he secured in Bonn for the Beethoven Festival of August 1845—the Festival Liszt did so much to support, for which he wrote a cantata, and at which he performed as soloist, accompanist, and conductor—"extremely comfortable before the arrival and after departure of the influx of [Festival] visitors." Yet even Smart complained about furnishings, especially about "a washing stand with a drawer which stuck fast so that it was of no use." Furthermore, Smart's hotel had no "good place for receiving letters[;] they are never placed in any spot where you can get at them but you must always ask for them." Finally

---

[48] Frances Trollope, *Belgium and Western Germany in 1833* (London 1834), Vol. II, pp. 89-95.

[49] Putnam, pp. 29 and 119.

Smart observes that "the house for an hotel [was] clean but
occasionally there were horrid smells, particularly at the back
where the ducks and fowls were enjoying themselves."[50]

No wonder Liszt travelled whenever possible with a personal secretary—after early 1841 with Gaetano Belloni, an unusually capable assistant; or, later, with the singer Ciabatta
mentioned below in Chapter III. Like modern-day businessmen, travelling artists in Vormärz Germany could scarcely
have found time to purchase tickets, haul luggage, and arrive
at points of departure "in plenty of time" merely to get good
seats on uncomfortable, crowded, and expensive coaches
leaving—as often as not—in the middle of the night, travelling
slowly from one provincial town to another, and arriving at
hotels of questionable cleanliness and character. Berlioz had to
travel across Germany in 1843 with a quarter-ton of orchestral
scores and parts, but Liszt made more and longer journeys than
Berlioz, and it is a testimonial to his tremendous endurance
that the rigors of of prolonged travel did not injure him permanently or even kill him.

Vormärz German Customs and Curiosities

To those who visited Germany during the Vormärz era
and left us their impressions, social ills and instabilities were
often less interesting than "the picturesque": scenery, sights,
customs, and clothes. Andersen, for example, described an
evening journey to a small Bavarian town as if he were intro-
ducing a story by Washington Irving:

> After passing Münchberg we were in the mountains; and the
> country around displayed a more romantic character. It was in
> the evening light. The mountain "der Ochsenkopf" the largest
> here, was quite hidden by the misty clouds; the road became
> narrower and dark; at Berneck it was quite enclosed by steep
> cliffs; to the left, at some yards above us, stood a ruined tower,
> which in ancient times certainly commanded the entrance to
> this place. Berneck itself, with its uneven streets, the light
> which moved about within the old houses; the postilion's music,

---

50 *Leaves from the Journals of Sir George Smart*, ed. H. Bertram and C. L.
E. Cox (London 1907), p. 332. Hereafter "Smart." Some of Smart's observations on the Festival are reprinted in LSae No. 25 (1979), pp. 116-119.

which sounded as melancholy as the tune of an old ditty —
everything breathed the spirit of romance.[51]

Sentimental he may have been, but Andersen usually got his
facts straight. Parts of Germany *were* lovely; even Berlioz, who
despised overblown descriptions of dark forests, monasteries,
lonely chapels, and other spooky things, praised Berlin and
found the Rhineland "grand and beautiful."[52] Another place often singled out for praise was "Old Nuremberg," largely destroyed by fire bombs in 1944-1945 (as were Hamburg,
Dresden, Frankfurt a.M., and Berlin). Andersen's jottings
about Dürer's town are enthusiastic as well as picturesque:

> Such things are not to be described, they must be drawn! Had
> I talent to have done it, I would have placed myself on the old
> stone bridge over the river whose yellow water hurries rapidly
> on, and there would have depicted the singular projecting
> houses. The old Gothic building yonder on arches, under which
> the water streams, stands prominently over the river, adjoining
> a little hanging garden with high trees and a flowering hedge!
> Could I paint, I would go into the market, force my way
> through the crowd, and sketch the fountain there; it is not so
> elegant as in the olden times with its rich gilding, but all the
> splendid bronze figures stand there yet. . . . Were I a painter,
> I would go to the tomb of St. Sebaldus, when the sunlight falls
> through the stained glass windows on the statues of the
> Apostles, cast in bronze by Peter Fischer, and the church and
> tomb should be drawn as they were reflected in my eyes.[53]

Other tourists wrote about historic Augsburg; Putnam even
visited "the printing offices of the celebrated *Allgemeine
Zeitung*, or Augsburgh Gazette—the *Times* of Germany, and

---

[51] Andersen, p. 19.

[52] See esp. Berlioz, p. 248. Berlioz also experienced in the Black Forest an
anguish that was "almost inexplicable" and writes in his memoirs about
"the cold, the funereal black and white aspect of the mountains, the wind
howling through the shivering pine trees, [and] the secret gnawings of
heart so powerfully felt in solitude" [Berlioz, p. 263]. All this from the
composer of the *Symphonie fantastique*, that masterpiece of the macabre!

[53] Quoted from Andersen, pp. 20-21. Liszt also found Nuremberg
"marvellous." See his letter of 12 November 1843 to the Comtesse
d'Agoult, reprinted in *Correspondance de Liszt et de la Comtesse
d'Agoult*, ed. Daniel Ollivier (Paris 1933-1934), Vol. II, p. 291. Hereafter
"Ollivier."

the most influential journal on the continent," a paper Liszt
often read and alternately praised and cursed during his
German tours. Like others, too, Putnam found Heidelberg's
"pretty gardens" and "venerable" university a delightful spot to
spend an afternoon.[54]

Sometimes, of course, travellers' accounts seem to contra-
dict each other. Beattie, for instance, stated that

> Bonn presents an agreeable and imposing aspect . . . which,
> like the *boulevards* of Brussels, Frankfort, &c., have been de-
> molished and transformed into tasteful and extensive walks for
> the inhabitants. . . . [The city] is now a favoured seat of the
> muses, and possesses a university in excellent discipline. The
> professors have individually gathered fame in the various de-
> partments of science and literature. The young men who here
> prosecute their studies under able and vigilant masters arrive
> in a few years at a degree of proficiency which was rarely
> known in the last generation.[55]

Sir Arthur Faulkner, on the other hand, formed a rather different impression a decade or so later:

> Christmas-day and the first of the new year [in Bonn] are here
> the dullest days in the three hundred and sixty-five. Neither
> balls, plays, nor concerts, not even a symptom of gaiety in the
> streets. The churches, which are the only places of resort, are
> open late and early, and, what is remarkable and
> unpardonable, the music below mediocrity, spite of all that
> might be expected from the birth-place of Beethoven, Salomon,
> Rees [sic], and Rhomberg [sic].

"It seems the Bonners prefer the more rational joys of domestic
life on such occasions; and in this they perhaps best consult the
spirit of true Christianity, which desires us to 'rejoice with
trembling'," Faulkner continues. Then he adds this disclaimer:
"For my own part I am equally independent of their festivity
or their dulness, enjoying, as I do, a quartet regularly once a
week."[56]

---

[54] Putnam, pp. 119 and 124.

[55] Beattie I, p. 181.

[56] Arthur Faulkner, *Visit to Germany and the Low Countries* (London 1833),
      Vol. I, p. 189.

The eastern portions of Germany were generally avoided by travellers; they were less heavily populated, transportation through them was more difficult to arrange, and they were considered wild, untamed regions.[57] (Berlin, of course, was the exception.) Railroads especially did not penetrate parts of Pomerania and East Prussia until quite late. Yet to Captain Edward Spencer, who visited central Europe during the 1830s, Silesia was well worth a visit:

> Breslau . . . is the most bustling, animated town in the Prussian dominions; and its advantageous situation on the Oder renders it one of the most important as a commercial position. The inhabitants are evidently wealthy; and the number of new buildings, ornamented villas, and pleasure grounds in the environs, eloquently tell that it is in a prosperous state. . . . Taken altogether, I should infinitely prefer residing here to Berlin. There is not that dreariness in its streets; the theatre is also good, the country beautiful, the manners of the people frank and friendly, without the desire to make the world believe that they are the owners of double the wealth they possess. There is also a good public library, a university, with literary institutions sufficient to supply the wants of those who have an appetite for learning; while good and cheap provisions will satisfy those whose desires are of a more sublunary character.[58]

"Above all," Spencer observes, Breslau "opens a wide field of interest to the antiquarian in a ramble through its numerous churches, as they are all more or less ornamented with monuments of the middle ages, and curious old paintings of the German school." As was often the case, the past (rather than the present) captured the traveller's attention: not the new buildings erected around Hamburg's harbor after the Great Fire of 1842, but the ancient paintings of Breslau's churches,

---

[57] They still are. Bailey, who claims to be fond of what once was East Prussia ("There is the bracing roughness and readiness and urgent humor of the pioneer"), quotes one Count von Flemming to the effect that "the farther east you go . . . the larger the schnapps glasses get and the smaller the washbasins. When you get so far that both are approximately the same size then you're right on—that's my home" [Bailey, p. 340].

[58] Edward Spencer, *Sketches of Germany and the Germans* (London 1836), Vol. I, pp. 136-137. Chorley, interestingly enough, agreed that Berlin could be dreary, at least when seen for the first time "by the light of very early day" [Chorley I, p. 141].

especially the "many exquisite ones by Willmans, usually
termed, par excellence, the Silesian Rembrandt."[59]

In their customs and habits, Vormärz Germans sometimes
seemed a motley crew: many of them were simple people with
direct, even heavy-handed accents and manners. Furthermore,
German men and women of that era often ate bad food, drank
to excess, smoked too much, and did not always keep themselves and their surroundings clean. "Things here [in
Hamburg] have a true German aspect," Edward Wilkey observed in 1839: "There are the same heavy, phlegm-indicating
countenances, and little unornamental caps, fitting close to the
head, that you see further south." Unlike Glassbrenner, Wilkey
and others of his kind were amused by the working-class customs they encountered. Pipes and cigars, for example, struck
Wilkey's fancy. "It is said," he observes, "that a hundred thou-
sand cigars [are] smoked daily in Hamburg, which I think is
very possible."[60] Nathaniel Parker Willis, that dandified American visitor of 1845, commented on some of the same sorts of
things:

> The *degree of resource* that smoking is, to the Germans of all
> ages and classes, is wonderful [sic], most of them having the
> pipe in the mouth literally three-fourths of the time, and flying
> to it from all kinds of annoyance and restlessness. . . . I should
> not be surprised if tobacco stood the Germans instead of
> newspaper virulence and highly-spiced politics—instead of the
> getting up of sham enthusiasms and the gladiatorship of pri-
> vate character—excitements which are wanting in Germany.[61]

Willis seems to have been ignorant of the censorship imposed
on the German press. Ignorance, however, did not necessarily
inhibit observation. At the table d'hote of his inn, for instance,
Wilkey regularly sat down with

---

[59] Spencer I, p. 137.

[60] Edward Wilkey, *Wanderings in Germany* (London 1839), p. 6.

[61] N. Parker Willis, *Rural Letters* (Detroit 1853), pp. 279-280. Other
      travellers also commented on German enthusiasms for liquor and tobacco;
      Putnam [p. 119], for example, described the common room of a "primitive
      inn" where German peasants were "drinking beer in quarts full, and
      smoking pipes till they couldn't see each other's noses."

fifty or sixty persons of different nations [to] dine daily at four o'clock. One of the plates to-day was too remarkable to be passed over in silence,—consisting, as it did, of a bit of raw *schinken*, or ham, a bit of clammy salt fish, some very buttery beans, and ditto peas—certainly a delightful olio!

"These little things I like occasionally to note down," Wilkey explains, "as they seem to me quite as *entertaining* as others of greater importance." Among them was the use of imported ice to cool the wine at the same table d'hote—"a great luxury," Wilkey astutely observes, especially during the "extremely warm weather" he encountered in Hamburg and Berlin that summer.[62]

In general, lower- and middle-class Germans seem to have been regular, even predictable in their habits. Several visitors commented on how early people got up in the mornings and how early they went to bed. Furthermore, almost everyone wore appropriate, traditional costumes: uniforms for soldiers, civic officials, and household servants; suits for businessmen; academic gowns for university professors; and so on. But Germans were scarcely "all of a piece" when it came to fashion. In 1845 Atkinson visited Hamburg; several years later he described that pleasant, well-ordered place and wrote that "the honest Hamburghers so arrange their amusements as not to clash and interfere with each other, and to allow time for the dance after the theatre." But Atkinson also encountered social climbers who aspired to sophistication and fashionable attire:

Who are these fair damsels flitting along so nimbly [on the way to the opera house], so gaily attired in short-sleeved dresses, black lace mittens, silken aprons, and with embroidered handkerchiefs, so tastefully held,—how smartly they are got up. But what is concealed under that mysterious shawl? Can it be a bouquet, or some token of love? No; pounds of sausages, a cabbage, with some garlick, and, perhaps, a bottle of creature comfort, savoury comestibles for Herr Von Stuffemfull's supper.[63]

Trinkets also fascinated visitors: Willis, who commented regularly on costumes, observed of the 1845 Leipzig Trade Fair that

---

[62] Wilkey, p. 7.

[63] Atkinson, p. 40.

Among other keepsakes [for sale] were . . . *garters with poetry
inscribed on them*. They were elastic and painted to imitate
wreathes of roses. I bought a pair for sixpence with a verse
upon each. . . . poetry where we are not in the habit of looking
for it, but, to the taste of the humble and virtuous, not misplaced. *Honi soit qui mal y pense*, as says the classic moral of
the garter.[64]

No one, of course, imagined that Germany was inhabited
exclusively by overweight, ill-dressed cigar-smokers and pretty
girls hiding poetic garters and garden vegetables under their
clothes. Merchants and other members of the German middle
classes looked down upon pretentious rustics, while aristocrats
despised social-climbing tradesmen and businessmen. Members
of the armed services, however, were virtually exempt from
criticism. "Here every man is, or has been, a soldier," Beattie
remarked in 1831, and his comments about enlisted men and
especially about career officers held true of German society
throughout the nineteenth century:

The profession of arms includes every class of the community.
The only road to preferment in the state runs through the
provinces of war, and is proportionally crowded by aspiring
delegates. [Indeed,] the passion for military glory is carried to
an extreme. It admits of no rival, or if it meets, extinguishes
it. . . . But in the time of peace, in retirement, such a passion
accommodates itself with difficulty to existing circumstances.
The gallant soldier is often a discontented citizen. . . . Thus a
predilection for arms, and a prejudice against commerce or ag-
riculture, grow up together, and strengthen with their
growth. . . . [Even the peasant] hears that to be a soldier is to
be every thing becoming a man, with an immeasurable distance
between the sword and the ploughshare.[65]

In Prussia, Wilkey observed, "every male inhabitant is obliged
to serve three years in the army, with a few exceptions for those
in peculiar circumstances, as *only sons* who are engaged in
business that they cannot delegate to another person, or who
have aged parents to support."[66]

---

[64] Willis, pp. 278-279.

[65] Beattie I, pp. 301-302.

[66] Wilkey, p. 29.

Musicians too became soldiers, and soldiers musicians. On one occasion Beattie watched from his hotel window as a group of performers, "composed of the *élite* of the military bands, and drawn up in the form of a crescent, commenced an opera [about] . . . some bold popular incidents in the life of Frederick the Great":

> The various pieces . . . went off with great *éclat* [and] repeated bursts of acclamation from the surrounding multitude fully attested with what interest they participated in the incidents and how highly they appreciated the music of the piece. . . . Some of the singers — all military — were in fine voice, and gave the occasional song or recitative with great taste and effect. Were I to judge of the merits of this performance by the impression it has left upon me, I should give it the preference over most productions of the kind I have ever heard. I have experienced less pleasure on a benefit night at the theatre San Carlos, than I did on the present occasion at Coblentz.[67]

Berlioz too encountered military bands; indeed, "one would have to be exceedingly cross-grained to avoid hearing any, for they parade about the streets at all hours of the day." He was deeply impressed by the musical abilities of such ensembles, especially Prussian ones:

> [The military bands of Berlin and Potsdam are composed of] all good readers, all well up in the mechanisms of their instruments, playing in tune, and favoured by nature with indefatigable lungs and lips of leather. Hence the extreme facility with which the trumpets, horns, and cornets give those high notes unattainable by our [French] artists.[68]

Other Germans aspired to intellectual instead of military glory. "In Germany there is more culture than in any other country," George Calvert remarked around the middle of the nineteenth century:

> Her high-schools, her universities, her libraries are the best in the world, the most numerous and the most accessible. Nowhere is knowledge more valued; nowhere are there so many men with empty pockets and full heads; and nowhere has more money less social weight [!]. The German is, moreover, sociable;

---

[67] Beattie II, p. 150.

[68] Berlioz, p. 325.

enjoying especially an after-meal talk. He excels, too, I think, in the rarest conversational talent—that of being a good listener.

Embroidering these themes, Calvert describes a dinner he attended in the public dining room of the Erbprinz Hotel in Weimar—the same hotel frequented by Liszt during his visits to that city in 1841, 1842, and 1844:

> Our little party . . . was as companionable as though we had been the assorted guests of a discriminating Amphytrion. Our chief talker was a young Lutheran ecclesiastic, who, voluble and well-informed, was carried forward by an inordinate momentum of animal spirits. . . . Another of our company was an inspector of baths at Marienbad, who was modestly proud of some autograph verses given him by Goethe. . . . On Monday morning I awoke with such pleasant recollections of the preceding afternoon and evening, that I resolved to stop a day or two in Weimar—at least until time should begin to press idly upon me.[69]

Nor were German women without intellectual ambitions (or, at least, pretentions). The Baroness Blaze de Bury, who visited Prussia in 1846, stated that

> the ladies of Berlin are . . . *"woundly learned,"* as Tony Lumpkin says, and it is lucky for you if you do not find yourself called upon to decide a knotty point concerning literature in the days of Rhâmesès, even whilst you are sucking an orange at a *Damen Caffee*, or if you do not have the smoked Hamburgh beef rammed down your throat by an unexpected shot from Hegel or Kant.[70]

But the Countess did not dislike German intellectuals, even feminine ones. On the contrary: she enjoyed engaging conversation, and she found well-bred Prussians every bit as entertaining as the aristocrats she encountered in other parts of Europe:

---

[69] George Calvert, *First Years in Germany* (Boston 1866), pp. 172-173. Weimar must have been one of the most pleasant places in Vormärz Germany: everybody praised it, even Berlioz [p. 273] and anonymous travel guides like *Allemagne et Pays-Bas* (Paris c. 1845).

[70] The Baroness Blaze de Bury, *Germania: Germany as it is* (London 1851), Vol. I, pp. 281-282.

The *salons* of Berlin are not, as in Paris, *salons de causerie*, where everything is talked of; no! they are, I repeat it, *salons* where everything is *discussed*; politics, philosophical subjects, the more learned questions of science, and the lighter questions of art, all are taken into serious consideration. . . . Now, it will be objected this must lead to heaviness and inevitable *ennui*, and that to hear the peculiarities of Jenny Lind's talent examined as ought to be a treatise on the Cunei-formed alphabet, must be insufferable—not a bit; but there is an originality about their way of treating every question, and a curious manner of diving after every pearl, no matter in what oyster it may lie hidden, which throws an unspeakable charm into the conversation of a well-bred, intelligent German, (I take the Berliner to be the quintessence of the *gelehrter Deutscher*), and which makes you feel, when you leave their society, that, though the subjects you have been talking over were every-day ones, every faculty of your intelligence has been called into play in treating them.[71]

Liszt received many honors during his German tours, but two granted him special distinction: the Prussian Order "Pour le Mérite" (reserved until 1842 for bravery on the field of battle), and the honorary doctorate conferred upon him immediately afterwards by the University of Königsberg. In the eyes of many Germans, the degree took precedence even over the quasi-military decoration,[72] and after March 1842 almost every German concert announcement and review referred to "Herr Dr. Liszt," evidently a man of intellectual as well as artistic distinction.

Finally, the nobility. Long before the nineteenth century began the Prussians had already acquired a reputation for stuffiness and an exaggerated sense of propriety. But the Bavarians were no Prussians, and proud of it: their kings and queens walked among the common people and enjoyed their subjects' amusements. "To an English traveller in Germany," wrote Mrs. Anna Jameson in 1839, "nothing is more striking

---

[71] Blaze de Bury I, pp. 283-284.

[72] This was not always true. The *Illustrirte Zeitung*, which otherwise ignored Liszt between July 1843 and September 1845, mentioned him in an article devoted to the new Prussian decoration; and in describing the 1845 Beethoven Festival, the same paper identified a portrait of Liszt with the caption "Ritter des Orden 'pour le mérite'" This portrait is reproduced as the frontispiece of the present volume. See LIZ Nos. 21 (1.1.1844), p. 11; and 116 (27.9.1845), p. 181.

than the easy familiar terms on which the sovereign and his
family mingle with the people."[73] Nineteenth-century Germans,
it should be remembered, were so conscious of class distinctions
that it was possible even for a king to chat with his subjects
and remain a king; no one, not even democratic American
travel-writers, believed otherwise. Thus German princelings
were far removed from Czar Nicholas I, who unbent only
enough to recognize Liszt's existence before insulting him.[74]
Beattie once "had the honour" of being presented to Ernest, the
Prince of Saxe-Meiningen, and his son:

> The hereditary Prince is a remarkably handsome young man,
> of six or seven and twenty, and wears the uniform of a colonel
> in the British-Hannoverian service. I have seldom met a young
> man of his rank who improved so rapidly upon acquaintance.
> In general, they are either fearful of committing an act of rash
> condescension, or of betraying some inferred ignorance in con-
> versation; but Prince Ernest freely risks the one, and has no
> cause to fear the other. He has made several visits to England,
> and is as much master of its language as he promises to be an
> honour to its service. This young Prince, and his cousin the
> Duke of Meiningen, are two of the handsomest *knights* I have
> met with in any country.[75]

Berlioz too was impressed not only with the cordial manners of the German aristocrats he encountered, but with their
love of music. In Hechingen he encountered the same prince
who made Liszt a "Hofrat" (or court counselor) in the fall of
1843, and referred to his cleverness and generosity.[76] And in
Berlin the Prince of Prussia invited Berlioz to a delightful
matinée:

> I was astonished at not seeing the orchestra, no sound betrayed
> its presence, when a slow phrase in F minor, well known to
> [me], made me turn my head towards the largest room in the
> palace, which was concealed from our sight by an immense

---

73   Anna Jameson, *Visits and Sketches at Home and Abroad*, 3rd ed. (London
     1839), Vol. I, p. 75.

74   See Walker, pp. 374-375.

75   Beattie I, pp. 112-113.

76   See Berlioz, pp. 265-266. In November 1843, as we shall see in Chapter
     III, Prince Ernest of Hohenzollern-Hechingen also gave Liszt a ride on his
     pleasure boat.

curtain. His royal highness had had the courtesy to order the
concert to open with the overture to the *Francs Juges*, which I
had never heard arranged thus for wind instruments. There
were three hundred and twenty players, directed by Wiprecht
[sic], and difficult as the music was, they performed it with
marvellous exactness, and that furious fire with which . . . the
Conservatoire perform[s] it on . . . great days of enthusiasm
and ardour.[77]

Mrs. Jameson wrote with similar sympathy about the family
and musical inclinations of Ludwig I of Bavaria. In the early
1830s she was present at a performance given by the Munich
Liederkranz and attended by the Bavarian Royal Family, and
she recounted that experience in glowing terms:

> The first rows of seats was assigned to [the royal family]; but
> no other distinction was made between [them] and the rest of
> the company. . . . At length a side door was thrown open: a
> voice announced "the king;" the trumpets sounded a salute; and
> all the people rose and remained standing until the royal
> guests were seated. The king entered first, the queen hanging
> on his arm. The duke Bernard of Saxe-Weimar, and his duchess
> [Ida of Saxe-Meiningen] followed. . . . The king bowed to the
> gentlemen in the orchestra, then to the company, and in a few
> moments all were seated. . . . Between the acts there was an
> interval of at least half an hour, during which the queen and
> the princess Matilda walked up and down in front of the or-
> chestra, entered into conversation with the ladies who were
> seated near, and those whom the rules of etiquette allowed to
> approach unsummoned and pay their respects. The king,
> meanwhile, walked round the room unattended, speaking to
> different people, and addressing the young bourgeoises, whose
> looks or whose toilette pleased him.

At about ten the concert ended, but "the king and queen remained a few minutes in conversation with those around them,
without displaying any ungracious hurry to depart; and the
whole scene left a pleasant impression upon my fancy."[78]

---

[77] Berlioz, pp. 325-326.

[78] Jameson I, pp. 70-74.

Music in Vormärz Germany

As historian Golo Mann has observed, people "looked back with a certain nostalgia to the days of the German Confederation . . . because those were comparatively harmless, quiet times" for residents and visitors alike.[79] And nostalgia can be cheerful, even comic. This was true too of the 1850s. Anyone, for instance, who compares Chapters 62-63 of *Vanity Fair* with many of the travellers's observations quoted above will see that Thackery did a good job of recalling as well as caricaturing the gentle Germany he himself visited during 1830-1831. "Pumpernickel," for example, is a good-natured lampoon of Vormärz Weimar and its occasional foreign guests: voracious eaters and cigar-smokers, pretty girls in picturesque costumes, and tourists like Mr. Jos who keep journals in which they record "elaborately the defects or excellences" of the inns they visit and the wines they drink.[80] Thackery's sense of fun was infectious, and some of his jokes appear in "real" accounts of Vormärz German travels. Chorley, for instance, makes use of a pun that occurs several times in *Vanity Fair* when he refers to "dames of high transparency" in describing Liszt's triumphs in 1840s Berlin.[81] But Thackery also admired the magnificence of the German Rhineland: its "scenes of friendly repose and beauty" and its "great castle-crested mountains" were the same scenes and mountains that other travellers admired, and that Liszt himself encountered whenever he made a Rhenish steamship voyage or ventured forth from his summer retreat at Nonnenwerth to give a concert in a nearby town. And Thackery's descriptions of musical occasions—of Wilhelmine Schroeder-Devrient singing the part of Leonora or, more delightful yet, of a German court performance of *Don Giovanni*—were evidently intended to awaken in the hearts of his readers the raptures of his heroine Emmy: "raptures so exquisite" that she (and they) would have to wonder "whether

---

[79] Mann, p. 54.

[80] See the Penguin Classics edition of William Makepeace Thackery, *Vanity Fair* (London and New York 1968), p. 717.

[81] See Chorley II, p. 246. This pun substitutes an English translation of the adjective "durchlässig" (i.e., "transparent") for the noun "Durchlaucht" (i.e., "Your Excellency" or "Your Highness").

it was not wicked" to take so much delight in the splendid music of Beethoven and Mozart.[82]

Germany during the 1830s and 1840s, then, was not only "comparatively harmless" and "quiet," but full of musical enthusiasm. If asked about that enthusiasm, almost every visitor would have given the same answer: the Germans loved music, and Germany was one of the most musical countries—if not *the* most musical—in the Western world. Supercilious he may have been, but even Willis took German music seriously. "Germany is the inner tabernacle of harmony," he wrote after his tour of 1845, "and the science of music is studied here with a philosophic depth that makes of it an intellectual profession."[83] Yet the Germans were musical enthusiasts as well as cogitators. "Dull and phlegmatic though the people who reside between the Vistula and the Rhine are generally considered," the Englishman John Strang wrote in 1831,

> I can assure you, that there are few hearts among them that cannot be roused to enthusiasm by a pealing chorus, or carried away captive by a soul-touching melody. The fact is, that in Germany, music, in all its branches, is thoroughly studied, practised, and worshipped by every one, from the peasant to the prince; affording, as it does, the most hallowed delight of the one, and the most favorite pastime of the other.[84]

Despite their musical enthusiasms, though, the Germans of the 1830s and 1840s were not uniformly sophisticated in their tastes, nor were their abilities as composers and performers uniformly remarkable. In the first of his four volumes devoted to the life and music of Richard Wagner, Ernest Newman describes Vormärz Germany as a country plagued by musical incompetence and indifference to new compositional styles.[85] Newman's observations were drawn from a number of first-hand accounts (including those of Berlioz), and there can be no doubt that many German musicians of that era, espe-

---

[82] Thackery, p. 719.

[83] Willis, p. 263.

[84] John Strang, *Germany in MDCCCXXXI* (London 1836), Vol. I, p. 244.

[85] See Newman I, especially Chapters VIII-IX ("The State of Music in Germany" and "The Economic and Social Status of the Musician").

cially orchestral musicians, were what Newman claims: poverty-stricken hacks who spent much of their lives warming benches in less-than-mediocre ensembles. But Newman's account was written to emphasize the difficulties Wagner faced when he first began to convert German audiences to his revolutionary musical and theatrical ideals; thus Newman emphasized what was wrong with the German musical world, not what was right with it. Others—Berlioz among them—did not share his views, especially about the standard German musical repertory and the respect accorded its composers. "In America," Willis remarks,

> the public at large makes little distinction between great composers and great players—all who are devoted to music, being, in common parlance, "musicians." But there is almost as much difference between composing harmony and playing it, as between making a horse and driving it. Liszt, Vieuxtemps, De Meyer, and other great players, it need hardly be said, are men of very different profession from Beethoven, Mozart, and Meyerbeer. . . . [E]ven in England, the two are superficially confused; and it is in Germany alone that the musical *composer* is of a recognized intellectual profession.[86]

Faulkner, himself (as we have seen) an amateur musician and a travel-writer who spoke up when something displeased him, attended a concert in Bonn directed by Professor Breidenstein—the man who helped organize the Beethoven Festival which Liszt underwrote and at which he participated as pianist and conductor. "The selection for the evening was from various authors of celebrity, more particularly . . . Beethoven; and truly, without straining at a compliment, so many sung well, that it was almost impossible to say who sung best [sic]."

The following day Faulker attended an instrumental concert given by a group of university students:

> The orchestral force, which was composed of thirty amateurs and professors, form[ed] three sides of a quadrangle. The horns, bassoons, and double-basses, occupied the back row, and immediately before them the clarionets and oboes. On the left wing were posted the first violins and flutes, and opposite to them the tenors and secondos, while the kettle-drums and

86 Willis, p. 263.

serpents were banished to the remotest left corner of the rear
rank, and the violoncellos occupied the centre. In front the
conductor stood, mounted on an elevated platform, in a position
equally conspicuous to the whole party. We had Beethoven's
"Jupiter" [sic] and the "Furianthe" [sic] of Weber, in a spirit
that would not have discredited the Frankfort opera. . . . You
were tortured by the discord of no "timeless, tuneless" scraper,
such as abound in my own land, who, utterly unconscious of
his vileness, throws a whole band into confusion as
irrecoverably as a raw recruit discomposes the movement of the
drill, equally the nuisance of the kibes before and corns behind.
The German amateur is no parrot or merely mechanical artist;
in the best sense of the word, he is a musician, as skilled in his
score as he is expert with his instrument.[87]

One aspect of music in Vormärz Germany, however, was
generally ignored by tourists: the profession of criticism.
Chorley, who found much to praise in the performances he
heard during the 1840s, was suspicious of journalists who sold
their opinions for money. In fact, Chorley was suspicious of the
German musical establishment as a whole: of its patron
princes, its court composers, its supercilious newspapers, and
its back-bench hacks. Against the dangers inherent in class
consciousness (the "Stände") and "the pleasures and the foibles
of what may be called small town life," Chorley warned, artists
and critics alike must be on their guard. Even in Berlin,
"notoriously the city of criticism," spite and malice—only just
masked by hypocritical "gallantry"—seemed to be the order of
the day:

[I]f I praised the hospitable attentions of —, I was chilled with
a direct "You go there? It is a hollow house." If I inquired in one
quarter for Mendelssohn's music, a dry, "Yes, he had talent as
a boy," discouraged a second question. — If I desired to know,
in a second, which of Marschner's works were most in favour,
"They perform none here," was the certain answer, and as certain a prelude to some story of cabal and quarrel, which it fa-
tigued the heart to hear.[88]

---

[87] Faulkner I, pp. 198-200.

[88] Chorley I, pp. 154-156.

Chorley also found fault with many individual German performances. In one production of Weber's *Freischütz*, for example, he encountered a quartet of horns that was "allowed to plod
through its work, with only the coarsest lights and shades
rubbed in, as one says of a painter's sketch." Furthermore,

> to say that the overture went correctly is tantamount to prais-
> ing the Lancashire chorus singers for going through the
> "Hallelujah" of the "Messiah" without utterly breaking
> down. . . . [And with the exception of one Herr Mantius], there
> was not a *solo* singer on the stage who did not sing with an
> impaired or inferior organ. Finish of style there was none; nor
> those traces of vocalization which give the most wretched
> Italian artist a certain air, and a certain hold upon the atten-
> tion.[89]

It is important to remember, however, that Liszt's German
experiences—like those of Chorley—were many and varied in
character. If some critics were frauds, others were not; if some
theater-goers happily swallowed anything they were given,
others did not.

Furthermore, different parts of Germany were informed
by different levels of experience and taste. Despite Chorley's
misgivings, Berlin seems to have been comparatively sophisticated musically, while Dresden—for all the love its rulers and
citizens had for music—was conservative in its tastes.[90] In the
hinterlands Liszt was almost always received as a kind of performing deity;[91] but in Leipzig and Berlin, where established
musical organizations like the Gewandhaus and the
Singakademie sponsored regular performances of excellent
music, he was (as we shall see) criticized almost as frequently
as he was praised. Nor should institutions like the Leipzig
Conservatory and the Gewandhaus be underestimated. Music
historians have sometimes made light of the Conservatory's

---

[89] Chorley I, pp. 150-152.

[90] See Berlioz, esp. pp. 288-289.

[91] A comparatively lengthy account of a Liszt concert in Neisse, Upper
Silesia (certainly "the hinterlands" as far as Rheinlanders and even
Berliners were concerned), appeared in an issue of the *Oberschlesischer
Bürgerfreund*. See ObBf No. 22 (18.3.1843), pp. 87-88. Much of this ac-
count is reprinted in Appendix D, which contains longer quotations from
1840s foreign-language sources. See Appendix D, quotation 13.

rather circumscribed musical milieu; Liszt himself later dismissed its faculty and students as "little Leipzigers," and Berlioz—ever wary of contrapuntal complexities—found the respect accorded Bach in Leipzig a little tiring.[92] But the Conservatory was a model of modern practice, and its director Mendelssohn was one of the finest composers of his day. And of the Gewandhaus concerts he heard in 1839, a few months before Liszt performed there for the first time, Chorley observed:

> [The directors and musicians of the Gewandhaus] opened their doors liberally to every new instrumental work of promise; taking good care, however, in cases of experiment, to assure the interest of the evening's performance by the repetition of some favourite and well-known production. . . I cannot pass over the performance of Beethoven's four overtures to "Fidelio" . . . or the series of three or more historical concerts, in which the effect meditated by Spohr, in his strangely incoherent symphony, was produced by progressive selections of instrumental music, beginning with Bach and Handel. We are still too far [in London] from being ripe for such performances as these—too largely apt to treat all public exhibitions as mere aimless amusements, where the most piquant novelty is the one thing best worth pursuing.[93]

The people of Leipzig may not always have appreciated Liszt's merits, but their opinions—shaped by performances that wrung praise from almost everyone, Chorley included—cannot be dismissed out of hand.

---

[92] See Berlioz, p. 324. For many Germans, however, Bach became during the mid-nineteenth century a symbol of the supremacy of their own musical culture. Heinrich von Treitschke, for example, claimed that among the achievements of Mendelssohn—that "thorough German" who repudiated Meyerbeer's *Huguenots*, a work that exercised "an irresistable influence over the masses" but lacked "the simple greatness of German art"—was the rediscovery of Bach's music, which revived "among the cultured the taste for the noble and *genuinely German* artistic forms of the symphony, the oratorio, and the sonata" [Treitschke, *History of Germany in the Nineteenth Century*, trans. Eden and Cedar Paul (Chicago 1975), pp. 299-300; italics added].

[93] Chorley II, pp. 30-31.

Liszt and the Vormärz Public

How, then, did Germany receive Liszt and his music during the 1840s? This question has no simple answer. Individual Germans must have thought and felt any number of things about Liszt, even though most of them seem to have thoroughly enjoyed his performances. Indeed, as a virtuoso—and, on most occasions, as a conductor and composer—Liszt was a phenomenal success. That a few critics were violently opposed to him is no surprise; given human nature, a few people will be opposed to almost anything one can think of, and a very few people—critics among them—will sell their opinions to the highest (or lowest) bidder. Liszt, then, was different things to different Germans in large part because there were different *kinds* of Germans, with differing national, political, and cultural attitudes.

To some, as we shall see below, Liszt was primarily, even exclusively a showman; to others he showman and artist combined. To some, he was a foreigner, whether "exotic" or merely undesirable; to others he was himself German, whether he acknowledged it or not. (To some, then, Liszt was a Frenchman, and many Germans had little use for the French; to others, he was an adopted patriot who set nationalist poems like "Was ist des deutschen Vaterland?" to music and, as a consequence, incurred the wrath of French critics.)[94] To some, Liszt was a poseur, the son of a sheepherder who put on airs along with the medals he often sported in public; to others, he was a democratic hero, a man whose genius made it natural for him to be entertained not only by kings, but also by crowds of university students (notorious as the most outspoken opponents of the status quo). To still others, he was Romanticism incarnate, an advocate and example of everything dangerous (and delicious) about that movement, everything from "the extraordinary, the mysterious, the irrational, [and] the fantastic," to "unconventional eroticism" as well as "sentimentalism mixed

---

[94] Issues of nationality and patriotism pertaining to Liszt's German tours are discussed elsewhere and at greater length by the present author. See Saffle, "Liszt und die Deutschen, 1840-1845," scheduled when the present volume went to press to be published in *Liszt und die Nationalitäten: Bericht über das internationale Symposion Eisenstadt, 10.-12. März 1994*, ed. Gerhard J. Winkler (in press).

with irony and self-derision," and "the peculiar features of a unique personality."[95] It goes almost without saying that he appealed powerfully to the fairer sex.

And to most Germans—indeed, to almost all of them—Liszt was a genial, charitable, charming young man. Whatever his artistic successes or failures, his generosity on behalf of so many causes (including "German" causes, like the completion of the Cathedral at Cologne) made it difficult in the last analysis to carp too much about the huge amounts of money his concerts took in. In short, Liszt was the idol of thousands and the enemy (or the disappointment) only of a few. Within the quiet, anxious social order of the Vormärz era—an era marvellously portrayed in Thomas Mann's *Buddenbrooks*, with its references to "real" people and places like members of student Burschenschaften and the great Hamburg fire of 1842—Liszt's music stood out in bold and often elegant relief.

In order to understand Liszt's German tours fully, however, we must grapple more fully with both the plaudits Liszt received from the many and the rebukes he received from the few. The evidence presented in newspapers and magazines, in concert programs, posters, and box-office records, and in reminiscences, letters, diaries, and documents of almost every description presents a complex but comprehensible picture of his German performances and their receptions by critics and audiences alike. It is to these sources of information—to their inherent characteristics, and especially to their limitations—that the next chapter will be devoted.

---

[95] See the remarks about "Romanticism and Politics" in Hertz, *Nationality in History and Politics* (New York c. 1966), pp. 353-355.

Frankfurter patriotisches

Wochenblatt

zum
Besten der Armen und des Waisenhauses.

(Redacteur Dr. C. W. Spieker.)

No. 7.

Den 25. Januar 1843.

Klavierkoncert
von
Dr. Liszt.

Am 19. Januar gab der größte Klavierspieler unserer Zeit, Herr Kapellmeister **Dr. Friedr.** Liszt, im Schauspielhause ein Konzert, das alle Gegenwärtige mit Bewunderung, ja mit Staunen erfüllte. Eine solche bis ins Unglaubliche gesteigerte Fertigkeit, verbunden mit einem seelenvollen Ausdruck tiefer Empfindung und ächt musikalischer Gedanken, ist noch nicht dagewesen. Die edle Musica wird leider in unsern Tagen oft zu einem sprühenden Feuerwerk mit Raketen und Brillantfeuer herabgewürdigt. Da sprühet und blitzt, da siedet und zischt es; da werden Schwierigkeiten gehäuft, pikante Passagen mühsam ausgegrübelt, die Reihe der Tasten en carrière durchstürmt und in wilder Raserei eine Masse von Tönen unter einander geworfen, daß dem bestürzten, gleichsam übergerannten Zuhörer Hören und Sehen vergeht.

Wäre Liszt's Klavierspiel nichts weiter als ein solches herkulisches Spiel mit Tönen, hätte man nur die Bildungsfähigkeit der Hand und die Schnellkraft der Finger zu bewundern, so würde man ihn kaum einen Künstler nennen dürfen; sein Spiel würde kalt lassen und nicht die Seele in ihrer Tiefe bewegen. Aber er versteht die starre Tastenreihe zu beleben und zu beseelen, den Hörer in den Strom seiner Gedanken und Gefühle hinein zu ziehen und eine innere Befriedigung zurückzulassen. In seinem Spiel ist etwas Edles und Gediegenes, Geistvolles und Erhebendes. Was er vorträgt, ist durch seine Seele gegangen, nichts Gesuchtes und Erkünsteltes, sondern Wahrhaftiges und Phantasiereiches.

> Er spielt in schönsten Weisen
> Recht aus des Herzensgrund,
> Und giebt in Sehnsuchtstönen
> Sein tiefstes Leben kund.

Plate 1

A page from Frankfurt an der Oder's
Patriotisches Wochenblatt (24 January 1843)

CHAPTER II

Liszt's German Experiences: Sources and Documents

Was man in der Zeitung liest ist manchmal auch wahr.
Bismarck

The most informative accounts of Liszt's performances in Germany during 1840-1845 appear in the contemporary press, especially in local newspapers and musical magazines as well as in contemporary books and pamphlets about Liszt and his career. Also of value are other kinds of documentary evidence, including advertising posters, playbills, business records, diplomas, and testimonials of various kinds. This is not to underestimate the importance of the information contained in Liszt's correspondence, especially the long series of letters he addressed to the Comtesse Marie d'Agoult, his lover during much of the 1830s and 1840s and the mother of his three children. Nor should reminiscences and related documents like diary entries be ignored, even those written down and published decades after the events they describe were over. Finally, a few other sources—poems, plays, pictures of various kinds, and inscriptions, as well as secondary sources (especially those published prior to World War II and based on archival evidence lost or destroyed during that war)—contain information today available nowhere else. Together, these sources tell us much about Liszt's German tours.

None of these sources is definitive, of course; the very idea of "definitive" historical evidence is untenable. But thousands of nineteenth- and twentieth-century documents refer to Liszt's German experiences, and the information they contain can be conflated to produce detailed accounts of many individual musical events as well as of Liszt's relationship with German audiences and the German musical establishment of the 1840s. The pages that follow describe these documents, reliable and otherwise, and evaluate some of the information they contain.

Newspapers

Daily and weekly newspapers constitute the single most substantial and reliable source of information about Liszt's performances in Vormärz Germany. Advertisements and announcements identify most of the dates, times, places, and admission prices of individual concerts, and some advertisements contain reliable concert programs. Newspaper reviews and notices assess Liszt's piano-playing, composing, or conducting, and many of them also describe audience reactions. Finally, "feature" stories of various kinds—anecdotes, personal announcements, comments in gossip columns, and occasional biographical articles and interpretive essays—provide a considerable amount of supplementary information. A typical German newspaper recital-review page is reproduced above as Plate 1. A second newspaper recital-review page is reproduced below as Plate 2. A newspaper advertisement for still another recital is reproduced as Plate 3.[1]

The Germans were among the first peoples to print and circulate newspapers; the *Frankfurter Ober-Postamts-Zeitung*, one of the publications that advertised some of Liszt's Rhineland concerts, may then have been the oldest daily newspaper in the world.[2] By March 1840, when he performed for the first time as an adult in Germany, Liszt would have been able to purchase and read more than 100 daily and weekly papers.[3] Until recently, however, nineteenth-century papers like the *Ober-Postamts-Zeitung* were rarely consulted by musicologists. Several factors have contributed to this situ-

---

[1] Like many other items referred to in the present chapter, these documents are also discussed in Chapter III and cited as sources in Appendix C.

[2] According to Robert W. Desmond, *The Information Process: World News Reporting to the Twentieth Century* (Iowa City, Iowa 1978), p. 33. In 1866 the *Postamts-Zeitung*, then some 250 years old, merged with the *Frankfurter Zeitung*, a newspaper established in 1855; both papers survive today in the form of the world-renowned *Frankfurter allgemeine Zeitung*.

[3] See Gert Hagelweide, *Deutsche Zeitungsbestände in Bibliotheken und Archiven* (Düsseldorf 1974). Virtually every German newspaper cited below is identified by siglum and title in Appendix A.

ation. For one thing, the political fragmentation of Germany prior to the 1870s prevented the establishment of a national newspaper archive comparable in scope and holdings, say, to the British Library's newspaper collections or the Newspaper Division of the Library of Congress.[4] Furthermore, early attempts at cataloging German newspaper collections produced reference works of uneven quality.[5] By the beginning of the twentieth century, however, the Deutsche Staatsbibliothek in Berlin had assembled a collection of German newspapers second to none in the world.[6] Unfortunately, Allied bombing raids during World War II damaged the Staatsbibliothek, as well as archives in Hamburg, Frankfurt, and other major cities. Then, after 1945, Hitler's Germany was divided into three new nations: the Federal Republic of Germany, the German Democratic Republic, and the People's Republic of Poland.[7] Only in 1974, with the publication of Gert Hagelweide's reliable guide to post-war collections of German papers, did up-to-date information about international holdings become readily available.[8]

In general, Vormärz German newspapers can be separated into four categories: 1) those devoted for the most part to political events, local happenings, vital statistics, and so on; 2) those devoted almost entirely to personal and commercial an-

[4] Information about the history of important German newspapers appears in *Zeitung und Bibliothek: Ein Wegweiser zu Sammlungen und Literatur*, ed. Hagelweide (Pullach bei München 1974).

[5] For example, *Die deutsche Presse. Verzeichniss der im Deutschen Reiche erschienenen Zeitungen und Zeitschriften*, Vol. I ["Politische Zeitungen, Amts-, Local- und Anzeigeblätter"] (Forbach 1885).

[6] See Hans Traub et al., *Standortskatalog wichtiger Zeitungsbestände in deutschen Bibliotheken* (Leipzig 1933). Traub identifies a number of papers omitted from Hagelweide's somewhat less comprehensive catalog.

[7] Portions of what was Vormärz Germany also belong today to Russia (formerly the Union of Soviet Socialist Republics). Research problems involving archives in present-day Poland, eastern Germany, and Russia are discussed below.

[8] Hagelweide's catalog is identified above. Other recent catalogs of German papers include Adelheid Schäfer, *Hessische Zeitungen* (Darmstadt 1978); Hans-Dieter Wüstling and Johannes Jandt, *Sächsische Zeitungen in Dresdner Bibliotheken und Archiven: Ein Katalog der Bestände bis 1945* (Dresden 1980); and Felicital Marwinski, *Zeitungen und Wochenblaetter* (Weimar 1968). NB: Marwinski's and Wüstling/Jandt's typescript catalogs refer only to holdings of local papers.

nouncements; 3) "Fremdenlisten" devoted almost entirely to information about the comings and goings of visitors in limited geographical areas; and 4) newspapers or newspaper supplements ("Beilagen") of a literary, scientific, fashionable, or other specialized character. To some extent these kinds of papers cannot be distinguished clearly from each other. The *Dresdner Anzeiger*, for example, was an advertising paper that also published a "Fremdenliste"; so did the *Leipziger Tageblatt und Anzeiger*. Only a few literary or scientific papers as such were published independently: Leipzig's *Illustrirte Zeitung*, for example. Instead, literary and scientific newspapers often appeared as supplements to daily papers. *Die Posaune*, which was devoted almost exclusively to fashion and the arts, appeared as a supplement to the *Hannoversche Morgenzeitung*.[9] *Mnemosyne* appeared as a supplement to the *Neue Würzburger Zeitung*, while the so-called "Schwäbische Chronik" supplemented Stuttgart's *Schwäbischer Merkur*. Exceptions to these classifications included Vormärz Germany's most important and "modern" daily papers: the *Augsburger Allgemeine Zeitung* (mentioned in Chapter I), the *Allgemeine Preußische Staats-Zeitung* of Berlin, and the so-called *Vossische Zeitung* and *Spenersche Zeitung*, also of Berlin. Other Vormärz papers can also be difficult to classify.

Liszt himself collected newspaper clippings associated with his German tours, and so did the Comtesse d'Agoult. Clippings from their collections survive today at the Goethe- und Schiller-Archiv, Weimar;[10] and in the so-called "Second Scrapbook" of Marie d'Agoult, owned by the Bibliothèque Municipale, Versailles.[11] Among these clippings are several items apparently available nowhere else in the world. The d'Agoult Scrapbook, for example, contains an article taken from the *Tribunal für Musik, Literatur und Theater*, a paper pub-

---

9   See Hagelweide, p. 176.

10 Especially D-WRgs Liszt Kasten 249ff. Other Weimar Liszt documents are cited below by shelf number(s) and contents.

11 F-Vm Shelf No. "Holmes J1." Hereafter the "d'Agoult Scrapbook" or simply "Scrapbook." NB: This document should not be confused with F-Vm Ms. F-766 (the so-called "First Scrapbook"), which also contains a few clippings—among them, one from the *Journal de Liège* (27 August 1843) about Liszt's appointment to the position of Kapellmeister at Weimar.

lished in the early 1840s at Frankfurt a.M.[12] Unfortunately, all known collections of the *Tribunal* as well as those of a few others like Ulm's *Wochenblatt* were wiped out during 1944-1945.[13]

Most of Liszt's biographers have made only sporadic use of these and other newspaper sources. Ramann, for instance, cites a small number of Berlin, Dresden, and Leipzig reviews in her accounts of Liszt's concert tours.[14] Lájos Koch, the most important early Liszt bibliographer, identifies a number of German newspaper articles in his invaluable "bibliographic essay."[15] Finally, Emile Haraszti and Peter Raabe collected press clippings associated with Liszt's activities. But Haraszti

---

[12] See Heinrich Meidinger, *Frankfurt's gemeinnüßige Anstalten* (Frankfurt a.M. 1845), p. 408, which describes the *Tribunal* as a musical newspaper published twice each week during 1839 and the early 1840s. A brief announcement about the *Tribunal* may also be found in Iris 11 (1840), p. 168. Like a very few other rare music periodicals, the *Tribunal* was omitted from Imogen Fellinger's *Verzeichnis der Musikzeitschriften des 19. Jahrhunderts* (Regensburg 1968). Other rare clippings preserved in the d'Agoult Scrapbook and in other collections are cited in Appendix C.

One problem confronting bibliographers is deciding whether a given serial publication is a "newspaper" or a "magazine." Quoting Emil Dovifat, Hagelweide [p. 22] defines a newspaper as a publication providing "the widest publicity with the shortest regular periodicity to most recent current events." For small Vormärz German towns, weekly newspapers would have fit this definition; so would the *Tribunal*, at least as far as music-lovers were concerned. Yet periodicals like *Das Rheinland* are sometimes called "newspapers," sometimes "magazines." See the *Bibliographie der Zeitschriften des deutschen Sprachgebietes bis 1900*, 3 vols.; ed. Joachim Kirchner (Stuttgart 1966-1977).

[13] Among such papers were the *Zeitinteressen* and the *Intelligenzblatt*, both printed in Ulm. Prior to 1945 runs of both papers were owned by the Württembergische Landesbibliothek, Stuttgart. Liszt is rumored to have visited Ulm during November 1843, but this rumor can no longer be verified.

[14] For example, the references to MzRh, DrWb, and VZ in Ramann II, pp. 65 and 168. Ramann's collection of newspaper clippings and copies is preserved in D-WRgs Liszt Kasten 364.

[15] See Lájos Koch, *Liszt Ferenc bibliográphiai kísérlet/Franz Liszt: ein bibliographischer Versuch* (Budapest 1936), esp. pp. 22-24. Several of Koch's citations cannot be verified today—among them, an article about Liszt and a concert of the Berlin Academic Men's Choral Society published in the *Berliner Figaro* on 18 February 1843. The present author could not find this article in the collections of the City Library, Budapest (where Koch worked), and the entire 1843 Deutsche Staatsbibliothek run of this paper was destroyed during World War II.

specialized in French-language documents; his work emphasizes French (rather than Hungarian or German) influences on Liszt's life and accomplishments.[16] Raabe, who placed more emphasis on German aspects of Liszt's career, unhappily relied to a considerable extent on handwritten copies of newspaper articles supplied somewhat sporadically by assistants.[17] Other scholars have made more consistent use of newspaper sources, especially those that describe Liszt's visits to other parts of Europe.[18] Descriptions of his life and accomplishments published in the nineteenth-century German press, however, remain largely unexamined.

Not all 1840s German papers, even those devoted to the arts and to local affairs, published musical news or concert reviews, and not all advertising papers carried concert announcements and notices. Furthermore, some parts of Vormärz Germany had no papers of their own, and a few papers known to have been published during the early 1840s seem to have disappeared completely.[19] Surviving runs of local newspapers, however, contain more detailed information about Liszt's performances in Germany than do any other kind of source material—more even than contemporary music magazines, which (as we shall see below) often relied on newspapers for their facts and figures.

16 For example, Emile Haraszti, "Liszt à Paris: Quelques documents inédits," *Revue musicale* 165 (1936), pp. 241-258; and 167 (1936), pp. 5-16.

17 D-WRgs Liszt Kasten 557 contains some of the copies Raabe used in his researches; unfortunately, many of these items cannot be identified today. The results of Raabe's researches appear not only in his two-volume Liszt monograph, but in newspaper articles like "Liszts erste Begegnung mit Leipzig: Auch ein Kapitel Gewandhausgeschichte," *Leipziger Neue Nachrichten* (16 December 1931).

18 See, for example, Dezsö Legány, *Franz Liszt: Unbekannte Presse und Briefe aus Wien* (Cologne and Graz 1984), as well as Allsobrook's account of Liszt's British tours identified in Chapter I. Information about other studies involving Liszt and the nineteenth-century press appears in Saffle, *Franz Liszt: A Guide to Research* (New York 1991), esp. pp. 113-116.

19 For example, the 1844-1845 issues of the *Rhein- und Mosel-Zeitung*. See Hagelweide, p. 199. Other papers reported missing still exist: for example, 1842 issues of Tilsit's *Echo am Memelufer*, which survive in the Deutsche Staatsbibliothek [*contra* Hagelweide, p. 289].

Münchener Tagblatt.

Siebenzehnter Jahrgang.

Montag   *№* **300.**   30. Oktober 1843.

Das Tagblatt erscheint täglich; hohe Festtage ausgenommen. Der Tränumerationspreis beträgt für ein J br 3 fl., für 1|2 Jahr 1 fl. 30 kr., vierteljährig 45 kr. Bei Inseraten kostet der Raum einer gewöhnlichen Spaltzeile 3 kr. Passende Beiträge werden mit Dank angenommen und gediegene honorirt.

Anzeigen für den folgenden Tag werden längstens **10 Uhr Vormittags** angenommen.

Salon.

Liszt wird, dem allgemeinen Wunsche entsprechend, heute Montag noch ein **viertes Concert**, gleich dem vorigen im k. Hoftheater, geben, und zwar abermals zu einem wohlthätigen Zwecke — zum Besten der in Griechenland befindlichen größtentheils aus Bayern bestehenden, dem Militär nicht angehörenden Deutschen, zu deren Unterstützung, da sie in Folge der jüngsten Ereignisse daselbst brodlos geworden sind, bekanntlich von Se. Majestät dem Könige eine Sammlung in allen größern Städten des Königreichs bewilligt worden ist. Der geniale Künstler begründet sich durch diese Wohlthätigkeitsakte in unserer Mitte ein nimmer verlöschliches Andenken, da er dem Ruhme seiner Meisterschaft den noch schöneren edler und großartiger Uneigennützigkeit und eines für fremde Noth warm fühlenden Herzens hinzufügt.

(Privat=Musik=Verein.) Der hiesige Privat=Musikverein feyerte am Montag den 13. ds. das allerhöchste Namensfest J. M. der Königin mit einem großen Vocal = und Instrumental=Concerte, welcher brillanten Abendunterhaltung nebst einer großen Anzahl Gesellschaftsmitgliedern, auch viele dazu geladene Personen von Distinction beiwohnten, worunter man mehrere der ausgezeichnetsten hiesigen Virtuosen bemerkte, die sich auf das vortheilhafteste über jene musikalische Soirée aussprachen. — Das Orchester, von dem k. Hofmusikadspiranten Hrn. Carl Huber dirigirt, war großartig besetzt und executirte mit größter Präcision und überraschendem Effecte die Ouvertüre zu Weber's Freischütz" so wie jene zur „Stummen von Portici" von Auber und ein sehr wohlgelungenes ansprechendes Potpourri von Carl Huber, dessen Bruder der k. Hofkapellsänger Michael Huber ein darin vorkommendes Lied mit Auszeichnung vortrug. — Eine Phantasie für das Violoncello von dem k. Hofmusikus Hrn. Menter jun. mit großer Kunstfertigkeit ausgeführt, wurde mit dem lebhaftesten Beifalle und Hervorrufen des Künstlers belohnt, welche Ehre auch der k. Hofschauspielerin Frl. Söltl nach dem Vortrage einiger Declamations=Stücke in der 1. und 2. Abtheilung des Concertes erzeigt wurde. — Der hier rühmlichst bekannte junge Violin=Virtuose Hr. Fr. Mayer spielte das Adagio und Rondo des Violin=Concerts Nr. 2. von Beriot und erregte durch den Ausdruck des Gefühls, sowie durch die Fertigkeit und Reinheit seines Vortrages allgemeine Bewunderung. Da der junge Tonkünstler dem Vernehmen nach, erst 16 Jahre zählt und es in der Kunst schon so weit gebracht hat, so berechtiget sein reiches Talent gewiß zu den schönsten Erwartungen für die Zukunft. Herr Mayer fand aber auch die lebhafteste Theilnahme und Anerkennung und wurde nach vollendetem Vortrage stürmisch hervorgerufen. — Ein Chor von jugendlich frischen Stimmen sang mit Beglei-

---

Plate 2

A page from the *Münchener Tagblatt* (30 October 1843)

baar mit 1 % Rabatt bereit. Die Obligatio-
nen sind sämmtlich zweifach und gut versichert
und 5%tig.
Ehrhardt's öffentl. Bureau.

(Parfümerie),

als Pommade, Oele, Seifen in verschiedenen
Sorten, wovon in Cartons assortirt zu passen-
den Geschenken sich eignen, habe stets in frischer
Waare am Lager
Friedr. Ackermann

(Empfehlung).

Hiermit bringe eine hübsche Auswahl geripp-
ter Strichen glatt u. façonirt sowie davon
gefertigte Chemissettes und Manchettes in em-
pfehlende Erinnerung.
Fried. Ackermann.

Geschäfts-Empfehlung. Ich beehre
mich einem hiesigen und aus-
wärtigen Publikum die Anzeige
zu machen, daß ich mein Ge-
schäft wieder angefangen habe
und empfehle mich im Repari-
ren aller Art Uhren, für das
früher genossene Zutrauen dan-
kend, bitte ich auch in meiner
neuen Wohnung um zahlreichen
Zuspruch, und werde mir alle
Mühe geben, meine werthen Kunden gut und billig
zu bedienen.
August Krämer, Uhrmacher
wohnhaft bei Herrn Rechtsconsulent Strauß
am Markt.

Privat = Verkäufe.

Zu verkaufen. Es ist eine Mehltruhe
oder auch zu einer Habertruhe tauglich, zu verkaufen; auch ist immer wieder Pfund weiß Bier-
hefe zu haben bei
Frau Münzing, wohnhaft
bei Bäcker Berg.

(Fett=Vieh=Versteigerung) Am
Montag, den 27. Novbr.
dss. J. Mittags 1 Uhr,
werden in meiner Fabrik
12 Stück fette Ochsen und
6 „ „ Kühe
im Wege des Aufstreichs verkauft, wozu die Liebhaber mit dem Bemerken hiemit höflich eingela-
den werden, daß das Vieh noch weitere acht
Tage unentgeltlich stehen bleiben kann.
Georg Friedrich Rund.

Amtliche Verleihungen.

[Güterverpachtung.] Samstag den
18. ds. M. Nachmittags 3 Uhr verpachtet die
unterzeichnete Stelle auf dem
Rathhaus in Sontheim
4 1/8 Mrg. 42 5/8 Rt. Acker,
den sogenannten Nonnenacker,
auf Sontheimer Markung, auf 18 Jahre, zu
4 gleichen Theilen im öffentlichen Aufstreich.
In der letzten Pachtperiode war Kupferschmied
Kunz von Heilbronn Pächter dieses Gutes.
Heilbronn den 14 Novbr. 1843.
K. Kameralamt.

Privat=Verleihungen.

Zu vermiethen. In der Neckarsulmer Vor-
stadt ist für eine einzelne Dame oder einen
Herrn ein äußerst freundlich gelegenes Zim-
mer nebst Alcoven, wozu auf Verlangen auch
eine Bühnenkammer abgegeben werden kann,
zu vermiethen und sogleich zu beziehen. Wo?
sagt Ausgeber dieß.

CONCERT
des
Dr. Franz Liszt

in Heilbronn, Mittwoch, den 15. Nvbr.

im Falkensaale.

Anfang Abends halb 7 Uhr.

Eintrittspreis 1 fl. 30 kr.

1. Ouvertüre aus „Wilhelm Tell.“
2. Andante aus „Lucie von Lammermoor.“
3. Fantasie über Thema's aus „Don
Juan.“
4. „Das Ständchen.“ } Lieder von
5. „Der Erlkönig“ } Schubert
6. Chromatischer Galopp

Sämmtliche Nummern werden auf
dem Flügel vorgetragen von dem Con-
zertgeber.

Gedruckt und verlegt unter der Verantwortlichkeit der Carl Schell'schen Buchdruckerei

Plate 3
A page from Heilbronn's *Intelligenz-Blatt* (11 November 1843)

DAS RHEINLAND

wie es ernst und heiter ist.

Fünfter Jahrgang. Redigirt von Dr. Fr. Wiest.

N: 106. Sonntag, 5. September 1841.

Ein billet doux des Teufels

an

Franz Liszt.

[Ein sehr seltenes Manuscript, mitgetheilt von Dr. Wiest.]

Satanasruh. In der Nacht vom
1. auf den 2. September 1841.

Sehr geehrter Herr College!

Ich habe Ihrem letzten Concerte in Mainz beige-
wohnt. Sie haben mir eine schlaflose Nacht verur-
sacht. Der Kopf wirbelte mir von Melodieen, Har-
monieen, von Ton-Combinationen, wie ich sie nie
gehört, und ich, der ich nur im Höllenlärm der Unter-
welt Ruhe finde, konnte in den Nachklängen, die Ihr
Spiel in mir aufkeimen ließ, zu keinem innern Frie-
den kommen. Es war mir, als wäre ich eine arme
Seele und Sie der Teufel hinter mir! Sie sprangen
mir in merkwürdigen Passagen nach, Sie machten
einen Griff nach mir, einen Griff, wie ihn nur Liszt
machen kann, natürlich hatten Sie mich gleich am
Genicke. Jetzt rissen sie mich hinauf zu jener Glet-
scherhöhe, wo der Aether waltet und die Sphären
klingen, dann schleuderten Sie mich wieder in die tiefste
Tiefe, in den Mittelpunkt der Erde hinein, wo die
Erdbeben fabricirt und die Metalle gekocht werden!
Jetzt schlugen Sie einen Triller mit mir an Felsen-
riffen, dann schleiften sie mich im tollen Fluge über
die Tastenfläche ihres Claviers, es ging Berg auf,
Berg ab, über Leichenfelder, Kirchhöfe und Blumen-
paradiese! Jetzt legten Sie mich auf einen Ambos
und hämmerten mit dem Centnergewicht Ihres kleinen
Fingers auf mir herum, dann dehnten Sie mich aus-
einander wie Gummielasticum vom Nord- bis zum
Südpole. Ihre eine Hand war am Nord-, die andre
am Südpole. Sie umfaßten für mich eine ganze
Welt von Schmerz und Wollust, von Todesgrauen
und Lebenswonne, und jetzt erst ließen Sie mich
verhauchen, verhauchen wie den Todes-
seufzer des Bischofmörders Kühnapfel, nachdem
Sie mich von unten hinauf gerädert hatten. Ich
danke Ihnen, Herr Liszt, für diese Nachgefühle
Ihres Concertspiels! Wie Sie mit den Seelen um-
springen, bald in der Galoppe chromatique, bald im

valse infernale, können Sie getrost jedem Teufel von
erster Qualität ein Douplé vorgeben.

Und dennoch, dennoch, obwohl Sie mir gezeigt,
daß ich in meinem Metier nur ein Stümper, daß ich
nur Fliegen-Seelen fange, da wo sie Adler-Geister
und Löwenherzen in Ihre Netze ziehen, dennoch muß
ich Ihnen meine Bewunderung ausdrücken. Nun weiß
ich freilich nicht, ob Ihnen an meiner Bewunderung
etwas liegt; Sie sind zwar gewiß schon von manchem
dümmeren Teufel als ich bin, bewundert worden, so
wie aber auch der geistreichste Mephisto vor Ihrem
Clavierspiele die Waffen der Satyre strecken muß, doch
wird Ihnen meine Bewunderung nicht völlig gleich-
giltig sein, wenn Sie erfahren, daß sie Ihnen ein
musikalischer Teufel darbringt. Ja! vor meinem
Falle war ich einer jener Cherube, die bestimmt sind,
die Orgel-Blasbälge zu treten, wenn der Alte da
oben seine Gewitter- und Sturmwind-Concerte zum
Besten gibt. Ich verstehe mich demnach auf die musikalischen Windmachereien der Gegenwart, ich weiß,
wie die Virtuosen der Gegenwart alle Register aufzie-
hen, um Lärm in der Welt zu machen, wie die Journalistik
getreten wird als Blasbalg, um künstliche Stürme des
Enthusiasmus hervorzubringen, dieß alles weiß ich nur
zu gut, als daß ich mit der graffirenden Bewunderungs-
Sucht der Welt den Künstler-Armeen gegenüber Hand
in Hand geben könnte. Aber bei Ihnen, sehr verehr-
ter College, Künstler und Teufel par excellence,
mache ich eine Ausnahme!

Als mir der Zettel, die Ankündigung Ihres Concertes zukam, war mir eben eine frische Sendung von
Seelen einiger Tausend falscher Spieler, Ballettän-
zerinnen, Pietisten, Wucherern und Volksbedrückern zu-
geschickt worden, gewiß die lockendsten Teufelsbraten
zum Soupé, die man sich nur denken kann, aber ich
ließ alles liegen und stehen und eilte zu Ihnen. Ich
schwitzte in Ihrem Concerte, daß mir die Schwefel-
pfühle meines Gebietes wie kühlende Luftbäder hätten vorkommen müssen, ich war den ganzen Abend
hindurch eingepfercht zwischen zwei sogenannte Kunstkenner und zwei sogenannte Clavier-Trommler,
die immer und immer behaupteten, das was Sie
machten, wäre eben keine Hexerei, nur Fingergeschick-
lichkeit; ich hätte aus der Haut fahren mögen, wäre
mir nicht um meinen neuen Frack leid gewesen, aber

Plate 4

A page from *Das Rheinland* (5 September 1841)

Breslauer Theater.

Dienstag den 31. Januar 1843.

Erstes Concert

des Hof-Kapellmeisters, Ritter etc. etc. Herrn

Dr. Franz Liszt.

Nach dem ersten Akte des Schauspiels:

1) Concert in Es-dur (Erster Satz) von L. v. Beethoven, mit Orchester Begleitung. - - - - - - - - - - - Fr. Liszt.
2) Ave Maria, Lied von Schubert, - - - - - Fr. Liszt.
3) Reminiscenzen aus Norma (Grosse Fantasie), - Fr. Liszt.

Nach dem Schlusse des Schauspiels.

4) Andante, Finale aus Lucia di Lammermoor, - - Fr. Liszt.
5) Ungarische Melodien und Marsch, - - - - Fr. Liszt.

Neu einstudirt:

Schwärmerei nach der Mode.

Schauspiel in 4 Akten von Karl Blum.

Personen:

Gräfin Angelika,	Madame Pollert.	Anton, Diener der Gräfin, — Herr Hofrichter.
Justizrath Hellbern,	Herr Henning.	Ein Pachter, — Herr Gleger.
Herr Julius von Senbheim,	Herr Reder.	Erster } Landmann, — Herr Hoffmann.
Potter Redum,	Herr Rottmayer.	Zweiter } Herr Muller.
Fabricius, Haushofmeister der Gräfin,	Herr Wohlbrück.	Erste } Landfrau, — Demoiselle Luders.
Christian, sein Neffe,	Herr Bercht.	Zweite } Madame Werthrad.
Pachter Freiburg,	Herr Seydelmann.	Dritte }
Johann, Diener des Grafen Senbheim,	Herr Rottmayer d. j.	Bediente.
		Landleute.

Scene: auf dem Gute Angelika's am Bodensee.   Die Handlung beginnt Morgens und endet Abends.

Regisseur: Herr Rottmayer.

Preise der Plätze.

Ein Platz in den Logen des I. Ranges, im Balkon, in den Parquet-Logen, im Parquet | Rthr. 20 Sgr.
Ein Platz in den Logen des II. Ranges, ein Sitzplatz im Parquet . . . . 1 — 7½
Ein Platz im Parterre . . . . — 25
Ein Platz in den Gallerie-Logen . . . . — 17½
Ein Platz auf der Gallerie . . . . — 12½

Zu den Concerten des Herrn Dr. Fr. Liszt können Billets für die Logen und festen Plätze im Theater-Bureau gelöst werden. Die Billets zu Stehplätzen auf dem Balkon und im Parterre, so wie die Gallerie-Logen und Gallerie-Plätze werden nur am Abende der betreffenden Vorstellung an der Kasse ausgegeben.

Das zweite Concert des Herrn Dr. Fr. Liszt findet Donnerstag den 2. Februar, das dritte Sonnabend den 4. Februar statt.

Einlaß 5 Uhr.   Anfang 6 Uhr.   Ende gegen 9 Uhr.

Morgen,
zum Benefiz des Herrn Hirsch:

neu einstudirt: „Die Zauberflöte," Oper in zwei Akten. Musik von Mozart. Die drei neuen Decorationen sind vom Decorateur Herrn Pape.

Herr Hof-Kapellmeister Dr. Franz Liszt wird die Güte haben, diese Aufführung zu dirigiren.

Plate 5

A poster for Liszt's Breslau concert of 31 January 1843

Salle de l'hôtel du Bazar.

Mardi le 21. Fevrier 1843.

CONCERT

donné par le Dr. F. Liszt.

PROGRAMME.

1) Andante de Lucie de Lammermoor.
2) Fantaisie sur des motifs de Don Juan.
3) Etude
4) Mazurek } de Chopin.
5) Erlkönig.
6) Galopp chromatique.

On commencera à 6½ heures.

Prix des billets à 2 Rtl.

On trouve des billets chez Messrs. *Bieczyński & Schmidt*, rue de Breslau No. 12.

Plate 6
A playbill for Liszt's Posen concert of 21 February 1843

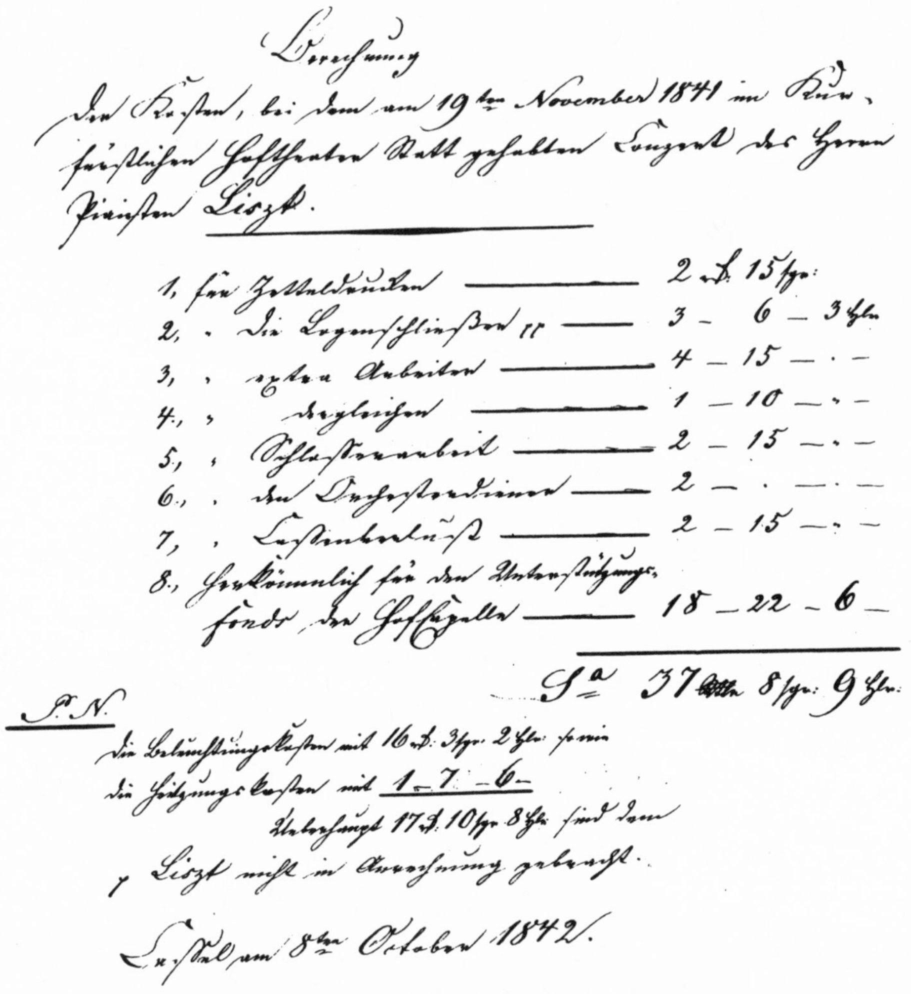

Berechnung

der Kosten, bei dem am 19ten November 1841 im Kurfürstlichen Hoftheater Saal gehaltenen Concert des Herrn Pianisten Liszt.

1, für Zetteldrucken	—	2 rt. 15 gr.
2, " die Logenschließer etc	—	3 – 6 – 3 hl.
3, " extra Arbeiter	—	4 – 15 – " –
4, " dergleichen	—	1 – 10 – " –
5, " Schlosserarbeit	—	2 – 15 – " –
6, " den Orchesterdiener	—	2 – " – " –
7, " Kastenverlust	—	2 – 15 – " –
8, herkömmlich für den Unterstützungsfonds der Hofkapelle	—	18 – 22 – 6 –

Sa. 37 rt. 8 gr. 9 hl.

P.N.

Die Beleuchtungskosten mit 16 rt. 3 gr. 2 hl. ferner die Heizungskosten mit 1 – 7 – 6 –
Überhaupt 17 rt. 10 gr. 8 hl. sind dem Liszt nicht in Anrechnung gebracht.

Cassel am 8ten October 1842.

Plate 7

Accounts for Liszt's Kassel concert of 19 November 1841
(courtesy Hessisches Staatsarchiv)

This bill and others like it document not only what Liszt paid to hire halls, light them, heat them, etc.; they also document the courtesy with which he was treated by many of his aristocratic hosts. In the case of his 19 November 1841 concert, most of the costs were waived by a local official.

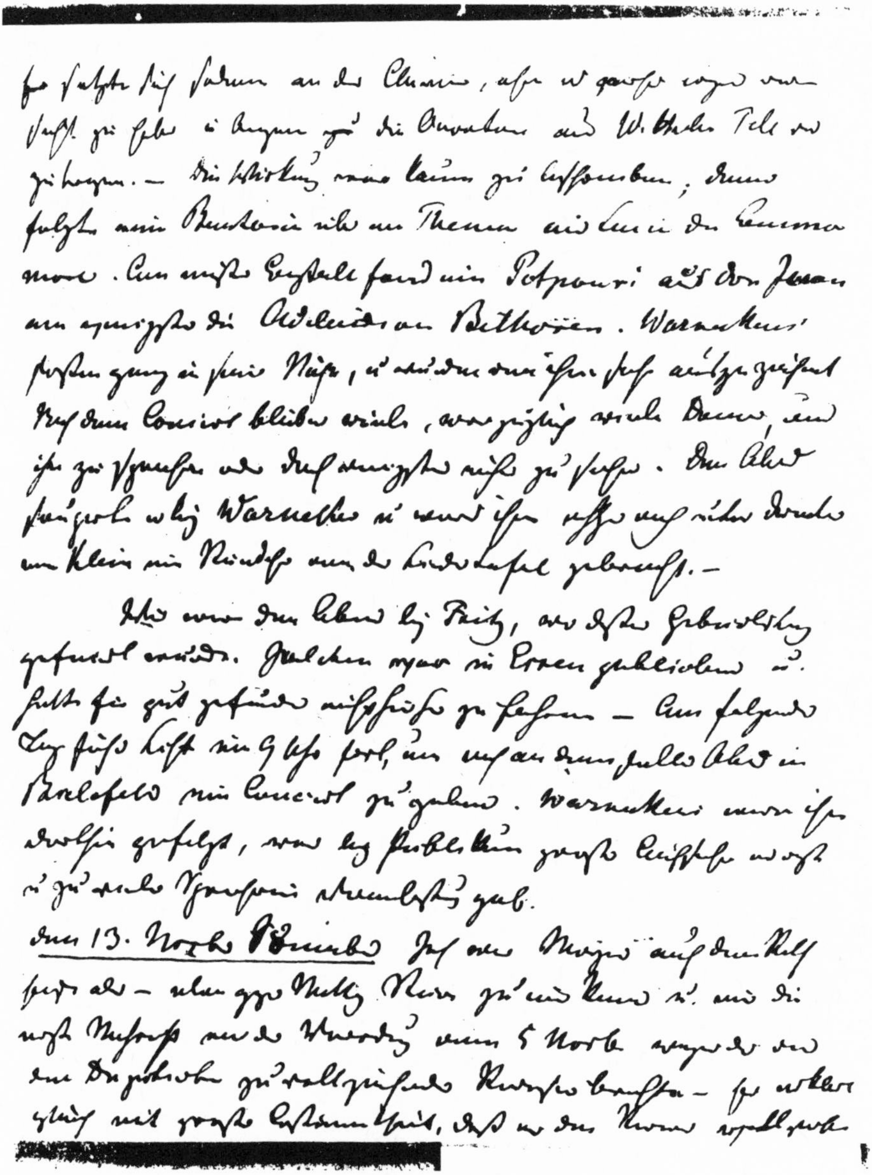

Plate 8

A page from the diaries of Albert Pagenstecher which describes
Liszt's Osnabrück concert of 12 November 1841

(courtesy Niedersächsisches Staatsarchiv)

Dienſtag   № **304**   München   den 31. Oft. 1843.

Der Bayeriſche Landbote.

Der »Bayeriſche Landbote« erſcheint täglich in Bälden, nach Umſtänden in ganzen Boyen, und wird hier und in Augsburg Nachmittags 5 Uhr für den andern Tag ausgegeben. Inſerationsgebühr iſt 2 kr. für die ſpaltige Petitzeile. Auskunft ertheilt die Erpedition unentgeltlich. Intereſſante Mittheilungen werden gerne angenommen und angemeſſen vergütet. — Der Abonnements-Preis iſt in München in der Erpedition des Landboten, Pfulagaſſe Nr. 4. | **Durch die Königl. Poſtämter halbjährig bezogen:** ganzjährig fl. 2, 42 kr., halbjährig fl. 1, 30 kr., vierteljährig fl.   45 kr. | im I. Rayon fl. 2, 38 kr., im II. Rayon fl. 2, 44 kr., im III. Rayon fl. 2, 59 kr.

An Dr. Franz Liszt.

Geſprochen bei dem am 28. Oktober 1843 ihm zu Ehren veranſtalteten Feſtmahle der Geſellſchaft der „Zwangloſen"
in München.

In einer Zeit, — die Vorzeit war es nicht,
    Nicht Orpheus' und Amphions Fabeltage;
Man that auf Wunderglauben ſchon Verzicht,
    Und aus auf Oſſianſche Seelenklage:
In einer Zeit, in der Metall und Erz
    Der Menſchen höchſte Dithyrambenlieder:
Es war in unſrer Zeit — uns ſagt's das Herz,
    In unſrer Zeit kehrt' ein Arion wieder.

Er kam vom Oſten, zog von Land zu Land,
    Ein Knabe noch und ſchon der Saiten Meiſter,
Und als die Jugend ihm die Kränze wand,
    Berief der Herrſcher — ſeiner Töne Geiſter;
Er lehrte ſie, was Sterbliche bewegt, —
    Dämoniſch ſeine Feuerſeele faſſen;
Und was entzückt, und was die Welt erregt,
    Er lehrte ſie zu lieben und zu haſſen.

Dem Einen gab er die Bacchantenwuth,
    Die andern mußten leis im Walde rauſchen,
Er tauchte den in Sonnen-Aufgangs-Gluth,
    Der mußte mit Sylphiden Flügel tauſchen.
Erlkönig rief er in der Nacht heran,
    Herrn Byron's Manfred hielt bei ihm die Wache,
Es ſtand der Schatten ihm des Don Juan,
    Und krönte ſeiner Töne Geiſterſprache.

Und wenn der Donner majeſtätiſch klang,
    Der Nacht entſtürzten hohe Waſſerfälle,
Und Wog' um Woge tönten im Geſang,
    Da warf der Meiſter Blitze in die Welle;
Und löſte mit kunſtfert'ger, ſich'rer Hand,
    Gleichwie ein Taucher Perlen aus dem Meere,
Und rollte ſie, wie ein entflatternd Band,
    Hin durch die harmonieenreiche Sphäre.

Denn liebend dient' ihm ſelbſt Titania,
    Wenn, wie im Mond die Silberfluth erbebte,
Wie durch den Blätterwald Sakontala,
    So zart ſein Finger durch die Saiten ſchwebte.
Es hielt im Nachhall ſeiner Töne Bild
    Noch feſt die Pſyche, die erſtaunend ſchweiget,
Gleichwie ein reizend blühendes Gefild
    Durch die Morgana in die Lüfte ſteiget.

Ein Magus ſtand er ſo in ſeinem Reich;
    Bewundernd warf die Welt ſich ihm zu Füßen,
Die er durchzog, erhabnen Fürſten gleich,
    Und Ton-Hero'n, die aus Walhalla grüßen.
Er ſchritt durch manches großen Königs Land,
    Die Harfe der Natur ihm vorzuführen,
Da kam er ſiegend auch an unſern Strand,
    Die Herzen zu ergreifen und zu rühren.

Und ſteht vor uns mit ſeinen Fantaſien,
    Vor uns mit allen ſeinen Lebensſonnen,
Mit ſeinen zauberiſchen Melodie'n
    Gebietend unſern Thränen, unſern Wonnen.
Wenn Saitenkunſt auch minder dauernd iſt,
    Als Malerwerk und marmorne Geſtalten,
Für immer lebt die Sage doch von Liszt
    Und ſeinen herzerſchütternden Gewalten.

         Carl Fernau.

Plate 9

**A poem about Liszt from Munich's *Bayerische Landbote*
(31 October 1843)**

This poem, presented to Liszt on 28 October 1843 at a banquet organized in his honor by a Munich musical society, was only one of many published in local newspapers around the same time. Other poems were sold in shops or street-side stands as souvenirs; enthusiasts could toss copies of such poems onto the stage during or after performances. The present author owns one of these odes, dated 31 October 1843. It was reprinted in the *Landbote* three days later. See Appendix C, entry (223).

Magazines

Other nineteenth-century periodical publications also contain valuable information about Liszt's German tours. Substantial articles, reports, and reviews appeared regularly in specialized music magazines, especially in the *Allgemeine musikalische Zeitung*, the *Neue Zeitschrift für Musik*, the *Blätter für Musik und Literatur* (after 1844, the *Kleine Musikzeitung*), and *Signale für die musikalische Welt*. Other important music magazines, albeit foreign ones, ran squibs about German musical matters: these include the *Revue et Gazette Musicale de Paris* (which Liszt served as an editor for a number of years), the *Gazetta musicale di Milano* (which carried a considerable amount of German musical news), and the *Wiener allgemeine Musik-Zeitung* (which printed brief reports about several otherwise obscure Liszt performances in Silesia and Saxony). Even periodicals published in London followed a few of Liszt's German performances; among these, the *Musical Examiner* is perhaps the most interesting.[20] The first page of a representative German magazine article about Liszt is reproduced below as Plate 4.

Although they did not run concert advertisements and announcements on a regular basis, nineteenth-century music magazines often published reliable and insightful concert criticism. In March 1840, for example, daily papers like the *Leipziger Zeitung* and the *Leipziger allgemeine Zeitung* reviewed most of the public concerts Liszt gave in Leipzig and Dresden. Reports of the same concerts which appeared in the *Allgemeine musikalische Zeitung* and the *Neue Zeitschrift*, however, are more informative and circumspectly written; in fact, they number among the finest accounts of Liszt's virtuoso career.[21] A similar situation holds true for his Weimar concerts

---

[20] Information about topics covered in the *Examiner* may be found in Diane Snigurowicz, *RIPM: The Musical Examiner, 1842-1844* (Ann Arbor 1992). Not all of this information is correct, however, and no report about Liszt at Bad Ems appeared in the *Examiner* for September 1844 [*contra* Snigurowicz, p. 72].

[21] March and April 1840 *Neue Zeitschrift* reviews have been quoted extensively in the Liszt literature, primarily because Schumann wrote them. See Ramann II, pp. 61ff.; and Walker, pp. 345-346 and 349-351. See also Leon B. Plantinga, *Schumann as Critic* (New Haven and London 1967), esp. pp. 214-218.

of January-February 1844. Prior to the 1850s the *Weimarische
Zeitung*, one of the stuffiest papers of its day, ran only one
front-page piece about Liszt: the official announcement of his
appointment to the local court as "Kapellmeister im
außerordentlichen Dienst."[22] Music-lovers who wanted information about Liszt's activities in and around Weimar had to
turn to the *Neue Zeitschrift* and especially to the *Allgemeine
musikalische Zeitung*, as we shall see in Chapter III.

Despite their value to researchers, nineteenth-century
magazines suffer from limitations. For one thing, they often
published accounts of events long over and far away, relying
on reports that were out-of-date even before they appeared in
print. For another, magazine editors and readers were more
easily fooled than their newspaper counterparts. Vormärz
newspaper readers must have heard some of the local news
before it appeared in print. Magazine readers, on the other
hand, were supposed to believe what they were told. A case in
point: the counterfeit Liszt letter that appeared in a February
1842 issue of *Das Rheinland*.[23] This letter was published in
Mainz—a long way from Berlin, where it was purportedly
written on 28 January 1842. No one knows whether Friedrich
Wiest, the *Rheinland* editor, considered the letter genuine. In
any event, it also appeared in the *Berliner Figaro*, but only after Liszt had left Berlin to visit Moscow and St. Petersburg.[24]
If the letter had been published in Berlin prior to Liszt's departure, it would have been unmasked instantly as a forgery.
As it was, Liszt published a disclaimer in the *Figaro*, but only
after the hoax had already fooled many Prussian readers.[25]

---

[22] See WrZ No. 87 (2.11.1842). Walker also commented on the attitude of this
paper when he observed that it "provided no hint of the importance of
[Liszt's 29 November 1841 performance], reporting merely that 'the famous pianoforte player Liszt gave . . . a concert that fully justified the call
that went out for him'" [Walker, p. 370].

[23] MzRh No. 18 (10.2.1842), pp. 69-71.

[24] See BFig Nos. 54-55 (5. and 7.3.1842), pp. 214-215 and 218-219.

[25] See BFig No. 68 (22.3.1842), p. 272. A reference to this document appears
in Suttoni, "Liszt Correspondence in Print: An Expanded, Annotated
Bibliography," JALS 25 (1989), entry 315. Hereafter "Suttoni." The text
of Liszt's disclaimer appears in Appendix E, which reprints complete six
little-known Liszt letters published in Vormärz periodicals. See Appendix
E, letter 4.

For more than sixty years, and especially since the mid-1960s, the *Allgemeine musikalische Zeitung*, the *Neue Zeitschrift*, and *Signale* have been subjected to careful scholarly study.[26] Other periodicals, though, especially those of a less specialized character, have been virtually ignored. Among these latter publications are *Der Salon*, *Der Sammler*, and the *Frankfurter Konversationsblatt*, all of them aimed at a broad, well-educated readership. In 1841, for example, the *Salon* carried two detailed accounts of Liszt's private and public appearances in Kassel. Koch overlooked not only these articles, but also several of the lengthy and amusing Liszt pieces that appeared in 1842 and 1843 in *Der Gesellschafter*, an important and entertaining Berlin periodical.[27] Invaluable accounts of Liszt's Berlin, Breslau, and Erfurt performances published in the *Blätter für Musik und Literatur* have also received less attention than they deserve, a subject dealt with at greater length below. Fortunately, nineteenth-century German periodicals like the *Blätter* have become more familiar to scholars during the last thirty years, thanks to several recent bibliographies and research guides.[28]

NB: The present author has been unable to locate a similar letter, dictated by Liszt to his secretary Gaetano Belloni and reportedly published in AuZ. See Ramann II, p. 167. NB: Ramann states that Belloni signed the AuZ letter [*contra* BFig No. 68 (22.3.1842), p. 272, which has Liszt's signature]. Still another Liszt letter, this one dated "Königsberg, am 11ten März 1842" and directed against Wiest, appeared in VZ No. 63 (16.3.1842).

26 In addition to Plantinga's work (identified above), see Marcello Conati, "Saggio di critiche e cronache verdiane delle 'Allgemeine musikalische Zeitung' di Lipsia (1840-48)," *Il Melodramma italiano dell'Ottocento. Studi e ricerche per Massimo Mila* (Torino 1977), pp. 13-43; Siegfried Kross, "Aus der Frühgeschichte von Robert Schumanns 'Neuen Zeitschrift für Musik'," *Die Musikforschung* 34 (1981), pp. 423-445; Reinhold Schmitt-Thomas, *Die Entwicklung der deutschen Konzertkritik im Spiegel der Leipziger "Allgemeinen musikalischen Zeitung"* (Frankfurt a.M. 1969); and Rudolf Vogler, *Die Musikzeitschrift "Signale für die musikalische Welt," 1843-1900* (Regensburg 1975).

27 For example, the review of Liszt's 8 January 1843 performance in BGes, "Kunst und Gewerbe Beiblatt" No. 1 (1843), p. 50.

28 In addition to Kirchner, see Fellinger's splendid catalog (identified above) and her article about music periodicals published in the *New Grove Dictionary of Music and Musicians*, ed. Stanley Sadie (New York and London 1980); Vol. XIV, esp. pp. 415-417 and 467-484. See also the ongoing series of RIPM ("Répertoire international de la presse musicale") publications,

Many magazines ignored Liszt's Vormärz tours or published very little about them. The important *Deutsche
Vierteljahresschrift*, for example, which covered important
events of many kinds, ran only one squib about his 1843 successes in southern Germany.[29] Between July 1843 (when it first
appeared in print) and the end of 1845, the *Illustrirte Zeitung*
mentioned Liszt only when he played for royalty or received
decorations from them,[30] even though it ran longer articles
about Mendelssohn and Wagner's *Rienzi*. Other magazines ignored Liszt utterly—among them publications like *Der
Volksbote* (during 1844-1845), *Mephistopheles* (during
1842-1844), the *Morgenblatt für gebildete Leser* (during
1842-1845), and the *Dresdner Abend-Zeitung* (during 1840).[31]
Nevertheless, magazine accounts of Liszt's German experiences
are generally informative and reliable sources. They deserve to
be consulted more frequently by the musicological community
and, in some cases, to be reprinted in part or even complete.

Books and Pamphlets

By 1848 a number of books and pamphlets devoted primarily or even exclusively to Liszt had appeared in print. Several of these publications contain valuable information about
individual German performances, even entire tours. Two of
them were written by Ludwig Rellstab, the well-known poet
and music critic.[32] Another valuable publication, albeit one that
says comparatively little about Liszt and Vormärz Germany, is
the 1844 biography written by Gustav Schilling.[33] These works

---

especially the guide to the *Wiener allgemeine Musik-Zeitung, 1841-1848*,
ed. James Deaville and Beverly J. Sing (Ann Arbor 1990).

[29] See the *Deutsche Vierteljahresschrift* 1 (1844), p. 354.

[30] For example, LIZ No. 21 (1.1.1844), p. 11; and Nos. 116-117 (20 and
27.9.1845), pp. 195-197.

[31] The present author has been unable to consult an 1842 *Abend-Zeitung*
article cited in Koch, p. 22.

[32] See Ludwig Rellstab, *Franz Liszt. Beurtheilungen — Berichte —
Lebensskizze* (Berlin 1842); and *Musikalische Beurteilungen* (Leipzig
1848). The former volume is hereafter referred to as "Rellstab." It is reprinted in facsimile in LSae Nos. 23-24, 27-28, and 32-34 (1978-1984).

[33] Gustav Schilling, *Franz Liszt. Sein Leben und Wirken aus nächster
Beschauung* (Stuttgart 1844). A second volume by Schilling, *Für Freunde*

have long been familiar to biographers—among them Ramann, Raabe, Haraszti, and especially Walker, all of whom refer to them on several occasions.[34]

Other volumes remain unfamiliar, even virtually unknown. Among them are two obscure pamphlets. The first, by F. J. A. Schreiber, is devoted to the concerts Liszt gave in 1843 in Breslau and surrounding towns;[35] the second, by an anonymous author, is devoted to Liszt's visit to Hamburg in October and November 1840.[36] Schreiber's pamphlet contains detailed accounts of several concerts, a catalog of the pieces Liszt played in Breslau prior to mid-February 1843, and a portrait of the artist at the keyboard overlooked by all of Liszt's iconographers.[37] The *Liszt in Hamburg* pamphlet, which may survive today only in the d'Agoult Scrapbook, deals primarily with the quarrel between Liszt and the management of Hamburg's Theater discussed below in Chapter III.[38]

Although interesting in and of themselves, books and pamphlets like Rellstab's, Schilling's, and Schreiber's contain

---

der Tonkunst (Kitzingen 1845), mentions some of Liszt's German concerts and describes the celebration in Liszt's honor held on 22 August 1841 [Schilling, *Für Freunde*, pp. 104-105].

[34] See Walker, pp. 4 and 372n-373n. Walker also mentions Johann Wilhelm Christern's biography *Franz Liszts Leben und Werk* (Hamburg 1841; hereafter "Christern"), as well as the annotations Liszt made in a copy of that volume owned by the Library of Congress. Information about annovations appears in Carl Engel, "Views and Reviews," *MQ* 22 (1936), pp. 354-361. Unfortunately, Christern says little or nothing about most of Liszt's 1840 and 1841 German performances.

Copies of Christern were presented free of charge in 1843 to *Blätter für Musik und Literatur* subscribers. See BML 4 (1843), p. 89.

[35] F. J. A. Schreiber, *Andenken. Dr. Franz Liszt und dessen Anwesenheit in Breslau* (Breslau 1843). Hereafter "Schreiber." A copy of the repertory catalog from Schreiber's pamphlet also survives in the d'Agoult Scrapbook.

[36] *Liszt in Hamburg* (Hamburg 1840).

[37] Information about a large number of Liszt portraits appears in André Csatkai, "Versuch einer Franz-Liszt-Ikonographie," *Burgenländische Heimatblätter* 5/2 (1936), pp. 34-67. Handsome reproductions of a number of portraits and other illustrations appear in Ernst Burger, *Franz Liszt: A Chronicle of his Life in Pictures and Documents*, trans. Stewart Spencer (Princeton, New Jersey 1989). Hereafter "Burger."

[38] Other copies of the pamphlet existed prior to 1900. See Josef Sittard, *Geschichte des Musik- und Concertwesens in Hamburg* (Hamburg 1890), p. 237n, for a summary of the pamphlet's contents. Contemporary newspapers also printed passages found in the pamphlet.

only a little "new" information about Liszt's German experiences. Most of Rellstab's 1842 volume, for example, consists of reviews that appeared originally in the *Vossische Zeitung*. Easily accessible in book form to nineteenth-century scholars, these reviews entered Liszt biography by way of Ramann, who passed some of them on to other experts.[39] On the other hand, an 1846 volume by Carl Gollmick reprints three reviews that appeared originally in Frankfurt's *Konversationsblatt*,[40] but these reviews have been overlooked in the Liszt literature. Gollmick's volume also contains a good, otherwise unavailable contemporary account of the Frankfurt Mozart Foundation and Liszt's benefit concert of 25 September 1841.[41] Books and pamphlets like these help round out our knowledge of his German performances and activities, although they only occasionally provide information about public concerts unavailable in the contemporary press.

Liszt's Letters of 1840-1845

Liszt was a voluminous correspondent, especially in later life. During the early 1840s, however, he wrote comparatively few letters; at least, comparatively few of them from those years have appeared in print. The most important published correspondence pertaining (at least in part) to his German tours is the collection of letters Liszt exchanged during the 1840s with the Comtesse d'Agoult.[42] Imperfectly edited by his

---

39 For example, compare Ramann II, pp. 152n-153n, with Burger, p. 140. Burger reproduces in facsimile Ramann's summary of Rellstab's information as if that summary were as "authentic" as other documents that appear in his handsome work. As we shall see, though, Rellstab deliberately ignored some of Liszt's Berlin performances in his newspaper reports. Because she relied almost entirely on Rellstab's book and ignored other sources, including the *Spenersche Zeitung*. Ramann inadvertently introduced errors into subsequent accounts of Liszt's 1842 triumphs.

40 See Carl Gollmick, *Feldzüge und Streitereien im Gebiete der Tonkunst* (Darmstadt 1846), pp. 223-247. Hereafter "Gollmick." The three articles in question appeared originally in FKB No. 209 (26.7.1840), pp. 835-836; Nos. 226-227 (16-17.8.1840), pp. 904 and 908; and Nos. 304 and 306 (4 and 6.11.1843), pp. 1213-1214 and 1218-1219. A copy of the 16-17 August 1840 article is also preserved in the d'Agoult Scrapbook.

41 See "Die Mozartstiftung in Frankfurt am Main" in Gollmick, esp. p. 143.

42 Hereafter "Ollivier," as in Chapter I.

grandson Daniel Ollivier, the Liszt-d'Agoult letters went through several editions during the 1930s. A number of other published letters also contain information about Liszt's German experiences. Some of them may be found in the turn-of-the-century anthologies edited by "La Mara," the pen-name of Marie Lipsius.[43] Others have appeared in a variety of books and magazines.[44] But even a few "published" Liszt letters remain virtually unknown. In March 1840, for example, a letter written by Liszt appeared in the *Dresdner Anzeiger* apologizing for the problems associated with tickets for his Leipzig concerts.[45] Although it also appeared in the *Frankfurter Konversationsblatt*,[46] this letter is mentioned in none of the standard biographies.[47] Other unfamiliar examples of published Liszt correspondence are cited in the pages below, and several letters are reprinted complete in Appendix E.[48] Other letters pertaining to Liszt's German tours undoubtedly exist and remain unpublished.

A surprisingly large number of Liszt's letters from the 1840s remain unpublished. Among them are two substantial series of documents. The first series, addressed to Heinrich Schlesinger (Liszt's publisher in Berlin) and to a few other individuals, belongs to the Library of Congress.[49] The second,

---

43 For example, *Franz Liszt's Briefe*, ed. La Mara; 8 vols. (Leipzig 1893-1902). Hereafter "Briefe."

44 See, for example, William Wright, "New Letters of Liszt," JALS 31 (1992), pp. 7-33. Wright's article contains the text of a fragmentary Liszt letter addressed to Mendelssohn shortly after March 1840, a letter also cited in William Little's study (see Chapter III below).

45 See DrAn No. 89 (29.3.1840).

46 See FKB No. 93 (2.4.1840), p. 372.

47 But see Suttoni, item 308.

48 For instance, the complete FKB text of Liszt's 1840 apology letter appears as letter 1. The DrAn version of Liszt's letter of apology appears in facsimile in Burger, p. 130.

49 See Elizabeth H. Auman et al, *The Music Manuscripts, First Editions, and Correspondence of Franz Liszt (1811-1886) in the Collections of the Music Division, Library of Congress* (Washington, D.C. 1991). Hereafter "Auman." Letters 8-15, 22-29, and 32 identified on page 96 of this catalog were written during Liszt's German tours. See also Jacqueline Bellas, "La tumultueuse amitié de Franz Liszt et de Maurice Schlesinger: Autour d'une correspondance inédite," *Littératures* 12 (1965), pp. 7-20. Among

addressed to Liszt's close friend Joseph Maria Lefebvre (a
well-known Cologne music publisher and piano manufacturer),
may be found in the collections of the Staats- und
Universitätsbibliothek, Hamburg ("Sammlung Franz Liszt").[50]
A few of the Liszt-Lefebvre letters have been quoted in print
or even published complete.[51] Others—for example, those dated
2 April, 1 June, and 10 October 1842—mention Berlin's
Vossische Zeitung, performances in East Prussia, a quarrel
with critics in the pages of the Augsburger allgemeine Zeitung,
and Liszt's relationship with the celebrated Italian tenor
Giovanni Rubini. Most of these letters are cited below in
Chapter III. References to other German individuals and
events also appear in the Washington letters; in a note addressed to Schlesinger on 26 December 1843, for instance, Liszt
describes his plans to visit Magdeburg, Hannover, and
Brunswick early in the following year.[52] The Hamburg and
Washington letters deserve to be published complete as soon
as possible, as do many other archival collections of Liszt correspondence.

Liszt's letters have been studied by a number of scholars,
several of whom have pointed out weaknesses in published
editions of his correspondence.[53] Comparatively little attention,
however, has been devoted specifically to letters associated

---

other items, Bellas reprints the text of an 1841 letter that refers to the
third North German music festival and to Liszt's plans to visit Frankfurt
a.M. in the near future [Bellas, pp. 16-17].

50 Hereafter referred to by library siglum (D-Hs) and letter number (when
the latter information is available). The present author regrets that complete texts of relevant H-Ds Liszt/Lefebvre letters cannot be reprinted
below. Permission to do so was not forthcoming, and a few of the letters
are especially difficult to transcribe.

51 See, for example, Philippe Autexier, Mozart & Liszt Sub Rosa (Poitiers
1984), pp. 62 and 122; Paul Ellmar, "Eck & Lefebvre Pianofortefabrik und
Musikverlag," Jahrbuch des Kölnischen Geschichtsvereins 33 (1958), pp.
221-233; and "Hitherto Unpublished Material from Private Collections"
[three Liszt-Lefebvre letters], LSae 45 (1990), pp. 34-37. The last item
contains the text of letters dated 49 August 1842, 5 September 1842, and
1 January 1844. The first of these letters appears in English translation
in LSae 44 (1990), p. 40. Autexier's monograph is referred to hereafter as
"Autexier."

52 Auman, p. 96, letter 26.

53 For example, Suttoni, esp. pp. 9-24.

with his German tours. To some extent these documents have been ignored because they are not especially interesting to read: many of them are short, somewhat cryptic in style, and deal abruptly—if at all—with "interesting" individuals and situations like love affairs, scandals, and so on.[54] If unpublished, they are often difficult to decipher; if published, they may be available only in bowdlerized editions.

Published or not, Liszt's correspondence of the 1840s rarely contains otherwise unavailable information about individual musical events. One exceptional letter, addressed to d'Agoult on 25 January 1842, mentions four private performances omitted from previous tallies of his Berlin activities.[55] On the other hand, consider the unusually detailed missive Liszt sent to Count Thaddäus Amadé on 4 September 1840.[56] This document—which mentions public performances in Leipzig, Dresden, Baden-Baden, Mainz, Ems, Wiesbaden, Frankfurt a.M., Mannheim, Bonn, Cologne, and Hamburg as well as Berlin—nevertheless contains only a little "new" information: the large number of pieces Liszt played in August 1840 at Ems for the Empress of Russia. What's more, this letter—like many others—contains characteristic mistakes and mentions plans that never came to pass. Liszt tells Amadé, for example, that he gave three concerts each in Leipzig and Dresden during March 1840. Even discounting his performances in private homes, he played four times in Leipzig's Gewandhaus: on 17, 23, 24, and 30 March. Liszt also mentions that he plans to visit Berlin during or immediately after October 1840, "if I have enough time left." In fact, he reached Berlin only in December 1841. Similar "errors" crop up in unpublished letters: for example, in the Liszt/Lefebvre letter of 2 April 1842 mentioned

---

[54] One exception is the angry epistle transcribed, translated, and discussed in Ophra Yerushalmi, "A Liszt Letter to Alexandre Weill (Frankfurt 1842)," JALS 30 (1991), pp. 71-73. The circumstances associated with this letter are unknown.

[55] "[Q]uatre matinées chez la Princesse de Prusse, dont j'ai fait moi seul, absolument et exclusivement les honneurs en jouant sept ou huit morceaux chaque fois" [Ollivier II, pp. 197-198].

[56] Published in German in *Franz Liszt in seinen Briefen*, ed. Hans Rudolf Jung (Frankfurt a.M. 1989), pp. 74-77. Amadé helped pay for Liszt's early musical education, and Liszt may have felt obligated to provide in return an unusually fulsome description of his activities.

above. In this note Liszt tells his friend that he gave three concerts in Königsberg during the previous month. In fact, he gave five: on the afternoon of 13 March and the evenings of 10, 11, 13, and 14 March 1842.

These observations are not intended as accusations of dishonesty. Liszt was no court reporter, and no one compelled him to stick to the "facts." Furthermore—as we saw in Chapter I—travel in Vormärz Germany was a difficult business, and Liszt's itineraries were rearranged frequently due to illnesses, delays, and pleas from patrons to linger in certain towns. But Liszt *was* occasionally careless in his correspondence, and this has muddied the biographical waters. In a letter addressed to d'Agoult on 15 February 1842, for example, we find statements to the effect that two different events—a supper for diplomats and other officials (complete with military music), and a concert at the Hotel de Russie—took place in Berlin on the same date (9 February 1842). They probably did not.[57] In his haste to jot down his impressions of "the last week" for the Comtesse—he was then an extraordinarily busy man, and his relationship with d'Agoult had already begun to deteriorate—Liszt did not stop to check his dates. Had Ollivier checked them, he might have noticed the discrepancy in question. In any event, he would have assigned Liszt's letter to "1842" instead of "1843."

When he describes in his letters his feelings about Germany and the Germans, though, Liszt tells us things we can learn from no other source. Nineteenth-century German newspapers rarely if ever ran "interviews" with individuals, even those as famous as Liszt, and reminiscences cannot always be trusted. Thus it is only from his letters that we learn how tired and discouraged Liszt often became during his tours and how often he masked his true feelings, even from his friends. "At 10 o'clock I left for Erfurt," he tells the Comtesse

---

[57] "Le soir du jeudi (9 [sic] février) j'ai donné un souper de 70 personnes. . . . Mercoredi [sic] 9 février à dix heures, plus de 500 artistes dramatiques, chanteurs, chanteuses, danseurs, danseuses, acteurs, actrices, se sont réunis das la salle de l'Hotel de Russie. Je leur ai joué quatre à cinq morceaux . . ." [Ollivier II, pp. 263-264]. The Hotel matinée took place on Wednesday, 9 February 1842 [VZ No. 36 (12.2.1842)]. The date of the "supper" cannot be determined so readily. It, too, may have been 9 February, when Liszt played privately in the evening at a Berlin "Beer-schen Haus" See AmZ 44 (1842), cols. 238-239. Or it may have been 8 February, when he played privately for the Royal York Masonic Lodge.

d'Agoult in a letter dated Weimar, 18 February 1844, where, he goes on to explain:

> I had to play in the evening. I was weighed down by sobs, but I played without anyone suspecting my feelings. Afterwards, though, I had an attack of nerves. I wept for a long time, quite alone, and now I am writing you my thoughts on this deplorable business.[58]

Of even greater interest, perhaps, are Liszt's epistolary remarks about the contemporary press. Most of these remarks are sarcastic, even angry: German newspapers are "malicious,"[59] and those who write for them are "scoundrels."[60] Nevertheless, newspapers kept Liszt informed even in out-of-the-way places. "So what sort of news from Germany do you want?" he asks d'Agoult in a letter dated 23 January 1844. "Me, I live a quite isolated life in Weimar and know nothing but what the *Allgemeine Zeitung* knows five days earlier than I do."[61] Furthermore, Liszt obviously enjoyed reading about himself in newspapers and magazines. In an unpublished letter to Heinrich Schlesinger, dated 6 February 1843, for instance, he expresses admiration for a lengthy essay devoted to his keyboard artistry and published anonymously the previous month in the *Frankfurter Konversationsblatt*.[62] The unusual length and detail of this essay, not to mention Liszt's endorse-

---

58 "A dix heures, je suis parti pour Erfurt. Il me fallait jouer le soir. Des sanglots m'oppressaient, j'ai joué pourtant sans que personne pût se douter de mon émotion, mais après ma crise nerveuse m'a pris. J'ai pleuré longuement, tout seul, et maintenant je vous écris mes réflexions au sujet de cette déplorable histoire" [Ollivier II, p. 331]. The "deplorable business" involved the troublesome Hermann Cohen—who, as we shall see in Chapter III, helped get Liszt into hot water with Leipzig's musical establishment in March 1840, and who never fulfilled the expectations Liszt had for him.

59 See Wright, p. 18. See also Little, pp. 120-121, which mentions an otherwise unknown review published in the *Eisenbahn*.

60 "Lumpen" [Ollivier II, p. 199]. The complete quotation appears in translation in Chapter III below.

61 "Quelle nouvelle d'Allemagne voulez-vous donc? Moi, je vis tout-à-fair confiné à Weymar et ne sais absolument que ce que l'*Allgemeine Zeitung* sait cinq jours plus tôt que moi" [Ollivier II, p. 322].

62 Auman, p. 96, letter 15. The article in question appeared in FKB No. 27 (27.1.1843), pp. 107-108.

ment of its contents, makes it one of the most important of Liszt documents—as we shall see in Chapter V.

Additional references to Liszt's letters are scattered throughout other portions of the present volume, including Appendix C. Several complete, little-known letters are reprinted in their original languages in Appendix E.

Posters and Playbills

Only a handful of concert posters and playbills survive from Liszt's German tours. These artifacts—which once existed in considerable numbers but, for the most part, were discarded long ago by cleaners-out of attics and cellars—belong today primarily to private collectors; only a few are preserved in collections accessible to the public. A handful of playbills have been reproduced in biographies and iconographical works, as have a small number of posters.[63] A previously "unpublished" poster for an 1843 Liszt performance in Breslau is reproduced as Plate 5.

Playbills seem to be scarcer than posters, and very few have been mentioned in biographies. One playbill, with the word "Fürstenwalde" written in ink across the top, contains the only "program" we have for Liszt's concert of 19 February 1843.[64] The existence of this undated playbill suggests that Liszt may have printed and distributed similar playbills for programs he played over and over again. On this recital, among other works, he performed Theodor (?) Kullak's fantasy on Weber's *Der Freischütz*, a piece he evidently played in Germany on only one other occasion: his recital of 25 January 1842 in Berlin.[65] We know, however, that Liszt's Fürstenwalde program

---

[63] Advertising posters for performances in Leipzig, Weimar, Breslau, and Munich, for example, are reproduced in Burger, pp. 128, 139, 148, and 150.

[64] See D-WRgs Liszt Kasten 240.

[65] For a number of reasons accurate identification of the Kullak piece—if it is *only* one piece—is impossible. Liszt himself may have omitted it from his own catalog of the compositions performed by him during the 1830s and 1840s (D-WRgs Liszt Ms. Z15); he mentions a "transcription et paraphrase de Kullak" evidently—but not necessarily—different from his own paraphrase (?) on Kullak's transcription of music from Act IV of Donizetti's *Dom Sebastien*. On this last point, see Rena Mueller's references to Walker's use of D-WRgs Liszt Mss. Z15 and Z15a information,

also included at least one number for euphonium and piano—a fascinating detail omitted from the playbill mentioned above, but remarked upon in contemporary reports.[66] Other playbills document Liszt's visit to Posen in February 1843. One of them, which identifies the program for his 21 February 1843 recital, is reproduced from a private collection as Plate 6. A second identifies the pieces Liszt himself played at the Hotel de Bazar three days later. A third, undated and owned by the Goethe- und Schiller-Archiv, bears the word "Posen" in Liszt's hand.[67] But none of the selections identified on this last playbill matches his regular repertory choices. Either Liszt appeared on this otherwise undocumented occasion as a last-minute guest, or—more probably—he simply sat in the audience and enjoyed the show.

Business Documents

Most of the contracts, receipts, income tallies, and other business documents associated with Liszt's German tours seem to have disappeared. Among surviving documents are several which pertain to his 19 and 22 November 1841 Kassel concerts and which belong to the Hessisches Staatsarchiv, Marburg.[68] One of these documents is reproduced as Plate 7, together with additional information about its significance. Receipts for most of Liszt's spectacularly successful series of 1841-1842 Singakademie concerts are owned by the Goethe- und Schiller-Archiv.[69] Scattered references to concert expenditures and other financial transactions also appear in his letters and in a few newspaper notices and reviews.

---

as published in the *Journal of the American Musicological Society* 37 (1984), p. 194. The most precise contemporary information about Kullak's *Freischütz* transcription and Liszt's German repertory appears in press reports of his 25 January 1842 concert, where it is identified simply as a transcription of the "Agathe-Aria." Walker [p. 372n] omits this transcription from Liszt's Berlin repertory, but Ramann and Burger both mention it. See, for example, Burger, p. 140.

[66] See, for example, VZ No. 44 (21.2.1843).

[67] A second copy of the Plate 6 playbill, together with the other playbills mentioned above, may be found in D-WRgs Liszt Kasten 240.

[68] Shelf Nos. A 5/12 Bd. 1; and 159 Nr. 15 Bd. II.

[69] D-WRgs Liszt Kasten 135.

Diplomas and Testimonials

In addition to the titles and decorations bestowed upon him by aristocrats and by organizations like the Prussian Academy of Arts and the University of Königsberg, Liszt held honorary memberships or directorships in several German musical organizations. Almost all of the diplomas that testify to these honors are preserved today in Weimar collections, including those of the so-called "Liszthaus": the former Hofgärtnerei, where Liszt lived intermittently between 1869 and his death in 1886.[70] One of the "Liszthaus" diplomas was awarded by the Verein der deutschen Hochschüle, Dortmund, on 1 September 1843.[71] In fact, Liszt played in Dortmund on 24 August 1843: local papers as well as the *Allgemeine Preußische Staats-Zeitung* and a commemorative pamphlet mention that performance, and Liszt himself mentioned his Dortmund "triumphs" in a undated letter to Prince Felix von Lichnowsky.[72] Liszt almost certainly performed in or, at the very least, on behalf of Dortmund on other occasions. Chorley, after all, claims that his idol toiled

> across the country (and German posting *was* then still a toil) to contribute his astounding "Hexameron" *fantasia*, and his "Tarantelles," and his "Galoppe Infernale," to the sober establishment of a *gymnasium* in Dortmund.[73]

[70] See Hedwig Weilguny, *Das Liszthaus in Weimar*, 6th ed. (Weimar 1973), pp. 11-13. Among items Weilguny discusses are programs for two January 1842 Berlin concerts, the Prussian Academy of Arts diploma mentioned below, a gold medal commemorating the same event, and a manuscript of the cantata Liszt composed for the Beethoven Festival held in Bonn in August 1845.

[71] D-WRgs Liszt Überformate 127.

[72] See (respectively) DoWB No. 35 (2.9.1843), p. 292; APSZ No. 63 (1.9.1843), p. 407; *Gymnasio Tremoniensi* . . . (Hamm 1844), p. 21; and Hans von Wolzogen, "Franz Liszt's Briefe an den Fürsten Felix Lichnowsky," *Bayreuther Blätter* 30 (1907), p. 31. See also "Franz Liszt in Dortmund," *Die Heimat* (1924-1930), p. 16.

[73] Chorley II, p. 245. The "Galoppe Infernale," of course, was Liszt's celebrated *Grande Galop chromatique*—possibly the most popular piece in his 1840s German repertory. None of the numbers Chorley mentions, however, seem to have appeared on Liszt's 24 August 1843 Dortmund program. Nor was Chorley correct in his assessment of why Liszt visited Dortmund. As we shall see in Chapter III, by 1843 the Gymnasium in question had already been in existence for three hundred years.

None of Liszt's biographers, however, mentions either his appearance in Dortmund or the existence of the Verein diploma. Other testimonials include a list of guests who attended a banquet celebrating Liszt's election to the Prussian Academy of Arts.[74] Still others document his lengthy involvement with Freemasonry and his membership in several German Masonic lodges.[75] Finally, a few diplomas attest to honors overlooked or ignored by most biographers. Among them are honorary memberships in the Albrecht Dürer and Mozart Societies, both of Nuremberg.[76] The press announced many of Liszt's awards, including some he received from foreign dignitaries,[77] but no contemporary reference to these honorary memberships seems to have appeared in print.

Reminiscences and Related Sources

Reminiscences of musical life in Vormärz Germany, especially of Liszt's private appearances as a performer, provide valuable information about performance practices and repertory choices as well as a few facts about his itineraries. Liszt reminiscences may be found in books, magazine articles, letters, diary entries, city chronicles, and other primary and secondary sources. No complete catalog of these sources has ever been compiled, although Koch provides information about a large number of books and articles which mention Liszt and which date from the nineteenth and early twentieth centuries.[78] Several scholars have published impressive col-

---

[74] D-WRgs Liszt Kasten 165. Guests at the banquet included Mendelssohn and Rellstab as well as Alexander von Humboldt, whom Liszt knew and corresponded with throughout 1842.

[75] See Autexier, passim. Additional information about this topic appears in Lennart Rabes, "Franz Liszt — The Freemason," Ars Quatuor Coronatorum 96 (1983-1984), pp. 140-145.

[76] D-WRgs Liszt Überformaten 151-152. The diplomas themselves are dated (respectively) 13 and 14 October 1843. See also Julius Kapp, Franz Liszt (Berlin 1908), p. 175. Hereafter "Kapp."

[77] See, for example, the notice "Liszt's vollständiger Titel," published in EuEut 4 (1844), pp. 167-168. Awards described in this notice include the Order of the Lion of Belgium, honorary citizenships in several Hungarian towns, and the medal of the Prussian Academy of Arts mentioned above.

[78] See Koch, pp. 45-56.

lections of Liszt documents, including lengthy quotations from reminiscences. The finest of these collections include Ernst Burger's handsome Liszt iconography and a Liszt "reader" compiled by Adrian Williams.[79] Reminiscences of individual performances may also be found in books devoted primarily to other topics. Among these is Ludwig Passarge's *Ostpreußisches Jugendleben*, which contains information about several matinée recitals Liszt presented in Königsberg in March 1842.[80] Another little-known account appears in the published reminiscences of K. C. von Leonhard, who invited Liszt to attend a soirée held at Leonhard's home immediately after the pianist's Heidelberg recital of 28 November 1843.[81] Reminiscences also crop up in magazine articles[82] and in collections of letters like those of Felix Mendelssohn[83] and Clara Wieck Schumann.[84]

Other reminiscences and similar kinds of documents, however (diary entries, city chronicles, and other kinds of archival material) have never been published and remain virtually unknown. On 12 November 1841, for instance, Liszt presented a public recital at Osnabrück. The only surviving

---

79   Adrian Williams, *Portrait of Liszt by Himself and his Contemporaries* (Oxford 1990). Hereafter "Williams." Burger's book is identified above.

80   See Ludwig Passarge, *Ein Ostpreußisches Jugendleben* (Leipzig 1906), pp. 118-121. Like other reminiscences, Passarge's are cited as sources in Appendix C and discussed in Chapter III below.

81   See K. C. von Leonhard, *Aus unserer Zeit in meinem Leben* (Stuttgart 1854-1856); Vol. II, pp. 259-261.

82   For example, in Carl Reinecke, "Erinnerungen an Franz Liszt," NZfM 78 (1911), pp. 570-573. The same Reinecke reminiscences of Liszt's 31 October 1840 Hamburg performance, taken from another source, appear in English in Williams, p. 145. NB: Reinecke remembered Liszt more clearly than the details of his Hamburg performance; he fails to mention, for example, that on that occasion Liszt and four local musicians played the Hummel Septet as a quintet—a good example of making do with available musical forces. See HZCor No. 260 (3.11.1840).

83   See, for instance, *Felix Mendelssohn: Letters*, ed. G. Selden-Goth (New York 1945), pp. 289-291

84   See Berthold Litzmann, *Clara Schumann: Ein Künstlerleben*, 3 vols. (Leipzig 1920), passim. Hereafter "Litzmann." This anthology also contains the texts of several letters written by Robert Schumann and a conclusion to one of Clara's letters written by Liszt himself. With regard to Liszt's correspondence with the Schumanns, see Kapp, "Franz Liszt und Robert Schumann," *Die Musik* 13-2 (1913-1914), pp. 67-85.

account of this performance—and of at least one private performance the same day—appears in the unpublished diaries of Albrecht Pagenstecher, which belong to the Niedersächsisches Staatsarchiv.[85] A page from these diaries is reproduced as Plate 8. Comments about Liszt performances also appear in city records and chronicles, including those of Frankfurt a.M. and Koblenz.[86]

Other Primary Sources

Among contemporary sources of information about Liszt's German tours are a few literary works, mostly poems written in honor of his appearances in various cities and towns. None of these poems can be considered a work of art (at least in the opinion of the present author), but some are amusing: acrostics on Liszt's name, for example, and verses published in "foreign" languages like English, probably to show off their authors' accomplishments in the German press. One of these poems, followed by additional information, is reproduced as Plate 9. Another appears in Chapter III, freely translated into doggeral English. A few plays about Liszt's Berlin triumphs of 1841-1842 received some attention in their day. These are satirical skits rather than full-blown comedies or dramas, and their subjects are more often Liszt's fans rather than Liszt himself. Poems and plays associated with individual performances and tours are identified in Appendix C.

Illustrations of various kinds (portraits, pictures of places and buildings, caricatures, and so on) also tell us something about Liszt's circumstances in the 1840s and how German audiences responded to him. Many of these illustrations appeared originally in works having nothing directly to do with music: in atlases, for example, or in travel books.[87] Others, especially

---

85 Shelf No. Ers A 12 Nr. 12 Bd. 18. NB: Pagenstecher's handwriting is quite difficult to read. The present author is grateful to James Deaville for help in deciphering the diary pages in question, and to Barbara Hassell for proofreading documentary transcriptions.

86 See, for example, J. J. Lucas's handwritten *Chronik der Stadt Koblenz* [Koblenz Stadtarchiv Shelf No. 997], p. 430, which contains information about several Liszt concerts in the Rhineland.

87 A few of these illustrations have been reproduced in articles about Liszt's German travels. See, for example, Autexier, "Franz Liszts Konzertbesuche

caricatures, were issued as "broadsides" and survive today primarily in private collections.[88] Still others appeared in works
devoted to music criticism, among them a portrait of Liszt
wearing the decoration of the Order "Pour le Mérite" that appeared originally in Leipzig's popular *Illustrirte Zeitung*. This
portrait is reproduced as a frontispiece to the present volume.
Another Liszt portrait was distributed in 1843 as a supplement
to the *Allgemeine musikalische Zeitung*.[89]

One work incorporates poems, plays, *and* pictures: *Das
Liszt-ge Berlin*, an anthology published in three parts during
or shortly after March 1842.[90] The title is a pun on "Liszt" and
"List" (which means "cunning" in German); the second and
third volumes contain poems (including a parody of Heine's
"Loreley," called "Des Mädchens Klage"), plays (including a skit
about Liszt's triumphal Berlin departure), and several colored
caricatures printed as frontispieces.

Finally, the Pierpont Morgan Library in New York City
owns a printed copy of Beethoven's "Kreutzer" sonata which
documents a private performance of that work by Liszt and the
violinist Franz Fesca on 18 March 1844. This score, inscribed
by both Fesca and Liszt, is the only evidence we have for that

---

in Frankfurt," *Frankfurter allgemeine Zeitung* "Rhein-Main-Blatt" (24
July 1986), p. 23. Autexier also reproduces a picture of the
"Komödienhaus," the theater where Liszt performed in August 1840 and
August-September 1841.

[88] The Goethe- und Schiller-Archiv, however, owns a number of caricatures.
Others are reproduced in Burger, pp. 143ff. Among them are illustrations
from *Berlin wie es ist und . . . trinkt*, a series of mostly literary satires
issued by Adolf Glassbrenner under the "Brennglass" pseudonym discussed in Chapter I. A pun on "ist" ("is") and "ißt" ("eats") appears in
Glassbrenner's title; the Liszt literature is full of puns. Several poems
published in Vormärz newspapers were based on them entirely.

Additional information about Liszt caricatures and their present
whereabouts appears in an exhibition catalog published several years ago
by the Liszt Ferenc Memorial Museum. See *Liszt Ferenc — Kárikatúrák*
(Budapest 1988).

[89] See AmZ 45 (1843), cols. 955-958, which discusses this portrait and
Liszt's life prior to the 1840s. The portrait itself has been reproduced several times; it has even appeared on postage stamps. See Victor Danek,
"Liszt (and his Contemporaries) on Stamps," JALS 23 (1988), pp. 3-18, esp.
pp. 6-7 and plate III/1.

[90] Albert Enssenhardt, *Das Liszt-ge Berlin*, 3 vols. (Berlin 1842). The New
York Public Library owns a complete copy of this rare work; the shelf
number is Drexel 2184.

performance.[91] A few other inscriptions and handwritten "album leaves" also document isolated German experiences. One of these "leaves" consists of the score for a short piano piece entitled "Ländler." Unfortunately, as we shall see below, neither this piece nor other sources of information tells us very much about Liszt's three-day visit to Donaueschingen in the fall of 1843.

Secondary Source Materials

Secondary sources occasionally provide otherwise unobtainable information about Liszt's German tours. Among the most valuable of these sources are pre-1939 publications that draw upon documents lost or destroyed during World War II. One example is Emil Jacobs's article about Liszt and d'Agoult at Nonnenwerth and other German places, including Berlin.[92] Jacobs's article consists primarily of quotations from a series of letters addressed by Marie von Czettritz und Neuhauß to her stepdaughter, the Baroness Isidore von Kitzing. The texts of these letters refer at some length to Liszt's 1841 Rhineland itinerary and to otherwise unknown private performances given at Nonnenwerth during August-October of that year. Unfortunately, the original letters were destroyed with the rest of Varnhagen von Ense's papers during World War II bombing raids. Another valuable secondary source is Paul von Ebart's account of two Liszt concerts in Coburg.[93] According to Ebart, Liszt first played in Coburg on 1 November 1842. The only contemporary reference for this performance is a short notice

---

91 The score in question, which belongs to the Pierpont Morgan Library's Cary Bequest, contains Liszt's signature and the date "18 März 44" in the upper-left-hand corner of the violin part. On the front endpaper of the piano part appear in Fesca's hand the words "Gespielt am 18. März 1844 // zu Magdeburg // von Franz Liszt // begleitet [sic] von Franz Fesca."

92 Emil Jacobs, "Franz Liszt und die Gräfin d'Agoult in Nonnenwerth, 1841-1842," *Die Musik* 11/1-2 (October 1911), pp. 34-45 and 93-112. Hereafter "Jacobs." NB: The title of this article is misleading: there is nothing in it about Liszt and d'Agoult at Nonnenwerth in 1842. Indeed, there seems to be very little evidence that Liszt even visited Nonnenwerth in 1842, although he returned there in 1843. The present author is indebted to Pauline Pocknell for sharing this hypothesis with him.

93 See Paul von Ebart, *Hundert Jahre Coburgische Theatergeschichte, 1827-1927* (Coburg 1927), p. 20.

in the *Neue Zeitschrift*.[94] Working with materials apparently unavailable today, Ebart was able not only to reproduce the program of this recital, but also that of a second concert presented in Coburg three days later.[95]

Without doubt, though, the most important pre-1945 "secondary" source of information about Liszt's tours—and one that stands in a class by itself—is Lina Ramann's three-volume biography. We have already seen that Ramann cannot always be relied on. Yet she made more systematic use of contemporary sources vis-à-vis Liszt's Vormärz performances than any other scholar. Ramann knew Liszt personally and solicited his corrections for the first volume of her work.[96] Not everything in Ramann's biography was approved by Liszt, but he unquestionably supplied some of her information and anecdotes. Indeed, because her facts are so often correct and can so often be verified by consulting contemporary magazines and newspapers, Ramann's every word deserves attention.[97]

A number of worthwhile secondary sources have also appeared in print since 1945. Among these is Wolfram Huschke's book about music in Weimar during the eighteenth and nineteenth centuries.[98] Working with archival materials withheld from most foreign scholars, Huschke has been able to

---

94 NZfM 17 (1842), p. 178. NB: An otherwise unpublished letter by Liszt, dated "Coburg den 7. November 1842," compliments the Coburg piano manufacturer G. F. Siller on the quality of his instruments. See *Regierungs- und Intelligenzblatt* (Coburg 1842), p. 991. See also Suttoni, item 317.

95 Liszt mentions both concerts in a letter dated 8 November 1842. See Ollivier II, p. 227.

96 Some of her questionnaires have been preserved, together with Liszt's answers in his own handwriting. See Ramann, *Lisztiana*, ed. Arthur Seidl and Friedrich Schnapp (Mainz and New York 1983), pp. 385-408.

97 Ramann [II, p. 269] claims, for example, that Liszt performed in Mannhein late in 1845. The present author was unable to verify whether this concert took place. In scanning October 1845 issues of Mannheim newspapers, however, he came across an advertisement for a previously unknown Liszt concert given in Heidelberg on 15 October of that year. See MnJ NO. 282 (15.10.1845), p. 1129. Perhaps Liszt told Ramann this event had taken place in Mannheim because it was advertised there. Or perhaps he confused Mannheim and Heidelberg because he played in both cities during the fall of 1843.

98 Wolfram Huschke, *Musik im klassischen und nachklassischen Weimar, 1756-1861* (Weimar 1982). Hereafter "Huschke."

cast new light on Liszt's 1841, 1842, and 1844 visits to Weimar and surrounding areas.[99]

Not all Liszt secondary sources are completely reliable, of course. This is true of biographies like Ramann's as well as of pre-World War II city music histories like Fritz Hartmann's account of the performing arts in historic Braunschweig.[100] Hartmann claims that Liszt gave four concerts in Braunschweig's Theater during his visit in March 1844. Contemporary newspapers, however, provide corroboration for only one: that of 25 March.[101] Even Alfred Dörffel's splendid history of Leipzig's Gewandhaus overlooks some of the numbers Liszt played in that hall during 1840 and 1841.[102]

Nor are post-1945 secondary sources always more reliable. A short history of music in Donaueschingen, written by Max Rieple and published in conjunction with music festivals held in the 1950s, mentions at least one performance Liszt presented during the fall of 1843 at the local palace.[103] But Rieple states that Liszt conducted in the local theater *and* played the piano in Donaueschingen.[104] Whether he did both things on only one occasion is not clear. Instead, Rieple quotes the diary of a local aristocrat which mentions that Liszt played his transcription of Schubert's *Ave Maria*, bringing tears to the eyes of his listeners. The source of this passage may be a pre-World War II history of court music in Donaueschingen, a photocopied page from which was mailed to the present author by an official

---

[99] Another valuable source of information, this one about Liszt's Kassel and Göttingen concerts of November 1841, is Herfried Homburg, "Kassel zu Füßen von Franz Liszt," *Hessische Blätter* No. 16 (19 January 1962). Hereafter "Homburg."

[100] See Fritz Hartmann, *Sechs Bücher Braunschweigischer Theater-Geschichte* (Wolfenbüttel 1905), p. 499.

[101] See BnAn No. 73 (25.3.1844). Hartmann also claims Liszt visited Braunschweig near the end of 1844, something he could not have done; beginning in August 1844, Liszt spent most of a year in France, Portugal, Gibraltar, and Spain.

[102] See Alfred Dörffel, *Geschichte der Gewandhausconcerte zu Leipzig* (Leipzig 1884), passim.

[103] See Max Rieple, *Musik in Donaueschingen* (Donaueschingen 1959), p. 12.

[104] "Liszt dirigirte im Theater eigene Stücke und versetzte seine Zuhörer durch sein virtuoses Klavierspiel in helles Entzücken" [Rieple, p. 12].

of the Fürstlich Fürstenbergische Hofbibliothek.[105] This history claims that Liszt played at least twice at the local palace, although it says nothing about his conducting an orchestra. Two additional sources supplement Rieple's remarks but do not always clarify them. First, an advertisement for a public Donaueschingen concert, evidently presented by Liszt sometime before 25 November 1843, is said to have appeared in the *Donaueschinger Wochenblatt*.[106] Second, an autograph manuscript of a "Ländler" written by Liszt in honor of the Princess of Hohenzollern-Hechingen and played in her presence has recently been described in print.[107]

Other modern histories are more disappointing than Rieple's. Lothar Hoffmann-Erbrecht's skimpy account of music in Silesia from the Middle Ages to the present day, for instance, ignores Liszt's 1843 Breslau triumphs entirely.[108] And many volumes, some of them popular Liszt biographies (which shall remain unnamed in these pages), contain thoroughly unreliable information about Liszt's German tours overall.

Documentary Problems and Perspectives

We have seen that primary and secondary sources of many kinds contain a great deal of information about Liszt's German tours of 1840-1845. We have also seen that these sources impose limitations on our knowledge of his performances and experiences. The most pervasive of these limitations is lack of information. For a number of public concerts, to take but one example, we know little or nothing about dates, times, places, admission prices, or programs. (A special problem involves the number of private performances Liszt gave in certain places. Comments to the effect of "several" or "a couple" have always

---

[105] See *Das Fürstlich Fürstenbergische Hoftheater zu Donaueschingen, 1775-1850* (Donaueschingen 1914), p. 101. In this source the diary quotation reads: "[Liszt spielte sein Ave Maria,] was alles zu Tränen rührte und ihn selbst so ergriff, daß er sich einen Augenblick entfernen mußte." The present author was unable to consult this diary in person.

[106] This source too was unavailable for examination.

[107] See Michael Kienzle, "Ein Liszt-Autograph in Donaueschingen," *Liszt Information* [European Liszt Centre] 12 (1982), pp. 10-12.

[108] See Lothar Hoffman-Erbrecht, *Musikgeschichte Schlesiens* (Dülmen 1986).

been understood throughout the present volume as referring to *two* performances unless other information is available.)[109] Nor do we know how German audiences reacted on a number of occasions. Newspapers, magazines, reminiscences, and even Liszt's own letters sometimes refer to comings and goings, dinners, suppers, parties, serenades, and other festive or note-worthy occasions. But no one followed Liszt about during the 1840s and wrote down everything he did, and on several occasions during his German tours he seems to vanish from view.

Contemporary newspapers and magazines are generally our most reliable sources of factual information about where, what, and how well Liszt played. Consider the following exemplary report of the artist's 24 March 1840 performance, which appeared in the *Leipziger Zeitung* two days later:

Leipzig, 25 March. Yesterday Herr Franz Liszt presented his second and, to the best of our knowledge, his last*) concert [in Leipzig] in the Gewandhaus hall, accompanied by the local orchestra. He played the *Konzertstück* of C. M. v. Weber (Op. 79) as well as a fantasy of his own and two songs by Franz Schubert (*Ave Maria* and *Ständchen*). We can only repeat what has already been written about the deep impression made by his extraordinary artistry. Only Liszt understands how to control his instrument with the utmost firmness and marshal the storm of sound it produces under his fingers. Applause of an intensity seldom heard here filled the hall. After the concert was over the singer Fräulein Schlegel presented a bouquet of flowers to the master amid cries of celebration, and the honored artist thanked his audience by returning to the piano and playing the *Erlkönig*. — On the evening of the 23rd our famous music director Dr. Mendelssohn-Bartholdy honored our visitor from abroad with a tremendous musical fête in the Gewandhaus hall. As part of the activities a concerto by [Johann] Sebastian Bach for three keyboard instruments was performed by Liszt, Mendelssohn-Bartholdy, and Ferd[inand] Hiller, with the accompaniment of a string quartet.

And then, at the bottom of the page:

[109] Consider, for example, a report in the Mainz magazine *Gutenberg* to the effect that, in early October 1843, Liszt played locally at several private parties: "Liszt . . . besuchte uns auf auf etliche Tage und spielte in *einigen* Privatzirkeln" [MzGut No. 161 (10.10.1843), p. 739; italics added]. We know he played in Frankfurt a.M. on 4 October, and it is probable that this report refers to at least one other performance in the same city.

*) We have just learned that Herr Franz Liszt will present a benefit concert on behalf of the pension fund for old and sick musicians on Monday, the 30th [of March]. (Editor)[110]

Reports like this one, which contain detailed program information (including the titles of encores) and even references to other events, are our most reliable guides to what really happened when Liszt appeared before Vormärz audiences.[111]

Yet even the contemporary press occasionally reviewed concerts without mentioning where or what he played. In November 1842, for example, the Frankfurt a.M. magazine *Didaskalia* ran a brief account of a concert Liszt gave with Rubini at Gotha. This account is dated "Gotha, 9. Nov." and runs as follows:

> Yesterday Liszt and Rubini arrived here and in the evening gave a concert in the Grand Ducal Court Theater which, despite the unusually high prices, was filled with listeners. It scarcely deserves to be mentioned that these heroes of art were accorded the same brilliant reception and caused the same excitement here that has greeted their appearance everywhere else. After the concert a group of local artists met at the "German Court" Hotel, and the joyous supper that followed did not fail to be enlivened by noble and witty toasts. Above all, Liszt's genial personality was treasured by everyone who came into contact with him and got to know him.[112]

Notices like this one, full of platitudes about "brilliant receptions" and "genial personality," say next to nothing about what actually happened.[113] Unfortunately, this notice may be the only surviving account of the concert it describes.[114]

---

110 LZ No. 74 (26.3.1840), p. 1061. See Appendix D, quotation 1.

111 The *Leipziger Zeitung* review is incomplete, however, in not identifying Liszt's fantasy as his *Réminiscences des Huguenots*. See AmZ 42 (1840), col. 298.

112 FDid No. 314 (14.11.1842). See Appendix D, quotation 10.

113 Liszt would have agreed. In his handwritten corrections to Christern, he observed that one purple, fact-free passage was "for newspaper articles very suitable, for biography impracticable" [Engel, p. 359].

114 Nothing about this concert appeared in Gotha's *Allgemeine Anzeiger* or *Regierungs- und Intelligenzblatt* during 1842. In his introduction to the first edition of Liszt's little-known piano piece *Die Gräberinsel der Fürsten zu Gotha* (Budapest ?1981), Friedrich Schnapp states that a short account

Also missing from contemporary accounts of his German concert tours is a great deal of information about Liszt's travels, schedules, and habits. Fortunately, many of his experiences—or something close to them—were described by other travellers, as we saw in Chapter I. We know Liszt led a remarkably active life in Germany, on as well as away from the concert platform. Indeed, the more one studies his activities, the more one wonders how many undocumented private performances Liszt gave in his "idle hours." During his Berlin sojourn of 1841-1842, for example, he performed constantly; Rellstab states that "scarcely a evening passes . . . without Liszt being heard at private soirées or matinées." Yet, as Rellstab goes on to point out, these events lay outside his own sphere of interest: Berlin's public musical life, especially its concerts, operas, and recitals.[115]

Nor were private performances the only Liszt events to which magazines and newspapers often closed their pages. We have already seen that censorship in Vormärz Germany forced the press to limit itself to "safe" material: news of the day, royal proclamations, public and personal advertisements, and so on. Magazines were not controlled as carefully as newspapers, but they also avoided dangerous topics, especially political ones. Consequently, journalists wrote nothing but respectful accounts of Liszt's relationships with German aristocrats. Even satires of Liszt and his fans avoided political issues of every kind. By contrast, the free French press lampooned Liszt as a "German patriot" and ridiculed his long hair, thin figure, elegant clothes, and decorations—above all, the Sword of Honor, which the Hungarians had bestowed upon him in January 1840

---

of the concert in question appeared in the 10 November 1842 issue of the *Gothaische Zeitung*. The present author has been unable to locate a copy of this review. Schnapp also suggests that Liszt may have played *Die Gräberinsel* "quasi improvvisando" on this occasion; again, it is impossible to verify such an hypothesis.

Schnapp's introduction to *Die Gräberinsel* appears in English translation in JALS 19 (1986), pp. 179-180.

[115] "Fast kein Abend vergeht,—ja die Vormittage werden zu Hülfe genommen—wo nicht Herr Liszt, wenn nicht öffentlich, doch vor so vielen Anwesenden, sich hören läßt, daß diese Privat-Soiréen oder Matinéen, in Bezug auf die Zahl der Zuhörer den öffentlichen gleich zu stellen sind. *Diese* musikalischen Ereignisse liegen indeß außerhalb unseres Kreises" [VZ No. 36 (12.2.1842)].

and which French caricaturists often depict him as wearing.[116]
Many Germans humorists abstained from similar lampoons,
perhaps because military or quasi-military honors were too
widely respected to be criticized openly. Or perhaps—and this
may have been true especially after early 1842—Liszt had begun to be perceived as a German "native son," even a patriot
whose musical settings of verses like "Was ist des deutschen
Vaterland?" were inappropriate subjects for "German"
ridicule.[117]

Another impediment to our knowledge of Liszt's German
tours also has its roots in politics: despite the recent
"democratization" of what used to be "Soviet" Europe, it is still
difficult to acquire information from archives in eastern
Germany, Poland, and Russia. The blockades imposed by
Communist regimes after World War II persist to the present
day, if only in the form of inadequate or even nonexistent pho-
tocopying equipment. In the case of the Weimar Staatsarchiv,
the blockade was and may still be a real one; because its re-
cesses conceal political material, including (so rumor has it)
information about former Nazis living in the immediate vicinity, very few researchers have been permitted to work there.

Not all Eastern European institutions, of course, continue
to function as secretively as the Staatsarchiv. For decades
Hungarian archives, including the National Széchényi Library,
have shared their treasures with the rest of the world. Since
1985, the present author has also received invaluable assistance from institutions like the former Deutsche
Staatsbibliothek of East Berlin (now Berlin's Staatsbibliothek
Preußischer Kulturbesitz), the Musikbibliothek der Stadt
Leipzig, the Sächsische Landesbibliothek, and especially the
library of the University of Wroclaw (formerly Breslau) in

---

[116] One of these caricatures, reprinted in Germany during the 1840s, reappears in Burger, p. 146.

[117] In an 1843 review of Liszt's four-part chorus *Das deutsche Vaterland*,
however, a critic for the *Allgemeine musikalische Zeitung* complained that
regions were represented in that work by less effective music and that,
overall, Liszt's piece was too operatic and complex for a "popular"
("volkstümlich") composition. See AmZ 45 (1843), cols. 711-713. See also
Cecilia Porter, "The 'Rheinlieder' Critics," MQ 63 (1977), pp. 87-88; and
Saffle, "Liszt und die Deutschen, 1840-1845" (identified above in Chapter
I).

Poland. Other organizations have been less helpful, though, especially when information was requested through the mails. In fact, the only way to examine certain sources—at least prior to 1989—was to visit these less helpful organizations in person and, occasionally, to grease bureaucratic wheels with bribes. The present author recalls occasions when a five-mark note and a pound of coffee beans led to the "discovery" of uncataloged newspaper clippings and other evidence about Liszt concerts in remote German towns.

In general, though, the greatest impediment to our knowledge of Liszt and Vormärz Germany has been a long-standing prejudice against periodicals as reliable sources of historical information. The simple truth is that accounts of Liszt's activities published in the contemporary German press are generally more accurate and more complete than accounts culled from other sources. Only with regard to private performances do letters, reminiscences, and occasional inscriptions or "album leaves" regularly tell us many things we cannot also learn from newspapers and magazines. Business documents, posters, playbills, poems, and so on, often supplement press records, but they rarely replace them altogether.

These generalizations, of course, are not always true, but they are often true—so often, in fact, that anyone studying Liszt's visits to Germany should be wary of "facts" that cannot be verified in the contemporary press. A case in point: Liszt's description in one of his "Bachelor of Music" letters of an evening he spent in Cuxhaven sometime after his tour of Denmark in July 1841. Liszt tells a good story in this letter: how his ship was forced into harbor by a storm, how a troupe of actors organized an impromptu show, and how much fun everybody had with the pretty Cuxhaven girls. What he doesn't mention is *when* the whole business took place and *what* he performed—or, for that matter, *that* he performed. Most of Germany's papers overlooked the incident, but one of them received a letter about it and ran a squib that made its way into the d'Agoult Scrapbook.[118] Still another squib, this one

---

[118] See Appendix D, quotation 4.

In reviewing *An Artist's Journey* several years ago, the present author assumed that Liszt claimed to have travelled from Copenhagen to Nonnenwerth by way of Cuxhaven. See *Notes* 47 (1990-1991), pp. 1133-1135, for the present author's review. Suttoni's assumption [see

less informative, appeared as a "miscellaneous" notice in a Rhineland paper.[119]

The press cannot *always* be relied upon, of course, but neither can other sources of information. Consider documentary problems associated with Liszt's participation in the 1845 Beethoven Festival held at Bonn. In 1984 Allan Keiler published an unfortunate review of Walker's *Virtuoso Years* volume, charging—among other things—that Walker failed to cite descriptions of the Festival published in the *Kleine Musikzeitung* (as the *Blätter für Musik und Literatur* was known after 1844).[120] Keiler's contention that the *Musikzeitung* presents the "most accurate"[121] available information is open to question (as we shall see below), but so is Walker's reply that the *Musikzeitung* account is "retrospective" and "cannot always be reconciled with reality."[122]

Instead of consulting newspapers and magazines, Walker relies primarily on the reminiscences of Festival visitors, documents no less "retrospective" than many accounts published in the contemporary press. There can be no doubt that reminiscences are extremely useful sources. Furthermore, press accounts of the Festival were not always correct. An example: Sir George Smart states categorically that the Festival rehearsal held on 8 August 1845 dealt with "parts of Beethoven's Mass in D and the Choral Sinfonia," while the afternoon rehearsal dealt with the Mass and that "nothing else was rehearsed" on that occasion; instead, Liszt met with the King of Prussia in

---

Liszt/Suttoni, p. 191], however, doesn't fit the facts: Liszt performed in Hamburg on 29 July 1841, and he gave an "unscheduled" performance in Kiel—on the far side of the Danish peninsula from Cuxhaven—one or two days earlier. Evidently Liszt travelled from Hamburg to Nonnenwerth via Rotterdam, as he mentioned he might in his letter to d'Agoult of 10 July 1841. See Ollivier II, p. 170. His Cuxhaven performance, therefore, must have taken place after 29 July, probably on Friday, 30 July 1841; the clipping in the d'Agoult scrapbook mentions "Freitag."

119 See MzRh No. 104 (31.8.1841), p. 415.

120 See Keiler, "Liszt Research and Walker's 'Liszt'," MQ 70 (1984), pp. 374-403.

121 Keiler, p. 403n.

122 Quoted from Walker's reply to Keiler in MQ 71 (1985), p. 219. NB: The Keiler/Walker exchange raises important issues in Liszt research, and it (especially Walker's part of it) deserves to be read with care.

Cologne to make final arrangements for Festival activities.[123] Liszt's first public rehearsal of his Festival Cantata, therefore, must have taken place on 7 August and not the following day, as reported in the *Hannoversche Morgen-Zeitung*.[124] A counter-example: the *Kleine Musikzeitung* (Keiler's favorite source) includes on the program of the 13 August 1845 concert Liszt's *Loreley* with Herr Götze as the soloist.[125] No other source mentions Götze's performance, and H. K. Breidenstein—the Festival director—later explained that Götze fell ill and was unable to fulfill his responsibilities.[126] Press acounts of the Festival made mistakes, but they almost always contain information missing from reminiscences per se. More: they tell us how Liszt was received by the audiences of his day. Most of all: they influenced—even *established*—his reputation with contemporary readers and, to a considerable extent, with the readers of subsequent generations. (We shall explore this last subject in Chapter V.) Only by taking *all* available evidence into account can events like the 1845 Beethoven Festival be reconstructed as thoroughly and accurately as possible.

Everyone knows, of course, that the press cannot always be trusted. Magazines and newspapers sometimes make mistakes, and occasionally they deliberately suppress or distort the truth. This, however, is no reason for ignoring them—especially since they often present information and opinions available nowhere else. Furthermore, writers of letters and reminiscences rarely correct themselves, while magazines and newspapers have always been to some extent self-correcting. Inaccurate advertisements, even in Liszt's day, were often superceded by published corrections or by apologies from editors to readers. Similarly, periodical reviews often served to "correct" advertised programs which, for one reason or another, were changed just before or even after those concerts began.[127]

---

[123] Smart, pp. 303-304.

[124] See HanMZ (31.8.1845), p. 556.

[125] See BML 6 (1845), p. 154.

[126] See H. K. Breidenstein, *Zur Jahresfeier der Inauguration des Beethoven-Monuments* (Bonn 1846), pp. 21-23.

[127] On some occasions, though, inaccuracies were simply forgotten. Rellstab, for example, never bothered to correct his announcement that Liszt would

More troublesome to historians are outright but unacknowl-
edged lies and slanders that appeared in *Signale* and other
anti-Liszt papers. Occasionally we can prove these calumnies
are untrue. One *Signale* contributor, for instance, gloated over
Liszt having just lost his fortune gambling in Breslau, only to
confess a couple of paragraphs later that he had not lost it: a
cheap trick familiar today to readers of the gutter press.[128]
Finally, periodicals—especially newspapers—can also be difficult to locate and consult; their use in historical research calls
for hard work, patience, a little luck, and a considerable
amount of time.

The greatest impediment to the use of newspapers and
magazines in Liszt research, however, has been the superior
attitude scholars have adopted (and continue to adopt) toward
periodicals as historical documents; they consider newspapers
and magazines too "superficial" or "popular" in character to be
trusted where "art music" is concerned. As Lucy Maynard
Salmon put it more than half a century ago: "The old proverb
'familiarity breeds contempt' [applies] to the newspaper since
its very accessibility [becomes] in the eyes of the public the best
of reasons for ignoring it."[129] Salmon readily acknowledges that
"danger lurks" when historians rely on newspapers for information they cannot be trusted to provide. But she also points
out that even the most dubious products of journalism have
their uses for historical scholarship:

> the historian may find both the authoritative and the unau-
> thoritative parts [of newspapers] of value. . . . The authori-
> tative parts are necessary in giving a connected account of past
> events, while the unauthoritative parts may be of value in de-
> termining ideals and standards, in gauging collective ignorance
> or intelligence, and interpreting the spirit of a time or of a lo-
> cality.[130]

---

be engaged for the following season as "Kapellmeister" in London. See Iris
12 (1841), p. 192. However, a correction did appear in BML 3
(1842), p. 12. Furthermore, Liszt apparently told one Magdeburg reporter
that he planned to write an opera with George Sand! See MbZ No. 65
(16.3.1844), p. 4. This plan is also mentioned in other Vormärz sources.

[128] See SmW 1 (1843), p. 69.

[129] Lucy Maynard Salmon, *The Newspaper and the Historian* (New York
1923), p. xxxix.

[130] Salmon, p. xli.

For Liszt researchers, the authoritative parts of newspapers are those that present *facts:* advertisements, announcements, and reports of dates, times, places, persons, particular pieces of music, and so on. The unauthoritative parts, of course, are those that present *opinions:* concert reviews, feature articles and biographies, poems, caricatures, and so on. Or are they? On the one hand, we may believe that critics like Schumann and Rellstab tell us precisely how Liszt played, but we can never know for certain. In this sense, even the opinions of a Schumann or a Rellstab cannot be considered "reliable," at least in the same sense that accurate statements about dates, times, and places can be said to be reliable. On the other, critics like Schumann and Rellstab have become authorities in their own right: their opinions have *become* facts and must be considered "reliable" both because they embody (or are believed to embody) artistic judgment of the highest order, *and* because our opinions have been formed by theirs.[131] Thus we must study both kinds of facts—those of history, and those of the history of reception (respectively, the provinces of "Geschichte" and "Rezeptionsgeschichte," to use technical German terminology) if we want to come as close as possible to understanding Liszt's concerts and career.

Only on a few occasions do newspapers and magazines fail us completely. We know virtually nothing, for example, about Liszt's performances in Donaueschingen and Memel, for example, although—as we saw above vis-à-vis Donaueschingen—a small about of indirect information has come down to us from the press.[132] Again, we know little about Liszt's visit to

---

131 That Schumann has been accepted more widely than Rellstab as an authority on Liszt is due to several factors, among them Schumann's excellence as a composer and the greater accessibility of his published criticism. One wonders, though, if his reservations about Liszt have helped make his observations "authoritative." As Salmon observes [pp. 329-330], "the public [tends] to take more kindly to censure than to praise and it is doubtless this that explains why the very word criticism has come to connote adverse judgment." On the other hand, neither Schumann nor Rellstab can reasonably be associated with "the advertiser, the business manager, the friend, the social circle, the technical language that may conceal poverty of thought, the lack of constructive listening, [and] the absence of standards"—all things that conspire "to perplex the historian in his efforts to reconstruct the music of an era from the contemporaneous criticism of music" [Salmon, p. 328].

132 An undated and unidentified clipping about Liszt's performance in Memel,

Tilsit—although, again, our best source of information is the press.[133] More complex is the situation associated with his Bautzen concert of February or March 1844. The *Budinisser Nachrichten*, Bautzen's principal Vormärz paper, published nothing about this event in its issues of February-March 1844. Furthermore, and for whatever reason, the division of the Dresdner Staatsarchiv in charge of Bautzen's city records denied in 1986 the existence of additional documentation. Interestingly enough, a second Bautzen paper called the *Erzähler an der Spree* mentions a Liszt recital scheduled for Zittau in March 1844 that was cancelled at the last moment.[134] Yet in March 1843 both the *Nachrichten* and the *Erzähler* advertised and reviewed a local recital presented by Wilhelmine Schroeder-Devrient, one of Liszt's favorite 1840s performance partners.[135] Perhaps the Bautzen press ignored Liszt because his own concert was underwritten by a group of local music-lovers who saw no need to take out ads. (Even today, the press is inclined to report events that have "paid their way," one way or another.) Fortunately for historians, Liszt's Bautzen concert caught the attention of *Signale* and the *Wiener allgemeine Musik-Zeitung*. These magazines ran squibs that document not only the invitation he received from Bautzen's music-lovers, but the fee he was offered in advance for his incomparable services.[136]

These and other details of Liszt's 1840s German tours will be explored chronologically and in greater detail in the following pages.

East Prussia, after the middle of March 1842, was supplied by the library of the University of Wroclaw, Poland.

133 In addition to contemporary reports in local papers, a feature article that appeared decades later in the *Vossische Zeitung* refers not only to Liszt's 15 March 1842 public Tilsit performance, but to what may have been a private performance at the home of one Katharina von Sanden's grandmother. See Sanden, "Franz Liszt und Bettina von Arnim," VZ (8.4.1933).

134 BauEr No. 11 (15.3.1844), p. 84.

135 See BauN No. 23 (22.3.1843), p. 150; and BauEr Nos. 12 and 14 (24.3. and 7.4.1843), pp. 96 and 110-111.

136 See SmW 2 (1844), p. 93; and WaMZ No. 42 (6.4.1844), p. 168.

CHAPTER III

A Short History of Liszt's German Tours

Er will bloß zeigen, wie es eigentlich gewesen ist.
Ranke

Liszt's performances in Germany between 1840-1845 can be divided among eighteen "tours," each ranging in length from a single concert to dozens of public and private appearances. To some extent these tours can be separated from each other only arbitrarily. Liszt did not leave Germany between August 1841 and March 1842, for example, but it is convenient to discuss his performances during those months in terms of three "tours": of central Germany (October-December 1841), of Berlin (December 1841—March 1842), and of eastern Prussia (March 1842). By discussing each tour in its turn, we can more easily trace Liszt's comings and goings. We can also more readily perceive how his reputation in Germany waxed and waned.

Table 1 provides a summary of Liszt's 298 documented German performances. Additional information about individual performances may be found in Appendix C.

Dresden and Leipzig: March 1840

Returning to Paris after triumphal appearances in Vienna and Prague, Liszt visited Dresden and Leipzig for the first time in March 1840. The fourteen public and private performances he gave in those German cities were his first as a mature artist.[1] More important, the reputation he acquired during his

---

[1] Travelling with his father from Vienna to Paris in 1823, Liszt performed in Munich and Augsburg. In honor of his triumphal return to Bavaria, several newspapers printed notices about his previous visit or reran the reviews he received in 1823. See, for example, AuTb No. 289 (21.10.1843), pp. 1241-1242.

visit made him a famous—if controversial—figure in German musical life for years to come.

Liszt arrived in Dresden on the morning of 14 March and secured rooms for himself and his entourage at the Hotel de Saxe. No sooner had he unpacked his bags, however, than he was asked to perform privately at two soirées (1-2).[2] At one of these events he joined Dresden violinist Karl Lipinski in a Beethoven violin sonata.[3] Gossip about Liszt must have whetted the appetites of Dresden concert-goers, for the crowded hall of his hotel fell silent, then burst into applause, when he stepped to the piano at his first public appearance on 16 March (3). In addition to his fantasies on *Les Huguenots* and *Lucia di Lammermoor*, he played his own *Grand Galop chromatique*; with Wilhelmine Schroeder-Devrient he also performed Schubert's *Ständchen, Ave Maria,* and *Erlkönig.* Liszt's virtuosity created a sensation. Johannes Heitmann, critic for the *Allgemeine musikalische Zeitung,* called him "the *non plus ultra* of musical art."[4] Robert Schumann, writing for his own *Neue Zeitschrift,* also praised him warmly.[5] In a shorter notice, the *Leipziger Zeitung* merely remarked that Liszt's enormous technical skill overcame every obstacle, and that he made an unprecedented impression upon his listeners.[6]

Liszt and Schumann left Dresden early the next day and travelled together by train to Leipzig, a journey of some three

---

[2] Throughout the present chapter, numbers in parentheses identify each of Liszt's 1840s German performances *and* the sources of information about them identified in Appendix C. See also Table 1.

[3] Which Beethoven sonata Liszt and Lipinski performed on this occasion remains unknown; we know they played several different sonatas on other occasions. The program advertised for Liszt's 27 March 1840 concert (10), for example, included the Sonata in a minor, Op. 23. See DrAn No. 83 (23.3.1840). At the concert itself, however, Liszt and Lipinski played the "Kreutzer" Sonata, Op. 47. See LZ No. 77 (30.3.1840), p. 1109. Moreover, sometime before 31 March 1840, Liszt and Gewandhaus concertmaster Ferdinand David played Beethoven's C-minor Sonata, Op. 30, No. 3, at a private party in Leipzig (13).

[4] "Mit Liszt mithin [ist] das *Non plus ultra* in der Kunst erreicht" [AmZ 42 (1840), col. 264].

[5] See Walker, pp. 345-346.

[6] "In der That erreicht die Fertigkeit Liszt's einen solchen Grad der Ueberwindung aller erdenklichen Schwierigkeiten . . . Den Eindruck Liszt's wird keiner hervorbringen können" [LZ No. 68 (19.3.1840), p. 969].

TABLE 1
Liszt's Concerts in Germany

In the following table "b" stands for a benefit performance, "g" for gratis (i.e., for a free performance), "m" for matinée, "p" for a private performance, and "reh" for an open rehearsal.

(1) DRESDEN p	?14.3.1840	
(2) DRESDEN p	?15.3.1840	
(3) DRESDEN	16.3.1840	
(4) LEIPZIG	17.3.1840	
(5) LEIPZIG p/m	20.3.1840	
(6) LEIPZIG p/m	22.3.1840	
(7) LEIPZIG p	23.3.1840	
(8) LEIPZIG	24.3.1940	
(9) DRESDEN p	?26.3.1840	
(10) DRESDEN	27.3.1840	
(11) DRESDEN m/b	29.3.1840	
(12) LEIPZIG b	30.3.1840	
(13) LEIPZIG p	before 31.3.1840	
(14) LEIPZIG p/m	31.3.1840	
(15) BADEN-BADEN	16.7.1840	
(16) BADEN-BADEN	21.7.1840	
(17) MAINZ	23.7.1840	
(18) EMS p	?25.7.1840	
(19) EMS	?27.7.1840	
(20) EMS p	28.7.1840	
(21) WIESBADEN	30.7.1840	
(22) FRANKFURT a.M.	5.8.1840	
(23) FRANKFURT a.M.	7.8.1840	
(24) MANNHEIM	8.8.1840	
(25) FRANKFURT a.M.	10.8.1840	
(26) BONN b	12.8.1840	
(27) COLOGNE	13.8.1840	
(28) HAMBURG	28.10.1840	
(29) HAMBURG	31.10.1840	
(30) HAMBURG ?m	2.11.1840	
(31) HAMBURG	2.11.1840	
(32) HAMBURG	6.11.1840	
(33) HAMBURG b	10.11.1840	
(34) HAMBURG	7.7.1841	
(35) HAMBURG m	9.7.1841	
(36) KIEL	?12.7.1841	
(37) KIEL	27.7.1841	
(38) HAMBURG	29.7.1841	
(39) CUXHAVEN p	30.7.1841	
(40) NONNENWERTH p	?9.8.1841	
(41) BONN	11.8.1841	
(42) NONNENWERTH p	13.8.1841	
(43) EMS	16.8.1841	
(44) NONNENWERTH p	22.8.1841	
(45) COLOGNE b	23.8.1841	
(46) KOBLENZ	25.8.1841	
(47) NONNENWERTH p	?26.8.1841	
(48) FRANKFURT a.M.	27.8.1841	
(49) FRANKFURT a.M.	29.8.1841	
(50) WIESBADEN	30.8.1841	
(51) MAINZ	1.9.1841	
(52) WIESBADEN	2.9.1841	
(53) MAINZ ?b	3.9.1841	
(54) MAINZ ?b	?5.9.1841	
(55) BADEN-BADEN	16.9.1841	
(56) FRANKFURT a.M. b	25.9.1841	
(57) NONNENWERTH p	after 2.10.1841	
(58) COLOGNE	5.10.1841	
(59) AACHEN	12.10.1841	
(60) NONNENWERTH p	22.10.1841	
(61) NONNENWERTH p	c. 22.10.1841	
(62) ELBERFELD	27.10.1841	
(63) DÜSSELDORF	28.10.1841	
(64) BONN p	1.11.1841	
(65) DÜSSELDORF	2.11.1841	
(66) ELBERFELD	3.11.1841	
(67) KREFELD	4.11.1841	
(68) WESEL b	7.11.1841	
(69) MÜNSTER	9.11.1841	
(70) MÜNSTER	11.11.1841	
(71) OSNABRÜCK p/m	12.11.1841	
(72) OSNABRÜCK	12.11.1841	
(73) BIELEFELD	13.11.1841	
(74) DETMOLD b	15.11.1841	
(75) KASSEL p/?m	17.11.1841	
(76) KASSEL p	18.11.1841	
(77) KASSEL	19.11.1841	
(78) KASSEL p	21.11.1841	
(79) KASSEL	22.11.1841	
(80) GÖTTINGEN	24.11.1841	
(81) WEIMAR p	?25.11.1841	
(82) WEIMAR ?p	26.11.1841	
(83) WEIMAR p	?27.11.1841	
(84) WEIMAR ?p	28.11.1841	
(85) WEIMAR b	29.11.1841	
(86) JENA m	30.11.1841	
(87) LEIPZIG p	1.12.1841	
(88) LEIPZIG p	2.12.1841	
(89) DRESDEN	4.12.1841	
(90) LEIPZIG	6.12.1841	
(91) DRESDEN	9.12.1841	
(92) DRESDEN p	11.12.1841	
(93) LEIPZIG p	12.12.1841	
(94) LEIPZIG	13.12.1841	

(95) ALTENBURG	14.12.1841
(96) LEIPZIG	16.12.1841
(97) HALLE	18.12.1841
(98) HALLE p	19.12.1841
(99) BERLIN	27.12.1841
(100) BERLIN	1.1.1842
(101) BERLIN p	3.1.1842
(102) BERLIN b	5.1.1842
(103) POTSDAM m	8.1.1842
(104) BERLIN b	9.1.1842
(105) BERLIN ?p	before 12.1.1842
(106) BERLIN b	12.1.1842
(107) BERLIN m	16.1.1842
(108) BERLIN m/?b	20.1.1842
(109) BERLIN	21.1.1842
(110) BERLIN	23.1.1842
(111) BERLIN	24.1.1842
(112) BERLIN m/p before	25.1.1842
(113) BERLIN m/p before	25.1.1842
(114) BERLIN m/p before	25.1.1842
(115) BERLIN m/p before	25.1.1842
(116) BERLIN b/m	25.1.1842
(117) BERLIN	30.1.1842
(118) BERLIN m/b	1.2.1842
(119) BERLIN	2.2.1842
(120) BERLIN p	?4.2.1842
(121) BERLIN	6.2.1842
(122) BERLIN p	8.2.1842
(123) BERLIN m/b	9.2.1842
(124) BERLIN p	9.2.1842
(125) BERLIN b	10.2.1842
(126) BERLIN b	16.2.1842
(127) BERLIN b	19.2.1842
(128) BERLIN	23.2.1842
(129) BERLIN m	25.2.1842
(130) BERLIN ?p	27.2.1842
(131) BERLIN b	28.2.1842
(132) BERLIN	2.3.1842
(133) BERLIN m/b	3.3.1842
(134) MARIENBURG p	8.3.1842
(135) ELBING	8.3.1842
(136) KÖNIGSBERG	10.3.1842
(137) KÖNIGSBERG	11.3.1842
(138) KÖNIGSBERG m	13.3.1842
(139) KÖNIGSBERG	13.3.1842
(140) KÖNIGSBERG p	
	before 14.3.1842
(141) KÖNIGSBERG p	
	before 14.3.1842
(142) KÖNIGSBERG m	14.3.1842
(143) KÖNIGSBERG	14.3.1842
(144) TILSIT	15.3.1842
(145) TILSIT m	16.3.1842
(146) MEMEL	after 16.3.1842

(147) LÜBECK p	before 3.6.1842
(148) LÜBECK b	3.6.1842
(149) BRÜHL p	10.9.1842
(150) COLOGNE p	12.9.1842
(151) COLOGNE m/b	13.9.1842
(152) AACHEN	17.9.1842
(153) WEIMAR	23.10.1842
(154) JENA b	26.10.1842
(155) ERFURT b	28.10.1842
(156) WEIMAR p before	29.10.1842
(157) WEIMAR p before	29.10.1842
(158) WEIMAR b	29.10.1842
(159) ERFURT	31.10.1842
(160) COBURG	1.11.1842
(161) COBURG b	4.11.1842
(162) GOTHA	9.11.1842
(163) FRANKFURT a.M.	15.11.1842
(164) COLOGNE m	?18.11.1842
(165) MÜNSTER	26.12.1842
(166) WEIMAR	29.12.1842
(167) BERLIN p	31.12.1842
(168) BERLIN	5.1.1843
(169) BERLIN	8.1.1843
(170) BERLIN	11.1.1843
(171) BERLIN p	12.1.1843
(172) BERLIN	15.1.1843
(173) BERLIN b	18.1.1843
(174) FRANKFURT a.d.O.	
	19.1.1843
(175) BRESLAU	21.1.1843
(176) BRESLAU	24.1.1843
(177) BRESLAU	26.1.1843
(178) BRESLAU	27.1.1843
(179) BRESLAU	29.1.1843
(180) BRESLAU	31.1.1843
(181) BRESLAU	1.2.1843
(182) BRESLAU	2.2.1843
(183) BRESLAU p/m	3.2.1843
(184) BRESLAU	4.2.1843
(185) BRESLAU p	before 6.2.1843
(186) BRESLAU p	before 6.2.1843
(187) LIEGNITZ	6.2.1843
(188) BRESLAU	7.2.1843
(189) BRIEG	8.2.1843
(190) BRESLAU	9.2.1843
(191) BERLIN p	12.2.1843
(192) LIEGNITZ	13.2.1843
(193) BERLIN b	16.2.1843
(194) POTSDAM p	18.2.1843
(195) FÜRSTENWALDE m/g	
	19.2.1843
(196) POSEN	21.2.1843
(197) POSEN	22.2.1843
(198) POSEN	24.2.1843
(199) POSEN	27.2.1843

(200) GLOGAU	1.3.1843	
(201) GLOGAU	3.3.1843	
(202) GLOGAU g	3.3.1843	
(203) LIEGNITZ	4.3.1843	
(204) BRESLAU	7.3.1843	
(205) NEISSE m	9.3.1843	
(206) HAMBURG	26.6.1843	
(207) SOLINGEN m/b	11.8.1843	
(208) BONN p	18.8.1843	
(209) DORTMUND b	24.8.1843	
(210) COLOGNE	12.9.1843	
(211) ISERLOHN b	23.9.1843	
(212) FRANKFURT a.M. p/m	4.10.1843	
(213) FRANKFURT a.M. p	c. 4.10.1843	
(214) WÜRZBURG	7.10.1843	
(215) NUREMBERG m	11.10.1843	
(216) NUREMBERG m	13.10.1843	
(217) MUNICH	18.10.1843	
(218) AUGSBURG	19.10.1843	
(219) MUNICH p	after 19.10.1843	
(220) MUNICH p	after 19.10.1843	
(221) MUNICH	21.10.1843	
(222) MUNICH b	25.10.1843	
(223) MUNICH b	30.10.1843	
(224) AUGSBURG	1.11.1843	
(225) AUGSBURG b	4.11.1843	
(226) STUTTGART p	?6.11.1843	
(227) STUTTGART b	7.11.1843	
(228) TÜBINGEN	11.11.1843	
(229) STUTTGART p/?m	before12.11.1843	
(230) STUTTGART m/b	12.11.1843	
(231) STUTTGART	14.11.1843	
(232) HEILBRONN	15.11.1843	
(233) STUTTGART	16.11.1843	
(234) LUDWIGSBURG	17.11.1843	
(235) HECHINGEN	18.11.1843	
(236) STUTTGART b	21.11.1843	
(237) DONAUESCHINGEN	before 25.11.1843	
(238) DONAUESCHINGEN p	before 27.11.1843	
(239) DONAUESCHINGEN p	before 27.11.1843	
(240) KARLSRUHE	27.11.1743	
(241) HEIDELBERG	28.11.1843	
(242) HEIDELBERG p	28.11.1843	
(243) KARLSRUHE p	29.11.1843	
(244) KARLSRUHE b	1.12.1843	
(245) MANNHEIM m	3.12.1843	
(246) KARLSRUHE b	4.12.1843	
(247) MANNHEIM m	6.12.1843	
(248) WEIMAR	7.1.1844	
(249) GOTHA	18.1.1844	
(250) WEIMAR	21.1.1844	
(251) RUDOLSTADT b	27.1.1844	
(252) WEIMAR	4.2.1844	
(253) JENA p	c. 5.2.1844	
(254) JENA	5.2.1844	
(255) ERFURT	17.2.1844	
(256) WEIMAR p	before 18.2.1844	
(257) WEIMAR p	before 18.2.1844	
(258) WEIMAR p	before 18.2.1844	
(259) WEIMAR p	before 18.2.1844	
(260) WEIMAR	18.2.1844	
(261) DRESDEN b	21.2.1844	
(262) DESSAU	24.2.1844	
(263) DRESDEN	27.2.1844	
(264) BAUTZEN	?before 1.3.1844	
(265) DRESDEN b	1.3.1844	
(266) BERNBURG	before 5.3.1844	
(267) BERNBURG p	before 5.3.1844	
(268) STETTIN	7.3.1844	
(269) STETTIN	8.3.1844	
(270) MAGDEBURG	14.3.1844	
(271) MAGDEBURG	15.3.1844	
(272) MAGDEBURG	17.3.1844	
(273) MAGDEBURG p	18.3.1844	
(274) BRAUNSCHWEIG	22.3.1844	
(275) BRAUNSCHWEIG	25.3.1844	
(276) HANNOVER	28.3.1844	
(277) HANNOVER	31.3.1844	
(278) HANNOVER g	31.3.1844	
(279) BONN reh	7.8.1845	
(280) BONN reh	9.8.1845	
(281) BONN reh	10.8.1845	
(282) BONN	12.8.1845	
(283) BONN m	13.8.1845	
(284) BRÜHL p	13.8.1845	
(285) COLOGNE	14.8.1845	
(286) STOLZENFELS p	16.8.1845	
(287) KLEVE ?b	18.8.1845	
(288) BADEN-BADEN p	before 26.8.1845	
(289) BADEN-BADEN p	?after 26.8.1845	
(290) BADEN-BADEN	21.9.1845	
(291) STUTTGART	29.9.1845	
(292) DARMSTADT	8.10.1845	
(293) STUTTGART	10.10.1845	
(294) ?STUTTGART p	?after 10.10.1845	
(295) DARMSTADT p	c.12.10.1845	
(296) DARMSTADT	12.10.1845	
(297) HEIDELBERG p/?b	15.10.1845	
(298) FREIBURG i.B.	17.10.1845	

to four hours. That evening Liszt performed for the first time at the Gewandhaus, one of Germany's most celebrated concert halls (4).[7] His program consisted of the "Scherzo and Finale" (actually the last three movements) of Beethoven's "Pastoral" symphony, his own fantasy on "I tuoi frequenti palpiti" from Pacini's *Niobe*, an etude, and his *Galop chromatique*. Appearing with him was one Madame Schmidt, who sang songs by Proch and Mendelssohn, and Liszt played his own *Valse di bravura* as an encore. Considerable excitement had been generated in Leipzig by reports of his recent triumphs,[8] but his first Gewandhaus concert was not altogether a success. Neither music-lovers nor critics found much to praise in his Beethoven transcription; Schumann, though, observed that the audience had at least heard some masterful playing and "seen the lion shake his mane."[9]

Much more unfortunate were the business arrangements made by Liszt and by his travelling companion Hermann ("Puzzi") Cohen. Tickets for Gewandhaus concerts, underwritten by Leipzig linen merchants, traditionally cost 16 groschen. Liszt demanded much higher sums for admission to his own concerts: 1 thaler for "regular" tickets (i.e., for tickets purchased before the concert), and 2 thalers for tickets sold "at the door." Furthermore, he advertised a few advance-purchase "Sperrsitz" (i.e., reserved-seating) tickets, thereby breaking another unwritten Gewandhaus law against assigned seats. Finally, complimentary tickets were withheld from newspaper critics and other local dignitaries.[10] The resulting brouhaha was

---

7   Ramann II, p. 61, gives 15 March 1840 as the date for this concert; the correct date is 16 March. Similar mistakes, scattered throughout the literature, are generally ignored below. NB: The most accurate account of Liszt's March 1840 tour appears not in the standard Liszt literature, but in William Little, "Mendelssohn and Liszt," *Mendelssohn Studies* (Cambridge and New York 1992), pp. 106-125. Hereafter "Little."

8   *Contra* Walker, p. 348. See AmZ 42 (1840), cols. 91-93: an account of Liszt's successes in Vienna late in 1839.

9   "Dennoch, versteht es sich, hatte man den Meister auf dem Instrumente herausgehört; man war zufrieden; man hatte ihn wenigstens die Mähnen schütteln gesehen" [NZfM 12 (1840), p. 119]. The entire passage is translated into English in Walker, p. 349.

10 Among those denied tickets was Friedrich Wieck, Schumann's father-in-law elect. See Litzmann I, p. 418.

heard hundreds of miles away.[11] Liszt was criticized for everything from the pieces he performed to the flowers he received
from a local singer at his second Gewandhaus appearance.[12]
The *Dresdner Wochenblatt* even ran an article complaining that
he had falsified his real name ("List"!) in order to appear as an
"exotic" Hungarian rather than an honest German.[13] On 29
March Liszt published a letter in the *Dresdner Anzeiger*, apologizing for business mistakes he blamed to some extent on
himself.[14] But his difficulties in Leipzig cannot be blamed exclusively on the ticketing fiasco. Widespread opposition to musical novelty as well as to his aristocratic airs and his
disinclination to speak German instead of French also upset
many people; they certainly irritated Schumann.[15] The results
were serious: by the end of March 1840 Liszt's reputation in

[11] For reports in the Karlsruhe and Frankfurt a.M. press, see (respectively)
      JdNVM 2 (1840), pp. 127-128; and MzRh No. 54 (1840), p. 215. Ramann
      II, p. 65, quotes part of the latter notice, which states simply that "Liszt
      hat in Leipzig keine Freikarten zu seinem Concerte ausgegeben. (Der
      Jammer darüber hat sich bereits 10 norddeutsche Blätter wörtlich
      mitgetheilt.)"

[12] Schumann mentions this last incident in a famous passage well-known to
      Liszt scholars. See NZfM 12 (1840), esp. p. 119. See also Walker, pp.
      350-351.

[13] See "Vorschlag an den Tonkünstler Fr. LISZT wegen Abänderung der
      Schreibart seines Namens," DrWb No. 23 (18.3.1840), p. 130. Liszt, of
      course, did *not* alter his name; Walker [p. 38] points out that it was prob-
      ably his father who adopted "the new orthography" of Hungarian spelling.
      The *Wochenblatt's* attack, however, may have inspired Liszt to appear in
      Hungarian national costume at the concert given in his honor on 23 March
      1840 (7). See "Max Müller und Liszt," *Familienblatt* [Leipzig] No. 245
      (20.10.1896), p. 980.

[14] See DrAn No. 89 (27.3.1840). Reprinted in FKB No. 93 (2.4.1840), p. 372.
      See also Appendix E, letter 1, where the *Konversationsblatt* text is re-
      printed complete. NB: Like other German-language quotations below, this
      one contains typographical errors and eccentricities of style. The present
      author is grateful to James Deaville and Barbara Hassell for pointing out
      these and related problematic passages.
          Local gossip held that "Herr Hofmeister," Liszt's Leipzig publisher,
      had something to do with the ticketing scandal. According to modern his-
      torians, though, the problems originated with Cohen. See Raabe I, pp.
      78-79. See also E. H. Müller von Asow, "Hermann Cohen, ein
      Lieblingsschüler Franz Liszts," *Österreichische Musikzeitung* 16 (1961),
      pp. 443-452. Tierney's biography of Cohen, cited in the bibliography, does
      not address these issues.

[15] See Litzmann I, p. 416.

Germany had suffered a setback from which it has never fully
recovered.

A second Gewandhaus concert, scheduled for the evening
of 18 March, had to be cancelled: Liszt had fallen ill. Confined
to his hotel bedroom for several days, he received visits from a
number of musical celebrities—among them, Schumann,
Mendelssohn, and Ferdinand Hiller. The *Dresdner Wochenblatt*
again attacked Liszt, accusing him this time of feigning illness
to avoid his public.[16] Several musicians rallied to his defense,
however, and challenged Adolph Schäfer, editor of the
Wochenblatt, to publish their spirited attack on that
individual's questionable ethics and artistic judgement.[17] By 20
March Liszt had recovered his strength, but his second Dresden
concert—originally advertised for the following day—had by
then been postponed twice.[18] Nevertheless, he felt well enough
to play privately for a small party held at Schumann's home (5).
Two days later he again performed privately in Leipzig (6), this
time at the home of Raimund Härtel. Both matinées were successes, and Schumann observed that Liszt's playing brought
tears to the eyes of one of his friends.[19] "I wish you could have
been with [us] early this morning," Schumann wrote Clara
Wieck. "He played some of the Novelettes, part of the Fantasie,
and of the Sonata, and I was really quite moved. A good deal
of it differed from my own conception, but it was always genial,

16 "Der Pianist Liszt in Leipzig," DrWb No. 24 (21.3.1840),
    "Außerordentliche Beilage." Schumann, who agreed with this rumor,
    called Liszt's illness "eine politische Krankheit" [Litzmann I, p. 418].
    Whether Schumann spread the rumor himself, however, is another mat-
    ter. In event, Liszt became ill on other occasions during his travels: in
    Berlin and Königsberg in 1842, for example, and during or after his visit
    to Bonn in 1845.

17 See DrWb No. 25 (25.3.1840), p. 174. The letter in question, dated 23
    March 1840 and signed only with a series of initials, states that Schäfer
    1) ridiculed Liszt without justifiable musical grounds, and 2) attacked him
    in order to increase *Wochenblatt* circulation. Schäfer denied both charges
    on pp. 147-148 of the same issue, but the repeated exploitation of Liszt's
    name in Schäfer's paper lends support to the second accusation. Ramann,
    incidentally, implied that only one article appeared in issues 24-26 of the
    Wochenblatt. See Ramann II, p. 65.

18 At first until 25 March, then until 27 March. See DrAn Nos. 78, 81, and
    83 (18, 21, and 23.3.1840).

19 "Nur Becker war dabei [am 20. März], dem standen die Thränen in den
    Augen, glaub ich" [Litzmann I, p. 414].

and full of such delicacy and strong feeling as he probably does not enjoy every day."[20]

On 23 March Hiller gave a dinner in Liszt's honor at the Äckerlein. And, in an attempt to restore his musical reputation, Mendelssohn arranged a "private" concert for him the same day (7). Complete with refreshments, the concert took place at the Gewandhaus. Liszt was treated to performances of several masterpieces (including Schubert's "Great" Symphony in C Major), and he participated in a performance of Bach's "Triple" Concerto; he also played several of his own works, including his *Lucia* fantasy and his transcription of Schubert's *Erlkönig*. Schumann was deeply moved by the three incomparable hours of music he heard that evening,[21] and his guest's local reputation took a turn for the better.

The following evening Liszt presented his second public Leipzig concert (8), collaborating with the Gewandhaus orchestra in Weber's *Konzertstück* and playing his *Huguenots* fantasy and three Schubert song transcriptions—including the *Erlkönig* as an encore. Schumann singled out his interpretation of the *Konzertstück* for special praise,[22] while the *Allgemeine musikalische Zeitung* marvelled over the astonishing technical brilliance and strength of his *Huguenots* performance and the smooth, tasteful presentation of his song transcriptions.[23] Finally, as we saw in Chapter II, the *Leipziger Zeitung* described his artistry in the most positive terms.[24] A complete

---

[20] Quoted from *Early Letters of Robert Schumann*, trans. May Herbert (London 1888), p. 298. Schumann's contention that Liszt played with different degrees of musical insight on different occasions will be referred to again in Chapter V.

[21] "Es schien alles wie aus dem Augenblicke hervorgewachsen, nichts vorbereitet; drei glückliche Musikstunden waren's, wie sie sonst Jahre nicht bringen" [NZfM 12 (1840), p. 119]. This review is quoted in Ramann II, p. 66; and in other biographies.

[22] "Webers Konzertstück . . . war und blieb die Krone seiner Leistungen" [NZfM 12 (1840), p. 119].

[23] "In der Fantasie über die Hugenotten . . . setzt die ungeheure Technik und ausdauernde Kraft des Herrn Liszts wahrhaft in Erstaunen. . . . Ganz anderes Interesse boten die Schubert'schen Lieder, welche Herr Liszt auf sehr geschickte und geschmackvolle Weise für die Pianoforte bearbeitet hat" [AmZ 42 (1840), col. 298].

[24] See Appendix D, quotation 1.

success, the concert concluded with a trumpet-and-drum fan-
fare and the presentation of a floral wreath; Liszt replied by
offering to give a benefit concert in Leipzig in the near future.

On 25 March Liszt returned to Dresden in order to visit
the King of Saxony and to give several more concerts. The following day, in all likelihood, he played the piano part of
Mendelssohn's Concerto in d minor at the home of Karl Krägen
(9), and on the evening of 27 March he gave a public concert
at the Hotel de Saxe (10). Sharing the stage, Liszt performed
Beethoven's "Kreutzer" sonata with Lipinski, accompanied
several songs for Schroeder-Devrient, and may have played the
first version of his own *Tarantelles napolitaines*—one of several
problematic repertory choices discussed in Chapter IV. Another
success, this concert helped advertise a benefit matinée presented at the same hotel two days later (11). Little information
survives about the matinée, but we do know that its proceeds
went to Dresden's poor.

On the morning of 30 March Liszt hastened to Leipzig to
rehearse for his third and final public Gewandhaus concert
(12). The program included the Mendelssohn Concerto, three
etudes by Hiller, ten selections from Schumann's *Carnaval*, and
the *Hexameron* variations composed collaboratively by Chopin,
Czerny, Herz, Liszt, Pixis, and Thalberg. Tremendous applause
greeted some of these numbers; others were less successful. The
Allgemeine musikalische Zeitung, for example, sharply criticized the Mendelssohn concerto performance, one evidently arranged in haste.[25] But the concert itself was an unquestioned
financial triumph, and over 640 thalers was raised for old and
ailing Leipzig musicians. The audience's response was enthusiastic, and Liszt played his *Galop chromatique* as an encore.
The following morning he played for the last time at
Schumann's home (14), entertaining his friend with Schubert
song transcriptions and several studies. His host played too,
albeit somewhat nervously. "Liszt's playing is full of spirit and

---

[25] See AmZ 42 (1840), col. 298. Claims that Liszt sightread the concerto at
his Leipzig concert are incorrect. We know he played through it at
Krägen's house in Dresden. See Little, p. 118. All this has nothing to do,
however, with Liszt's skill as a sightreader, and stories about his abilities
are legion. Evidently, for instance, he sightread Mendelssohn's Op. 25
Concerto in Paris—and in the composer's presence. See Ramann II, p. 58.

life," Schumann later wrote.[26] And of the previous evening's Gewandhaus concert, he proclaimed that his colleague was "unquestionably a tremendous performer, like no other."[27]

Liszt's first German tour was not an unqualified success. Sickness, "scandal," unfortunate program choices, sometime inadequate rehearsal, and vicious attacks by local newspapers marred his visits to Dresden, and especially to Leipzig. Nevertheless, both of the most important German musical magazines—the *Allgemeine musikalische Zeitung* and the *Neue Zeitschrift*—praised his pianism, and he proved he could play magnificently even after debilitating illness. These accomplishments to his credit, and a considerable amount of money in his (and others') pockets, he left Leipzig for Paris late on 31 March 1840 and a few days later, travelling by way of Metz, met the Comtesse d'Agoult a short distance outside the French capital.

A Rhineland Tour: July-August 1840

Returning from a trip to England, Liszt undertook his first tour of the Rhineland during July-August 1840. Although some of his Rhenish concerts were poorly attended and others received only perfunctory attention in the press, he managed to earn critical praise as well as a lot of money. During August 1840 he also contributed heavily to the Beethoven Memorial fund, a charity that occupied his attention intermittently until August 1845.

Liszt travelled to Baden-Baden by way of Brussels and Mainz to begin a working holiday at Germany's most famous spa. (On this occasion, alone among his cross-country German travels, he was accompanied by d'Agoult.) His arrival was announced for the first time on 8 July by the *Badener Wochenblatt*, a local newspaper,[28] but he actually reached Baden-Baden only on 16 July, the date of his first concert at the Salle de Réunion (15). The program for this event included his

---

[26] Quoted in Litzmann I, p. 421.

[27] Quoted in Litzmann I, p. 420.

[28] BdWb No. 61 (8.7.1840), p. 668. Quoted in: Ernst Ihle, "Liszt-Besuche und Liszt-Konzerte in Baden-Baden," *Badeblatt* No. 140 (19.6.1926). See also BdWb No. 69 (17.7.1840), p. 833.

transcription of the overture to Rossini's *Guillaume Tell* and
his own *Galop chromatique*. The Grand-Duke of Baden and
other "royals" were in attendence, and ticket sales resulted in
a profit of 1,500 francs. Liszt gave a second concert in the same
hall on 21 July (16). Sharing the platform on this occasion was
Valerie de Rupplin, a singer from Konstanz; together, the two
artists presented arias from *Lucia di Lammermoor* and *Robert
le diable*, and Liszt played a "Marche hongroise" as well as the
Hexameron variations. The audience was small but the applause enthusiastic.[29] Neither concert was reviewed by local
critics, but the *Wochenblatt* boasted that his visit affirmed the
importance of the arts in Baden-Baden.[30]

Together with d'Agoult and the notorious Cohen,[31] Liszt
travelled to Mainz, where lodgings were secured the Hotel de
Russie. On the evening of 23 July he gave a concert at the Hof
zum Gutenberg (17). Appearing with Madame Duflot-Maillard,
he accompanied an aria from *Robert le diable* and played his
own *Puritani* fantasy and his *Galop*. A small audience, composed of "elite" citizens from surrounding towns, waited impatiently from 4:30 p.m. until 7 p.m. for the concert to begin.
Disgruntled by this experience, Carl Gollmick tempered his
praise for Liszt's technical skill, energy, and extravagent ex-
pressiveness by asserting in the *Frankfurter Konversationsblatt*
that the virtuoso was no composer in his own right, and that
"all of his reminiscences, his orgies, his grand galops, etc.,"
would never earn him a place in the Pantheon of Art.[32] Dr.

---

29 "Baden, 22. Juli. Gestern gab Liszt ein zweites, nicht sehr besuchtes
    Concert unter großem Beifall" [Iris 1 (1840), p. 140]. Remarks in the
    French press about the "enthousiasme extraordinaire" that greeted Liszt
    may refer to his 16 July performance. See RGMP 7 (1840), p. 410.

30 See BdWb No. 71 (19.7.1840), p. 884.

31 Cohen accompanied Liszt on several of his Vormärz tours, although he
    does not seem to have meddled in his teacher's affairs after March 1840.
    Instead, he occasionally gave recitals of his own. On 14 July 1840, for in-
    stance, he himself gave a Baden-Baden recital, playing a simplified ver-
    sion of Liszt's *Réminiscences de Lucia di Lammermoor* and *Hexameron*.
    See BdWb No. 75 (23.7.1840), p. 946.

32 "Liszt ist kein selbstständiger Componist . . . und alle seine
    Reminiscensen, seine Orgien, seine Galops chromatiques, u. s. w. mit noch
    so räthselhafter Technik, Geist, Weltschmerz oder Koboldorie
    vorgetragen, reichen nicht hin, ihm eine Stelle in das Pantheon der
    Aesthetik zu verschaffen" [FKB No. 209 (30.7.1840), p. 836].

Friedrich Wiest, on the other hand, gave him a much more flattering review in *Das Rheinland*, but he also made fun of the "Lisztomania" that had already befallen concert-goers in other German cities.[33]

Liszt may have left Mainz as early as the following morning; in any event, he arrived at Bad Ems two days later. Almost as soon as he registered at the Hotel Englischer Hof,[34] he was asked to play privately for the Empress Alexandrova of Russia and a number of distinguished guests, including the composer Giacomo Meyerbeer (18). Liszt acknowledged his colleague's presence with a fantasy on melodies from *Les Huguenots*, and his performance of Schubert's *Ave Maria* so moved the Empress that she invited him to visit Russia—an invitation he accepted in 1842. Little is known about his public concert at the Ems Kursaal (19), but we do know he played no fewer than ten pieces privately for the Empress on the afternoon or evening of 28 July (20).

Liszt probably left Ems on 29 July in order to travel by steamboat to Wiesbaden, where he gave a concert at the city theater the following evening (21). His program included a work identified only as "Tarentelles napolitaines" as well as the *Hexameron* variations, the latter possibly with orchestral accompaniment.[35] Next he visited Frankfurt a.M., probably travelling there on the Taunuseisenbahn mentioned in Chapter I. In Frankfurt Liszt performed three times at the city theater during a week-long visit. His first Frankfurt concert took place

---

[33] See Appendix D, quotation 2.

[34] The Princess Belgiojoso, an influential figure in Liszt's early life, was also registered at the same hotel; Meyerbeer was registered in the Darmstädter Hof nearby. See EmsLK (26-28.7.1840). With regard to the Princess herself, see Walker, pp. 237-238.

[35] A program for this concert is preserved in D-WRgs Liszt Kasten 240. This program also advertises Weber's *Jubel-Overture*, a work Liszt performed later both as pianist and conductor.

No one knows whether Liszt himself prepared a piano-orchestral version of *Hexameron* prior to the 1840s. In any event, he played *Hexameron* with orchestra in Vormärz Germany on many occasions. Several early solo-piano editions of *Hexameron* contain orchestral cues. See, for example, those of Haslinger (Plate No. T.H. 7700) and Troupenas (D-Bds Busoni Collection 38/7; no plate number). Additional information about *Hexameron* editions appears in Schnapp, "Verschollene Kompositionen Franz Liszts," *Von deutscher Tonkunst*, ed. Alfred Morgenroth (Leipzig 1942), p. 129.

on the evening of 5 August (22). Accompanied by the Theater orchestra, he played Weber's *Konzertstück*, and he also performed his fantasy on *Lucia di Lammermoor*, the *Tarantelles*, and the almost inevitable *Galop*. Two days later he appeared again with orchestra, performing Hummel's Concerto in b minor as well as several solo works (23). The program of his last Frankfurt concert on 10 August (25) included Beethoven's Fantasy for piano, chorus, and orchestra, Op. 80, a mazurka by Chopin, and an improvised fantasy on themes submitted by his audience. Liszt also found time to visit Mannheim on 8 August, where he gave a recital that evening at the local Theater (24).[36]

Liszt's Frankfurt concerts were received with considerable enthusiasm. One local magazine observed that the second concert was poorly attended because other events were also taking place,[37] but periodicals far and wide praised his musicianship. The *Konversationsblatt*, for example, applauded his dexterity and precision, which bordered "on the incredible" and which one had to witness in order to believe.[38] Even the *Augsburger allgemeine Zeitung*, then Germany's most prestigious and influential newspaper, reported that his first Frankfurt performance was "of course" the most brilliant of successes.[39]

Liszt left the Frankfurt area in time to reach Bonn on 12 August. That evening he presented a benefit concert in the hall of the local literary society (26).[40] Most of the pieces he played on that occasion also appeared on his other Rhenish programs.

---

[36] No account of this performance seems to have survived, but one local paper printed a German translation of an article about Liszt taken from London's *Morning Post*. See MnDP No. 97 (14.8.1840), pp. 385-386.

[37] "Das zweite Conzert war verschiedener Privat-Soiréen wegen nur sehr schwach besucht" [FKB No. 226 (16.8.1840), p. 904]. The third, however, was packed. See AuZ (1840), p. 1815.

[38] "Die ans Unglaubliche [sic] grenzende Fertigkeit und Präcision des Künstlers vermag keine Feder zu schildern; man muß hören und *sehen*, ja sehen *muß* man, um zu sehen, daß es für die Finger Liszt's keine Schwierigkeiten giebt" [FKB No. 219 (9.8.1840), p. 875].

[39] "Liszt gab [am 5. August] in unsrem Theater ein Concert, das natürlich den glänzendsten Erfolg hatte" [AuZ (1840), p. 1781].

[40] This recital was originally advertised for 4 August 1840. See BnWb No. 92 (2.8.1840). A corrected announcement appeared in the following issue of that paper.

In honor of the Beethoven Memorial fund, though, he also performed his transcription of Beethoven's *Adelaïde*, the concluding movements of his "Pastoral" symphony transcription, and
all of the "Moonlight" sonata. The following day Liszt travelled
to near-by Cologne, where he completed his tour with a concert
in the hall of the Casino (27). Unfortunately, no local reviews
of his 1840 Bonn and Cologne concerts have survived,[41] and
even the program he played at the Casino appears to have been
lost. Several months later, however, the *Jahrbücher des
deutschen National-Vereins* mentioned the Bonn recital, referred to his "incomparable talent," and reported happily that
he had contributed 10,000 francs on behalf of a monument to
be erected to Beethoven's honor.[42]

Hamburg: October-November 1840

Returning to Germany from a second trip to England,
Liszt visited Hamburg during October and November 1840.
There he gave six concerts, received generally favorable reviews

---

[41] Apparently a Bonn newspaper published a general attack on "virtuosos"
after Liszt left the immediate area. See Theodor Henssler, *Das
musikalische Bonn im 19. Jahrhundert* (Bonn 1959), p. 172. The *Bonner
Wochenblatt* published a short notice, ostensibly quoted from the *Journal
de Francfort*, which mentions Liszt's 7 August 1840 concert in a favorable
light. See BnWb No. 96 (11.8.1840). See also Henssler, *Das musikalische
Bonn*, p. 171. The present author was unable to locate the JdF notice in
question.

[42] "Endlich hat uns auch der geniale Liszt durch sein unvergleichliches Talent in Entzücken versetzt. . . . Seinen großartigen Sinn und Charakter
bewies er aber noch besonders dadurch, daß er dem Comité für
Beethovens Monument eine Anweisung von 10,000 Franken übergab als
'vorläufigen Beitrag'" [JdNVM 2 (1840), p. 376]. Other references to
Liszt's donation appeared around the same time in AmZ 42 (1840), col.
798; and NZfM 13 (1840), p. 72. His eventual contribution, translated into
Prussian currency, amounted to 2,666 thalers. See H. K. Breidenstein,
*Festgabe zu der am 12ten August 1845 stattfindenden Inauguration des
Beethoven-Monuments* (Bonn 1845), p. 10. NB: Breidenstein's book is reprinted in German in LSae 25 (1979) without page numbers. It appears
in English translation in LSae 27 (1981), pp. 28-40.
      Liszt/Suttoni, pp. 188-190, discusses Liszt's early interest in the
Beethoven project. Reports of his activities on behalf of it appeared frequently in the German press prior to 1845. See, for instance, AmZ 45
(1843), cols. 333-334; and NZfM 17 (1842), p. 16. Other reports about the
project ignored Liszt altogether, however. See AmZ 45 (1843), col. 398;
NZfM 16 (1842), pp. 7-8; Iris 11 (1840), pp. 187-188; and SmW 1 (1843),
p. 224.

from local papers, and earned a tremendous amount of
money—much of it donated to a local pension fund. Furthermore, it was in Hamburg that Liszt demonstrated for the first
time his ability to resolve professional disputes through patience, generosity, and sheer musicianship. As a consequence,
he earned the lasting respect of that city's artistic community.

After leaving Paris and stopping in Liège and Aachen,
Liszt celebrated his twenty-ninth birthday on 22 October 1840
in Düsseldorf. Three days later he reached Hamburg, secured
lodgings at the Hotel zur alten Stadt London by 9 p.m., ate a
late dinner with several old friends (including his Hamburg
publisher Schuberth), and only then retired to his room to write
two important letters.[43] His first Hamburg recital took place on
28 October in the Apollo-Saale (28). The sensation he created
on this occasion was due in part to his spirited interpretations
of pieces like the *Lucia* fantasy and the *Galop*, performances
likened by one admiring critic to a proud horseman mastering
a noble steed.[44]

Unfortunately, Liszt owed some of his Hamburg celebrity
to a quarrel which began that evening with the management
of the city's theater. The officials in question refused to permit
one of the Theater's musicians to perform with him and, after
playing the three concluding movements of his "Pastoral" symphony transcription,[45] he apologized to his audience for "a certain monotony" ("eine bedeutende Monotonie") in his program,
and for his lack of musical accomplices. At least some of his

---

43 In addition to a lengthy missive addressed to the Comtesse d'Agoult, he
    wrote a letter of complaint to the editor of the *Revue des Deux Mondes*
    about a lampoon of himself and the "Sword of Honor" he received in Pest
    the previous January. That he would write this second letter so soon after
    a difficult journey—indeed, that he simply did not collapse after five days
    and nights of coach travel—testifies to the strength of his feelings about
    the *Revue* lampoon. With regard to the letter itself, see Ollivier II, pp.
    40-42; and Briefe I, pp. 38-40. A complete English translation of the letter
    appears in Walker, pp. 327-328. A partial translation appears in Williams,
    pp. 146-147.

44 "[Liszt] verhält sich zu seinem edlen Instrument wie der Reiter zu seinem
    edlen Rosse, beide sind Eins, der Reiter versucht seine Kraft, wie ist er
    stolz auf seinem Renner!" [HNZ No. 254 (29.10.1840)].

45 Not afterwards, as Sittard states in his *Geschichte des Musik- und
    Concertwesens in Hamburg*, p. 237. See instead BML 1 (1840), p. 19. Most
    of the *Liszt in Hamburg* pamphlet mentioned above in Chapter II also
    deals with the "Theater affair."

listeners responded with cries of "Bravo!" and considerable excitement ensued. Many Hamburgers sided with Liszt; others, however, attacked him for "actions unbecoming a musical genius."[46] But the furor over the "Theater affair" didn't interfere with public enthusiasm. On 6 November Liszt himself wrote the Comtesse d'Agoult that the Hamburg was wild about him, and that his next concert was already sold out.[47]

On 31 October Liszt gave his second Hamburg recital in the hall of his hotel (29). He played the piano in an arrangement of Hummel's Septet and performed etudes by Chopin and Moscheles, Beethoven's *Adelaïde*, and *Hexameron*. The artistry he demonstrated on this occasion silenced at least some of his opponents.[48] Furthermore, he responded to requests from his audience and performed the entire "Moonlight" sonata by memory—a feat we take for granted today, but one which amazed Hamburg amateurs and professionals alike.[49] Hans Christian Andersen, who attended one of Liszt's Hamburg recitals, seems to have been as impressed as local music-lovers with the pianist's transcendent spirit, energy, and skill:

[46] See "Herr F. Liszt und die Direction unsers Stadt-Theaters," HNach No. 270 (13.11.1840). See also BML 1 (1840), pp. 17-18; and *Liszt in Hamburg*, passim.

[47] "Le public de Hamburg est furieux pour moi. Depuis onze heures du matin on refuse des billets pour mon concert de ce soir" [Ollivier II, p. 49]. Hamburg's *Correspondent* also reported that Liszt's 31 October concert attracted as large a "versammelte ein eben so zahlreiches Publicum wie das erste" [HZCor No. 260 (3.11.1840)], and *Der Freischütz* described his 6 November concert in terms of large crowds and tremendous success. Only his performance with Cohen on 2 November "war sehr sparsam besucht" [HFrs No. 45 (7.11.1840), col. 720].

By October 1840 Liszt had apparently become sensitive to newspaper heckling of every kind. In a letter addressed to Schumann on 4 November 1840, for example, he refers to his quarrel with the Theater management, mentions the indignities he suffered at the hands of the Leipzig press, and laments that "les mêmes journaux vous auront appris combien ces petits misères ont été impuissants et ridicules" [Kapp, "Franz Liszt und Robert Schumann," *Die Musik* 13-2 (November 1914), p. 74]. One wishes Liszt had identified the "journaux" in question. Throughout his 1840 visit, Hamburg papers indulged in some sarcasm at Liszt's expense, but none of them launched full-scale attacks against him as the *Dresdner Wochenblatt* had the previous spring.

[48] One critic even used the words "seine Neider und Feinde zum Schweigen gebracht" [BML 1 (1840), p. 24].

[49] See BML 1 (1840), p. 24. This anecdote reappears in Christern, p. 36.

Any one who admires art in technical facility must bow before Liszt; he that is charmed with the genial, the divine gift, bows still lower. The Orpheus of our day has made tones sound through the great capital of machinery, [because] . . . "his fingers are simply railroads and steam-engines." His genius is more powerful to bring together the great minds of the world than all the railroads on earth. [Liszt] has made music echo in the trade-emporium of Europe, and (at least for a moment) the people believed the gospel. The spirit's gold has a mightier ring than that of the world.[50]

On 2 November, Liszt performed again at his hotel (30), repeating much of his 31 October program. For the most part the press ignored this event, but *Der Freischütz* published a short account of his participation the same day in a concert presented by one "Herr Herrmann"—in fact, none other than "Puzzi" Cohen (31). According to this account, Liszt and Cohen gave an inspired performance of the *Hexameron* variations in a two-piano version.[51] Cohen himself played Liszt's *Lucia* fantasy and the piano part of Beethoven's Op. 97 "Archduke" trio, another work also included in his teacher's German repertory—in this instance, on the program of Liszt's third recital at his Hamburg hotel (32). Presented on the evening of 6 November, this recital featured a piano transcription of Schubert's *Lob der Thränen*, Weber's "Invitation to the Waltz," and an improvised fantasy on themes borrowed from Beethoven's Seventh Symphony, Donizetti's *Lucrezia Borgia*, and Mozart's *Don Giovanni*.[52]

---

50 Quoted from Andersen, "Liszt," *Monthly Musical Record* (1 April 1875), p. 49. Part of this review also appears in a different translation in Williams, p. 146. The entire review appears in *A Poet's Bazaar*, pp. 8-11.

51 "Herr Liszt enthusiasmirte von neuem durch den Vortrag . . . des Hexamerons, für 2 Flügel arrangirt, mit dem Concertgeber [i.e., Cohen] ausgeführt" [HFrs No. 45 (7.11.1840), col. 720].

52 Liszt may have drawn inspiration for this improvisation from the "Fantasie de Lucrezia" he was then in the process of writing. See Ollivier II, p. 47.
  Der Freischütz referred to the 6 November concert as Liszt's third in Hamburg. See HFrs No. 46 (14.11.1840), cols. 734-735. It was actually his fifth, the tendency in the Vormärz press having been to count only highly-publicized and/or solo Liszt performances as "concerts." Even the *Neue Zeitschrift* referred to his 10 November concert as his "fourth." See NZfM 13 (1840), p. 168.

Perhaps his successes won over the Theater directors with whom he had quarreled, or perhaps those gentlemen appreciated his offer to donate the proceeds from his "farewell concert" to the musicians' pension fund. In any event the concert itself, originally scheduled to be presented at Liszt's hotel, took place on 10 November at the much larger Theater (33). Appearing with the Theater orchestra, Liszt played Hummel's B-minor Concerto, Weber's *Konzertstück*, and an arrangement of *Hexameron* for piano and orchestra. A tremendous success, the concert earned him the renewed respect of Hamburg artists and audiences alike and contributed more than 2,000 thalers to a worthy cause.[53] If Liszt had not committed himself to a second tour of the British Isles with impresario Louis Lavenu, he certainly could have continued making money—and giving it away—in Hamburg.[54]

Like all of his 1840 German tours, Liszt's Hamburg visit was a thoroughgoing popular success. It was less successful artistically, though, at least according to certain critics. One journalist complained, for example, that his subject played too few works by classical masters.[55] Other negative but nonetheless characteristic responses to his playing were summarized many years later by Carl Reinecke:

[At his 31 October 1840 concert Liszt] began with Beethoven's Sonata in c-sharp minor, *quasi una fantasia*, and I remember very well both my delight with his incomparable performance

---

[53] Sittard, p. 238, reports Liszt's contribution as almost 2,300 thalers; *Liszt in Hamburg* reports it as 2,296 thalers, 13 groschen. *Der Freischütz*, on the other hand, gives the sum as 3,400 thalers—possibly an exaggeration. [HFrs No. 47 (21.11.1840), col. 750]. Liszt seems to have done well in Hamburg: consider the 1,500 francs he earned from his 28 October recital. See Ollivier II, p. 43. Even the subsequent sale at auction of his "Hamburg" Erard piano brought in "14,600 marcs": the equivalent of 21,000 French francs [RGMP 8 (1841), p. 24] or 3,189 German thalers [Ramann II, p. 87].

[54] Invitations to Liszt to remain in Hamburg appeared in several newspapers. See, for example, HZCor No. 272 (17.11.1840). Nor did Hamburg's women forget their idol: during his tour of England they sent him a silver drinking cup. See NZfM 14 (1841), p. 26.

[55] "Bei der Beurtheilung eines Virtuosen ist es durchaus nöthig und wird es durchaus verlangt, daß der Concertgeber einige classische Compositionen zu Gehör bringt" [HNach No. 258 (30.10.1840)]. As we shall see below, however, Liszt was also criticized in Germany for his Beethoven performances.

of the first two movements and my astonishment at the rhythmic liberties he took with the last. My impressions were just
as mixed during his other performances. When he played like
the authentic Liszt, he played as no one else has ever played
before. . . . Boldness, passion, grace, elegance, wit,
straightforwardness of expression: all were present at appropriate moments and called forth boundless admiration. If,
however, he decided to entertain the mob, he would permit
himself the liberty of indulging in all kinds of tricks, at which
I, even as a boy, had to shake my head. I remember well my
astonishment, for example, when—in his otherwise marvellous
performance of the overture to [Rossini's] *Guillaume Tell*—he
hammered out the *ranz-des-vaches* with the side of his right
first finger![56]

But Liszt did not long continue to play so many tricks on his
listeners. By the time he returned to Germany in 1841 from
further adventures in the British Isles, his playing seems to
have improved and become more reliable as well as
interpretively even more brilliant and satisfying.

Hamburg, Kiel, and Cuxhaven: July 1841

After months of wandering through England, Ireland,
Scotland, and parts of continental Europe, Liszt travelled to
Hamburg to participate in the third North German Music Festival. Hamburg and Kiel also served as his points of departure
for Copenhagen and several enormously successful, highly
publicized performances at the Danish court. Yet most of the
concerts Liszt gave on his way to and from Denmark remain
among the least well-documented of his career.

He reached Hamburg on 5 July 1841 and again lodged at
the Hotel zur alten Stadt London. On 7 July he took part in one
of the three principal concerts of the Festival, performing the
solo part of Beethoven's Fantasy for piano, chorus, and orchestra (34). He also played at least two solo numbers, one of them
Weber's fantasy *Oberons Zauberhorn*. Critical response to his
playing was mixed. On the one hand, the *Allgemeine
musikalische Zeitung* called his Beethoven performance less
than outstanding and reported that local music-lovers were

---

[56] Translated from Reinecke, "Erinnerungen an Franz Liszt," NZfM 78
(1911), p. 570. A somewhat different translation appears in Williams, p.
145.

disappointed with it.[57] On the other, Hamburg's *Correspondent* stated that, under Liszt's fingers, Beethoven's masterpiece produced an effect unprecedented among local performances.[58] And Christern, a few months later to become the author of the biography mentioned in Chapter II, complimented his subject on several things, including a new, livelier style of playing in the *Neue Zeitschrift:*

> In general we must admit that his recent appearances in the capitals of Europe seem to have transformed Liszt utterly [as a performer]. What formerly was fixed, melancholy, and prudent has become vigorous, fresh, youthful, and full of artistic bravado.[59]

Unfortunately, Liszt scarcely mentions his own Festival activities in the "Bachelor of Music" letter he subsequently addressed to Léon Kreutzer, devoting more of his attention to his activities in Denmark and to his adventure in Cuxhaven (mentioned in Chapter II and described below).[60]

Two days later Liszt gave a solo recital in Hamburg's Apollo-Saale (35). In addition to his fantasies on *La Somnambula* and "God Save the Queen" (known in Germany

---

[57] "Liszt spielte die Beethoven-Fantasie mit Chor, aber nicht ausgezeichnet, so dass es Musikkenner weit unter ihrer Erwartung [sic] fanden" [AmZ 43 (1841), col. 576].

[58] "Dieses Meisterstück machte einen um so größeren Effect, als es in solcher Ausführung hier nie zu Gehör gekommen" [HZCor No. 160 (9.7.1841)]. As we shall see, however, Liszt was also complimented by many critics for his Beethoven performances—perhaps, overall, the most controversial of his German career.

[59] "In allgemeiner Hinsicht muß man sagen, Liszt scheint sich seit seiner neuen Anwesenheit in den Weltstädten völlig umgewandelt zu haben. Früher Alles stille, melancholische, tiefe Besonnenheit des Spieles; jetzt Alles Leben, Frische, Jugendkühnheit und Kunstübermuth" [NZfM 15 (1841), p. 51]. Other reviews appeared on pp. 15 and 41-42 of the same journal. The *Blätter für Musik und Literatur* agreed: "Liszt's physische Natur scheint in England neue Lebenskraft gewonnen zu haben" [BML 2 (1841), p. 128].

[60] See Liszt/Suttoni, pp. 192-196. Liszt's brief account of the Festival as a whole may also be found in Ramann II, pp. 113-114.
    Notices of Liszt's Danish adventures also appeared in contemporary German newspapers. See, for example, KlCb No. 58 (21.7.1841), p. 240; and the *Flensburger Zeitung* No. 59 (26.7.1841), p. 234. Liszt's Danish tour is also described in detail in Bengt Johnsson, "Liszt og Danmark," *Dansk Musiktidsskrift* 37 (1962), pp. 79-82; and 38 (1963), pp. 81-86.

as "Heil Dir im Siegerkranz" and a favorite of his British tours), he participated in a performance of Beethoven's Quintet for piano and winds. Sponsored by J. Schuberth and Co., his Hamburg publisher, this recital was ignored by most of the local newspapers. Der *Freischütz*, though, complimented the pianist on his fantasy-playing before reading him a little lecture about taking liberties with Beethoven's tempos.[61] The *Blätter für Musik und Literatur* was more positive, asserting that Liszt had never before performed so well in Hamburg, and that his 9 July matinée was full of delightfully artistic playing.[62]

Liszt apparently left Hamburg for Denmark around 11 July. He may have given his first performance in Kiel the following evening (36). Little information survives about this event; neither of the local papers published advertisements or announcements for it, although the *Kieler Wochenblatt* printed a "fragment of a letter" which probably describes a local enthusiast's response.[63] Having promised to give a second concert in Kiel, Liszt left for Copenhagen on 14 July aboard the *Christian VIII*.[64] Returning on 27 July, however, he found that only 72 tickets had been sold. and that Kiel officials had taken it upon themselves to cancel this event. The *Wochenblatt* describes his subsequent actions as follows:

---

61 See Appendix D, quotation 3. Criticism in the press may have bothered Liszt, but it rarely interfered with his career, though. Soon after his 1841 Hamburg visit he was made an honorary member of the North German Musical Union. See D-WRgs Liszt Überformate 124.

62 "Mit solchem naiven Feuer der Begeisterung hat er noch niemals gespielt, wenigstens nicht wie wir ihn im Herbst v. J. kennen lernten. . . . [J]etzt haucht jede harrende Passage das Entzücken der Kunstlust" [BML 2 (1841), p. 128].

In this instance, as in many others, biographers have oversimplied the critical picture. Ramann, for example, implies that Liszt's 9 July 1841 Beethoven performance was received with exceptional enthusiasm in Hamburg but criticized by "remote" magazines like the *Allgemeine musikalische Zeitung*. See Ramann II, p. 115. In fact, Liszt's performance was also criticized by Hamburg's *Freischütz*. It is important to remember that different Vormärz critics had different tastes in Beethoven. They were not always out to "get" Liszt, merely to describe and evaluate his work.

63 See "Franz Liszt (Brieffragment)," KlWb No. 58 (21.7.1841), pp. 235-236.

64 As reported in KlCb No. 57 (17.7.1841), p. 236.

When Herr Liszt arrived on Tuesday, he discovered what the real truth was, viz., that most of the population wasn't interested in his offer. Nevertheless, a few music-lovers were unhappy, and he announced immediately that anyone who could be informed in time and was still interested in attending [the previously advertised event], would be welcome that evening to hear him play.[65]

Praising the fine performance that followed (37), the *Kieler Correspondenz-Blatt* proclaimed that the performer himself was applauded warmly by the small but grateful audience that enjoyed the unexpected pleasure of his music.[66]

Returning to Hamburg the following day, Liszt presented a final concert at the Theater on 29 July (38). His program included Weber's *Oberons Zauberhorn*, his own fantasy on *Les Huguenots*, and Schubert's *Ständchen*. This time the local press all but ignored him, although *Der Freischütz* made another joke at his expense, remarked offhandedly that a downpour of events had made him too tired to pay attention to Liszt's latest performance.[67] Then, on the way to Rotterdam and the Rhineland the following morning, Liszt's ship was forced by bad weather to put up in Cuxhaven for a few hours. That evening he entertained a party of travelling artistes also stranded by the bad weather (39), playing dances on a piano fetched especially for the occasion.[68] As soon as the weather improved,

[65] "Da Herr Liszt am Dienstag [i.e., 27. Juli] anlagte, und erfuhr, wie es der Wahrheit gemäß war, daß das größere Publicum seine Leistungen zu würdigen nicht vermöge, eine geringe Zahl von Musikfreunden aber um so schmerzlicher empfinde, welchen Genuß sie entbehren müssen, erklärte er sogleich, wenn man diejenigen noch benachrichtigen könne, welche sich für sein Spiel interessirten, würde er mit Vergnügen den Abend vor ihnen spielen" [KlWb No. 61 (31.7.1841), p. 247].

[66] "Am Dienstag Abend hatten wir den ganz unerwarteten Genuß, Herrn Franz Liszt in einem zweiten Concert zu bewundern, in welchem er mit außerordentlicher Gefälligkeit . . . herrliche Musikstücke vortrug zum Entzücken des nicht zahlreichen aber aufrichtig dankbaren Publicums" [KlCb No. 61 (31.7.1841), p. 252].

[67] "Thut mir leid, lieber F[ranz], daß ich Deiner Aufforderung heut nicht genügen kann. . . . In diesem Sommer werden wir von Regen- und Musikgüssen so überschwemmt, daß ich ganz notenmüde worden bin" [HFrs No. 32 (7.8.1841), col. 510].

[68] See Appendix D, quotation 4. Documentary problems associated with Liszt's visit to Cuxhaven are discussed in Chapter II.

though, his ship set out once more for the mouth of the Rhine, where he caught a steamer to take him to Nonnenwerth, his home for most of the summer.

A Second Rhineland Tour: August-October 1841

Throughout 1840, and even during July 1841, Liszt managed to run afoul of German critics on an occasional basis. With the assistance of Gaetano Belloni, his new-found secretary, however, and with careful attention to the public-relations of professional concertizing, he began to prepare—however unwittingly—for the "Lisztomania" of 1842 Berlin. Small wonder, then, that despite some critical opposition, his second Rhineland tour was more successful than the first. After establishing a temporary home for himself and d'Agoult on Nonnenwerth, an island south of Bonn, he visited such nearby cities as Aachen, Cologne, and Mainz. The reviews he received for many of these performances reflect his steadily increasing fame throughout Germany as well as Britain and the rest of Europe.

Travelling to Nonnenwerth via Düsseldorf and Cologne, Liszt reached Bonn in time to attend the local theater on 10 August.[69] The following evening he presented a solo recital there, possibly at the same theater (41). But Liszt did much more during the next few weeks besides give public concerts. He also played privately to small groups of guests at Nonnenwerth on a number of occasions. The first took place shortly after his arrival in early August (40), the second on 13 August (42), the third about two weeks later (47), the fourth sometime after the beginning of October (57), and the fifth and sixth on or around 22 October 1841, his thirtieth birthday (60-61).

For Liszt, Nonnenwerth served as a quasi-restful retreat and as a base of professional operations. Travelling via steam boat, he arrived in Ems in mid-August, stopping for several

---

[69] See BnWb No. 96 (10.8.1841). Liszt may have arrived at Nonnenwerth as early as 7 August; a letter from Marie von Czettritz to Isidore von Kitzing, dated 15 August 1841, mentions that d'Agoult arrived on a steam boat from Mainz nine days earlier (i.e., on 6 August) and that Liszt himself arrived the following night. See Jacobs, p. 36; and Williams, p. 168. Therefore the letter from d'Agoult to Liszt, dated "10 August 1841" in Ollivier's edition [II, pp. 175-176], is probably misdated.

days at the Gasthaus Englischer Hof.[70] On 16 August he gave a concert at the Ems Kursaal (43), where he played a Chopin mazurka, his own transcription of the "Polonaise" from *I Puritani*, and his ever-popular *Galop chromatique*. Returning to Nonnenwerth, he spent a few quiet days before he was entertained on the evening of 22 August by the Cologne Liedertafel. After making an excursion with joyful Liedertafel members and their guests to Rolandseck, a village almost directly opposite his island retreat, he performed for the entire party in the hall of the abandoned Nonnenwerth nunnery (44). Several detailed descriptions of the outing appeared in German periodicals, but the best account of Liszt's role in this affair appeared in the *Blätter für Musik und Literatur*:

> After the end of the banquet the party returned to Nonnenwerth, where a large number of people had gathered from the surrounding area. Liszt surrendered to requests to hear him play, had a grand piano brought into the chapel, and proceeded to display his indescribable talents to the assembled, attentive, excited crowd. Once again the abandoned cloister was filled with soul and spirit, and it is certain that the nuns, who once directed their prayers to heaven from this place, could not have encountered anything more truly divine than did this worldly assembly through Liszt's electric performance.[71]

The company then left on a steamship for Cologne; during the trip music was provided by orchestral musicians and Liedertafel members, who performed German songs as well as a cantata based on tunes from Liszt's own works.[72] The party was greeted on their arrival with cheers and fireworks, and the guest of honor was taken to a hotel to spend the night.

---

[70] See EmsLK (15-17.8.1841), p. 360. The only other surviving information about Liszt's 1841 Ems concert appears in Heinrich Wagner, "Unter Künstler und Künstlerinnen im Kursaal," *Emser Fremdenliste* (10.7.1926).

[71] See Appendix D, quotation 5. This passage is quoted in part in Christern as well as in Ramann II, pp. 127-128. Other accounts of this event imply both that it took place on the evening of 23 August (i.e. immediately after the concert on behalf of the Cologne Cathedral building fund), and that Liszt did not play.

[72] "Während der Fahrt sangen die etwa 380 starken Mitglieder [des Philharmonischen Gesellschafts] die besten teutschen [sic] Lieder und eine zu diesem Zwecke eigens gedichtete Kantata nach Melodien aus Liszts Werken" [AmZ 44 (1842), col. 822].

The following evening Liszt gave a concert in Cologne at the local Casino (45). His program was made up of stand-bys, including the *Puritani* "Polonaise" and a "Tarantelle" (probably his transcription of "La Danza" from Rossini's *Soirées musicales*). The *Kölnische Zeitung* described his playing in superlatives,[73] and Liszt donated 380 thalers to the Cathedral fund.[74]

Travelling to Koblenz several days later, Liszt gave a recital at the Saale des Jesuiten-Kollegiums on 25 August (46). Appearing before a large and brilliant audience which applauded him vigorously, he played part of his "Pastoral" symphony transcription, his *Robert* fantasy, and his *Galop*. Next he stopped at nearby Frankfurt, where he presented two concerts at the local Theater. Despite lovely weather and sharply increased ticket prices, a large crowd turned out on 27 August to hear his first performance (48).[75] Liszt distinguished himself on this occasion in the solo part of Beethoven's "Emperor" concerto; he also played several operatic fantasies, including one on *Robert*. At his second concert, which took place on 29 August (49), he played Weber's *Konzertstück* and the *Hexameron* variations, both with orchestral accompaniment. On this latter occasion Adelaide Kemble also sang arias by Pacini and Mercadante, probably without his assistance. Ticket sales for the 27 August concert alone came to more than 1,200 florins.

Local newspapers overwhelmed Liszt with praise. The *Konversationsblatt*, for instance, stated that his agility conquered the most difficult passages with ease,[76] while *Didaskalia* proclaimed that even the best pianists had to marvel at his playing, which combined enormous facility, strength, and endurance with expressive power and tenderness to such an ex-

---

[73] See Klaus Körner, *Das Musikleben in Köln um die Mitte des 19. Jahrhunderts* (Cologne 1969), p. 82. The *Zeitung* issue from which Körner quotes was unavailable to the present author.

[74] See AmZ 43 (1841), col. 822; and Ramann II, p. 128.

[75] "Trotz des herrlichen Wetters und der stark erhöhten Eingangspreise [war das Schauspielhaus] überfüllt" [FDid No. 243 (31.8.1841)].

[76] "Wir fügen . . . daß Liszt unerreichbar dasteht, daß er mit der fabelhaftesten Leichtigkeit die schwierigsten Passagen besiegt" [FKB No. 242 (2.9.1841), pp. 966-967].

tent that it could not be surpassed.[77] Only the *Allgemeine musikalische Zeitung* took exception:

> Eight days ago Franz Liszt presented two concerts in the Frankfurt Theater and triumphed as always, although the second concert was not well attended. Accounts of this virtuoso are taking on the character of a unanimous verdict: in short, that Liszt's playing—with all due respect to his fiery talent, genial interpretations of established masterpieces, and a fabulous technique which deals with difficulties like a giant handles a baby—is, nevertheless, incomprehensible rather than clear, astonishing rather than satisfying, [and] more deified by the mob than received with the quieter, more contemplative applause of connoisseurs.[78]

(We shall see below that opinions like these tempered the "Lisztomania" that began to spread throughout Germany during the fall of 1841, then developed into real critical opposition or indifference a couple of years later.)

On 30 August Liszt appeared in Wiesbaden (50), and three days later he gave a second recital there (52). Between these events he performed in Mainz at the Hof zum Gutenberg (51). Riding several of his favorite warhorses on this last occasion—the *Tell* overture, the *Puritani* "Polonaise," and the "Marche et Cavatine" from *Lucia*—he deeply impressed Friedrich Wiest, editor of *Das Rheinland*. In 1840, as we saw above, Wiest complimented Liszt's piano-playing (albeit with tongue in cheek).[79] In 1841, however, the good doctor showered the virtuoso with praise in the form of a "Love Letter from the Devil." Marvelling at the infernal brilliance of Liszt's *Robert le diable* fantasy, Wiest—who published his letter under the pseudonym of "a poor devil, born a German scribbler"—also acknowledged the nun-like holiness of his Satanic superior's *Ave Maria* transcription.[80] Two more concerts in Mainz followed

---

[77] "Selbst bedeutende Klavierspieler stehen mit Bewunderung vor [Liszts] Leistungen, in welchen ungeheure Fertigkeit, Kraft und Ausdauer, Stärke und Lieblichkeit in so hohem Maße vereinigt sind, daß man wohl annehmen darf, es sey hier nichts mehr zu erreichen übrig" [FDid No. 243 (31.8.1841)].

[78] See Appendix D, quotation 6.

[79] See Appendix D, quotation 2.

[80] "Wo Sie aber ganz die Höhe und Tiefe Ihrer genialen Teufels-Natur als

LISZT IN GERMANY, 1840-1845

in quick succession (53-54). Liszt shared the first of them with Adelaide Kemble, and the two artists won additional praise in *Das Rheinland*'s pages.[81] After this concert was over, Liszt was treated to a serenade at his hotel by members of a local choir.[82]

After leaving Mainz (and, possibly, after another visit to Nonnenwerth), Liszt and Belloni headed for Baden-Baden, where they arrived on 14 September and lodged at the Hof von Holland Hotel.[83] Two days later Liszt gave a concert at the Salle de Réunion (55). The turn-out was disappointing—perhaps because visiting notables distracted potential listeners, perhaps because Anton Rubinstein (then making a German tour of his own) had presented many of Liszt's favorite pieces only weeks before.[84] Liszt left Baden-Baden on the morning of 17 September in order to be inducted on the following evening into the Frankfurt Masonic Lodge "Zur Ewigkeit."[85] His sponsors included Wilhelm Speyer, a local composer with whom Liszt had corresponded sporadically for several years.[86] The ceremony completed, Liszt probably rested in Frankfurt for a few days before presenting his third and final concert there on 25 September (56). Announced as a benefit performance on behalf of

---

Clavierspieler fund gaben, das war in der Phantasie über die Motive aus 'Robert le diable' . . . [und] Sie sangen das *Ave Maria* auf dem Piano wie eine Nonne, die der Heiligsprechung entgegensteht!" [MzRh No. 106 (5.9.1841), p. 422].

81 See MzRh No. 106 (5.9.1841), pp. 423-424.

82 See MzRh, "Album für Scherz und Ernst" No. 107 (7.9.1841), p. 427.

83 Belloni generally accompanied Liszt on his tours after early 1841, but contemporary sources often state merely that Liszt "and retinue" were travelling together or had checked into certain hotels.

84 Information about Rubinstein's 1841 tour appears in Ernst Ihle, "Liszt-Besuche und Liszt-Konzerte in Baden-Baden." Rubinstein's Baden-Baden concert took place on 31 August 1841, a day after Liszt's first 1841 Wiesbaden recital.

85 See D-WRgs Liszt Überformate 120, 1M: Liszt's diploma of enrollment in the Frankfurt lodge. This document is reproduced in facsimile in Walker, p. 369. NB: Liszt's Masonic interests are important to any student of his German concert tours because, as we shall see below, he gave several performances for Masonic organizations and causes. See Autexier, passim.

86 See, for example, Liszt's letter to Speyer of 10 September 1841. This letter is reprinted in Eduard Speyer, *Wilhelm Speyer der Liederkomponist* (Munich 1925), pp. 229-230; and in Autexier, p. 82.

the newly-formed Mozart Foundation, this event featured performances of the Hummel Septet and, more important, the premiere of Liszt's fantasy on themes from *Don Giovanni*—an appropriate choice for the occasion and one, according to Frankfurt's *Didaskalia*, that revealed not only the complete range of its composer's technical accomplishments, but the poetic elements of Mozart's original.[87] The concert was also a financial success; proceeds equalled 900 florins, and articles about the event appeared in many music magazines.[88] *Didaskalia*, however, also suggested that the money might better have been used for a German conservatory, a project Liszt himself might have found insupportable.[89] Finally, as was often his wont, Liszt published a note in the *Konversationsblatt* complimenting Ludwig Beck, the manufacturer of the piano he had played on several of his Frankfurt concerts.[90]

Returning to Nonnenwerth, Liszt spent part of October in comparative seclusion. On 5 October, though, he played again in Cologne, this time at the Royal Theater (58). A week later he visited Aachen, where he gave another "Theater" performance (59). On both occasions he shared the stage with Kemble and, in Cologne, with other vocalists. In addition to some of his stand-bys, he also played his *Réminiscences de Don Juan* and Weber's *Aufforderung zum Tanz*. The local press complimented him on both occasions, and the *Kölnische Zeitung* proclaimed that Liszt—that veritable cauldron of "ideas, associations, and

---

[87] "Die zweite große Piece war eine neue, hier zum Erstenmale öffentlich gespielte Phantasie über Motive aus Don Juan, in welcher Liszt nicht nur die ganze Fülle seiner technischen Virtuosität im vollsten Glanze zeigte, sondern auch die poetischen Elemente des Mozart'schen Tonwerkes heraufbeschwor" [FDid No. 272 (29.9.1841)].

[88] One notice also relates a rather confusing anecdote associated with the "Don Juan" fantasy and the *Galop chromatique*. See BML 2 (1841), p. 183.

[89] See FDid No. 272 (29.9.1841). Liszt's opposition to a national German music school cannot be taken for granted during the Vormärz era, but we know he came to dislike and disapprove of the Leipzig Conservatory and its "products" during the 1850s. See Walker, p. 348. Throughout the 1870s, on the other hand, Liszt devoted himself enthusiastically to the cause of a national Hungarian conservatory in Budapest. See Dezsö Legány, *Ferenc Liszt and his Country, 1869-1873* (Budapest 1984), esp. pp. 43ff. And, as we shall see again below, Liszt did much in 1843 to promote education in Dortmund.

[90] See FKB No. 269 (29.9.1841), p. 1073. See also Appendix E, letter 2.

difficulties"—had accomplished a veritable revolution in piano-playing.[91]

Liszt returned from Aachen to Nonnenwerth and secluded himself briefly before beginning his first cross-country tour of Germany's heartland. At a surprise birthday party given for him on 22 October by the Comtesse, however, he played for family and friends (60).[92] On another occasion (61) he played his "Don Juan" fantasy for Frau von Czettritz. Surrounded by the Comtesse and their children, as well as by companions like Prince Felix Lichnowsky and Joseph Maria Lefebvre, the Cologne music publisher and piano manufacturer, Liszt probably did not suspect that fame was about to engulf him in the months ahead.

From Elberfeld to Halle: October-December 1841

Abandoning his comparative seclusion near the end of October 1841, Liszt began a tour of central Germany which lasted almost two months and which brought him to the doorstep of his triumphs in Berlin. In all, he performed on thirty-five occasions prior to late December of that year, appearing publicly at least twice each in Düsseldorf, Elberfeld, Münster, Kassel, Leipzig, Dresden, and Halle. Many of these appearances remain unfamiliar today, even to scholars.

He began his tour in Elberfeld, where he presented a recital at the Saal des Casino on 27 October (62). His program included the *Tell* overture, his "Andante finale" from *Lucia di Lammermoor*, and his *Galop chromatique*. The Casino hall was crowded, and nearby Wuppertal's *Täglicher Anzeiger* reported that the genial and talented artist received applause and amazement from his fans.[93] So great, in fact, was his popularity

---

91 "[Liszt's Compositionen, d]ieser . . . Crater voll Ideen, kühner Verbindungen und Schwierigkeiten . . . stehen mehr oder minder immer mit der Revolution im Pianofortespiel, die [Liszt] so riesenkräftig verfolgt und zu Ende führt, in genauer Verbindung" [KZ No. 280 (7.10.1841)].

92 See Marie von Czettritz's description of this event. Quoted in E. Fleckner, "Franz Liszt feierte seinen 30. Geburtstag auf der Rheininsel Nonnenwerth," *Mitteilungen der Arbeitsgemeinschaft für rheinische Musikgeschichte* 38 (1972), pp. 143-144.

93 "Ein sehr zahlreiches Auditorium gab dem genialen und talentreichen Künstler seinen Beifall, sein Staunen und seine Bewunderung laut zu erkennen" [WpTA (29.10.1841)].

that local music-lovers implored him to return for a second concert, a proposal he accepted soon after his concert ended.[94] The next day Liszt travelled to Düsseldorf to give a recital at the Gurter'schen Saal (63). After playing excerpts from his "Pastoral" symphony transcription as well as his solo-piano transcription of Mendelssohn's *Auf Flügel des Gesanges* and his ever-popular *Galop*, he received another tumultuous reception. Agreeing to give a second concert in Düsseldorf, he returned to Bonn where, on the evening of 31 October, a banquet in his honor was given at the "Lese" by prominent Bonn citizens. Ostensibly a late birthday celebration, the banquet was actually a tribute to his activities on behalf of the Beethoven Memorial. Leopold Kaufmann, a patron of the arts and sometime mayor of the town, described the occasion as follows:

> The hall was gorgeously decorated and Liszt's bust fitted with a laurel wreath. The assemblage was a mixed one, seeing that the entire citizenry took part. . . . There were many toasts, the best of them delivered by Professor Breidenstein in Liszt's honor. It was very interesting to hear how Liszt replied. German was pretty difficult for him, as a result of which he spoke haltingly and asked us to excuse him for doing everything off the cuff, including some musical things. His toast honored the city of Bonn which, although small and little-known, had on Beethoven's account become great and celebrated. Champagne flowed like water ["Der Champagner floß wahrhaftig"] and everybody had a wonderful time.[95]

The following evening eight local choristers visited Liszt, who was stopping at Bonn's Hotel Trierscher Hof. After listening to their serenade, he played a piano arrangement of his four-part chorus *Das deutsche Vaterland* (64). According to Kaufmann, this arrangement was so demanding that only a Liszt could play it: although written throughout in octaves, each finger was nevertheless assigned a melodic task. Kaufmann felt the hotel's piano suffered under Liszt's powerful attack, and that

---

[94] That is, by 28 October 1841. A notice that "in den ersten Tagen der künftigen Woche wird Herr F. Liszt die Ehre haben, ein zweites Concert . . . zu geben" appeared in WpTA (29.10.1841).

[95] Translated from Paul Kaufmann, "Franz Liszt am Rhein," *Die Musik* 26-2 (1933), p. 119. The original German text is given in Appendix D, quotation 7. The text of Breidenstein's toast appears in BriefeHZ III, pp. 10-11.

the evening's music-making brought the poor instrument's end that much closer.[96]

Returning to Düsseldorf on 2 November, Liszt gave a concert the same evening at the city's Theater (65). No record survives of his program, but he is known to have shared the platform with two singers—one of whom, a Madame Ernst-Seydler, presented an aria from Mozart's *La Clemenza di Tito*.[97] The following morning he returned to Elberfeld, where he played that evening at the Casino hall (66). In his absence—or, perhaps, because of his or Belloni's carelessness—this concert had been advertised for the previous evening. A local newspaper corrected the mistake in time,[98] though, and Liszt performed before a responsive audience. No reviews of this event appeared in Elberfeld papers, but the *Düsseldorfer Kreisblatt* reported that his second Düsseldorf concert led to the same enthusiasm as the first.[99]

Then his travels began in earnest. Up to this time Liszt had been able to make use of steam boats on the Rhine, Main, Mosel, and Lahn rivers, and to shuttle back and forth between Mainz and Frankfurt or Düsseldorf and Elberfeld by train. Now he boarded a coach and set out for Krefeld, where he had been invited by Wilhelm von Beckerath, an occasional friend, to give a recital on 4 November at the Rump'schen Saal (67). There Liszt played a solo-piano arrangement of Weber's *Konzertstück* as well as Beethoven's Op. 101 Sonata and several smaller works. Travelling on to Wesel, he presented a benefit concert on 7 November (68) that included his *Tell* overture and *Adelaïde* transcriptions and his first known performance of Bach's extraordinary "Chromatic Fantasy."

---

[96] "Doch kann auch nur ein Liszt spielen, indem immer in Oktaven jeder Finger eine eigene Melodie zu spielen hatte. . . . [Liszt] geriet so in Feuer, daß er das arme Instrument, welches leider schon genug an Alter litt, an dem Abend dem Tode nahegebracht hat" [Kaufmann, p. 120]. Quotations from Leopold Kaufmann's letters also appear in Henssler, *Das musikalische Bonn*, pp. 179-180.

[97] See DüsKb No. 300 (4.11.1841).

[98] See EfZ No. 302 (2.11.1841).

[99] "Gestern ließ Herr Liszt in einem zweiten Concert auf hiesiger Bühne sich hören, und erweckte gleichen Enthusiasmus wie das Erstemal" [DüsKb No. 300 (4.11.1841)].

Liszt received a warm welcome in Wesel, and a critic for the *Niederrheinische Correspondent* proclaimed him a "true artist" instead of a mere virtuoso.[100] Nevertheless, he left town on the midnight post coach in order to reach Münster the following morning, where he put up at the Hotel König von England and prepared for a recital announced for 9 November at the Saale des Kremeramthauses (69). This performance too was enormously successful; he was applauded enthusiastically and asked to give a second concert at the Münster Theater. Herr Pichler, the director, acceded to this request, and Liszt played at the Theater two days later (70). Both Münster programs included operatic paraphrases and song transcriptions, and both concluded with the familiar *Galop*. After thanking Pichler for his assistance, the *Westfälische Merkur* prophesied that Liszt's appearance within the town's walls was an experience that local connoisseurs and music-lovers would treasure for a long time to come.[101]

Travelling toward Kassel, Liszt stopped in Osnabrück on 12 November in order to perform at the Großerklub (72). The only description of this event survives in the diaries of Albrecht Pagenstecher, a local civic official and ardent music fan. Pagenstecher's remarks give us a good idea of the arduous schedule Liszt maintained throughout the fall of 1841. Having arrived in Osnabrück at 6 a.m. by post coach, he caught three hours' sleep at a local hotel before breakfasting and beginning social calls that resulted in an impromptu matinée performance at the home of an Osnabrück citizen (71). Liszt probably snatched a quick dinner before his concert began at 7 p.m. After playing several difficult numbers, including his *Adelaïde* transcription, he caught another coach for Bielefeld very early the following morning.[102] There he presented another solo recital (73), then left at once for Detmold, arriving on 14 November. The following evening, after what we can safely assume was a

---

[100] "Liszt ist nicht virtuos — Liszt ist wahrhaft Künstler" [WesNC No. 194 (9.11.1841)].

[101] "Die Anwesenheit dieses genialen Tonkünstlers in unseren Mauren ist ein Ereigniß, welches allen Musikkennern und Musikfreunden lange in freundlicher Erinnerung bleiben wird" [MünWM No. 272 (13.11.1841)].

[102] Pagenstecher's diaries are discussed at some length in Chapter II. See also Plate 8.

day's well-earned rest, he gave a concert at the Detmold Hoftheater (74).

Two documents describe Liszt's Detmold concert in very different terms. A notice in the *Allgemeine musikalische Zeitung* proclaimed it as successful as his performances everywhere else.[103] But local critic Karl Ziegler attacked Liszt in one of the most brutal reviews he received during his virtuoso career—a review which condemned him and virtuosity in general as "the sickness of the nineteenth century."[104] Whatever his playing may have been like, Liszt's Detmold income was 2,500 thalers, a fabulous sum by local standards.[105]

Boarding another coach early on 16 November, Liszt managed to reach Kassel by nightfall and to secure rooms for Belloni and himself at the Hotel Römischer Kaiser. The following day he called on Louis Spohr, conductor of the local Orchestra and leader of Kassel's thriving musical life. After sight-reading some Bach chorale harmonizations at the piano in Spohr's home (75), Liszt was honored at a concert featuring one of Spohr's violin concertos.[106] The next evening he played at a soirée given at Spohr's home (76). Liszt astonished everyone with his sight-reading, and he also played some of his Schubert song transcriptions. Friedrich Nebelthau jotted down fragments of conversation, including Liszt's confession that, after Beethoven, he most admired Schubert.[107]

On the evening of 19 November Liszt gave his first public Kassel performance at the Hoftheater (77). In addition to Weber's *Konzertstück*, he played his own "Don Juan" fantasy and his *Galop chromatique*. The theater was filled to the brim

---

[103] "Am 15. November hat Liszt in Detmold ein Konzert mit demselben Erfolg gegeben, den er überall hervorgerufen hat" [AmZ 43 (1841), col. 1102].

[104] "Zu solchen hinreißenden excentrischen Dingen [i.e., Liszt's music and playing] gehört allerdings eine gewisse Fieberglut, eine gewisse Krankheit, die Krankheit des Jahrhunderts" [Karl Ziegler, *Dramaturgische Blätter* (Lemgo 1861), p. 14].

[105] Reported in H. L. Schäfer, "Franz Liszt in Detmold," *Lippische Blätter für Heimatkunde* No. 1 (1972).

[106] See Homburg, whose valuable article is identified above in Chapter II.

[107] "Es war im hohen Grade interessant, daß Fr. Schubert den Gegenstand bildete, da Liszt denselben neben Beethoven am meisten zu verehren scheint" [KasS No. 36 (4.12.1841), p. 323].

with dilettanti who responded with thunderous applause to his powerful performances, and the *Kasseler allgemeine Zeitung* reported that the "famous virtuoso" was cheered as vigorously when he was called back to the stage as he had been when the concert began.[108]

Eager to hear more of his music, a group of prominent citizens, including Spohr, persuaded Liszt to give a second concert in Kassel. For the program the two musicians selected Beethoven's "Emperor" concerto, a work never previously played by the local orchestra. No parts were available in the immediate vicinity, so one of Spohr's students was dispatched to Göttingen to fetch them. In the meantime Liszt attended a performance of an Auber opera, and on 21 November he played at another Kassel soirée, this one held at the home of Caroline von der Malsburg (78). Here he participated in a more-or-less spontaneous run-through of Spohr's Quintet in c minor for piano and strings, playing magnificently from an unfamiliar, hand-copied score. Frau Nebelthau, a member of the von der Malsburg family—and, one would assume, wife of the Friedrich Nebelthau mentioned above—left us her impressions of this "most elegant and tasteful" event.[109]

The Beethoven concerto parts having arrived, Liszt joined the Kassel Hoftheater orchestra on the evening of 22 November in both *Hexameron* and the "Emperor" (79). As solos he also played several Schubert song transcriptions, and he accompanied local musicians in songs for voice, clarinet, and piano. In another enthusiastic review, the *Kasseler allgemeine Zeitung* boasted that Liszt's "authentic German musical training" placed him a notch above the Paganinis, Ole Bulls, and other less impressive virtuosos of his day.[110] Remarks about his edu-

---

108 "Daß der lebhafteste Beifall von allen Seiten sich wiederholte und [der berühmte Virtuos] zuletzt wieder auf die Bühne gerufen und wie bei seinem ersten Erscheinen rauschend begrüsst wurde, brauchen wir wohl nicht zu sagen" [KasZ No. 321 (21.11.1841), p. 2248].

109 "[Liszt] spielte, wo nicht prima vista, doch gewiß sehr flüchtiger Bekanntschaft, Spohrs schönes Klavier-Quintett (c-Moll), aus einem geschriebenen, fremden Exemplare: die Auffassung war die genialste, der Vortrag der eleganteste und geschmackvollste, der Erfolg der hinreißendste, den man sich denken kann" [Quoted in Homburg].

110 "In nichts erschien [Liszt] uns größer, als in Beethovens Klavier-Konzert Es-Dur. Noch glühen wir von der großartigen Darstellung dieses

cation aside, the same paper was correct in asserting—as did the *Salon*—that Liszt's visit to Kassel was among the most welcome in the city's history.[111] His two public Kassel concerts earned him a total of 880 thalers, 34 groschen.

On 23 November Liszt travelled to nearby Göttingen. C. F. Lueder, a Kassel music enthusiast, accompanied him on this trip and wrote a description of the recital Liszt presented a the "Aula" of Göttingen's university on 24 November (80).[112] Local residents and students called for a second concert, and such an event was announced for Saturday, 27 November. But Liszt backed out when Lichnowsky arrived unexpectedly at his hotel. The two friends had planned to meet in Gotha; instead, they celebrated their reunion in Göttingen, then left for Weimar on the morning of 25 November.[113] Reaching Weimar the same evening, Liszt prepared for his introduction to the ducal court. During the days that followed he performed privately at least four times at the palace, or "Schloß" (81-84). Then, on the evening of 29 November, he presented a public concert at the Hoftheater (85). Among the works he performed was his own fantasy on *Robert le diable*. Public enthusiasm for this performance cannot be judged, but the stuffy *Weimarische Zeitung* unbent enough to run a short notice about his success.[114] Grand Duke Carl Friedrich even awarded Liszt the Order of the White Falcon, first class.[115] More important, the Grand Duke's son

---

Prachtwerkes, bei der Liszt zeigte, daß er hat, was allen Paganinis, Ole Bulles, u.s.w. abging; eine echte deutsche musikalische Bildung, die beste von allen" [KasZ "Beiblatt" No. 48 (29.11.1841)].

[111] "[Liszts] Erscheinung war uns um so willkommner, als wir nur selten ein solch eminentes Talent in unsern Mauern sehen" [KasS No. 35 (27.11.1841), p. 316].

[112] See Homburg.

[113] Homburg has Liszt and Lichnowsky arriving on different days in Göttingen, while the local "Fremdenlist" has them arriving on the same day. See GötWb No. 48 (27.11.1841), p. 439. Furthermore, according to Ramann, "In den Jahren 1841/42 begleitete der Fürst den Künstler auf seinen Reisen an den Rhein, über Weimar, Dresden, Leipzig, und anderer Städte nach Berlin" [Ramann II, p. 93]. But Lichnowsky arrived in Berlin only on 5 February 1842. See APSZ No. 36 (5.2.1842), p. 145.

[114] See WrZ No. 96 (1.12.1841), p. 383. The review itself is reprinted in Raabe I, p. 87.

[115] Although this award was widely publicized at the time, Walker ignores it. Instead, he reproduces in *Franz Liszt: The Weimar Years, 1848-1861* (New

Carl Alexander was so impressed with his artistry that he eventually offered him the position of "Kapellmeister im außerordentlichen Dienst"—an appointment confirmed, as we shall see below, in November 1842.

Not everyone, though, was thrilled by Liszt's Weimar performances. After praising his technical mastery, a critic for the *Neue Zeitschrift* remarked that

> despite everything, we just weren't satisfied. There is more of the contrived than the heartfelt in Liszt's own works. The fire of his feeling is volcanic, glittering, but destructive—it is not something that warms and enlivens. And all of his poetry is our own day's poetry of confusion. . . .

The same critic also took offense at Liszt's rhythmic liberties, although he did distinguish between what he considered a more successful *Hexameron* performance and less successful performances of Weber's "Invitation to the Waltz" and Schubert's *Erlkönig*.[116] Given as a benefit, Liszt's 29 November concert earned almost 530 thalers for the Frauenverein, a charity favored by Weimar's Grand Duchess.

The following afternoon Liszt performed in Jena (86), where he was subsequently made an honorary citizen.[117] He then left immediately for Leipzig, where he played twice for the Schumanns in their new home (87-88).[118] A few of the public and private concerts that followed remain virtually unknown—for example, those he gave in Altenburg on 14 December (95), and in Dresden on 4, 9, and 11 December (89 and 91-92). Others were celebrated, even controversial affairs. Among these were the programs he shared with Clara

---

York 1989), p. 249, a diploma, dated 13 February 1854, naming Liszt to the same order, *second* class. Generally speaking, decorated individuals move up—not down—in rank as their careers progress. Liszt himself, for example, was "promoted" in 1861 from Officer to Commander of the French Legion of Honor. See Walker, *Franz Liszt: The Weimar Years*, p. 541. Geraldine Keeling has shown that Liszt received the title of Officer in 1845—not 1860, as Walker claims elsewhere—but both scholars agree that the title of Officer came first. See Keeling, "Liszt and the Legion of Honor," *Liszt Society Journal* 10 (1985), p. 29.

[116] See Appendix D, quotation 8.

[117] The certificate survives as D-Wrgs Liszt Überformate 131.

[118] Robert Schumann and Clara Wieck were married shortly after Liszt's Leipzig visit of March 1840.

Schumann at the Leipzig Gewandhaus on 6 December (90) and
13 December (94). On both occasions the two pianists collab-
orated in an arrangement of the *Hexameron* variations, and on
13 December Liszt accompanied one "Signor Pantaleoni" (a
man destined to become his friend) in an Italian aria and
played Hummel's Septet as a piano solo as well as
Beethoven's *Adelaïde* and Schubert's *Erlkönig*. The 6 December
concert was so successful that the audience—some 900
strong—called for a repeat of *Hexameron*.[119] At the intermission, Liszt gave his partner a bouquet of flowers and, after
the concert, he hosted a dinner that included oysters and trout.
(Clara never really warmed to Liszt, though, and later she
seems to have resented his success.)[120]

On 13 December, however, Liszt's solo numbers met with
a mixed response. The *Leipziger allgemeine Zeitung* complained, for example, that two concerts which both featured the
same performers—and, in the case of *Hexameron*, the same
work—should not have taken place within a week of each other.
The *Neue Zeitschrift* also criticized the way Liszt played other
composers' works, complaining that he made everything sound
the same and often played pieces in anything but an authentic
manner.[121] Yet the *Leipziger allgemeine* also complimented the
"Don Juan" fantasy on its dramatic truthfulness and fidelity to
Mozart's drama.[122] And the *Neue Zeitschrift* praised Liszt's
Rheinweinlied, one of several works for male chorus the composer used to flesh out his German programs. Finally, on 16
December, Liszt appeared alone at at the Gewandhaus (96),
performing the "Emperor" concerto with Ferdinand David and

---

[119] See NZfM 15 (1841), p. 199.

[120] See Clara Schumann's diary entry for 5 [sic] December 1841. It is translated into English in Williams, p. 175.

[121] "Liszt spielt eigentlich nur die Noten fremder Compositionen, der sie
belebende Geist aber ist sein eigen; dadurch gestalten sich natürlich die
Muskstücke oft ganz anders, als sie in der Seele des Componisten
aufgegangen sein mögen" [NZfM 15 (1841), p. 199].

[122] "Die Fantasie über Themen aus Don Juan . . . mit einer dramatischen
Wahrheit der Auffassung, mit einer treffenden Treue der dialogischen
Details vorgetragen . . . bildet die Hauptbestandtheile derselben" [LAZ
No. 351 (17.12.1841), p. 4131]. Clara Schumann also praised Liszt's "Don
Juan" paraphrase. See Williams, p. 175.

the Gewandhaus orchestra.[123] Liszt also presented several other works, including his *Galop chromatique*. The following evening he attended a party at the Schumanns' for which, unhappily, he arrived late. Then, travelling on to Halle, he gave a recital on 18 December in the hall of the Kronprinzen Hotel (97). After playing a second time in Halle (98), he departed at last for Berlin—and "Lisztomania."

Berlin and "Lisztomania": December 1841 — March 1842

The performances Liszt presented during his first visit to Berlin became the most celebrated of his German tours, perhaps the most celebrated of his entire "transcendental" career. Between December 1841 and March 1842 he gave twelve solo recitals, appeared on at least fifteen additional public programs, and played privately on many other occasions. The "Lisztomania" that seized the usually self-satisfied and ordinarily reserved Berliners, especially the women and girls, received international attention. In certain respects, Liszt never surpassed his triumphs in Berlin; in other respects, he never lived them down.

He arrived in the Prussian capital on 26 December 1841; Meyerbeer, Mendelssohn, and Spontini were on hand to greet him. The following evening he presented his first solo recital at the Singakademie (99). His program consisted of his *Tell* overture transcription, the "Andante finale" from *Lucia*, his *Robert* fantasy, his *Adelaïde* and *Erlkönig* transcriptions, and his *Galop chromatique* as well as Bach's Chromatic Fantasy and Fugue. Liszt had already played these pieces a number of times in Germany, yet Berlin's response to them was unprecedented. More than 800 people (among them the King of Prussia, the Count of Nassau, and the Crown Prince of Württemberg) applauded enthusiastically, even ferociously. That evening Varnhagen von Ense wrote in his diary that Liszt's playing had been "marvellous, unexampled, magical,"

---

[123] Of this occasion, Clara Schumann wrote that Liszt played the "Emperor" concerto "in masterly fashion, but the *Robert le diable* fantasy dreadfully crudely." This passage is mistranslated in Williams, p. 175, who makes it appear that the "Robert" fantasy was a fantasy written by "Robert" (i.e., Schumann). See AmZ 44 (1842), col. 18. See also Litzmann, *Clara Schumann: An Artist's Life*, trans. Grace Hadow (New York 1913), Vol. I, p. 330.

and that he had received an unparalleled reception.[124] "Succés inouï," Liszt himself wrote Marie d'Agoult immediately after the concert was over.[125] But it was only the beginning of a triumphal ordeal.

During January-March 1842 Liszt gave thirty-four additional and documented public and private performances in Berlin. Altogether he performed at the Singakademie ten more times, not always alone: on 1 January (100), 5 January (102), 9 January (104), 16 January (107), 21 January (109), 23 January (110), 24 January (111), 30 January (117), 2 February (119), and 6 February (121). At the Hotel de Russie, his Berlin lodging-house, he gave or participated in concerts on 12 January (106), 9 February (123), 25 February (129), and 3 March (133). He played for students of Berlin's university on 25 January (116) and 1 February (118). He appeared as a pianist at the Royal Theater and the Berlin Opera on 10 February (125),[126] 16 February (126), 19 February (127), 23 February (128), 28 February (131), and 2 March (132). (He also made his German debut at the Theater as an orchestral conductor.) He performed privately or semi-privately on a number of occasions throughout January and February—for unknown audiences (101, 105, 124, and 127), for members of the Prussian royal family (112-115 and 120), at benefit concerts (130), and for the Royal York Masonic Lodge (122).[127] Finally, he travelled to Potsdam to present a concert on 8 January at the Casino (103), and on 20 January he apparently participated in a matinée benefit held at the Englisches Haus Hotel (108).

Daily life in 1842 Berlin must have been exhilerating as well as exhausting for Liszt. As he wrote to d'Agoult:

---

[124] "Abends im Saale der Singakademie Konzert von Liszt ohne Orchester; er spielte ganz allein, wunderbar, beispiellos, zauberhaft, mit allgemeinem heftigsten Beifall. Seit Paganini habe ich keinen solchen Meister gehört" [K. A. Varnhagen von Ense, *Tagebücher* (Leipzig 1861), Vol. I, p. 385]. See also Williams, pp. 176-177; and Ramann II, p. 150.

[125] Quoted from Ollivier II, p. 190.

[126] This concert was advertised originally for Monday, 7 February 1842, but presented on Thursday ("Donnerstag"), 10 February. See VZ and SZ Nos. 29 and 36 (4 and 12.2.1842).

[127] During his Berlin visit Liszt also joined the "Eintracht" Masonic Lodge. See D-WRgs Liszt Überformate 120.

I get up every day at about nine o'clock. From nine to one or
two o'clock about fifty people come and go in my [hotel] room.
[One of my friends] was telling me the other day that whenever
he happens to take a stroll on the Linden (it's the center of
Berlin) after leaving my room, the Linden strikes him as de-
serted. What do all of these people want of me? Most of them,
money; some of them (especially the young people) just to see
me in any way, shape, or form; others to be able to say that
they have seen me and that they visit me; still others (and especially the scoundrels) in order to be able to write newspaper
articles. While chatting and smoking I dictate to Lefèvre [sic]
(for writing tires me terribly), or to Schober, or Villers, the in-
dispensable replies to the hundreds of letters which I receive;
I arrange my programs, sort out my music and, now and then,
when an idea strikes me, scribble down notes.[128]

Afternoons, as we know from published accounts of his activities, Liszt regularly attended parties and matinées; evenings
he attended dinners and theatrical events and, of course, gave
concerts. No wonder he was tired: thirty concerts in two months
in a single city, not to mention his other activities, seemed almost unbelievable at the time.[129]

His impact on Berlin audiences was undeniable, but the
pros and cons of that impact were hotly debated in the press.
According to a critic for the *Allgemeine Preußische Staats-
Zeitung*, Liszt's successes revitalized Berlin's flagging musical
enthusiasms.[130] Other critics complained that he was a disrup-
tive fad, and Heinrich Heine went so far as to call his demonic
effect on his fans a kind of spiritual sickness.[131] Or, as
London's *Musical World* put it:

[128] Translated from Ollivier II, pp. 199-200.

[129] "Es klingt unglaublich: 30 Concerte in unserer Stadt!" [BML 3 (1842), p.
40]. A similar remark appeared in AuZ (1842), p. 416.

[130] "Die Konzertlust unseres Publikums, die in der letzten Zeit etwas
abgekommen zu haben schien, ist durch die geniale Virtuosität Franz
Liszt's neu geweckt worden" [APSZ No. 9 (9.1.1842), p. 34].

[131] "Die elektrische Wirkung einer dämonischen Natur auf eine
zusammengepreßte Menge, die ansteckende Gewalt der Ekstase, und
vielleicht der Magnetismus der Musik selbst, dieser spiritualistischen
Zeitkrankheit, welche fast in uns allen vibriert — diese Phänomene sind
mir noch nie so deutlich und beänstigend entgegengetreten wie in dem
Concert von Liszt" [Heine, *Historisch-kritische Gesamgausgabe der
Werke*, Vol. XIII/1, ed. Volkmar Hansen (Hamburg 1988), p. 126]. Heine,
however, made it abundantly clear that he also admired Liszt, and that

The reception given to M. Franz Liszt, when in Berlin, surpassed in extravagance, in madness, and in exaggeration, every
thing in the way of theatrical and musical *éclat*, that has
hitherto been seen in any of the countries of the terrestrial
globe. . . . The least remarkable incidents of this extraordinary ovation, consisted of fêtes, crowns, billets-doux, verses,
magnificent presents, almost daily the unharnessing of his
horses, and the raising of the artist on the shoulders of the
students to the sound of the academical songs (the same which
are sung in honour of the most celebrated professors of the
university), and the medal struck on the occasion, with the
portrait of Liszt and the inscription, "Zum unsern
Jahrhundert's Genius . . . [To the Genius of our Age']."[132]

Liszt's Berlin repertory was remarkable for its scope. In
all he played more than eighty works for piano: sonatas, prel-
udes and fugues, variation sets, dance pieces, etudes, and
operatic fantasies, as well as chamber works and concertos.
Much of his repertory was made up of "warhorses" like his
Schubert song transcriptions and his *Galop chromatique*. Other
works he performed only in Berlin: movements from
Beethoven's "Hammerklavier" sonata, for example, and pieces
by Handel and Scarlatti. As a conductor he directed an overture
by Spontini and a Beethoven symphony, and he appeared on
several occasions as an accompanist and ensemble musician.
Never before in the history of music had one performer demonstrated so much skill in so many situations as Liszt did in
1842 Berlin.[133]

"Lisztomania" (Heine's own term) had as much to do with the virtuoso's
audiences as with the virtuoso himself. These subtleties continue to be
misunderstood by scholars. See, for example, Andreas Ballstaedt and
Tobias Widmaier, *Salonmusik* (Stuttgart 1989), p. 46. NB: The comments
by Heine quoted above refer to Liszt's Paris performance of April 1841.
This does not mean, though, that Heine thought the Parisians were
crazier about Liszt than the Germans. On the contrary: Heine himself
marvelled in 1844 that Liszt could have so great an impact on a Parisian
audience, since "da[ß] war kein deutsch-sentimentales, berlinisch-
anempfindendes Publikum!" [Heine, *Historisch-kritische Gesamtausgabe*,
Vol. XIV/1, ed. Hansen (Hamburg 1988), p. 131]. See also Kapp, p. 183.

[132] Quoted from World 17 (1842), p. 188. The medal alluded to in this passage
is described somewhat differently in Ramann II, pp. 170-171.

[133] Nevertheless, even his most devoted admirers have slighted his Berlin
accomplishments. Walker, for example, overlooked the Singakademie
benefit at which Liszt accompanied soprano Marie Shaw in an aria from
Donizetti's *Lucia di Lammermoor* (111). Discrepancies also exist in published accounts of his Berlin repertory. Ramann, for example, claims that

His concerts quickly became the best-known and more celebrated of his "transcendental" tours, and most of his biographers have described them in some detail; Ramann alone devoted more than thirty pages to them and to his private life in the Prussian capital.[134] But contemporary accounts are almost always more accurate. The reviews written by Ludwig Rellstab for the so-called *Vossische Zeitung*, for example, contain many valuable insights into Liszt's piano-playing and conducting. Other reviews appeared regularly in the so-called *Spenersche Zeitung*. Almost all of these reviews came to similar conclusions, especially about the high quality of his performances, but each paper had its own slant. Two examples must suffice: On 7 January 1842, Rellstab described a performance of Schubert's *Ständchen* in the following way:

> In the middle of his program the artist offered us two more delicate works: the *Ständchen* and *Ave Maria* by Schubert. The reviewer wishes to point out that the former work is based on one of his own early efforts, to which the composer's talent has given long life, and which will be prolonged still further by our own artist's virtuosity. The gentle yet lively touch with which [Liszt] handles his instrument, especially in the delightful passage where the melody is presented in imitation, was enchanting.[135]

The same day the *Spenersche Zeitung* published this account of the same performance:

Es war ein Ratt was performed by a student chorus on 25 January 1842. Contemporary sources identify the work in question as *Es war ein König in Thule*, sung by a soloist (i.e., the "Hofsängerin").

[134] See Ramann II, pp. 145-177. Walker, pp. 373-374, pays special attention to Liszt's friendships with Charlotte von Hagn and the remarkable Bettina von Arnim.

[135] "Zur Mittelgabe bot uns der Concertgeber zwei zartere Stücke, *Ständchen* und *Ave Maria* von Schubert dar. Bei dem ersten ist Ref selbst betheiligt, da es die Composition eines seiner Jugendgedichte ist, dem das Talent des Musikers diese lange Lebensdauer verschaffen hat, die jetzt wiederum durch das der Virtuosität unseres Künstlers verlängert wird. Der leichte, lustige Hauch in der Behandlung des Instruments, besonders in der reizenden Stelle, wo die Melodie fortwährend imitirt wird, war bezaubernd" [VZ No. 7 (10.1.1842)]. Rellstab was celebrated in his own day as novelist and poet, and the opening numbers of Schubert's *Schwanengesang* are settings of Rellstab's poems.

During [Liszt's] playing, however, the enthusiasm and attention of the audience were directed toward the genial artist
himself, who moved his listeners to vigorous applause through
his charming presentation of the two Schubert songs:
Ständchen and *Ave Maria* (in the last of which one can hear the
chiming of evening bells).[136]

As these passages demonstrate, Rellstab usually took
more interest in purely musical matters (i.e., in what Liszt
played and how he played it). The critic for the *Spenersche
Zeitung*, on the other hand, often took more interest in the effect of Liszt's playing (i.e., in audience response). In the case
of the 12 January benefit recital given by Pantaleoni, however,
Rellstab left us a more interesting account of how
Lisztomaniacs behaved when their idol suddenly appeared
among them. Completely upstaging his colleague, Liszt walked
to the front of the hall and informed the enraptured crowd that
he had been requested to play something prior to his *Galop
chromatique*, which had been announced as the evening's final
number. He asked his audience to choose: should he play his
transcription of Schubert's *Erlkönig* or Weber's *Aufforderung
zum Tanz*? People went wild, shouting at the tops of their
voices for the numbers of their choice; written ballots were cast,
but the result was almost a tie: 350 votes for Schubert and 351
for Weber. Generous to a fault, Liszt played both pieces and
fantasized on the second, to the delight of his besotted fans.[137]

Virtually every contemporary account of Liszt's visit to
Berlin testifies to unbroken, astonishing public success. This
success, or "Lisztomania," expressed itself through unbridled
adulation for Liszt-the-man as well as Liszt-the-artist. Fanny
Lewald, who in her youth met Liszt during his Berlin sojourn,
confessed as much.[138] Many of the "Lisztomaniacs" were

---

[136] "Doch war Geist und Sinn immer nur auf den genialen Concertgeber
gerichtet, der dann auch durch den reizenden Vortrag der beiden Lieder
von Schubert: "Ständchen" und "Ave Maria" (im letztern die Klänge der
Abendglöcke andeutend), die Zuhörer auf Neue zum enthusiastischen
Beifall hinriß" [SZ No. 5 (7.1.1842)].

[137] See Appendix D, quotation 9. A less detailed account of the same scene
appears in SZ No. 11 (14.1.1842).

[138] "[I]ch hatte . . . eigentlich mehr Interesse für Liszt als Menschen, denn
für den Musiker gehabt" [Fanny Lewald, *Meine Lebensgeschichte*, Vol. III
(Berlin 1861), p. 200].

women, and "Lisztomania" itself was steeped in sexuality. Ladies and girls laughed and wept, threw handkerchiefs at their idol and themselves at his feet, scrambled for souvenirs, and sometimes fainted dead away. These goings-on not only turned artistic events into public circuses, but sickened Liszt himself.[139] Yet he lingered in Berlin for more than nine weeks, twice postponing his departure.[140] Evidently the wealth and acclaim Prussia had to offer him was too good to pass up.

At least nine of Liszt's concerts were devoted to worthy causes, though: the Cologne Cathedral fund, for example, as well as benefits for other artists and for Berlin's poor. His 25 January concert on behalf of aid to university students, for instance, raised more than 300 thalers.[141] But these donations, generous though they were, did little to interfere with his own money-making. Records for his Singakademie concerts prove that Liszt's "benefits," establish his *minimum* gross income between 27 January 1841 and 6 February 1842 as 8,817 thalers.[142] And money was only part of the story: he also received rings, watches, and other trinkets; he was showered with invitations to parties and soirées (some of which must have been pleasant enough); and the Prince of Prussia gave him a musical autograph written by Friedrich the Great. Banquets were thrown for him; the most famous, held on 18 Feb-

---

[139] "Je suis malade de concerts et de succès," he wrote d'Agoult on 6 January 1842. But Liszt was also physically ill for two days around the same time: "J'ai été malade deux jours. Par moments il me semble que ma tête et mon coeur se brisent" [Ollivier II, p. 191]. He also became ill during his 28 February benefit concert at the Berlin Theater, and another accompanist had to take his place for the final number.

[140] Originally Liszt planned to leave Berlin around 8 February 1842, but he postponed his departure for at least two days in order to perform at the Royal Theater. See APSZ Nos. 36-39 (5-8.2.1842), pp. 148ff. This may explain why his Singakademie concerts stopped on 6 February: he was probably too late to hire that hall again after deciding to remain longer in Berlin. Rescheduled for 26 February, his departure was again postponed so he could take part in another Theater concert. See APSZ No. 55 (24.2.1842), p. 230.

[141] See APSZ No. 38 (7.2.1842), p. 155. The precise figure given in this source is 318 thalers, 22½ groschen.

[142] See D-WRgs Liszt Kasten 240. The most profitable of the Singakademie concerts—that of 16 January—earned him a total of 1,134 thalers. Another—this one a benefit for Berlin's poor—netted 1,794 thalers, or 5,382 marks. See Ramann II, p. 163.

ruary, included a number of toasts, a short speech by Liszt in praise of German students, and performances in his honor of selections from Mendelssohn's oratorio *Paulus* and Meyerbeer's popular *Huguenots*.[143] He was followed everywhere, students serenaded him,[144] and even small children sang for him. He was elected to the Prussian Academy of Arts[145] and to several professional societies,[146] and the King of Prussia awarded him the order "Pour le Mérite"—the highest decoration the Kingdom could bestow on soldier or civilian alike.[147] No performing artist ever received so many honors in so short a time as did Liszt in 1842 Berlin.

On 3 March Liszt gave his final Berlin performance, a matinée in the hall of his hotel.[148] Cheering crowds were on hand to see him off, and he was escorted from the city in a coach drawn by six white horses, with Prince Lichnowsky by his side. The Berliners, however, quickly got over their "Lisztomania," and satires on Liszt and his hysterical fans appeared at once in newspapers and in pamphlet form.[149]

---

143 See Ramann II, pp. 169-170.

144 In 1843 students at Breslau's University honored Liszt with a torchlight procession. This was forbidden by the Rector and Senate of Berlin's university after his second "student" concert, however, and Liszt's fans had to settle for serenading him; evidently the authorities were afraid of a demonstration. See BML 3 (1842), p. 21.

145 See D-WRgs Liszt Überformate 121a.

146 For example, to the Men's Choral Society or "Männergesang-Verein." See D-WRgs Liszt Überformate 121.

147 The diploma, preserved as D-WRgs Liszt Überformate 126, is dated 16 June 1842 and signed by Alexander von Humboldt. Like his other titles and decorations, Liszt's "Pour le Mérite" award was widely reported in the European press. See, for example, WaMZ Nos. 69-70 [double issue] (9 and 11.6.1842), p. 288. See also the frontispiece to the present volume.

148 Accounts of this event overlook its musical character. That it was intended to be a benefit performance as well as a gala farewell may be seen in an announcement that appeared in the *Vossische Zeitung* the day after the event. See VZ and SZ No. 53 (4.3.1842). This announcement contains the text of a letter Liszt addressed to Maurice Schlesinger, his Berlin publisher. See Appendix E, letter 3.

149 A number of Liszt satires and caricatures from 1842, including *Das Liszt-ge Berlin*, are discussed above in Chapter II. See also Ramann II, pp. 174n-176n. Other satires have not been located by the present author—among them, pieces published in the *Zeitung für die elegante*

Disgruntled journalists could write what they liked, but they could not extinguish the legend of "Lisztomania" and the most successful single concert tour up to that point in musical history.

From Elbing to Memel: March 1842

Following his triumphal departure from the Prussian capital, Liszt embarked on his first trip to Russia. Travelling overland to St. Petersburg, he interrupted his journey with visits to Elbing, Königsberg, Tilsit, and Memel. In addition to money and applause in these places, Liszt received an honorary doctorate from the University of Königsberg—an honor almost unprecedented at that time, and an especially important one from the perspective of his German reputation.[150]

Liszt arrived at Elbing on 8 March and visited Marienburg palace that afternoon, where he gave a private performance (134). That evening he returned to Elbing and presented a public recital at the local Gymnasium (135). The hall began to fill with music-lovers about 4 p.m.; by 6:30 p.m., half an hour before the recital was scheduled to start, at least 350 people were on hand to hear the artist announce a program that included a fantasy on Mozart's *Don Giovanni*. Yet the *Elbinger Anzeiger* suggested that Liszt's appeal lay in his fashionableness and that, despite his astounding technical brilliance, he failed to reach the hearts of his listeners.[151] After the concert was over, he dined with a cherished colleague ("geschätzter Kunstfreund"), probably one Herr Krueger, a local government official who invited the pianist to visit Elbing

---

Welt, Komet, Rosen, and *Bemerker,* which were identified by Koch in various parts of his 1936 bibliography. Nor are most of these periodicals cited elsewhere in the Liszt literature or identified in modern reference works.

[150] A statement to this effect appeared in the musical press immediately after the degree was conferred: "Der Enthusiasmus, den der Große Künstler in Königsberg erregte, soll dem in Berlin geglichen haben; an Ehren-Auszeichnungen hat Liszt aber die größte erlebt, nämlich die philosophische Fakultät hat ihm das Doctor-Diplom überreicht" [BML 3 (1842), p. 60].

[151] "Woher der Enthusiasmus für Liszt's Spiel, wenn diesem wirklich das denselben bedingende Haupterforderniß abgeht, entstanden ist? — [Diese Frage] kann am treffendsten wohl mit drei Worten beantwortet werden: 'Er ist Mode' . . . Seine unbegreifliche Fertigkeit erregt Erstaunen, aber sie dringt nicht bis zum Herzen des Hörers" [ElbAn No. 20 (12.3.1842)].

and who later submitted information about his visit to local papers.

The following day Liszt travelled to Königsberg, where he performed at least eight times in five days. His first public recital took place at the local Theater on 10 March (136); his second recital was presented in the same place the following evening (137). Both recitals included familiar numbers like the fantasies on *Robert le diable* and *Don Giovanni*, but the second featured two novelties: the Prelude and Fugue in c-sharp minor from Book I of Bach's *Wohltempirirtes Clavier*, and a free fantasy on Weber's *Auffordering zum Tanz*. Friedrich Raabe, who reviewed the second recital, knew that Liszt had been criticized in Elbing for placing technical proficiency ahead of "spiritual" values. Consequently, Raabe did his best to defend the musician's artistic reputation in the pages of Königsberg's *Hartungsche Zeitung:*

> [Liszt's] technical facility is astonishing and heretofore unequalled, but such facility is *only one* of his accomplishments. It belongs to his playing as one of its essential aspects, but it isn't everything. Rather, it is a means to an end, not—as some would claim—empty show. . . . His virtuosity is not mere tinkling, but a kind of spiritual creativity; it is the poetry of piano-playing.[152]

Two days later, on 13 March, Liszt presented a pair of recitals: a matinée for students at the University (138), and an evening concert at the Theater (139). The programs for these performances have not survived, but we do know the *Grand Galop chromatique* was especially well received by the Theater audience. He also played privately in at least two Königsberg homes (140-141); Ludwig Passarge, then a boy, never forgot

---

[152] "Die technische Fertigkeit des Virtuosen ist erstaunlich und bis jetzt unerreicht, aber diese technische Fertigkeit ist nur Eine Seite [sic] des großen Pianisten. Sie ist freilich wesentlich, weil sie mit zu der Charakteristik seines Spieles gehört, aber sie ist nicht alles. Sie dient ihm nur als Mittel zu seinem Zweck, und ist nie, wie bei Anderen, leere Form. . . . Seine Virtuosität ist nicht ein bloßes Spielen auf dem Instrument, sondern ein geistiges Schaffen, es ist die Poesie des Fortepianos" [KönPZ No. 61 (14.3.1842), p. 484].

Vormärz critics east of Berlin seem to have been especially sensitive to the "transcendent" character of Liszt's virtuosity. With regard to this topic, see Saffle, "Liszt und die Deutschen, 1840-1845" (identified above in Chapter I).

those occasions and recalled them more than forty years later in his reminiscences. Finally, on 14 March, Liszt stood before a large crowd in the University's main hall to receive his honors. First he was presented with a valuable gold medal bearing the likeness of the Markgraf Albert; then he received a diploma certifying him an honorary "Doctor of Music" of Königsberg.[153] The degree was conferred upon him by Professors Jacobi, Rosenkranz, and Dulk. After the presentation was over Jacobi described Liszt's achievements at some length,[154] and Liszt seems to have "replied" with a brilliant keyboard fantasy (142).

That evening Liszt appeared for the last time at the local Theater (143), where he played his "Don Juan" fantasy and his *Erlkönig* transcription to thunderous applause. As soon as the concert was over he was treated to a banquet at the "Deutsches Haus" hotel, then escorted with his secretary Belloni and several other people to a coach. He ate breakfast in nearby Tapiau, then changed coaches and arrived in Tilsit in time to perform that evening in the hall of his hotel (144). On this occasion one Fräulein Müller shared the stage with him and gave dramatic readings between his keyboard performances. The following afternoon (i.e., 16 March) he gave a matinée performance for a local literary society (145). When he left Königsberg, however, Liszt was ill,[155] and by the time he and his party reached Memel the illness had become widespread. There was little to do but lie in bed and write letters;[156] only when health had returned was it possible to push on to St. Petersburg and new adventures. Nevertheless, he found

---

[153] For the original Latin text of this diploma, see Ramann II, p. 182.

[154] Jacobi's speech is reprinted in K. Lehrs, "Franz Liszt: Ehrendoctor," *Wissenschaftliche Monats-Blätter* 4 (1876), pp. 175-176. See also Ramann II, p. 183.

[155] See KönPZ No. 63 (16.3.1842), p. 501.

[156] Several of these letters, addressed to Lefebvre, remain unpublished. See Chapter II above. Others have appeared in print several times—among them, a letter of thanks to the faculty of Königsberg University for their generosity toward him. This letter exists in two somewhat different forms. See BFig No. 74 (31.3.1842), p. 296 [dated "Königsberg," 14.3.1842]; and Briefe I, p. 46 [dated Mittau, 18.3.1842]. The second version also appears in Lehrs, "Franz Liszt: Ehrendoctor," p. 175. See also *Eduard von Simson: Erinnerungen aus seinem Leben*, ed. Bernhard von Simson (Leipzig 1900), p. 69.

time and energy in Memel to present or participate in at least
one musical program (146).

Liszt's tour of East Prussia was unquestionably successful,
but it also evoked a certain consternation. Elbing was apparently both thrilled and shocked by his visit, and two articles in
a single issue of the *Anzeiger* were devoted to it, albeit after the
fact. "Lisztiana" jeered at Raabe's favorable reviews in the
Hartungsche Zeitung, while "Die Liszt-Periode in Berlin" described Liszt himself in most unflattering terms.[157] Nevertheless, a biography of Liszt also appeared in the same *Anzeiger*
issue, and the review of his Elbing recital quoted above was less
than damning. In spite of "Lisztomania" and its aftershocks, in
spite of illness and the hardships of travel through what was
mostly desolate country in the middle of winter, Liszt managed
to leave East Prussia with a doctor's degree in hand and with
most of his Berlin reputation intact.

Lübeck: June 1842

Returning from Russia, the *Nicolai* put into port in the
Hanseatic city of Lübeck—at that time one of Germany's free
cities.[158] On an evening in very early June Liszt gave a private
concert for the passengers who had accompanied him from
Russia on that ship (147). He improvised, played at least one
fantasy, and accompanied Pantaleoni in several numbers, including Pantaleoni's own "Venetian barcarolle"—a piece many
listeners found "heavenly."[159] The first page of music from this
"Barcarolle" is reproduced below as Plate 10. One or two days
later Liszt gave a benefit concert in Lübeck (148). He played
several numbers, including his "Don Juan" fantasy, and accompanied Pantaleoni in an aria from *Niobe*. Presented as part
of the city's "Liebhaberkonzert" series,[160] this concert was

---

157 Both articles were published in ElbAn No. 21 (16.3.1842).

158 According to one report, however, his ship docked at Travemünde. See
NZfM 16 (1842), p. 200.

159 "Hr. Pantaleoni . . . (welcher bekanntlich Liszt nach Petersburg
begleitete), entzückte durch den herrlichen Vortrag seiner *Barcarole
venetienne*, welcher ihm Liszt accompagnirte" [BML 3 (1842), p. 85].

160 The series, which began in 1780, introduced Lübeck music-lovers (or
"Liebhaber") to such works as Mozart's *Nozze di Figaro* in 1820 and

Plate 10

A page from Liszt's arrangement of Pantaleoni's
"Venetian Barcarolle"
(Leipzig: J. Schuberth: Plate 5692)

scarcely acknowledged by the local press.[161] Nevertheless, the
Revue et Gazette Musicale of Paris ran a short notice about it,
and the *Blätter für Musik und Literatur* printed a longer one.[162]
The concert itself raised 830 thalers for Lübeck's poor. Then,
accompanied by some of his shipmates from the *Nicolai*, Liszt
travelled on to Hamburg—and from there, one would imagine,
overland to Paris, where he spent much of the following summer.[163]

A Third Rhineland Tour: September 1842

Despite numerous claims to the contrary, we have already
seen that Liszt probably did not visit Nonnenwerth during the
summer of 1842. Instead, in late July of that year he received
in Paris a letter from Lefebvre, his friend in Cologne, asking
him to return to the Rhineland and perform on behalf of the
Cologne Cathedral fund.[164] Liszt had many reasons not to
undertake such a trip, but he told Lefebvre he would do so if
he received an official invitation from the fundraising committee.[165] Some five weeks, on 9 September, he arrived at Brühl
and performed privately there the following morning (149). Two
days later he gave a concert on behalf of the "Agrippina"
Masonic Lodge in Cologne (150). Finally, his benefit recital for

---

Beethoven's masterful "Eroica" symphony in 1834. See Johann Hennings
and Wilhelm Stahl, *Musikgeschichte Lübeck* (Kassel 1951), Vol. I, pp.
156-159.

[161] Only an advertisement appeared in the *Lübecker Anzeiger*, a newspaper
omitted in Appendix A. See instead Hennings and Stahl, *Musikgeschichte
Lübeck*, p. 159.

[162] See RGMP 9 (1842), p. 245; and BML 3 (1842), pp. 85-86.

[163] Liszt's Lübeck itinerary remains obscure. He arrived no later than 1 June,
because an unpublished letter of his addressed to Lefebvre bears that date
(D-Hs). Another letter in the same collection was written on board the
Nicolai, misplaced, then rediscovered. Still another letter, addressed to
the Comtesse d'Agoult on 1 June 1842, appears in Ollivier II, p. 215.
Whether Liszt proceded from Lübeck directly to Paris, however, is uncer-
tain.

[164] See Liszt's letter to Lefebvre of 28 July 1842 (D-Hs). This letter is published in Paul Ellmar, "Franz Liszt und der Kölner Dom," *Kölnische
Rundschau* No. 12 (20.1.1957), "Der Sonntag," p. 5.

[165] Liszt evidently received his invitation. In any event, he was subsequently
made an honorary member of the committee itself. See APSZ No. 255
(14.9.1842), p. 1090.

the Cathedral fund took place two days later at Cologne's Temple House (151). In addition to his fantasies on *Robert le diable* and *God Save the Queen*, he performed his own song *Angiolin dal biondo crin* with Pantaleoni.

Prior to his departure for Koblenz,[166] Liszt's friends treated him to a banquet, then transported him to the nearby train station in a wagon. At the station, however, an altercation broke out when officials and passengers waiting for the train to arrive were shocked to see the pianist's cart pulled all the way up to the tracks. Fists, walking sticks, and umbrellas were used as weapons, and Liszt's party was driven from the station in disgrace.[167] Afterwards he proceeded to Aachen, where he and Pantaleoni performed on 17 September (152) before he himself left for a brief visit to Paris.

From Weimar to Cologne: October-November 1842

When Liszt reached the French capital, he found a letter waiting for him which summoned him to Weimar on 20 October. He thought for a while about bypassing Liège and Cologne and travelling to Weimar via Frankfurt a.M.,[168] but several weeks later he informed Lefebvre that he had decided to visit Cologne after all, that he hoped there to meet with several dignitaries (including Breidenstein), and that he intended to arrive on 18 October.[169] Travelling by way of the Rhineland,

---

[166] See Ollivier II, p. 220.

[167] See BML 3 (1842), p. 203.

[168] See Liszt's unpublished letter to Lefebvre of 26 September 1842 (D-Hs).

Liszt probably did not make plans to visit Weimar as early as 25 August 1842, the purported date of a letter written by Meyerbeer to Wilhelm von Redern. See *Giacomo Meyerbeer: Briefwechsel und Tagebücher*, 3 vols.; ed. Heinz and Gudrun Becker (Berlin 1960-1973), Vol. III, pp. 412-414. Hereafter "Meyerbeer." Instead, Meyerbeer's letter probably dates from the following month. Among other topics it mentions a recent bout of illness of Liszt's part in Aachen (where, as we just saw, he played on 17 September 1842), and Liszt's decision to collaborate that fall with Rubini (one Liszt conveyed to his friend Lefebvre only on 10 October 1842).

[169] See Liszt's unpublished letter to Lefebvre of 10 October 1842 (D-Hs). In this letter Liszt states that he will not be able to visit either Bonn or Nonnenwerth on his trip ("m'arrêter ni à Bonn ni à Nonnenwerth"). In point of fact, he reached Cologne on 19 October, where he may have visited Lefebvre briefly before leaving for Weimar early the following day. See APSZ No. 296 (25.10.1842), p. 2161.

therefore, he reached Weimar by 20 October, where that afternoon the ducal heir Carl Alexander and his bride Sophie were
married "to the accompaniment of thunderous music."[170] Liszt
obviously was summoned to Weimar for the wedding cele-
brations, but he took no official part in the wedding itself.
Three days later, though, he participated in a concert held in
the ducal palace (153). Hundreds of local residents crowded into
the balconies of the palace hall to listen to him as well as to
Giovanni Rubini and Pantaleoni. The *Allgemeine musikalische
Zeitung* assumed that its readers would be bored with another
account of Liszt's successes; nevertheless, it reported that his
Weimar performances were as wonderful as ever.[171]

On 26 October, he gave a benefit concert in the Saale der
Rose in nearby Jena (154). Proceeds were donated to a local
orphanage with which the Grand Duke was associated. Again
Liszt met with tremendous success.[172] At this concert, according
to one source, he conducted a student chorus in a performance
of a well-known patriotic work identified only as "Sie sollen ihn
nicht haben."[173] Performances of patriotic songs in Vormärz
Germany were interpreted by some French critics as danger-

---

[170] See ErZ No. 140 (29.10.1842), which reported the event at some length and
employed the phrase "unter rauschender Musik" to describe the cele-
brations.

[171] "Wie [Herr Liszt] spiel[t], ist aller Welt bekannt, daher würde es die Leser
langweilen . . . Nur sei es bemerkt, dass . . . Herr *Liszt* auch diesmal,
wie früher, zu Bewunderung hinriss" [AmZ 45 (1843), col. 73].
    Giovanni Batista Rubini became Liszt's travelling partner sometime
around 20 October 1842, and the two artists performed together regularly
for about half a year before separating, apparently with some ill-will. In
his unpublished letter to Lefebvre of 10 October 1842 (D-Hs), Liszt an-
nounces that their partnership would begin on 1 November and that, although it would not bring him any financial rewards, he accepts it "for
reasons I will tell you later by word of mouth" [translation courtesy of
Pauline Pocknell]. What those reasons were remain a mystery.

[172] "In Jena gab Liszt, der immer wohlthätige, ein Concert zum Besten der
Kleinkinderbewahranstalt, die daselbst zum Andenken an die
Vermählung des Erbgroßherzogs gestiftet werden sollte . . . [Der]
Enthusiasmus . . . braucht kaum beigefügt zu werden" [NZfM 17 (1843),
p. 154].

[173] Almost certainly a setting of Nicholas Becker's "doggerel" poem *Das
deutsche Rhein*. See Porter, "The 'Rheinlieder' Critics," p. 77n. Which setting of Becker's poem Liszt conducted, however, remains unknown; dozens, even hundreds of German patriotic choruses appeared in print
throughout the Vormärz era.

ous, even treacherous; the words to this one defy Germany's enemies to seize the Rhineland, long considered by many Frenchmen as part of their own nation. No wonder a few journalists wondered whether Liszt really was a German, albeit one who often went about in Hungarian disguise.[174]

Around the same time he was treated to a banquet in Jena at which the famous Professor Wolff toasted him in good German style—that is, with respect to *all* of his titles—as "knight, doctor, master, and friend."[175] Liszt also made friends with a number of Hungarian students attending Jena's university, because two days later he invited them to his public benefit concert held at the Weimar Hoftheater on 29 October (158).[176] This event, which included performances of arias by Mozart and Rossini, Beethoven's *Adelaïde*, the *Puritani* "Polonaise," and *Erlkönig*—numbers which, for the most part, also appeared on Liszt's and Rubini's 23 October program—was "obviously" a glittering success.[177] During the days preceding this event Liszt also played privately for the ducal family (156-157), and on 28 October he presented a concert with Rubini and Pantaleoni at the Schlehendorn Hotel in Erfurt (155). Officially a benefit for Pantaleoni, the concert itself was enormously successful; more than 600 people turned out for it. The *Blätter für Musik und Literatur* called Liszt's performance "masterful,"[178] and a local paper affirmed that he drew from his

---

[174] This is not to imply that the French press always lampooned or attacked Liszt for his German sympathies. At least one French magazine described a Liszt benefit performance on behalf of the Cologne Cathedral fund (151) in glowing terms. See MRm No. 71 (29.9.1842). Furthermore, Liszt several times denied he was a German patriot. See Suttoni, entry 316. See also Saffle, "Liszt und die Deutschen, 1840-1845."

[175] "Unserm Ritter, Doktor, Meister, // Jenas treuem Freunde Liszt" [Adolf Mirus, *Das Liszt-Museum zu Weimar und seine Erinnerungen* (Leipzig 1892), p. 10]. In 1842 Liszt held no hereditary title, but anyone who had been awarded the Order "Pour le Mérite" deserved in Germany to be called a "knight." In any event, he was later given a patent of nobility by the Emperor of Austria. See Walker, pp. 30-32.

[176] Liszt's letter of invitation is reprinted in *Franz Liszt: Briefe aus ungarischen Sammlungen*, ed. Margit Prahács (Kassel 1966), p. 52.

[177] "Dass der Erfolg [von Liszt und Rubini] höchst glänzend war, versteht sich von selbst" [AmZ 44 (1842), col. 1013].

[178] "Wir enthalten uns jedes Lobes über die Leistungen de[s Herrn] Liszt . . . da es eines solchen bei ihre[r] längst anerkannten Meisterschaft von

listeners stormy exclamations of delight and raised them to the highest imaginable pitch of excitement.[179]

Three days later Liszt returned to Erfurt and presented a second recital there (159) that may have featured his "Don Juan" and "God Save the Queen" fantasies.[180] The *Erfurter Zeitung*, which had advertised but not reviewed his previous performance, congratulated him on both events and even published a lengthy excerpt from a letter by him addressed on 8 November 1842 to his friends in the Erfurt area:

> Because it gives me such joy, I am all the happier to take this opportunity to tell all of you again how genuinely thankful I am to Erfurt citizens for the warm reception I received from them. Please give my personal thanks especially to Herr Kappellmeister Golde and rest assured, that my memory of the D-Major Symphony so splendidly arranged and performed will never fade. In the course of the coming year I hope to have the pleasure of travelling from Weimar to visit you. So farewell! dear friend[?s]! Remember me fondly, etc.,
>
> F. Liszt[181]

Liszt's reference to Weimar in this letter is a meaningful one. During his 1842 visit to that town he negotiated an appointment as "Kapellmeister im außerordentlichen Dienst" (i.e., Court Music Director Extraordinary). In return, he asked for nothing except whatever financial renumeration the Grand Duke chose to give him.[182] For almost two decades Liszt main-

Seiten der erster Kunstrichter nicht bedarf und damit überflüssig wäre" [BML 3 (1842), p. 186].

179 "Herr Liszt zeigte sich in diesem Concert in seiner höchsten Größe, und mit einer solchen ihm nur eigenen Liebenswürdigkeit, daß er die anwesenden Zuhörer, mehr als 600 an der Zahl, zu den stürmischsten Exclamationen und zu der höchsten Begeisterung hinriß" [ErZ No. 140 (29.10.1842)].

180 See AmZ 45 (1843), col. 253, which mentions these works but not the date of their performance.

181 Quoted from ErZ No. 149 (17.11.1842). See Appendix E, letter 5. The present author has been unable to determine to which symphony Liszt refers in this letter, or to whom the letter was addressed.

182 Liszt's contract, written in French and dated 31 October 1842, is reprinted in Ramann II, p. 197. The official diploma of appointment, signed by Carl Friedrich and dated 2 November 1842, is reproduced in facsimile in Burger, p. 175. Its text also appears in Ramann II, p. 198; and in other biographies.

tained an official association with Weimar and, despite statements to the contrary, honored his contract—which, after all, was rather loosely worded—whenever possible. As we shall see, he returned to Weimar during the winter of 1844; he also visited Weimar briefly in 1846, and he moved there to take up his duties full-time in 1848.[183]

Leaving Erfurt immediately after his second concert there, Liszt travelled with Rubini to Coburg, where the two artists presented joint recitals on 1 November (160) and 4 November (161). The former event was widely reported in the European press, because both Rubini and Liszt received the "Order of Ernestine" from the Duke of Saxe-Coburg-Gotha.[184] The two artists also enjoyed several banquets in Coburg before travelling to nearby Gotha on or about 8 November, where they gave a concert in that town's Theater the following evening (162).[185] Next they travelled to Frankfurt a.M., where their joint recital at the Weidenbusch Hall on 15 November (163) was applauded by a glittering throng and earned 1,900 guilden—a sum at least one magazine considered excessive.[186] Afterwards they probably

---

[183] Liszt evidently planed to visit Weimar *every* year after 1844, because on 1 January 1845 he wrote a long letter to Carl Alexander, apologizing that his travels in Spain had prevented his return to Germany. See Raabe, *Großherzog Carl Alexander und Liszt* (Leipzig 1918), pp. 4-7.

[184] In a letter written on 8 November to the Comtesse d'Agoult, Liszt expressed his happiness on Rubini's behalf as well as his own. See Ollivier II, pp. 226-227.

  The "Order of Ernestine" was a so-called "House Order"—that is, it was honored wherever members of the family that bestowed it reigned. Since the House of Saxe-Coburg-Gotha produced Queen Victoria's consort Albert as well as a host of other nobles, the Order conferred its privileges during the 1840s in England, Belgium, Portugal, and France. The diploma and other souvenirs Liszt received as part of his investiture are preserved in D-WRgs Liszt Kasten 124.

[185] See Appendix D, quotation 10.

[186] See BML 3 (1842), p. 207. Rather surprisingly, local magazines and newspapers all but ignored this event. Only the *Journal de Francfort* had anything positive to say about Liszt and his celebrated colleague, observing that "[L]es succès de l'art qui marche de triomphe en triomphe, voilà ce qui caracterise les concerts de MM. Liszt et Rubini" [JdF No. 318 (18.11.1842)]. On the other hand, the *Allgemeine musikalische Zeitung* called Liszt's behavior in Frankfurt "arrogant" and maintained that the pianist "habe [sic] nie so wegwerfend gespielt" [AmZ 45 (1843), col. 90]. The latter magazine also reported Liszt's and Rubini's Frankfurt earnings as "1,500 fl[orins]."

took a train to Mainz, where they booked passage on a steamship bound for Rotterdam. Stopping briefly in Cologne, they presented a matinée concert on or around 18 November (164), then proceeded to Holland and still greater success.[187]

From Münster to Neisse: December 1842 — March 1843

Returning to Germany shortly before Christmas,[188] Liszt and Rubini visited Münster, where a program they presented with Rubini's pupil Marie Ostergaard on 26 December 1842 (165) featured several vocal selections as well as Liszt's *Norma* and "Don Juan" fantasies. Then, stopping briefly in Weimar, Liszt played privately for the ducal family on or around 29 December (166) before travelling with Rubini to Berlin for a series of highly successful musical events.[189] "Lisztomania" had ended in Berlin months before, but the pianist was still a welcome guest. During January 1843 he appeared on five public programs: the first took place at an unspecified location on 5 January (168), the second at the Singakademie on 8 January (169), the third at the Theater on 11 January (170), the fourth at the Singakademie on 15 January (172), and the fifth at the Theater on 18 January (173). On each of these occasions Liszt shared the platform with other artists, including Ostergaard and pianist Theodor Döhler, and on 5 January he conducted members of the Berlin Männergesang-Verein in at least one

---

[187] For details of Liszt's 1842 Dutch tour, see Peter Scholcz, "Liszts eerste concerten in Nederland, 1842," *EPTA Piano Bulletin* (1986), pp. 20-29.

[188] A letter Liszt wrote to his daughter Blandine is dated Münster, 23 December 1842. See *Correspondance de Liszt et de sa fille Madame Emile Ollivier*, ed. Ollivier (Paris 1936), pp. 23-24.

[189] Near the end of 1842 Liszt also met Richard Wagner in Berlin, an event described rather hazily by Wagner himself in the "authentic" edition of *Mein Leben* (Munich 1963), pp. 284-286. This meeting, an extremely important one for both artists, is more straightforwardly described in Newman I, pp. 348-349. Evidently Liszt and Schröder-Devrient were rehearsing for the private court concert of 12 January 1843 mentioned below when Wagner encountered them. In any event, Wagner's penchant for memory slips is well-known, and it is possible he heard Liszt and Schroeder-Devrient rehearsing for some other event.
　　NB: The music Wagner heard when he met Liszt in Berlin ("die berühmte Passage des Basses in der Rache-Arie der 'Donna-Anna' in Oktaven rapid auf dem Klavier" [*Mein Leben*, p. 285]) was being rehearsed, not performed. Consequently, it has not been counted in the present volume as one of Liszt's German performances.

number. Furthermore, he also participated in a private performance for Berlin's royal family held on 12 January at a local
palace (171).[190] And on New Year's Eve (i.e., 31 December 1842)
he played his fantasies on *Don Giovanni* and *Figaro* for Ludwig
Rellstab, his favorite Berlin critic (167).

Liszt's 1843 Berlin successes seem at least to have ap-
proximated those of the previous year. The *Blätter für Musik
und Literatur*, for example, wrote that he stood on the highest
step of artistic accomplishment—indeed, that no higher level
could be imagined.[191] And in the *Vossische Zeitung* Rellstab
stated that Liszt was greeted at his 8 January performance
with the same joy and enthusiasm accorded him the previous
year; furthermore, Rellstab affirmed that Liszt's audience was
as large as those of 1842 and filled the hall to overflowing.[192]
Success also greeted him in Frankfurt an der Oder, where he
presented a concert at the local Theater on the evening of 19
January (174). Heralded by a long series of advertisements in
local newspapers, this concert was a triumph. Liszt played
many of his most popular numbers, including Weber's
"Invitation" as an encore. The editors of the local *Telegraph*
marvelled at his unbelievable dexterity and thanked one Herr
Boettner profusely for bringing the pianist to their city.[193] An-

---

[190] Although mentioned in several press notices, this concert remains obscure.
We know only that it was held "am Hof" [SmW 1 (1843), p. 24] and in
honor of the King of Hannover and Count of Dessau. See FOPZ No. 17
["Beilage"] (17.1.1843), p. 138.
   Meyerbeer III, p. 424, has Liszt returning to Berlin from Breslau to
take part in this event. Evidently Meyerbeer's editors confused 12 January
with 12 *February* 1843.

[191] "Er stand, als wir ihn das erste Mal hörten, schon auf einer solchen Stufe
der künstlerischen Vollendung, bei welcher ein höherer Grad nicht mehr
gedacht werden kann" [BML 4 (1843), p. 24].

[192] *Contra* Walker, p. 373. "In der That, derselbe Andrang von Besuchern, der
den Saal bis auf den letzten Platz füllte, dieselbe Spannung von und
Theilnahme während des Concerts, dieselbe freudige Begrüßung des
Künstlers beim Erscheinen, derselbe Enthusiasmus nach denjenigen
seiner Kunstleistungen die für die Mehrzahl eine fesselnde Kraft haben"
[VZ No. 8 (10.1.1843)].

[193] "Das es Künstler, wie z. B. Thalberg, geben mag, die in ihrem Vortrage
mehr zum Herzen sprechen, mehr auf das Gefühl wirken, das wollen wir
nicht bestreiten; daß Dr. Liszt aber in dieser eminenten, ja fast
unglaublichen Fertigkeit . . . das halten wir für unbestreitbar" [FadOT
No. 9 (21.1.1843), p. 38].

other, much longer review—and one that affirms Liszt's status
as an artist as well as a dexterous virtuoso—appeared in
Frankfurt's *Patriotisches Wochenblatt* a few days later.[194] The
first page of the *Wochenblatt* review is reproduced at the beginning of Chapter II as Plate 1.

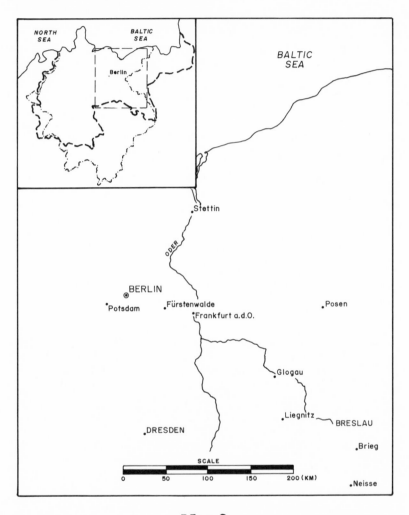

Map 2

Prussia and Silesia: Cities and Towns where Liszt Performed (1843)

[194] See FadOWB No. 7 (25.1.1843), pp. 77-79. This review will be reprinted
complete in Saffle, "Liszt und die Deutschen, 1840-1845."

Nevertheless, these successes paled into insignificance compared with Liszt's triumphs in Silesia. Map 2 above identifies the cities and towns where he played during his 1843 winter tour. Leaving Frankfurt as soon as his concert was over, Liszt reached Breslau, the Silesian capital, early the following morning.[195] There, at least in some of the publications that described his enormous successes in and around Breslau, "Lisztomania" became virtual idolatry. Articles about him flooded local papers, the students turned out to honor him with a torch-lit procession, and his success was in every way enormous.[196] Liszt came to be regarded by some of his followers not only as the greatest of virtuosos, but also as a veritable saint.[197]

In all, Liszt gave twelve public concerts in Breslau, one more than he presented at Berlin's Singakademie in 1842. Two of these concerts were presented in the music hall of the local university: the first on 21 January (175), and the second three days later (176). Three others were held in the Aula (or great hall) of the Leopoldina Gymnasium: the first on 26 January (177), the second on 29 January (179), and the third—his farewell concert—on 7 March (204). Still another took place in the hall of the "King of Hungary" Hotel on 27 January (178). Most of his performances, however, were presented in the city's Theater: on 31 January (180), 2 February (182), 4 February (184), 7 February (188), and 9 February (190). At several of his Theater concerts he played concertos with orchestra, and on two occasions—those of 1 February (181) and 7 March—he also appeared as a conductor. The more significant of these events was his performance of Mozart's *Magic Flute*, his first appearance as a full-fledged opera director. Finally, on 6 February he

---

[195] According to Schreiber, p. 8; and to BrZ No. 19 (23.1.1843), p. 133.

[196] Not according to *Signale*, however, which mocked the student procession as the work of a handful of disaffected young men out to stir up a rumpus. See SmW 1 (1843), p. 51.

[197] A few reports of Liszt's Breslau successes were a little less enthusiastic, however. One commentator observed that the pianist "erregte das allgemeinste, durch alle Classen der Gesellschaft gehende Interesse, aber nicht jene Sorte des Berliner Enthusiasmus [von 1842]" [AmZ 45 (1843), col. 299]. A reporter for *Signale*, on the other hand, claimed that the Breslauers were as "crazy" (närrlich) over Liszt as the Berliners had been the year before [SmW 1 (1843), p. 51].

made an excursion to nearby Liegnitz, where he presented a piano recital (187).

Virtually without exception the people and press of Breslau raved about Liszt as man *and* as virtuoso. After his concert of 24 January, for example, the *Breslauer Zeitung* applauded his poetic, tuneful, tender, and graceful interpretation of Beethoven's Sonata in A-flat Major, Op. 26—a beautiful composition of "the great Master's" which, according to the *Zeitung* critic, only Liszt could bring adequately to life.[198] Papers in nearby towns also praised his artistry to the skies. The *Oberschlesischer Bürgerfreund* reported that Liszt was received in Neisse on 9 March (205) by a music-loving, thankful, and satisfied audience that demonstrated through its applause a high level of respect for his artistry.[199] Large audiences were also on hand for his performances in Posen.[200] Indeed, his success there was so pronounced that periodicals all over Europe commented on it, and the *Augsburger allgemeine Zeitung* reported that local music-lovers had virtually deified him and crowned him with a laurel wreath.[201] In point of fact, Liszt earned only 1,000 thalers in Posen—far less than he had made in Berlin, but nevertheless a sum that caused the *Zeitung* to marvel over his financial success and his predecessors' failures.[202] And even the *Breslauer Figaro*—which, virtually alone at that time, seems to have held less extreme opinions about him—proclaimed him a tyrant of the piano who tri-

---

[198] "Welch eine Poesie! welch ein Gesang! welch eine Zartheit und Grazie! In solchem Glanze kann diese schöne Composition des hohen Meisters nur durch Liszt ins Leben treten" [BrZ No. 23 (27.1.1843), p. 162].

[199] "Herr Liszt hat hier ein musikliebendes, dankbares, aber auch ein sehr vernünftiges Publikum vorgefunden, das mit seinen Beifallsbezeugungen . . . einen um so höhern Werth erhalten" [ObBr No. 22 (18.3.1843), p. 88]. Additional excerpts from this review may be found in Appendix D, quotation 13.

[200] According to a Posen journalist. See Donath, "Franz Liszt und Polen," p. 55.

[201] "Mit dem berühmten Claviervirtuosen Liszt wird [in Posen] eben solche Abgötterei getrieben wie anderswo; man hat ihn vielfach angesungen und im Theater sogar feierlich mit einem Lorberkranze gekrönt" [AuZ (1843), p. 543]. Around the same time Liszt was also made Honorary Director of the Breslau Musical Union. See D-WRgs Liszt Überformate 124.

[202] "Thausend Thaler in einer einzigen Stunde verdient! Mozart kam zu *Fuß* nach Berlin!" [AuZ (1843), p. 543].

umphed over every difficulty his instrument might place in his way.[203]

In addition to his performances and personality, the press in Silesia marvelled over Liszt's large repertory. Besides his standbys—the *Grand Galop chromatique,* the *Ständchen, Ave Maria,* and *Erlkönig* transcriptions, the fantasies on *Robert, Norma, Don Giovanni, Lucia di Lammermoor,* and so on—he played in Breslau his arrangement of the "Serenade" and "Orgy" from Rossini's *Soirées musicales,* his fantasy on Pacini's *Niobe* (no longer part of his regular repertory), Beethoven's "Moonlight" sonata, the solo piano part of that composer's Concerto in c minor, and the first movement of his "Emperor" concerto as well as his transcription of Schubert's *Mélodies hongroises,* his own *Marche hongroise,* and one of his own "Paganini Etudes."[204] On 26 January Liszt also conducted his *Rheinweinlied* for men's chorus; on 27 January he accompanied Pantaleoni in three arias from operas by Pacini, Mercadante, and Meyerbeer; and on 7 March he led the orchestra of the Breslau Theater in performances of Beethoven's *Weihe des Hauses* overture and Weber's *Jubel-Overture.*

Nor did Liszt linger without interruption in Breslau during February-March 1843. He returned to Berlin to perform twice as pianist and conductor: the first time on 12 February (191), and the second four days later, on 16 February (193). Between those two events he sandwiched a second appearance at the city Theater of nearby Liegnitz (192); and five days later, on 18 February, he performed privately at the Potsdam Casino (194). Then, leaving the Berlin area, he travelled by train to Fürstenwalde, where he presented a benefit recital on behalf of the local poor (195). On his way back to Breslau, he gave four concerts in Posen (196-199), three concerts in Glogau (200-202), and a third concert in Liegnitz (203). Finally, he performed in Brieg (189) and, following his Breslau farewell—as we have

---

[203] "Er ist der *Tyrann* des Pianoforto's [sic], er *vernichtet,* was ihm Widerstand leistet, er überwindet spielend alle Schwierigkeiten seines Instrumentes" [*Breslauer Figaro,* p. 244]. The clipping from which this quotation was taken is preserved in D-WRgs Liszt Kasten 240.

[204] See BrPSZ No. 36 (11.2.1843), p. 253, for a complete list of Liszt's Breslau keyboard repertory prior to mid-February 1843. A somewhat less complete list, based only on his concerts prior to 6 February, appears in the end of Schreiber's pamphlet.

seen—he visited Neisse and gave a matinée recital there on 9
March. In all he appeared on more than twenty-five programs
in or near Silesia, not counting his February performances in
Berlin and Potsdam. Only in 1842 in Berlin did he perform
more often in a restricted geographical area.

It is the anecdotes about Liszt, though—especially about
the private performances he gave in Breslau for poor and dis-
advantaged people, and the language used to describe
them—that helps us understand how sincerely he was
venerated during his Silesian sojourn. On 3 February, for instance, he played three virtuoso works for Breslau
schoolchildren at a private matinée presented in the local
Catholic school (183). In what, in effect, is a Liszt hagiography,
Schreiber describes that matinée in terms of the "limitless joy"
that streamed from the eyes of the blessed pianist's youthful
listeners, and the shouts of praise with which they rewarded
their idol for the "unforgettably lofty honor" his presence conferred upon them.[205] And on at least two other occasions Liszt
also rewarded faithful but improverished admirers with private
performances. First, he played for a little boy who, himself a
budding pianist, had been presented to Liszt by the boy's parents (185). Second, he performed at his hotel for a poor cantor
who, visiting the big city with scarcely a penny in his pockets,
found himself unable to obtain a ticket to one of his idol's public
recitals (186).[206]

The obverse of these beatific occasions was a debacle that
seems to have taken place on 7 March in nearby Hirschberg.
A crowd of several hundred people heard that Liszt would be
arriving to perform there and rushed to the railway station,
where they waited for several hours until all of the scheduled
trains had arrived and they realized with chagrin that the
guest of honor had not been not on any of them. The farcical
tone of the article that describes this fiasco suggests, however,
that it may have been written in a spirit of carnival fun.[207] We

---

[205] "Die jugendlichen Gemüther, Verehrer und Anhänger der Kunst waren
tief ergriffen, die unbegrenzte Freude strahlte aus ihren beredten Augen
und lauter Dank für diese unvergeßlich hohe Ehre strömte dem
Scheidenden nach" [Schreiber, p. 11].

[206] The complete anecdote appears in Appendix D, quotation 12.

[207] See BrPSZ No. 36 (11.2.1843), p. 252. Liszt may also have played or

saw in Chapter II, however, that Liszt cancelled a concert in Zittau early in 1844, and we saw above that he cancelled one in Göttingen in November 1841. It is perfectly possible that he planned to perform in Hirschberg, only to change his mind at the last minute.

Liszt's 1843 performances in Prussia, Posen, and Silesia were tremendous critical and financial successes. Like those of 1842 Berlin, they call to mind the "Liszt legend": that the artist was far more saint than sinner.[208] What Liszt himself thought of the adulation heaped upon him in Breslau and surrounding towns has not come down to us. What we do know is that he left Neisse shortly after his concert on 9 March 1843 and, travelling by way of Cracow and Warsaw, proceeded to Russia to undertake a second, less successful tour of that forbidding country.

Hamburg: 26 June 1843

Returning from Russia three months later, Liszt stopped in Hamburg and performed as a guest of that city's music festival (206). For once even *Der Freischütz* resisted the temptation to take potshots at him and his partner Ciabatta. Instead, that periodical described their program—the "Don Juan" and *Somnambula* fantasies, a Chopin etude, Wallweiler's *Marche héroïque*, and two arias from operas by Mercadante—in relatively straightforward terms. The "Don Juan" fantasy, for example, wrung from the *Freischütz* critic what passed for unqualified praise.[209] The *Allgemeine musikalische Zeitung* also praised his fantasy but complained that Ciabatta didn't make

---

planned to play in nearby Teschen. See Ramann II, p. 86n.

Liszt himself seems to have enjoyed Carnival events, and he may have composed some carnival music. In March 1843 the *Vossische Zeitung* announced in an advertisement for a "Bal paré, masqué, et travesti" that Liszt had composed for that occasion a "Polonaise-Galop" for chorus on themes from three of Meyerbeer's operas, including *Les Huguenots*. See VZ No. 44 (21.2.1843). And *Signale* proclaimed a year later that "Liszt will die Weimaraner carnavalisiren" [SmW 2 (1844), p. 29].

208 The "Liszt legend" was defined by Ernest Newman, only to be attacked with more enthusiasm than accuracy. See Newman, *The Man Liszt* (London 1934), esp. pp. 2ff.

209 "Die Ausführung der [Don Juan] Fantasie war ganz besonders meisterhaft und auch die Composition nicht ohne glückliche Momente" [HFrs No. 26 (1.7.1843), p. 208].

a very good impression on his audience.[210] Soon afterwards
Liszt left for the Rhineland, where he spent part of the summer
in or around Nonnenwerth with the Comtesse d'Agoult.

Solingen, Bonn, Dortmund, Cologne, and Iserlohn: August-September 1843

In August and September 1843 Liszt made excursions
from Nonnenwerth to several nearby towns, where he appeared
publically and privately on four little-reported occasions. The
first of these, a matinée concert at the Solingen Casino, took
place on 11 August (207). Net proceeds of 427 thalers were
given to the local Masonic lodge and to other worthy causes.[211]
Interestingly enough, Liszt visited Solingen two more times,
but he apparently never performed there again. A week later,
however, he visited Bonn and played privately for Leopold
Kaufmann in the latter's home (208). In Bonn Liszt also heard
a student ensemble sing and enjoyed their performance so
much that he introduced them to the Comtesse.

On 24 August 1843 the city Gymnasium of Dortmund celebrated its tricentenary anniversary. Liszt again left
Nonnenwerth, this time at the invitation of Gymnasium officials, to present a benefit concert in Dortmund on behalf of the
school and its history (209). Arriving at the last minute, he was
just in time to attend a pre-concert banquet and, perhaps, other
anniversary events. His concert, presented to an enthusiastic
crowd at the local Casino, was followed by an anniversary ball.
Among Liszt's listeners in the Casino was a young boy named
Wilhelm Lübke, who recalled decades later that he had never
heard anything like the artistic individuality and power of his
idol's Dortmund performance, and that he never heard its like
again.[212]

---

210 "Von [Liszts] Vorträgen war die Ausführung seiner Don Juan-Fantasie
ganz ausgezeichnet und gehört diese zu seinen gelungensten
Leistungen. . . . Aber [Ciabatta], obgleich Liszt selbst am Piano
begleitete, keinen günstigen Eindruck hervorbringen [konnte]" [AmZ 45
(1843), col. 617].

211 Autexier, pp. 120-121, documents the division of Liszt's contributions as
well as those of one Samuel Küll, who gave 60 thalers of his own. The total
sum donated by Liszt was reported in SolKIB No. 69 (26.8.1843).

212 "Von einer solchen Beseelung des Instrumentes, von einer solchen Macht

On 12 September Liszt took part in a chamber-music concert at the Saal des Neuen Kuhberg in Cologne (210). On this occasion he performed a "Duo" for two pianos by Pixis, sharing the platform with Mortier de Fontaine. Finally, on 23 September he gave a concert at the "Trois Globes" Masonic Lodge in Iserlohn (211). Although the *Iserlohner Wochenblatt* ignored this event, the much more influential *Allgemeine Preußische Staats-Zeitung* described the affair (a benefit on behalf of German high-schools) in some detail. The *Staats-Zeitung* even reprinted a short speech Liszt gave after the concert was over, reminding his listeners that people without a spiritual life of their own were as good as dead.[213]

From Frankfurt to Mannheim: October-December 1843

Liszt's tour of central and southern Germany in the autumn of 1843 was in many ways the culmination of his German career. Within some eleven or twelve weeks he gave at least thirty-three public and private performances and earned almost unanimous praise from the press as well as a number of awards and decorations and a tremendous amount of money. The outright furor that accompanied his Berlin triumphs of early 1842, however, seems to have been absent during fall 1843. Liszt, then, is perhaps better represented as a successful—rather than notorious—concert artist by the reviews and accolades he earned in Munich, Augsburg and Stuttgart than by those of his other German concert tours.

He began his tour with a visit to Frankfurt a.M., where he played—and even sang!—at a private matinée hosted on 4 October 1843 by his friend and fellow Freemason Wilhelm Speyer (212). Liszt also played privately in or around Frankfurt on one other occasion (213). The Speyer matinée was widely reported, but the real beginning of Liszt's tour took place three days later when he performed publically with enormous success

---

der künstlerischen Individualität hatte ich bis dahin keine Ahnung gehabt. Ich habe auch später nie wieder einen ähnlichen Eindruck empfangen" [Wilhelm Lübke, *Lebenserinnerungen* (Berlin 1893), pp. 74-75].

213 "Ohne Seele und Geist kein Volk, nur todte Masse" [APSZ No. 102 (10.10.1842), p. 629]. The *Staats-Zeitung* mistakenly gives the date of Liszt's Iserlohn concert as 24 September.

at Würzburg's city Theater (214). The *Würzburger Abendblatt* reported the following morning that Liszt was the "man of the hour," and that he was greeted with thunderous applause at the completion of each number he played.[214]

A similar triumph greeted him in Nuremberg, where he presented two matinée performances: the first on 11 October (215), and the second two days later (216). On the former occasion he played the same program he had presented in Würzburg: his transcription of the overture to *Guillaume Tell*, the *Lucia* "Andante finale," his own transcriptions of Schubert's *Ständchen* and *Erlkönig*, and his *Galop chromatique*. (In Nuremberg he may also have played his *Ungarischer Sturmmarsch* as an encore.) A charming review in the local *Kurier* praised him and his playing in the strongest possible terms: no one else's performances, not even Thalberg's, had thrilled the *Kurier* critic as much as had Liszt's. Furthermore, the same review maintained that one only had to study his scores to experience the depth of his feelings and the intellectual appeal of his artistic integrity.[215] The same day the *Kurier* also published a poem in his honor, and two days later the paper announced with delight that he had received a laurel wreath from the mayor, Dr. Binder, after his second matinée.[216] Finally, as we saw in Chapter II, Liszt was also admitted to Nuremberg's Albrecht Dürer Society and made an honorary member of the local Mozart Society.

After spending several pleasant days in Nuremberg—a city, we saw in Chapter I, that he wrote about with enthusiasm to d'Agoult—Liszt proceeded via coach to Munich, where he gave four public concerts and played privately on at least two

---

214 "Liszt, der Mann des Tages, hat . . . auch hier durch seine außerordentliche Kunstleistung die lebhafteste Sensation erregt. . . . Der rauschendste Beifall begleitete alle Piecen des Concertgebers" [WürzAb No. 279 (8.10.1843)].

215 "Man studire nur einmal die großartigen Tonschöpfungen Liszt's, und man wird finden, daß in diesen Kompositionen . . . so viel Fülle und intensive Wärmekraft für das Gemüth, als richtig berechnete Kunstgerechtigkeit für den Verstand enthalten sind" [NürnK No. 286 (13.10.1843)].

216 The poem published in the *Kurier* was only one of several printed up in hundreds of copies for Liszt's performances and thrown at his feet, a kind of testimonial he also received from enthusiastic Munich music-lovers. The Nuremberg poems were also printed in NürnK Nos. 286 (13.10.1843) and 288 (15.10.1843).

occasions, probably at his hotel. His first Munich recital took place on the evening of 18 October at the Odéon (217) and, alone of all his late 1843 performances, began inauspiciously. Although local music fans had waited impatiently for the event to begin, the hall was not sold out, and the audience remained quiet as Liszt walked to the piano and began the overture to Rossini's *Tell*. Only then did his listeners realize the power of his piano-playing which, as a critic for the *Bayerische Landbote* put it, created the effect of an entire orchestra.[217] The rest of the program, the same one he was to present on his first recitals in Augsburg and Stuttgart, was applauded with enthusiasm. The King and Queen of Bavaria were especially pleased and received him after his performance was over. A small party followed and, according to Maxe von Arnim, Liszt played privately several times during the days that followed (219-220).[218]

We have seen that Liszt visited Augsburg as a boy and gave two recitals there: the first on 30 October 1823, the second on 8 October of the same year. The *Augsburger Tagblatt* reintroduced him to local audiences with a front-page reminiscence of those performances that was also a review of his triumphal return,[219] presented on 19 October in the hall of the Hotel Goldenen Traube (218). Almost as soon as this concert was over, though, he returned to Munich to present a second recital at the Odéon on 21 October (221). On this occasion he played a Bach fugue (probably the Fugue in e-flat minor from Book I of the *Wohltempirirte Clavier*) and the first movement of Beethoven's "Pathétique" sonata. His performance of the former number was admired by critics, but the latter number itself left some of his listeners cold.[220] The rest of his program, however, was an unqualified success: in addition to a Chopin

---

[217] "Plötzlich verliert er sich in rauschenden Accorden und alsbald erheben sich da und dort Einzelne, dann Gruppen, zuletzt das halbe Publikum, um sich mit dem Auge die Ueberzeugung zu verschaffen, daß wirklich nur ein Meister an seinem Instrumente sitze und *allein* dieses zu einem ganzen Orchester mache!" [MLb No. 294 (21.10.1843), p. 1212].

[218] See Williams, p. 202.

[219] See "Dr. Franz Liszt," AuTb No. 289 (21.10.1843).

[220] "Das Beethoven'sche Sonate ließ die Kunstkenner ziemlich kalt . . . [aber Liszt] spielte . . . die Bach'sche Fuge ganz im Geiste der Komposition" [MTb No. 294 (24.10.1843), p. 1413]. Similar words, evidently written by the same critic, also appear in Appendix D, quotation 14.

mazurka, he played his *Somnambula* fantasy, the "Polonaise" from *I Puritani*, and Weber's *Aufforderung*. He may well have been inspired to play especially well by the presence of the Bavarian royal family in the audience.

Liszt's third Munich concert took place four days later at the Hof- und Nationaltheater (222). Appearing with orchestra, he took part in an ensemble performance of Weber's *Konzertstück* twice: once at the beginning of the evening, and again as an encore. He also seems to have played *Hexameron* as arranged for piano and orchestra, and he certainly played his *Réminiscences de Don Juan*. Advertised as a benefit on behalf of a local home for the blind, this concert was a great success: 1,500 florins were raised for that institution, and a kind of endowment, established permanently in Liszt's name, was announced in the musical press.[221] The *Münchener Morgenblatt* observed that the "celebrated artist" received from a packed house the same triumphal reception that had already greeted him everywhere else in Europe.[222] In a longer, more comprehensive account of his Munich successes to date, the *Bayerische Landbote* wrote in part:

> A few words in general about his appearance and achievements here: Liszt has come, has played, and has conquered. . . . His *Grand Galop chromatique*, his "Andante finale" from *Lucia*, his Schubert song transcriptions, and above all other numbers his overture to *Guillaume Tell* and his reminiscences of *Don Giovanni*, have raised the applause he received to an utterly astonishing level because of the individuality of his playing and the incomparableness of his interpretive artistry. . . . His triumph in this, his third concert here [i.e., his concert of 25 October] has if anything been even greater, and it has become evident why he has been called the "Supreme Master of the Piano."[223]

---

221 See AmZ 46 (1844), col. 198. During 1843 and 1844 more and more of Liszt's activities were publicized widely, even internationally. This may have been due to Belloni's skill as a factotum; many of these notices are identical and must have come from the same "source."

222 "Der berühmte Künstler hat bei gedrängt vollem Hause einen jener glänzenden Triumphe gefeiert, die ihn durch ganz Europa begleiten" [MMb No. 86 (28.10.1843)].

223 Quoted from MLb No. 303 (30.10.1843), p. 1251. See also Appendix D, quotation 14.

On 28 October a banquet was held in his honor, and the *Münchener Morgenblatt* announced among its leading news items that he had received an invitation to return to Copenhagen and perform again for the royal Danish family.[224]

At his fourth and final Munich concert (223), a benefit on behalf of German civilians trapped by political uprisings in Greece, Liszt played Beethoven's "Emperor" and his own fantasy on *La Somnambula*, and he improvised a second fantasy on several tunes submitted by his listeners: melodies from Mozart's *Zauberflöte* as well as from *Norma* and *Euryanthe*. Another 1,200 florins were raised for charity, and the *Tagblatt* reported that "storm of jubilation" which broke out during the improvised fantasy—as well as after the other numbers—simply wouldn't end.[225] Fräulein Zehetmayer and Herr Piatti, his accomplices on this occasion, also distinguished themselves in (respectively) a concerto for 'cello and orchestra and an operatic aria. On his 25 October program, Liszt appeared with Fräulein Heßneker, Fräulein Rettich, and Herr Pellegrini, who sang or played solos of their own.

Leaving Munich the morning after his 30 October concert, Liszt travelled by train to Augsburg to give two more concerts: the first on 1 November (224), and the second—a benefit for poor and sick people in the immediate area—on 4 November (225). Little information survives about these events, although the *Augsburger Tagblatt* reported that tempestuous applause followed every number on 1 November, and that he received two curtain calls—evidently a sign of unusual enthusiasm.[226] And Augsburg's *Zeitung* reported of the same event that the magic of his playing would have instantly transformed even a sombre mood into one of good cheer.[227]

---

[224] See MMb No. 87 (1.11.1843), p. 345.

[225] "Er waren Jubelstürme, die ihn unterbrachen und nach jeder Nummer nicht enden wollten" [MTb No. 303 (2.11.1843), p. 1449].

[226] "Wir würden doch nur ein schwaches Bilt [sic] entwerfen, wollten wir den Beifallssturm mit Worten malen, welcher dem Vortrage Liszt nach jeder Piece folgte; der gefeierte Virtuose wurde jedesmal gerufen und am Schlusse sogar zwei Mal, eine Seltenheit, die auch von Rechtswegen nur den Koryphäen der Kunst, wie Liszt, gebührt" [AuTb No. 302 (3.11.1843), pp. 1295-1296].

[227] "[Liszt hat] mit dem Zauber seines Spiels auch das düsterste Gemüth auf Augenblicke erheitert" [AuZ (1843), p. 2452].

Travelling overland to Stuttgart, Liszt arrived during the evening of 5 November and settled into the Hotel Marquardt. There he was serenaded by a local choral ensemble—probably the "Gesellschaft des Glocke," which made him an honorary member five days later.[228] Soon after his arrival he was also invited to perform at court for the King of Württemberg (226), and on 7 November he presented a full-length recital at the Redoutensaal (227). The *Schwäbische Merkur* raved about his performance, especially about his manly strength as an artist and about his ability to play everything with genuine musical understanding and sincere emotion.[229] His listeners were just as enthusiastic, and they cheered each of his other public Stuttgart appearances: on 12 November (230), 14 November (231), 16 November (233), and 21 November (236). The 12 November matinée concert, presented at the hall of the local citizens's society, raised 645 gulden for the local high-school. The 21 November concert, officially a "farewell," was followed by a banquet at his hotel and, as guest of honor, he was awarded the Order of the King of Württemberg.[230] At several of his Stuttgart concerts Liszt performed alone, but on 16 November he shared the platform with Pantaleoni, and with Wilhelm Krueger he performed a piano four-hand fantasy on themes from Meyerbeer's *Huguenots*. Liszt also played privately in Stuttgart on at least one occasion: a matinée presented prior to his 12 November concert (229).

Although based in Stuttgart, Liszt did not linger there. On 11 November he visited nearby Tübingen, where he gave a recital (228). Several days later he travelled to Heilbronn, where he presented the same program he had already given in Munich and several other cities (232). On 17 November he stopped in Ludwigsburg, where he played a somewhat different

---

228 See D-WRgs Liszt Überformate 166.

229 "[Liszt hat] den kräftigen männlichen Charakter des Meisters . . . [Er] spielte alles mit einem in die Ideen der Musik eingehenden Verstand, mit dem tiefen Gefühle, wie es die verschiedenen reichen Stimmungen verlangen" [SSM (1843), pp. 1206 and 1214]. The present author would like to thank the officials and librarian of the *Stuttgarter Zeitung* for this material.

230 See D-WRgs Liszt Kasten 132. The diploma itself is dated that very evening.

program at the hall of the Waldhorn Hotel (234).[231] Finally, the following day he travelled on to Hechingen, where his performance (235) evidently was so successful that the Prince of Hohenzollern-Hechingen elevated him to the rank of "Hofrat" and soon thereafter conferred upon him the so-called "Haus-Orden," a decoration comparable in prestige to the Order of the White Falcon Liszt had previously received from the Grand-Duke of Weimar.[232] Most of Liszt's concerts outside Stuttgart during mid-November 1843 went largely unreported in the local press, but the *Ludwigsburger Wochenblatt* ran a comparatively lengthy review which compared him to Orpheus and his playing to the power of that legendary artist of ancient Greece.[233] And the *Verordnungs- und Intelligentz-Blatt* of Hechingen declared that "Liszt is not merely one of the greatest living virtuosos; he is also one of the most educated, talented, spirited, and noble of men."[234]

After leaving Stuttgart, Liszt spent several days sailing the Danube with the Prince of Hohenzollern-Hechingen and his retinue. Stopping in Donaueschingen sometime between 23 and 27 November, the pianist played his transcription of Schubert's *Ave Maria* and other numbers privately for local aristocrats (238-239) and—as we saw in Chapter II—may have conducted at a public concert presented a few days earlier (237). His visit with the Prince completed, Liszt proceeded quickly to Karlsruhe, probably by train, and gave a concert in the hall of the town Museum on 27 November (240). The following day he travelled to Heidelberg, where he presented a public recital in that town's museum on 28 November (241), then played at a party held at the home of Karl Gustav Leonhard (242). At his Karlsruhe and Heidelberg concerts Liszt

---

[231] A detailed account of this event appears in Hans Krämer, "Ein denkwürdiges Konzert in Ludwigsburg," *Ludwigsburger Geschichtsblätter* 40 (1987), pp. 191-196.

[232] Liszt, however, only received the decoration in question "third class." See EuEut 4 (1844), p. 80. The diploma is preserved in D-WRgs Liszt Kasten 124.

[233] "Wir hätten in Liszt gerne den Orpheus gehört . . . [und] wir hätten gerne die Macht der Töne im Gemüth erfahren" [LudWb No. 139 (21.11.1843)].

[234] "Liszt ist unbedingt nicht nur einer der größten lebenden Virtuosen, sondern auch einer der gebildetsten, talent- und geistvollsten, edelsten Menschen!" [VIb No. 48 (2.12.1843), p. 322].

performed essentially the same program: the *Tell* overture transcription, the *Lucia* "Andante finale," the *Réminiscences de Don Juan*, a Chopin mazurka, transcriptions of Schubert songs, and Weber's *Aufforderung zum Tanz*.

Liszt completed his tour of southern Germany with two additional concerts in Karlsruhe and two in nearby Mannheim. He also played privately for Karlsruhe nobility on 29 November (243). The public Karlsruhe concerts, presented on 1 December (244) and 4 December (246), won praise from local journalists, as did the Mannheim concerts of 3 December (245) and 6 December (247). On these occasions Liszt varied his repertory somewhat, performing his transcription of Schubert's *Lob der Thränen* and his fantasy on Meyerbeer's *Robert le diable* (respectively) on his first and second Mannheim recitals. The *Mannheimer Journal* announced that he received 600 gulden for his 27 November Karlsruhe concert, 559 gulden for his 1 December concert, and a special gift of 40 Louis d'or for his private performance on 29 November. In Karlsruhe he also donated 470 gulden to a local charitable institution.[235] Then, after a brief visit to Frankfurt, where he may have fallen ill,[236] he returned to Paris before beginning his first season as a "German" music director.

In and Around Weimar: December 1843 — February 1844

Most accounts of his life imply that Liszt assumed the duties of Weimar's Kapellmeister in 1848, only after he had abandoned the concert stage and the career of a travelling virtuoso for a life devoted to composing large-scale works like the Sonata in b minor and the first twelve symphonic poems. In fact, he served a full season as "Kapellmeister" in 1844. During January and February of that year he presented four major public concerts in Weimar, played privately several times for the ducal family (256-259), and also performed in several nearby towns. Only after his court duties were done did he travel to Dresden, Dessau, Magdeburg, and other cities to complete yet another cross-country tour.

---

[235] See MnJ No. 336 (9.12.1843), p. 1342.

[236] According to an article in the *Neue Zeitschrift*. See NZfM 19 (1843), p. 208 [issue dated 28.12.1843].

Liszt arrived in Weimar shortly before Christmas 1843 and spent several weeks preparing for his first official concert there as conductor and keyboard virtuoso. Presented on 7 January 1844 (248), this performance involved his conducting Beethoven's Fifth Symphony and playing the solo part in Hummel's Concerto in b minor. (Other numbers on the same program were conducted by Hyppolyte Chélard, an artist at the Weimar court and "the Frenchman" who ridiculed Liszt at the banquet that brought the 1845 Beethoven Festival to an acrimonious close.) At the end of the evening and by popular acclaim he also improvised a fantasy on the "La ci darem la mano" theme from Mozart's *Don Giovanni*.

Three more Weimar concerts followed: the first on 21 January (250), the second on 4 February (252), and the third on 18 February (260). At the 21 January concert Liszt conducted Beethoven's "Eroica" symphony and the incidental music for *Egmont* (Emil Genast was the reader); on 4 February he conducted Weber's *Jubel-Overture* and Beethoven's Seventh Symphony, and he led the orchestra while Wilhelm Krueger performed the solo part of Beethoven's C-minor concerto; and on 18 February Liszt conducted at least one movement from Schubert's C-Major Symphony as well as Berlioz's *King Lear* overture.[237] Nor did Liszt neglect the piano: on 21 January he played the solo part in Weber's *Konzertstück*; on 4 February he played a "Tarantelle," a "Mazurka," and a "Polonaise"—the latter probably from *I Puritani*; and on 18 February he accompanied Franz Carl Götze in *Angiolin dal biondo crin* and other vocal numbers and played the *Hexameron* variations, probably in their original solo form. Finally, with Carl Stör, Weimar's most celebrated violinist, Liszt performed a fantasy by Thalberg on themes from *Les Huguenots*.

As usual, Weimar's newspaper did not acknowledge Liszt's local success, but several magazines published fulsome and highly flattering review articles. Among these, the *Allgemeine musikalische Zeitung* showed greater enthusiasm, especially for his future as a conductor:

---

237 According to AmZ 46 (1844), col. 293, Liszt also conducted other works, including overtures by Lobe and Lambert. Other sources do not mention these last works, but some biographers do. See, for instance, Ramann II, pp. 223-224.

We had often heard and read that our Liszt, so highly celebrated as a piano virtuoso, was pretty poor as a conductor—or,
to put it another way, nothing much as a captain of his troops.
Yet in his performance of [Beethoven's] C-minor Symphony,
everything was fine except the second movement, which was
played too quickly. . . . If Herr Liszt can learn to combine calm
and secure control with patience and endurance in works like
this (we would especially like to hear under his direction
Beethoven's Ninth Symphony, a work never yet performed in
Weimar), we would be delighted to listen to him lead our local
musical forces more often.

Julius Kapp, the critic who wrote this passage,[238] also affirmed
that Liszt's Weimar concerts were warmly received and the
artist himself enthusiastically applauded, despite rumors of
empty halls, unfriendly audiences, and a less than honorable
reception as a conductor.[239] Furthermore, according to Kapp,
Liszt the conductor seemed to embody "the very spirit of music
itself."[240] No wonder the *Wiener allgemeine Musik-Zeitung* announced that he had completed his duties as Kapellmeister to
the complete satisfaction of all concerned.[241]

Using Weimar as a base of operations, Liszt travelled on
several occasions to nearby towns and gave concerts with or
without the assistance of other musicians. Unfortunately, most
of these events were virtually ignored by the press. On 18
January, for example, he and Herr Prüm, a Weimar 'cellist,
presented a recital at the Court Theater in Gotha (249). The
Weimarische Zeitung unbent enough to acknowledge the event,
but two subsequent public concerts—the first given at
Rudolstadt on 27 January (251), the second at Jena on 5 February (254)—remain obscure; only a few words survive about
Jena and little more than a program about Rudolstadt. Liszt
also played privately in Jena (253), improvising music to scenes
fr .n Goethe's *Faust* during a reading of that work, given by

---

[238] Not to be confused with the Julius Kapp whose biography of Liszt and
other studies are cited above.

[239] See Appendix D, quotation 15.

[240] "Liszt ist die verkörperte Musikseele" [quoted in Ramann II, p. 225; and
Kapp, p. 196].

[241] "(Liszt) [sic] hat seine Function als Capellmeister in Weimar mit eben
solchem Nachdruck als Erfolg angetreten" [WaMZ No. 28 (5.3.1844), p.
112]. See also WaMZ No. 23 (22.2.1844), p. 92.

his acquaintance Wolff at the personal request of Carl Alexander of Weimar and Russia's Prince Radziwil.[242] In Rudolstadt Liszt and Pantaleoni performed in the hall of the Hotel zum Ritter and presented, among other numbers, "I tuoi frequenti palpiti" from *Niobe* and Schubert's *Erlkönig*, the latter in piano transcription. No report describes how the artists were received, although we know that the proceeds went to Pantaleoni. But a poem, possibly intended to be sung to the tune of the Austrian (i.e., "Greater German") national anthem, appeared in a local newspaper and was devoted exclusively to Liszt:

> God preserve the art of Liszt!
> For years to come it shall be miss'd,
> That art the world has made its own;
> Thanks, Liszt, for coming to our home!
>
> Welcome to our valley dear
> Although it be no Belvedere;
> We'll listen to the best you offer
> And long we'll treasure what you proffer.
>
> Welcome where, beneath one's nose,
> The Danube river stately flows,
> We welcome you within our midst:
> God preserve the art of Liszt![243]

On 9 February Liszt travelled to Dresden to hear Wagner's *Rienzi* for the first time.[244] Then, on 17 February, he and members of the Weimar court orchestra presented an ambitious concert in Erfurt's Theater (255). The program included the overture to Beethoven's *Fidelio*, Weber's *Konzertstück* played by Liszt (and probably accompanied by the assembled orchestra), several numbers by Stör, Genast, Götze, and other artists, Liszt's own *Réminiscences de Norma*, and—again by Liszt—an improvised fantasy that brought the evening to a

---

[242] See Ramann II, p. 226.

[243] Freely translated into doggerel (and with attention to rhyme as well as to "reason") by the present author. The original German-language text appears in Peter Gülke, "Musik und Musiker in Rudolstadt," *Rudolstadter Heimathefte* 9 (1968), pp. 53-54. NB: Rudolstadt does not lie on the Danube; this bit of poetic license belongs to the author of the poem in question, not to its translator.

[244] See Newman I, p. 455.

close. A series of expensive advertisements for this concert appeared in the *Erfurter Zeitung*, advertisements that praised the court's decision to dispatch so rich a cultural delegation to a nearby town. And Augsburg's *Zeitung*, describing his departure from the Weimar area, expressed the hope that Liszt might inspire the young Grand-Duke Carl Alexander to renew the cultural tradition of the area, and might even attract youthful talent to Weimar herself.[245] Things, of course, did not work out uniformly well for Liszt in Weimar during the following decade, but his presence and activities there, including his productions of Wagner's *Tannhäuser* and *Lohengrin*, helped restore Weimar's reputation as a capital of German culture.[246]

From Dresden to Hannover: February-March 1844

On 19 February 1844, Liszt travelled to Dresden, where he lodged at the Hotel de Saxe—the same hotel where he stayed in March 1840. In Dresden he presented three concerts: the first and second at the Theater on 21 February (261) and 27 February (263), and the third at his hotel on 1 March (265). On 24 February he made an excursion to Dessau, where he played a concert that went all but unmentioned in the press (262). Around the same time he also performed publically in Bautzen (264), and on 5 March he played in Bernburg (266), where he also treated local music-lovers to an impromptu recital in the hall of his hotel as soon as his "official" performance was over (267). Only after those events and a visit to Stettin on the North Sea did he return to Germany's heartland.

Liszt's 21 February and 1 March Dresden concerts were benefits performances; the former, presented on behalf of the Naumann Foundation, earned some 1,300 thalers,[247] while the

---

245 "Franz Liszt hat uns seit dem 19. Febr. wieder verlassen. . . . Das Bedürfniß einer geistigen Regeneration wird von dem besseren Theile des hiesigen Publicums täglich mehr empfunden, und man tröstet sich mit der Hoffnung daß der junge Fürst — in dem lebhaften Vorsaß den alten Ruhm Weimars nicht ganz erlöschen zu lassen — zeitig darauf bedacht seyn werde wieder einige bedeutende jüngere litterarische Talente hierher zu ziehen" [AuZ (1843), p. 564].

246 Walker's *Franz Liszt: The Weimar Years* contains by far the best account of Liszt's relationship with Weimar's princes and people.

247 As reported in AuZ (1844), p. 558. See also LAn No. 64 (4.3.1844), p. 483; and Ramann II, p. 228.

proceeds from the latter went to Pantaleoni. For the first time in his German career, however, Liszt received uniformly un-flattering reviews—and for benefits, which previously seem to have been "off-limits" to the press. The most vicious attack came from *Signale für die musikalische Welt*, still a new pub-lication in 1844 and one that would take many potshots at Liszt in the years to come. On this occasion *Signale* mocked almost everything he did in Dresden, claiming that his playing was a caricature of real music, that he was unable to produce an au-thentic and attractive keyboard tone, that he held his fingers about the keys in an unnatural or affected manner, and so on and so forth.[248] What's more, the *Neue Zeitschrift* implied that his Dresden performances were deficient, even though they re-sembled those from his triumphal past. "Today the public has grown indifferent" to Liszt, that periodical proclaimed; and whereas once he could have destroyed ten pianos in an evening and wrung cries of "Heavenly!" and "Divine" from his enraptured listeners, now people merely complained about how cruelly he mistreated his instrument.[249] The absence of notices in local papers lends credibility to one of these assertions: that Liszt was no longer so newsworthy. Neither the *Dresdner Wochenblatt* nor *Anzeiger* nor even the *Leipziger Zeitung* re-viewed any of his 1844 performances, and even the *Leipziger Tageblatt und Anzeiger* reported only the proceeds raised on 21 February as 1,300 thalers. Finally, as we saw in Chapter II, Bautzen newspapers remained silent about his visit.

In Stettin things were somewhat different. Liszt may have travelled to that Baltic port simply to make money,[250] and he succeeded—at least if reports in the *Stettiner Zeitung* are cor-

---

[248] See SmW 2 (1844), pp. 68-69. See also Appendix D, quotation 16.

[249] "Aber das Publicum ist kälter geworden, das Alles ist ihm nichts Neues mehr, jetzt hat es ein Auge, und mehr als eins, für die Fehler seines verhätschelten Schoßkindes. Damals hätte er zehn Flügel zerschlagen können: das war himmlisch, göttlich! Sprengt er jetzt nur eine Seite: wie kann er nur das Instrument so maltraitiren!" [NZfM 20 (1844), p. 188].

[250] See the letter Liszt addressed to d'Agoult on 24 February from Dessau: "Je ne ferai que traverser Berlin pour remettre mon exemplaire de dédicace à la Princesse de Prusse, refuserai les offres de concert et me fourrerai dans le wagon de Stettin où il doit se trouver un millier de thalers" [Ollivier II, p. 334]. A report in *Signale* implies that Liszt agreed to visit Bautzen only after local music-lovers had raised the enormous "honorarium" of 800 thalers. See SmW 2 (1844), p. 93.

rect. But he was also a critical success in that northern town. Travelling via Berlin, he was serenaded by citizens of the Prussian capital but gave no concerts during that visit, possibly because at that moment his Berlin reputation was at a comparatively low ebb.[251] Then, in Stettin, he presented the first of two recitals at the Hotel de Bavière on 7 March (268). Accompanying Ciabatta in several numbers, Liszt also played his *Norma* and *Somnambula* fantasies, his *Erlkönig* transcription, and all of Beethoven's "Appassionata" sonata as well as his own *Galop chromatique*. For a moment "Lisztomania" returned: girls rushed from their chairs to cluster around the piano that stood in the center of the hotel's hall, while others were forced simply to stand and marvel that such sounds could be produced by just two hands. As an encore Liszt played *Erlkönig* for a second time. Despite a fine reception, though, he seems to have been exhausted; the *Zeitung* critic observed that the *Galop*, which Liszt played consummately, might—both in its wildness, and in its capacity to tire even a valiant virtuoso—reflect its author's experiences.[252] A second concert, presented in Stettin the following evening (269), went all but unnoticed by the press.

The last portion of his 1844 German tour took him to three important but not necessarily "musical" cities: Magdeburg, Braunschweig, and Hannover. Travelling by train from Stettin via Berlin,[253] Liszt arrived in Magdeburg on 13 March and

---

251 "(F. Liszt) [sic] hat sich zum Leidwesen seiner Verehrer in Berlin nicht aufgehalten, sondern ist sogleich nach Stettin abgereist, wo er ein Concert geben will. Man sagt, der berühmte Clavierspieler würde sich in Berlin nicht hören lassen; indeß wird er wohl dem Andringen seiner Verehrer und namentlich *Verehrerinnen* nachgeben" [WaMZ No. 38 (28.3.1844), p. 152]. A correspondent for *Signale*, for example, remarked sarcastically: "Liszt war in Berlin [in 1844] und kein Mensch nahm Notiz von ihm. Welcher Unterschied zwischen dem Liszt von 1842 und 1844. — Er hat sich die Haare abschneiden lassen, und kein Blatt berichtet darüber! Unerhört!" [SmW 2 (1844), p. 99].

252 "[D]ie jungen Damen sich von ihren Plätzen erhoben und dem Instrumente räherten, andere müheten sich, die Klaviatur zu überschauen, da sie es vielleicht für unmöglich hielten, daß diese Fülle von Tönen von nur 2 Händen hervorgebracht. . . . Nach dem jedesmaligen Vortrage schien der Künstler sehr erschöpft und fürchten wir beinahe, daß der *Galoppe chromatique*, den er in höchster Vollendung vortrug, das Bild seines Lebens ist" [StKPZ No. 32 [13.3.1844].

253 Liszt visited Berlin at least twice during March 1844. On 7 March he was

presented his first concert there on the following evening in the hall of the City of London Hotel (279). During the days that followed he made two public appearances at the Magdeburg Theater: the first on 15 March (271), and the second on 17 March (272). Finally, on 18 March he played Beethoven's "Kreutzer" sonata privately with Franz Fesca, a well-known local violinist (273). Overall Liszt's Magdeburg performances seem to have been successful; even *Signale* reluctantly admitted that he received the same loud applause—indeed, the same reception overall—that people everywhere had come to expect.[254] Moreover, in a brief but highly enthusiastic review the *Magdeburgische Zeitung* praised Liszt's spirit, even his genius, and claimed that the Beethoven sonatas he played on his 14 and 15 March recitals were among the most beautiful known to that newspaper's anonymous contributor.[255]

In Brauschweig, however, Liszt met with tremendous public acclaim but little in the way of critical recognition. Neither of the recitals he gave there—the first on 22 March in the "Medicinisches Saal" (274), the second three days later in the city Theater (275)—was reviewed in the *Braunschweigischer Anzeiger*. A brief notice in the *Berliner Figaro*, however, men-

---

serenaded by Berlin's Männergesang-Verein, of which he had already been named honorary director. Then, after performing in Stettin, he returned immediately to Berlin to attend a Männergesang-Verein concert. See APSZ Nos. 68 and 72 (8 and 12.3.1844), pp. 410 and 434.

Liszt made it clear that he could have performed in Berlin if he had wished to, and that he visited that city in 1844 (and certainly on other occasions) to make use of the railway lines that linked that city with Fürstenwalde, Potsdam, Magdeburg, and other nearby towns. He was even invited to perform in Fürstenwalde *because* of its railway station. While changing trains there in January 1843, he was accosted and invited to return and play. Evidently he accepted on the spot. See VZ No. 19 (23.1.1843). See also Ollivier II, p. 334. Liszt may also have remained in Berlin until 12 March to perform at a private court concert. The present author has been unable to locate reports about this last event in Berlin papers, but a squib in London's *Musical Examiner*, dated "Berlin, 12 March," announced that "Listz [sic] has arrived here, after giving three concerts in Dresden, and is to perform at the contemplated concert shortly to take place at Court, where also the sisters Milanollo and Miss Birch have received orders to attend" [MEx No. 73 (23.3.1844), p. 491].

[254] "[I]n Magdeburg fand der jetzt schon regelmäßig gewordene Liszt-Cravall statt. Man sollte meinen, Liszt müßte den lauten Beifall, das Belagern seines Hotels [etc.] herzlich satt haben" [SmW 2 (1844), p. 110].

[255] MgZ No. 66 (18.3.1844). The entire review is reprinted in Appendix D, quotation 17.

tioned that regular ticket prices were trebled for the second concert, and that the first, scheduled to begin at 7 p.m., drew listeners as early as 2 p.m. and was sold out two hours later.[256]

Finally, Liszt reached Hannover on 25 March and gave a public recital three days later in the Ballhofsaale (276). A second recital followed on 31 March at the Hannover Theater (277). Sometime after 28 March he was treated to a supper at which, without invitation, he also played several numbers on a nearby grand piano (278). One of these, a song he had evidently just written, impressed one listener with its quiet simplicity.[257] Performing alone on both public programs,[258] he presented a "Tarentelle," two of his Schubert song transcriptions, a Beethoven sonata, the *Tell* overture, the "Polonaise" from *I Puritani*, the *Lucia* and "Don Juan" fantasies, Weber's *Aufforderung zum Tanz*, and the ever-popular *Galop*. Both concerts were popular triumphs, and Liszt's playing impressed the kingdom's crown prince—according to one magazine, a man of artistic sensibility and sensitivity—who discussed music with the virtuoso as soon as his first Hannover recital was over. Liszt returned the compliment after a fashion by letting it be known that he considered Hannover's audiences the best in northern Germany.[259]

But critical approval was slipping from his grasp, at least in Germany. A long and intelligently written review of Liszt's Hannover concerts, published in *Der Posaune* (a local newspaper supplement devoted to opinion and the arts), addressed his weaknesses in some detail. Among other topics, the *Posaune*

---

256 See BFig No. 77 (30.3.1844), p. 308.

257 "[Er spielte] mit der einnehmendsten Laune, gab uns unter andern [sic] ein von ihm neu componirtes Lied von rührender Einfachkeit" [NZfM 20 (1844), p. 140].

258 Ciabatta, who sang in every other city his partner visited during February and March 1844, is mentioned in none of Liszt's Hannover reviews. Yet he evidently travelled to Hannover with Liszt. See HanZ (27.3.1844), p. 445, where Ciabatta's arrival on 27 March 1844 is duly noted.

259 "Der Kronprinz nahm Gelegenheit sich dem Virtuosen gegenüber auf eine denselben hoch ehrende Weise auszusprechen, und wer da weiß, wie kunstsinnig und kunstverständig dieser hohe Herr ist, wird dessen Beurtheilung gewiß die rechte Bedeutung geben. . . . Hr. Liszt . . . selbst [nennt] unser Publicum das beste von Norddeutschland" [NZfM 20 (1844), p. 139]. See also Ramann II, p. 231.

critic commented on the small size of the audience for his first Hannover concert,[260] the extravagent price he charged for tickets (two thalers, the same price charged in Stettin)[261] and, at greater length, on his repertory and abilities as a composer:

> The program for [Liszt's 28 March 1844 concert] consisted of seven selections, presented without assistance from other artists. . . . These seven works, however, were no masterpieces; rather, with the exception of a piece by Beethoven, they were for the most part arrangements of popular operatic tunes. Only the fantasy on Bellini's "Somnambula" displayed any artistic value and overshadowed a fantasy on "Lucia di Lammermoor" which opened the program and which was nothing more or less than a mere transcription. . . . [The last piece], the "Galop chromatique" is truly an infernal work, a real witches' dance. Perhaps it conveys enthusiasm, but it didn't entirely please [Liszt's] peaceful audience and it would have thrown a music theorist into complete confusion. . . . [Liszt's] technical equipment is complete . . . but we have been unable to discover anything original or truly individual in his style of performance [or in his own works].[262]

Not everyone agreed with opinions like these; the *Hannoversche Volksblatt*, for example, implied that the *Posaune* review was altogether too negative. Yet the *Volksblatt* went on to reprint a lampoon of Liszt—originally entitled "Les héroes du piano en 1854," but translated into German—which describes a virtuoso of the future who plays a sonata for four hands by Chopin with his left foot, etc., etc.[263] A reference to the same caricature appeared later in *Signale* and summed up the "artist of the future's" last number (a "Galoppe olimpique" for a piano supported on the backs of three horses) as "not too bad."[264] Liszt had been "discovered" by his Vormärz detractors:

260 Other periodicals disagreed with this assessment. See, for example, HanVb No. 52 (5.4.1844), p. 208.

261 Here other papers agreed. See, for example, BFig No. 58 (8.3.1844), p. 232.

262 Quoted from HanP No. 39 (31.3.1844), p. 155. NB: Portions of the passage translated above are quoted out of order. See Appendix D, quotation 18.

263 See HanVb No. 56 (12.4.1844), p. 224.

264 The present author was unable to verify the date and page number of this *Signale* caricature, which was mailed to him in the form of an undated clipping. But *Signale* also attacked Liszt with equal fervor on other occasions. One squib—published, interestingly enough, in March 1844—tells

his enormous reputation, showy style, and favorite warhorses—no pun intended—had proven themselves irresistable objects of ridicule. It was probably an auspicious moment for him to head for France, Portugal, Spain, and other friendlier southern climes.

Bonn and After: July-October 1845

Liszt returned to Germany in 1845 primarily to participate in the ceremonies associated with the dedication of the Beethoven memorial in Bonn. We have already seen that he played an important role in financing the memorial, and his reputation also attracted attention to the ceremonies themselves. Furthermore, Liszt ended up supervising much of the affair single-handed,[265] and the cantata he composed for the final concert was the first of his works for large-scale forces to receive public performance and recognition. Then, collapsing after the activities were over, he spent something like a month recuperating and giving the last of his 1840s German performances.

Near the end of July 1845 Liszt arrived in Bonn.[266] He may have planned to make his visit to the Festival a working holiday, but he soon discovered that no adequate facilities had been

of a young notary from Berlin who overtends himself playing the *Galop chromatique* and dies a week later "am Nervenfieder" [SmW 2 (1844), p. 104]. A second, somewhat longer squib pokes fun at Liszt's and Rubini's performances and incomes during their 1842-1843 tour of Dutch and German cities. See SmW 3 (1845), pp. 177-178.

265 Despite his own claims to the contrary. Early in 1843, for example, Liszt published a letter in the *Allgemeine Preußische Staats-Zeitung* protesting his "innocence" of anything more than artistic involvement with the Festival. This letter is reprinted complete with several questionable choices of wording in Appendix E, letter 6. It appeared originally in APSZ No. 19 (19.1.1843), p. 75.

266 According to several sources, he arrived about fourteen days prior to 9 or 10 August, possibly on 26 July. See WaMZ No. 100 (21.8.1845), p. 398. See also Breidenstein, *Zur Jahresfeier*, p. 8. NB: This last book is cited above in Chapter II. It is reprinted in German in LSae 25 (1979) without page numbers, and it appears in English translation in LSae 31 (1983), pp. 23-49.

Liszt also may have visited Nonnenwerth just before the beginning of the Festival. A comparatively lengthy squib in the *Revue et Gazette Musicale*, dated "Dusseldorf (Prusse), 3 août [?1845]," states that "M. Liszt vient de passer quelques jours à l'île de Nonnenwerth, dont il est propriétaire" and describes a serenade similar to the one performed as

prepared for the important concerts. With his help and that of Zwirner (the architect in charge of rebuilding the Cologne Cathedral), however, a wooden auditorium was hastily constructed and decorated—apparently quite handsomely—and other last-minute details taken care of. By 7 August the hall was finished, although Liszt and his fellow musicians had to rehearse that day before a small audience in a nearby riding school (279). Other open rehearsals were held in the new hall (280), though, and a final dress rehearsal (281) preceded the beginning of "official" Festival events.[267] The hall itself, incidentally, survived only until November 1845, when it was broken up and sold at auction.[268]

In addition to banquets, boat launchings, excursions, royal comings and goings, and the unveiling of the monument itself, the Festival included four concerts. The first was presented on Monday, 11 August; the second and third (respectively) on the morning and afternoon of Tuesday, 12 August; and the fourth on the morning of Wednesday, 13 August.[269] Liszt participated in two of these concerts. At the matinée on 12 August (282) he performed the solo part in Beethoven's "Emperor" and conducted three Beethoven works: the Fifth Symphony, the Canon from *Fidelio*, and the Act II Finale from that opera. At the morning concert on 13 August (283) he conducted his own cantata composed in honor of the occasion, and he accompanied one Fräulein Kratky in a performance of Beethoven's *Adelaïde*.

---

part of the festivities accompanying Liszt's 22 August 1841 boat trip to Cologne [RGMP 12 (1845), p. 272].

[267] Like other aspects of Liszt's visit to Bonn, the erection of the impromptu hall has already been described several times. See, for example, the "Liszt als deus ex machina" chapter in Henssler's *Das musikalische Bonn*, pp. 169-172. Walker and Ramann offer colorful accounts of the Festival as a whole. In a few places, however, Walker confuses the order of events. For example, he implies that the "Emperor" concerto was played on the "artists' concert" of 13 August [Walker, p. 423]. See Walker, pp. 417-426; and Ramann II, pp. 254-265.

[268] See AmZ 47 (1845), col. 847.

[269] Discussions of programs and program changes for these concerts may be found in Breidenstein, *Zur Jahresfeier*. Generally reliable information also appears in J. W. Davison's accounts of the Festival, which are discussed below.

Reports of the Festival were as varied in character and
color as its participants. Many visitors seem to have enjoyed
themselves; others did not. Poor planning by the Festival
Committee (supervised by Breidenstein), unsettled weather,
cramped hotels with indifferent food and uncomfortable beds,
and difficulties of many other kinds—including a bit of pushing
and pulling in public places, and a lot of theft—caused considerable hardship and confusion. We saw in Chapter I, for example, that Sir George Smart was quite disappointed with the
arrangements made on his behalf by the Festival authorities.
Less familiar than Smart's account of the Festival but equally
engaging are the reports written by J. W. Davison, the celebrated British critic, that appeared in seven issues of *The Musical World*. According to Davison,

> [Sunday, 10 August, was] the first day of the Beethoven Fête,
> and I have just returned to the *Hotel de l'Etoile d'Or*, situate
> in the market-place . . . where I have partaken of a fine din-
> ner. In a magnificent room, which the enterprising landlord,
> Herr Schmidts, has built for the occasion, and which he has
> appropriately entitled the *Salle Beethoven*, five tables of im-
> mense length were laid out to accommodate no less a number
> than five hundred persons. . . . [I perceived] Dr. Liszt at the
> head of the table, and near him Dr. Spohr, with his amiable
> and intelligent wife. . . . Champagne was the order of the
> day—and, of course, at Rome, you must be a Roman. I therefore
> drank champagne with the rest—and subsequently coffee—and
> finally added my little cloudlet to the gorgeous company of va-
> pors that choked the atmosphere in every direction—issuing
> from not less than two or three hundred cigars. . . . By the
> way, the dinner was not of the best, though assuredly of the
> plentifullest—but then, as I said before, anything will go down
> with the salt of such events and such society.[270]

Davison seems usually to have looked on the bright side
of things; he describes at length the pleasures of his journey,
the "politeness and civility" of the German customs authorities,
and the pretty girls he met on his travels.[271] But his de-

---

[270] Quoted from Davison's "Letters on the Bonn Festival"—in this case, from
World 20 (1845), pp. 409-410. Throughout this chapter "Davison" refers
by page number(s) to his reports for *The Musical World*.

[271] Compare, for example, Davison's account of entering Prussia [Davison, p.
411] with that of Chorley I, p. 419. NB: Chorley's reminiscences of the
Festival have been reprinted in LSae 25 (1979), pp. 104-116.

scriptions of the concerts themselves are not uniformly flattering to the artists involved. Of the 12 August afternoon performance, for example, Davison states that this event "in honor of the great Beethoven was seriously injured in the solo vocal department" by excessive demands upon some of the singers; and that "the recitative in [Beethoven's] *Mount of Olives*" was "a task of too great difficulty, and the result was its omission altogether from the program."[272] Other phrases are equally dismissive.

Davison's descriptions of Liszt's piano-playing, however, are not only positive, even sympathetic; they are also unusually detailed:

> The concerto in E flat, the *cheval de bataille* of all the Beethoven pianists, fared nobly in the hands of Liszt. It is almost as superogatory to speak now of the merits of Liszt's pianoforte playing as of the beauties of the composition he interpreted. I shall merely, in answer to the abuses of sundry of his quondam friends, who feasted and lived at his expense (not for the first time), give a direct denial to their statements in regard to his manner of rendering the concerto on this occasion. Instead of altering and exaggerating *almost every passage*, he altered but few, and exaggerated none. Instead of giving way to gestures and affectations of manner, he was remarkably quiet and unassuming. In short, I never heard him play in better style—with more of the air of a master and less of the grimace of an *etudiant*. . . . The only thing that surprised me was that Liszt—a thing unusual with him—played from *book*—yet when we reflect on the turmoil and fatigue to which he had been exposed, day after day, by the blunders of the committee and the importunity of visitors and applicants for favors of every kind, it is matter for admiration that he could play at all—much more that he could play with energy and *aplomb*.

Furthermore,

> [Beethoven's] symphony in c minor was, on the whole, an excellent performance. Liszt conducted with spirit, and a manifest comprehension of the score—which as he knows the symphony by heart is not to be wondered at. The *tempi* of the various movements, however, appeared to me to be taken too slow, especially in the *Finale*—but Spohr, Moscheles, and Sir George Smart (three excellent authorities) assured me that I

[272] Davison, p. 470.

was wrong, and that I had been accustomed to hear them in London too fast.[273]

Like most informed participants, Davison felt that some of the performances, even some of Liszt's, were better than others. On the whole, though, he praised Liszt as solo pianist and conductor, and he testified indirectly to the quality of Liszt's artistry when he stated that Beethoven's "*Adelaida* [was] indifferently sung by a Mlle. Kratky, though accompanied by Liszt." Davison also admired Liszt's Festival Cantata, even though he considered it less than a masterpiece:

> My impression of this composition is decidedly favourable. It is in the modern German style [sic]—by which do not understand Mendelssohn or Spohr, but Lindpainter or Wagner—and is, I think as good a work of its kind as nine out of ten of the present composers of Germany could have written. . . . The instrumentation is exceedingly brilliant, remarkably clear, and displays many bold and successful attempts at novelty. The voicing for the choir is admirable, and there is enough *idea*, both of melody and harmony in this composition, to authorise the opinion expressed by many distinguished artists present—that when Liszt ceased to be professedly a pianist he would become a composer.[274]

Nor was Davison the only critic to make positive remarks about Liszt's cantata. The *Zeitschrift für Deutschlands Musik-Vereine* explained at some length that the work contained a few eccentricities and dull sections, but also (and rather surprisingly) other passages that were highly effective and even beautiful.[275]

---

[273] Davison, p. 470. As we saw above, Liszt was criticized in 1844 for conducting the slow movement of Beethoven's Fifth too quickly—an unusual instance of a journalist (Kapp, in this case) correcting a great artist, and with positive results.

[274] Davison, p. 472. Ironically, Liszt completed work on his cantata with the held of the young Joachim Raff; the two musicians rode together by coach to Bonn and copied parts for eight to ten hours a day. See August Göllerich, *Liszt* (Berlin 1908), pp. 107-108. Later Raff attempted to take credit for many of his benefactor's achievements in orchestral composition. See Walker, *Franz Liszt: The Virtuoso Years*, especially the chapter entitled "The Raff Case" (pp. 199-208).

[275] See Appendix D, quotation 19. Foreign papers were more inclined to criticize Liszt's cantata than were German ones. The *Musical Times*, for instance, stated that "[t]he musicians appear to be all of one mind as to the character of the [cantata], viz: that it possesses indications of an un-

After it had already been performed at the beginning of the 13 August concert, the cantata had to be repeated because Queen Victoria and other royal visitors arrived only in time to hear the final measures. The second performance seems to have been better than the first, but the concert as a whole was an exhausting experience, and Davison called the event "altogether a mistake."[276]

Davison and others have called the 1845 Beethoven Festival a "personal triumph" for Liszt.[277] It *was* a triumph, but almost a tragic one. Liszt struggled to make the Festival work, only to bear the brunt of gossip associated with its failures and fiascos: hotel rooms that were deliberately overbooked, tickets that were promised to foreign journalists and then withheld from them, and monies that were misspent or lost. No individual could have solved all of these problems, but Liszt did his best to remedy some of them. For this he received gratitude and respect from many people, but jealousy and antagonism from a few:

> Liszt has been throughout the [Festival the] scape-goat of the Committee, than whom a greater set of bunglers were never before entrusted with an affair of such importance. Liszt had no power whatever vested in his person of giving away tickets, or of otherwise promoting the laudable endeavours of the press of distant countries to obtain information. . . . [But, w]henever he was applied to, sooner than expose the folly and meanness of the Committee (who made a trading speculation, and nothing better, of the entire Fête) *he bought tickets for the applicants and paid for them out of his own pocket.* . . . I am not aware how the English journals have treated Liszt, but the conduct of some of the Parisian prints has been utterly despicable. The greater number of these gentlemen lived the whole time at Bonn at the expense of the man they abuse, and some of them, (I have their names) actually borrowed money from him to take them home again. . . . Liszt's bill at the *Hotel de l'Etoile d'or* amounted to something less than eleven thousand francs—which, with what he gave towards the expenses of the inauguration, the erection of the statue, and the building of the new concert-room (which was wholly his idea) leaves him about *twenty-five thousand francs out of pocket* . . . for which

---

doubted, but, at the same time, of a self-willed and irregular genius" [MT No. 16 (1.9.1845), p. 118].

[276] Davison, p. 472.

[277] For example, see Walker, p. 426.

he is rewarded by a quantity of petty abuse, and a stroke of the
yellow jaundice. Poor Liszt has his faults it is true, and . . . I
have never numbered among his blind worshippers; but it must
not be forgotten that, but for Liszt, Beethoven might yet be
waiting for his statue. . . . [He] did his possible for the best,
and if his colleagues on the committee had been *musicians* instead of men wholly ignorant of art, things would have gone
very differently.[278]

Davison's observations confirm what others also observed:
that Liszt suffered during August 1845 from exhaustion and
weakened health.[279] Before taking to his bed, though, he performed privately for the Festival's royal guests: first at a soirée
presented in honor of Queen Victoria at Brühl on 13 August
(284), then at a concert held in the Stolzenfels castle near
Koblenz three days later (286). At the first of these events,
which took place only hours after the last Festival concert
ended, he played a fantasy on Bellini's *Norma* and a "Spanish
Fantasy" of his own creation. The soirée, which began at 9 p.m.
and did not end until midnight, was interrupted for
refreshments and everyone—including a cheerful King of
Prussia—was especially delighted with the performers.[280] At

[278] Davison, pp. 445 and 482. The financial outcome of the Festival is difficult
to determine. Liszt claimed a profit for the Festival of 1,700 thalers. See
Walker, p. 417n. Management, on the other hand, claimed a loss of 2,893
thalers that was made good only through the generosity of royal patrons.
See Breidenstein, *Zur Jahresfeier*, p. 29. That Liszt and Breidenstein held
different opinions about the Festival's outcome is scarcely surprising; as
Michael Härting has implied, a clash between two such imposing person-
alities was all but inevitable. See *Rheinische Musiker*, ed. Karl Gustav
Fellerer (Cologne 1960-), Vol. V, p. 13.

[279] Liszt became ill during or immediately after the Festival. Yet he visited
Brühl, Cologne, Koblenz, and Kleve before he wrote on 25 August to
Christian Lobe in Weimar that he had succumbed to a serious attack of
jaundice: "Wie Sie vielleicht schon vernommen haben, bin ich seit den
Bonner Festen mit einer *eclatanten* Gelbsucht und gänzlicher Abspannung
beglückt; jede Austrengung ist mir verboten" [Briefe VIII, p. 44]. Perhaps
Liszt ignored his doctor's orders prior to 25 August, or perhaps his disease
grew worse around that time. In any event, he seems to have made no
public appearances as a performer for several weeks after 25 August: the
longest hiatus in his Vormärz German tours.

[280] "[U]nser König zeichnete den Künstler [including Liszt] besonders aus"
[FOPZ No. 226 ["Beilage"] (17.8.1845), p. 2224]. Liszt was also asked by
the King to dedicate a memorial plaque at the Bonn Beethovenhaus on
13 August. See FOPZ No. 222 (13.8.1845), p. 2187-2188.

Stolzenfels Liszt participated in a program that also included an aria from *Don Giovanni* sung by Jenny Lind and a violin solo played by Pauline Viardot-Garcia.[281] Between these concerts he also performed in Cologne on 15 August (285), and afterwards he found the time and energy to travel to Kleve, where he gave what may have been a benefit concert on 18 August at the local Treasury (287). His program on this last occasion included all or part of Beethoven's Op. 26 Sonata. *Caecilia*, a Dutch music magazine which ran a squib about the Kleve concert, complimented Liszt on his use of a fine piano manufactured by Lefebvre's firm.[282]

The rest of his time in Germany seems a little hazy. We know Liszt visited Baden-Baden to recuperate at leisure; there he performed on at least three occasions: at a public recital presented with Lind on 21 September (290), and at two private functions that may have taken place several weeks earlier (288-289). About one of these latter functions Léon Kreutzer wrote a charming article for the *Revue et Gazette Musicale* full of praise for Liszt's playing and for the difficult program he presented: Rossini's "Tarantelle," the *Mélodies hongroises*, an improvisation based on a Chopin mazurka, and his own difficult fantasy on Meyerbeer's *Robert*.[283]

Then, abandoning his cure, Liszt travelled to Stuttgart, where he took part in a concert at the Redoutensaal on 29

---

[281] Meyerbeer evidently proposed Liszt as a participant for Brühl or Stolzenfels or both. See Meyerbeer III, p. 603. According to one newspaper, though, Meyerbeer and Liszt shared in the leadership of the Brühl concert. See FÖPZ No. 219 (10.8.1845), p. 2157. NB: The Stolzenfels concert seems to have been arranged at the last minute when a performance of *Norma* with Lind and Meyerbeer fell through. See FÖPZ No. 227 ["Beilage"] (18.8.1845), p. 2234.

[282] "Een schoon Staarstuk uit de beroemde Fabriek van Eck en Lefevre [sic] te Keulen wekte hier de algemeene bewondering" [CAmtN 2 (1845), p. 194]. Liszt often played on Eck & Lefebvre pianos during his German tours, especially in 1844-1845. See Ellmar, "Eck & Lefebvre Pianofortefabrik," esp. pp. 227-229.

[283] See RGMP 12 (1845), p. 292. See also Appendix D, quotation 20.
    Apparently at least one of Liszt's private Baden-Baden performances took place prior to 26 August, the date of Davison's letter that mentions this event. See Davison, pp. 469 and 473. A notice in the *Neue Zeitschrift* also refers to private performances in Baden-Baden but gives no dates; it also implies that Liszt gave no *public* performances there, which was not true. See NZfM 23 (1845), p. 148.

September (291). Sharing the platform with Jenny Lutzer, a local singer then currently employed by the Vienna Opera and engaged to be married to his colleague Franz von Dingelstedt, Liszt played what may have been his *Ungarische Nationalmelodien* and also presented a "Fantasie à capriccio" of undetermined authorship as well as his "Andante finale" from *Lucia* and his fantasy on Bellini's *Norma*. The *Schwäbische Merkur* reported that Stuttgart music-lovers had lost none of their enthusiasm for Liszt since 1843, and it expressed hope that, at his next Stuttgart concert, he would perform his *Erlkönig* transcription and his *Réminiscences de Don Juan*.[284]

From Stuttgart Liszt travelled to Darmstadt, where he gave a recital at the Saale der vereinigten Gesellschaft on 8 October (292). On this occasion he played seven works, including the *Tell* overture, the "Tarantelle" from Rossini's *Soirées*, and a Chopin mazurka. A host of dignitaries, including the Grand Duke and several visiting princes, attended this recital, which was presented before an overflowing auditorium. "In Liszt virtuosity has reached its pinnacle," the *Großherzogliche Hessische Zeitung* proclaimed three days later,[285] and in another notice the same paper announced that he would present a second Darmstadt concert at the local Theater on 12 October (296).[286] The program for this last event included Weber's *Konzertstück* for piano and orchestra and the *Robert* fantasy as well as several Schubert songs sung by Agnes Pirscher. Although the hall was less than packed, the concert seems to have been successful. According to the *Hessische Zeitung*, Liszt

[284] "Seit Liszt uns zum lezten Male besuchte, sind nun auch schon zwei Jahre vorüber; die Herzen der Stuttgarter sind ihm in dieser Zeit nicht fremd geworden: den es war der gleiche Enthusiasmus, der ihn, wie damals, so auch [am 29. September] wieder empfing. . . . Möge er noch länger weilen und noch mehrmals uns den Genuß seines Spiels gönnen; dann hoffen wir, im nächsten Konzert auch den Erlkönig und die Fantasie über Motive aus Don Juan zu hören" [SSM No. 268 (1.10.1845), p. 1069]:

[285] "Das Virtuosenthum hat in Liszt seinen Gipfelpunkt erreicht" [quoted in Philipp Schweitzer, *Darmstädter Musikleben im 19. Jahrhundert* (Darmstadt 1975), p. 155]. According to Schweitzer, the review in question appeared in the *Großherzogliche Hessische Zeitung* "Beiblatt" of 11 October 1845. The present author, however, has been unable to consult that issue of the *Zeitung*.

[286] See DmGHZ No. 281 (10.10.1845), p. 1515.

played Weber's work most beautifully, and he accompanied Fräulein Pirscher with considerable skill.[287] Around the same time he seems also to have performed privately for the King of Bavaria, possibly in Stuttgart (294), and he also played privately in Darmstadt (293) and Stuttgart (293) on other occasions.

Leaving Hesse behind, Liszt paused in Heidelberg to participate in a benefit for his sometime partner Pantaleoni (297). Then, on 17 October, Liszt gave his last German concert at the Kaufhaus-Saale in Freiburg i.B. (298). On this occasion he played his *Tell* overture, the "Andante finale" from *Lucia*, his own "Don Juan" fantasy, the "Andante con variazione" movement from Beethoven's A-flat Major Sonata, *Erlkönig*, the "Polonaise" from *I Puritani* and, almost inevitably, the *Grand Galop chromatique*. He was serenaded by the local Liedertafel before and after his performance, and the *Freiburger Zeitung* observed that his fabulous playing was rewarded by enthusiastic applause from an astounded audience.[288] Moreover, the *Oberrheinische Zeitung* called his appearance in Freiburg a new triumph for his truly colossal talent.[289]

On 18 October Liszt wrote a letter to his mother explaining that he would be arriving in Paris in about four days.[290] Then, after a vacation there of about a week, he began another tour of the French provinces. Liszt was to return to Weimar the following winter and to live there, sometimes for years at a

---

[287] "Das Concert von C. M. von Weber spielte Liszt ausgezeichnet schön. Ebenso lobend müssen wie die bescheidene Art anerkennen, mit welcher er die Schubert'sche Lieder, welche Mad. Pirscher sehr schön sang, accompagnirte" [quoted in Schweitzer, *Darmstädter Musikleben*, pp. 156-157].

[288] "[Liszt gab] das angekündigte Concert im Kaufhaussaale und es bedarf wohl nicht der Erwähnung, daß sein ausgezeichnetes großartiges Spiel von einem enthusiastischen Beifall der staunenden Zuhörer begleitet war" [FbZ No. 293 (19.10.1845), p. 1689].

[289] "Das Concert, welches dieser hochgefeierte Künstler uns in Freiburg nach langem Zaudern bot, *ein neuer Triumph seines wahrhaft gigantischen Talentes* . . . erregte" [FbOZ No. 293 (20.10.1845), p. 1225]. See also RGMP 12 (1845), p. 355; and other sources.

[290] See *Franz Liszts Briefe an seine Mutter*, ed. La Mara (Leipzig 1918), p. 65: "Ich werde höchstwahrscheinlich den 22. Oktober morgens in Paris eintreffen."

time, between 1848 and his death in 1886. Never again as a pianist, though, would he undertake a German concert tour.[291]

291 Liszt did perform occasionally in Germany as a pianist after 1845, however. On 16 October 1848, for example, he took part in a concert at the Halle Theater and played his "Don Juan" fantasy and his arrangement of the "Tarantelle" from Auber's opera *La Muette di Portici*. See Walter Serauky, *Musikgeschichte der Stadt Halle II* (Halle 1942), p. 608.

CHAPTER IV
Liszt's German Repertory

Génie oblige!
Liszt

Liszt's repertory as a performer, especially as a virtuoso pianist, poses special historical problems. It is not so much that the quality of his programs was sometimes "low."[1] It is rather that we often cannot identify the contents of those programs at all. And if we cannot tell *what* he played, we certainly cannot evaluate reports of *how* he played. The following pages are devoted to a review of Liszt's German repertory and to historical and critical problems associated with it.

Liszt's Keyboard Repertory

During his 298 documented performances in Germany, Liszt presented about 100 different keyboard, chamber, and orchestral compositions. Yet his working keyboard repertory was comparatively small. His legendary reputation as a "transcendental virtuoso" was based primarily on repeated performances of fewer than two dozen compositions written or arranged by himself or by Beethoven, Chopin, Hummel, Rossini, Schubert, or Weber.[2] Seventeen pieces or groups of pieces comprised the backbone of his piano repertory. These

---

[1] See Walker, p. 291, who also contends that Liszt generally permitted others to choose his repertory for him. Insofar as we know, however, Liszt chose at least some of the music for virtually every program in which he participated.

[2] Philippe Autexier has also studied Liszt's German repertory in terms of what he played and how often he played it. See Autexier, "Musique sans frontières?" *Revue musicale* 405-407 (1987), pp. 297-305. Autexier, however, discusses only some of Liszt's German concerts; his statistical statements about performances, therefore, are meaningless. Similar statements are avoided throughout the present chapter. On the other hand, Autexier's conclusions about Liszt's "French" vs. "German" repertories are

pieces are identified in Table 2. Abbreviated titles for these and other works and information about them may be found in Appendix F.

Of the seventeen pieces or groups of pieces listed in Table 2, only the *Grande Galop chromatique* was composed by Liszt entirely on themes of his own devising. Two works by Weber—the *Aufforderung zum Tanz* ("Invitation to the Waltz") of 1819, and the *Konzertstück* for piano and orchestra of 1821—are also "original" compositions, as are Chopin's mazurkas and etudes, and the etudes of Hiller, Moscheles, and Liszt himself. Of the fourteen remaining works, thirteen are transcriptions or paraphrases by Liszt on music written by other composers. The fourteenth, *Hexameron*, consists of variations on a tune from *I Puritani* composed jointly by Chopin, Czerny, Herz, Liszt, Pixis, and Thalberg. Liszt played each of these "primary" keyboard repertory selections at least twenty times in Germany during the 1840s. They represent about four-fifths of the music he is known to have performed as a solo pianist during his visits to that country.

Liszt regularly supplemented this primary repertory with other selections of "secondary" importance. Of ten or so secondary works (each of which was performed some five to twenty times), four are original compositions: Beethoven's "Emperor" concerto and "Moonlight" sonata, Hummel's Septet, and Liszt's own *Marche hongroise*. Two are transcriptions of Beethoven: *Adelaïde* and the "Scherzo and Finale" from the *Pastoral* symphony. The remaining works include Liszt's fantasies on *God Save the Queen* and paraphrases on themes from *Les Huguenots, Niobe,* and *Lucia di Lammermoor*.

Still other selections, performed on fewer than five occasions, formed Liszt's "tertiary" repertory. Of these infrequently-played pieces, Beethoven's Fantasy for piano, chorus, and orchestra, Op. 80, received five performances, Beethoven's Sonata in A-flat Major, Op. 26 (also known as the "Andante con variazione," from the subtitle of its first movement), five performances; Weber's piano fantasy *Oberons Zauberhorn* three performances; and so on. Liszt's tertiary repertory accounted for a surprisingly large number of the

---

true: Liszt was much more likely to play pieces like the *Réminiscences de Don Juan* in Germany than in France.

TABLE 2
Liszt's Primary German Repertory

In the following table selections are identified both by title and by entry number or numbers from Raabe's catalog {in curved brackets}. Names of composers other than Liszt on whose themes or music individual works are based are also given [in square brackets].

1. Liszt, *Grand Galop chromatique* {R. 41}: some 70 performances.

2. *Erlkönig* by Schubert/Liszt {R. 243/4}: more than 65 performances.

3. Liszt, *Réminiscences de Don Juan* [Mozart] {R. 228}: more than 55 performances.

4. Liszt, *Réminiscences de Robert le diable* [Meyerbeer] {R. 222}: more than 50 performances.

5. Liszt, *Réminiscences de Lucia di Lammermoor* [Donizetti] {R. 151}; and the related "Marche et Cavatine" {R. 152}: more than 40 performances. NB: This pair of works should not be confused with the "Andante finale" listed below.

6. Overture to *Guillaume Tell* by Rossini/Liszt {R. 237}: almost 40 performances.

7. Weber, *Aufforderung zum Tanz*: more than 35 performances.

8. Liszt, *Réminiscences de Puritains* [Bellini] {R. 129}; and the related *Introduction et Polonaise* from *I Puritani* by Bellini/Liszt {R. 130}: more than 35 performances altogether.

9. *Ständchen* by Schubert/Liszt {R. 245/7}: more than 30 performances.

10. Liszt et al, *Hexameron* variations [Bellini] {R. 131}: more than 30 performances in versions for solo piano, two-pianos/four-hands, and piano-orchestra.

11. Chopin mazurkas (usually unidentified): more than 30 performances.

12. *Ave Maria* by Schubert/Liszt {R. 243/12}: almost 30 performances.

13. "Andante finale" from *Lucia di Lammermoor* by Donizetti/Liszt {R. 151}: more than 25 performances.

14. Etudes by Chopin, Hiller, Liszt, and Moscheles (generally otherwise unidentified): more than 20 performances altogether.

15. Weber, *Konzertstück*, Op. 79: more than 20 performances.

16. "Tarantelle" {?R. 236/9} and/or "Tarantelles napolitaines" {?R. 10d/4 or R. 117}: more than 20 performances altogether.

17. Liszt, *Réminiscences de Norma* [Bellini] {R. 133}: about 20 performances.

various pieces he played in Germany, even though none of them appeared on more than a handful of programs. It is the breadth and depth of his musical interests, not his fundamental programming strategy, that is reflected in many of Liszt's tertiary repertory choices.

Liszt drew much of his keyboard repertory from the works of Beethoven. In addition to the pieces mentioned above, he played parts or all of at least five other Beethoven sonatas: those in c minor, Op. 13 (the "Pathètique"); d minor, Op. 31, No. 2 (the "Tempest"); f minor, Op. 57 (the "Appassionata"); A Major, Op. 101; and B-flat Major, Op. 106 (the demanding "Hammerklavier").[3] He also participated in performances of at least four Beethoven chamber works: the sonatas for violin and piano in c minor, Op. 30, No. 3; and F Major, Op. 47 (the "Kreutzer"); the Quintet in E-flat Major for piano and winds, Op. 16; and the Trio in B-flat Major for piano, violin, and 'cello, Op. 97 (the "Archduke"). Finally, he played his transcription of the "Marche funèbre" movement from Beethoven's "Eroica" Symphony and the solo part of Beethoven's C-minor Concerto. (As we saw in Chapter III, he also conducted the orchestral part of this last work.)

Liszt drew somewhat less frequently upon the works of Johann Sebastian Bach, although he played at least three Bach compositions in something like their original form: the Chromatic Fantasy and Fugue in d minor (BWV 903); the Prelude and Fugue in c-sharp minor from Book I of the *Well-Tempered Clavier*, and one of the solo parts for the Concerto in d minor for three keyboard instruments (BWV 1063).[4] Liszt also played two piano transcriptions of Bach organ works: probably those of the Prelude and Fugue in a minor (BWV 543), and the Prel-

---

3   Of these sonatas, the most poorly documented is the Op. 101. A single primary source identifies this work by key for Liszt's recital of 4 November 1841. See Ernst Klusen, *Das Musikleben der Stadt Krefeld* (Cologne 1979), Vol. I, p. 50. Apparently Liszt performed the Op. 101 sonata on at least one other occasion. See William S. Newman, "Liszt's Interpreting of Beethoven's Piano Sonatas," MQ 58 (1972), p. 192.

4   The *Niederrheinische Correspondent* identifies the first work simply as the "Chromatic Fantasy." See WesNC No. 133 (6.11.1841). Walker, p. 372n, identifies the second work as the Prelude and Fugue in "C" minor. Berlin's *Spenersche Zeitung*, however, gives "Cis" (i.e., c-sharp) minor. See SZ No. 26 (1.2.1842). Ramann II, p. 152n, also gives c-sharp minor.

ude and Fugue in e minor (BWV 548).[5] Finally, he presented three other Baroque keyboard works on his programs in Berlin: a sonata and the so-called "Katzenfuge" of Scarlatti, a fugue in e minor by Handel, and a set of variations from one of Handel's keyboard suites.

Liszt drew more sparingly on the compositions of his contemporaries, at least during his German tours. Schumann, for instance, was represented on public occasions by two performances of excerpts from *Carnaval*. Mendelssohn was represented in public by three works: the Concerto in d minor for piano and orchestra, Op. 40; the *Capriccio* in f-sharp minor, Op. 5; and Liszt's keyboard transcription of *Auf Flügel des Gesanges*. In addition to the other Weber works he played so frequently, Liszt also played that composer's *Momento capriccioso*, Op. 12; the A-flat Major Sonata; and an arrangement of the *Konzertstück* for piano solo. Most of Liszt's remaining German repertory was drawn from his own compositions and transcriptions, including—on only one clearly documented occasion—two selections from the *Album d'un voyageur* {R. 8}. Among the paraphrases of his own that he performed infrequently were the *Réminiscences de Lucrezia Borgia*, the fantasy on *Gaudeamus igitur*, and a fantasy—still unpublished in its proper form—on themes from Mozart's *Le Nozze di Figaro*.[6] Finally, Liszt played his transcription of Schubert's *Lob der Thränen* on several occasions, and he may have performed still

---

5 On 15 November 1842 in Frankfurt a.M., Liszt played a Bach Prelude and Fugue "mit Pedal," probably BWV 543. See FJ No. 315 (15.11.1842). On 21 October 1843, he played a Prelude and Fugue identified by a critic for the *Münchener Tagblatt* as a "Bach'sche Fuge" in the key of "es Moll" or e-flat minor [MTb No. 294 (24.10.1843), p. 1413]. Which fugue this was cannot be determined.

Whether the piano transcriptions of Bach organ works Liszt played in Vormärz audiences were the same ones he published later cannot be determined. See the "Verzeichnis aller Werke Liszts nach Gruppen geordnet" published in Raabe II (pp. 261-364). This catalog cites Ramann in support of 1842 as a possible *terminus ad quo* for all six Bach/Liszt prelude-and-fugue transcriptions. See Raabe II, pp. 268-269. NB: References to entries in Raabe's catalog appear hereafter in the form of "R." numbers {in curved brackets}. Thus the Bach/Liszt transcriptions entries in that catalog would be given as {R. 119/1} and {119/5}.

6 See Kenneth Hamilton, "Liszt Fantasizes — Busoni Excises: The Liszt-Busoni 'Figaro Fantasy'," JALS 30 (1991), pp. 21-27.

another Schubert song or song transcription.[7] Pieces by Heller, Hiller, Pixis, Vollweiler, and a number of other, less familiar composers rounded out his solo keyboard repertory.

The problems associated with Liszt's virtuoso keyboard repertory are many and varied. First, for more than eighty-five public and private performances we have no concrete repertory information whatsoever. Second, the information that survives for other performances is often incomplete. For none of his German recitals, for example, do we know which Chopin etudes he played, and for only one event—and that one poorly documented by date—do we know which Chopin mazurkas.[8] On several occasions we do not even know which Beethoven sonatas he performed. And—as we saw above—we cannot tell whether he played any Schubert song transcriptions besides *Ave Maria, Erlkönig, Lob der Thränen*, and *Ständchen*, at least in Germany.

One reason we do not always know what Liszt played is that individual works were often called different things on different occasions. The *Grande Fantaisie sur des thèmes de l'opera Les Huguenots* (1836), for example, was never identified in contemporary concert advertisements or reviews by its full title. Instead, it was sometimes called a "Fantasie" on Meyerbeer's opera, sometimes "Erinnerungen" or "Souvenirs" (i.e., "reminiscences") of that work, and sometimes "Réminiscences des Huguenots."[9] Other works are more difficult to pin down because Liszt published fundamentally different compositions with similar titles, or different versions of the same composition with identical titles. Consider his fantasies on tunes from Donizetti's *Lucia di Lammermoor*. During the 1830s Liszt completed two related works based on that opera:

---

[7]   One of these works was announced as "Auf Verlagen." See HZCor Nos. 257-258 (30-31.10.1840). No Schubert song, however, bears this title; the phrase probably should have read "auf Verlangen" (i.e., "by request"), as it did in announcements for one of Liszt's Breslau recitals. See BrPSZ No. 30 (4.2.1843), p. 210.

[8]   On 18 January 1843 in Berlin Liszt is reported to have played three Op. 50 mazurkas, then recently published at the time by Wessel and Stapledon of London. See MEx No. 19 (11.3.1843), p. 138.

[9]   Liszt himself used this last title for the holograph draft of his *Huguenots* fantasy preserved in D-Wrgs Liszt Ms. U56. It is also used occasionally throughout the present volume.

the *Réminiscences de Lucia di Lammermoor*, and a transcription of the "Marche et Cavatine" from *Lucia*. Printed programs from 1842-1843 indicate that he sometimes played the "Marche et Cavatine" in Germany as an independent work.[10] On other occasions, though, he is reported only to have performed a "Fantasie" on themes from *Lucia*, or only his *Andante finale de Lucia*, a simplified version of his *Réminiscences*. Yet Liszt himself had intended the "Marche et Cavatine" to be published as part of the *Réminiscences*, not as an independent paraphrase. In Table 2, therefore, performances of the "Marche et Cavatine" are counted together with those of the *Réminiscences de Lucia*, while "Andante finale" performances are counted separately. Vis-à-vis the "Andante finale": perhaps (and this is only an hypothesis) Liszt played simpler versions of certain works more and more frequently during the 1840s, perhaps because they could be sold more easily in sheet-music form. If this is true, his performances "advertised" simplified versions and helped make them popular.[11]

Similar problems are associated with performances of works based on themes from Bellini's *I Puritani*. Liszt completed and published three compositions associated with this opera: the *Réminiscences des Puritains*; a transcription of the "Introduction et Polonaise"; and the introduction, second variation, connecting material, and conclusion for *Hexameron*. Most programs for his German performances distinguish between *Hexameron* and the *Réminiscences* per se, although the latter work is often identified simply as a "Fantasie." A few advertisements, however, imply that *Hexameron* was written by Liszt alone. Other advertisements and reviews refer only to the "Polonaise" from *I Puritani*, or only to a "Polonaise." On 30 January 1842, though, Liszt apparently played both the *Réminiscences* and the "Puritani Polonaise" on the same pro-

---

10 See BrPSZ No. 23 (27.1.1843), p. 163.

11 It is only natural that Liszt was concerned about sales of his music, although not so concerned that he pandered to a mob of would-be virtuoso-manquées. Contemporary critics also understood which Liszt works were easier to play and sell. In a review of the *Lucia* "Marche et Cavatine" published in the *Blätter für Musik und Literatur*, for example, one reviewer proclaimed that "Diese Composition gehört übrigens zu den weniger Schwer auszuführenden Liszts" [BML 2 (1841); p. 168].

gram.[12] To complicate things still further, he often played *Hexameron* in arrangements for piano and orchestra, and for two pianos/four hands.[13] In Table 2, all of Liszt's German *Hexameron* performances, whether for solo piano, two pianos, or piano and orchestra, are tabulated under a single heading.

Still other compositions are virtually impossible to identify. Consider the so-called "Marches hongroises." Today we cannot tell whether these pieces were drawn from Liszt's own *Magyar Dallok, Magyar Rhapsodiák,* or *Ungarische Nationalmelodien* (some of which at least were drafted by 1840), or from his transcription of Schubert's *Mélodies hongroises* (1838), or whether the title "Marche hongroise" refers to another work altogether.[14] Nor can we be certain which of his own marches he may have played: his *Seconde Marche hongroise* (also known as his *Ungarischer Sturmmarsch*), his *Heroischer Marsch im ungarischen Styl* or, again, an unknown composition.[15] Furthermore, we cannot always determine

---

12 An advertisement in the *Allgemeine Preußische Staats-Zeitung* announced the *Réminiscences* as "1ster Theil: Quartett. 2ter Theil: Marsch und Polonaise" [APSZ No. 28 (28.1.1842), p. 112].

13 Liszt's two-piano arrangement of *Hexameron* was published only in 1870, and he may have played another arrangement during the 1840s. Contemporary sources, however, state only that the work was "für 2 Flügel arrangirt" [HFrs No. 45 (7.11.1840), p. 719]. See also Schnapp's useful "Verschollene Kompositionen Franz Liszt," p. 129.

14 An unpublished "Marche héroique" is preserved in D-WRgs Liszt Ms. U20. References to these and other marches appear in D-WRgs Liszt Ms. Z15.
   The problems associated with Liszt's "Hungarian marches" and "melodies" are considerable. On one occasion, for example, the *Revue et Gazette Musicale de Paris* reported that he played both "une marche héroique [et] marche hongroise" in Berlin [RPGM 10 (1843), p. 88]. Local accounts of the same event (i.e., the concert of 18 February 1843) mention neither work, and both "marches" have been omitted from Appendix C. Related to this is a contemporary question about the authenticity of the *Ungarischer Sturmmarsch.* An announcement by the firm of Bote & Bock, published in the *Vossische Zeitung* in 1844, claims that the *Sturmmarsch* was the work of a man named Joseph Gungl. See VZ No. 61 "Beilage" (12.3.1844). Interestingly enough, Liszt may have been in Berlin on 12 March 1844 and seen the announcement, but we do not know whether he replied to his publishers.

15 The *Allgemeine musikalische Zeitung,* for example, identifies one of the works performed in Berlin on 1 January 1842 as "Liszt's grandioses 'Ungarisches Marsch'" [AmZ 44 (1842), col. 145]. Other papers identified the same work as his "Marche hongroise."
   References to otherwise-unknown Liszt compositions crop up from

whether the "Tarantelles" mentioned in several advertisements and reviews were Liszt's own *Tarantelles napolitaines* from the first version of his *Album d'un voyageur*, or his transcription of *La Danza: Tarantella napolitana* from Rossini's *Soirées musicales*.[16] We also cannot determine, at least on some occasions, whether he played his *Serenata et l'Orgia (Grande Fantasie sur des motifs des Soirées musicales)*, or his somewhat less complex transcriptions of the "Serenade" and "Orgy" movements from the *Soirées* published separately around the same time. It is more likely that Liszt probably played the more complex transcription during his earliest German tours (early reviews refer more often to "Serenata" and "Orgia"), but he may also have played it later.[17] Finally, we cannot tell whether the work identified simply as "Campanella" and/or "Carnival of Venice" was taken from the *Etudes d'éxecution transcendante d'apres Paganini*, whether it may have been the *Grande Fantaisie de Bravoure sur la Clochette de Paganini* based on the "Campanella" theme, or whether it—or part of it—may have been a different work altogether.[18]

Similar problems exist for works by other composers. The appearances of Beethoven sonatas on Liszt's programs, for example, did not imply that he performed these works complete.[19] On 21 October 1843 in Munich, for instance, he

---

time to time in the Vormärz press. One of the most intriguing concerns a "Polonaise-Galop" based on themes from Meyerbeer's operas *Margarethe, Robert le diable,* and *Les Huguenots.* This novelty, arranged for voices, was announced for a "Bal paré, masqué et travesti" held as a Carnival celebration in Berlin on 25 February 1843. See VZ No. 42 (18.2.1843). Evidently the performance took place: Rellstab confessed himself satisfied with the music he heard on that occasion! See VZ No. 49 (27.2.1843).

16 In most cases, certainly, they were Rossini's. For his concert of 6 December 1843, for example, Liszt advertised the dance "aus Rossinis Soiréen" [MnJ No. 332 (5.12.1843), p. 1327].

17 According to one Frankfurt a.M. paper, for example, Liszt played the "Grande fantaisie" version of his Rossini transcription on 23 July 1840 in Mainz. See FOPZ Nos. 200-202 (21-23.7.1840), pp. 1664, 1672, and 1684. According to a Berlin paper, though, he played "La Serenata et l'Orgia" in that city as late as 30 January 1842. See APSZ No. 28 (28.1.1842), p. 112.

18 An incomplete "Carnaval de Venise" for piano {R. 665}, written in Liszt's hand, survives as D-WRgs Liszt Ms. J56.

19 Walker, p. 317, implies through omission that his subject played the entire "Hammerklavier" sonata during his Berlin concerts of 1841-1842. In fact, Liszt performed only two movements.

presented only the first movement from the "Pathètique" sonata;[20] on another occasion he played movements from several different sonatas on the same program.[21] Nor can we always determine whether Liszt performed more of Beethoven's Op. 26 Sonata than its first movement.[22] This is true of other works as well: on at least one occasion he played only the first movement of the "Emperor" concerto, and he occasionally interrrupted the order of movements in other works to play songs, short piano pieces, or even operatic fantasies.[23] No wonder critics occasionally thought he had written *all* the pieces he played—or, in some cases, merely embellished. Even those reporters who knew which work was which understood that Liszt's colossal talent transformed all music into his own.[24]

Liszt's Repertory as Conductor and Accompanist

Throughout his German tours Liszt accompanied singers and instrumentalists in operatic and chamber works. Beginning in 1842, he also appeared publically as an orchestral and operatic conductor. His orchestral repertory was small, though (at least prior to the late 1840s), and almost all of it has been mentioned in Chapter III. Beethoven was Liszt's favorite orchestral composer, and during the 1840s in Germany he conducted the Beethoven Third, Fifth, Sixth, and Seventh symphonies, the overtures to *Coriolan* and *Fidelio*, and the *Weihe des Hauses* overture, Op. 115. Other Beethoven works

---

20   *Contra* Newman, "Liszt's Interpreting of Beethoven's Piano Sonatas," p. 192.

21   See the *Memoirs of Hector Berlioz*, trans. David Cairns (New York 1969), p. 552 [*contra* Newman, "Liszt's Interpreting of Beethoven's Piano Sonatas," p. 193n].

22   On 17 October 1845, he performed the entire Op. 26 sonata, even though advertisements identify only the "Andante con variazione" movement. See FbOZ Nos. 287-288 and 293 (14-15 and 20.10.1845), pp. 1203, 1208, and 1225.

23   On 31 October 1840, for example, he scattered movements from the Hummel Septet throughout a Hamburg concert. See HNZ No. 255 (30.10.1840).

24   "Wir hörten Liszt in sieben Nummern . . . aber durch [Liszts] unvergleichliche und überreiche Transcription[en] für das Pianoforte wirklich ein Miteigenthum Liszt's geworden" [DmGHZ (1845); reprinted in facsimile in Burger, p. 158].

conducted by Liszt included the incidental music to *Egmont*, portions of *Fidelio* proper, and the orchestral accompaniment of the C-minor Concerto, Op. 37. Liszt also conducted a number of works by Weber (including the *Oberon* and *Jubel* overtures), a symphonic movement by Schubert, an overture by Berlioz, another by Lambert, and the whole of Mozart's opera *Die Zauberflöte*. Finally, he conducted the premiere performance of his own cantata written in honor of the 1845 Beethoven Festival held in Bonn, and he also appeared in Bonn as an accompanist and conductor of other works.

As a pianist Liszt frequently shared programs with other musicians, participating in performances of a number of sonatas as well as in large-scale chamber performances of various kinds. Among the works closest to his heart as an ensemble pianist were Beethoven's "Archduke" trio, Op. 97, and so-called "Choral Fantasy," Op. 80. Liszt also accompanied a variety of songs, operatic arias, and choral numbers, and in one instance—as we saw in Chapter III—he even arranged a "Barcarolle" by Pantaleoni {R. 644}. A page from this song, complete with Liszt's accompaniment and different melodic lines for different stanzas of its texts, is reproduced above as Plate 9.

In contemporary advertisements and reviews, unfortunately, many of Liszt's performances as chamber musician and accompanist are described only in the vaguest terms. In March 1844, for example, Liszt and Pantaleoni presented at least two different "Romances" on their Magdeburg programs; which "romances" these were, however, is unknown.[25] Unidentified arias and ensemble numbers from operas by Donizetti, Meyerbeer, Mozart, and many other composers also appear on advertisements and playbills. A few vocal and instrumental works were precisely identified, however. On half a dozen occasions, for example, Liszt accompanied performances of a cavatina from Pacini's *Niobe* entitled "I tuoi frequenti palpiti"—the same melody Liszt used in his own "Grande Fantasie" on Pacini's tune. On other occasions, we know only that Liszt participated in performing a Beethoven violin

---

[25] Liszt and Pantaleoni could have performed as many as four different piano-vocal compositions in Magdeburg, since two "Romances" are listed for each of two programs. See MbZ Nos. 64-65 (14 and 16.3.1844).

sonata, or that he played "part" of an opera like *Lucia di Lammermoor* on the piano.

We also cannot always determine whether Liszt played certain pieces as an accompanist or as a soloist. We know, for instance, that on several occasions he accompanied singers in performances of Schubert's *Ständchen* and *Erlkönig*. On the other hand, the fact that songs appeared on some of his programs had little to do with how individual Schubert songs were performed on those occasions. On 21 July 1840, for example, Liszt gave a concert in Baden-Baden with Valerie Ruppelin. Advertisements for that event mention only the title "Erlkönig"; they say nothing about whether Mlle. Ruppelin sang that work or Liszt played it by himself, and no reviews appeared in local newspapers.[26] We have seen, though, that on many occasions Liszt played Schubert songs as piano solos, even though famous singers shared the platform with him.

"Alternate" Liszt Editions and Other Repertory Problems

Liszt was at heart an improviser, and his enthusiasm for spontaneous music-making carried over into his career as a composer. Most of the compositions he published between the middle 1830s and the early 1840s appeared in two, three, or even four variant or "alternate" editions, and we simply cannot tell today which edition(s) he may have performed from during his German tours. In programs and reviews, for example, we find repeated references to his fantasy on themes from Meyerbeer's *Huguenots*. But Liszt did not publish *one* fantasy on that work; he published *three* significantly different fantasies, all of which have been described, in effect, as "one" work by compilers of dictionary articles and thematic catalogs.[27] As

---

[26] See, however, BdWb No. 73 (21.7.1840), p. 907.

[27] See, for example, Raabe II, p. 279 (i.e., {R. 221}). According to this source, only two, evidently quite similar versions of the *Huguenots* fantasy exist: those published by Hofmeister and Schlesinger. In fact there are at least three versions: the first published by Hofmeister (Plate No. 2269), the second published by Schlesinger of Paris (Plate "M.S. 2332"; see D-WRgs Liszt Ms. U56), and the third published by Schlesinger of Berlin (Plate No. 2136).

The present author is completing a study of these and other "alternate" Liszt editions, a few of which have been reprinted or mentioned to date in the Editio Musica/Bärenreiter *Neue Liszt Ausgabe* begun

far as we know, on the other hand, Liszt published only one transcription of the overture to Rossini's *Guillaume Tell* and only one paraphrase on themes from Bellini's *Somnambula*.

Yet, although he also published only one fantasy on themes from Mozart's *Don Giovanni*, Liszt seems to have improvised others. In fact, he improvised a number of fantasies during his German tours, sometimes on themes suggested by members of his audience.[28] Through improvisation he may also have tried out ideas for new "published" works. On 6 November 1840, for example, Liszt improvised a fantasy based partly on a tune from *Lucrezia Borgia*, thereby almost certainly beginning or, at the very least, continuing work on his *Réminiscences de Lucrezia Borgia*.

Liszt's Programming Strategies

The character of Liszt's German programs was influenced by a number of factors. One was the participation of other musicians. When an orchestra was available, Liszt could play concertos or conduct. When vocalists or instrumentalists were on hand, he could take part in chamber performances or accompany soloists. On many occasions, of course, he appeared alone, whether by choice or circumstance. Thus the presence (or absence) of other musicians determined many of his programming choices. Concertos by Bach, Beethoven, Hummel, and

---

during the 1960s. Furthermore, two teams of researchers are currently working on new catalogs of Liszt's music. The first team is headed by Mária Eckhardt of Budapest, the second by Leslie Howard and Michael Short of Great Britain. With regard to the first team's efforts, see Eckhardt, "A New Thematic Catalog of Liszt's Compositions," JALS 27 (1990), pp. 53-55. See also *Die Projekte der Liszt-Forschung*, ed. Detlef Altenburg and Gerhard Winkler (Eisenstadt 1991), which contains reports by Klaus Wolfgang Niemöller, Serge Gut, and Eckhardt about the "Eckhardt" catalog. Finally, see Eckhardt, "The Liszt Thematic Catalogue in Preparation: Results and Problems," *Studia Musicologica* 34 (1992), pp. 221-230; and other articles in this conference report.

28 The fact that he asked his audiences for themes does not necessarily mean that the fantasies Liszt subsequently "improvised" were not already worked out or even written down. As far back as April 1823, he arranged in advance of his second Vienna concert for Pixis to submit a theme for improvisation during his performance. When Pixis and the theme failed to appear at the proper time, the young artist found himself unable to improvise satisfactorily on a different theme. See *Der Sammler* [Vienna], 29 April 1823. The *Sammler* review is reprinted complete in Saffle, "Liszt Research Since 1936," p. 279.

Weber, for example, as well as chamber works like
Beethoven's Quintet for piano and winds, or Hummel's Septet
in something like its original form could be presented only with
the cooperation of his colleagues.

His listeners also influenced some of his programming
decisions. On 8 January 1842, for example, Liszt played in
Berlin before an audience that included Prince Louis
Ferdinand. Small wonder that on this occasion, and this occasion alone, Liszt participated in a performance of a piano
quartet written by the Prince himself. The presence of Hiller,
Mendelssohn, and Schumann in the audiences of his March
1840 concerts gave Liszt reason to present excerpts from
Carnaval and several of Hiller's etudes—pieces which he
rarely, if ever again, played in public during his German
tours.[29] Finally, the pieces he performed at private affairs seem
at least sometimes to have been chosen with regard for those
around him. In July 1840, for example, he may have played his
Huguenots fantasy because Meyerbeer was also present at the
Empress of Russia's Ems reception. When Liszt visited Kassel
and Ludwig Spohr the following year, he read through works
by Spohr, including the piano part for a Quintet in c minor. And
Liszt took part in performances of Wilhelm Speyer's songs in
1843 when he visited Speyer's Frankfurt home.

For the most part, however, Liszt seems to have established his own performing strategies and chosen his own solo
repertory. The programs for virtually all of his solo recitals
consisted of four, five, six, or seven showy compositions, arranged to create a sense of musical variety. A typical recital
might open with a large-scale, "serious" work—perhaps Liszt's
own transcription of the overture to Rossini's *Guillaume Tell*,
perhaps a Beethoven sonata or sonata movement. One or more
smaller pieces would separate that work from another large-
scale composition, perhaps an operatic fantasy or Weber's

---

[29] On 20 March 1840 Liszt played a Schumann fantasy (?the C-Major Fantasy) privately for Schumann himself. See Litzmann I, p. 414; and other
sources. Furthermore, Liszt performed works by Mendelssohn (e.g., the
Concerto in d minor) when that composer was not in the audience (e.g.,
on 16 February 1843 in Breslau). But Liszt didn't play much Schumann
or Mendelssohn later on in Germany, and by the mid-1840s he had apparently fallen out with both composers. See Walker, "Schumann, Liszt,
and the C Major Fantasie, Op. 17: A Declining Relationship," *Music &
Letters* 60 (1979), pp. 156-166. See also Little.

Aufforderung zum Tanz. The rest of the program, presented with or without intermission, would repeat that pattern. A large number of recitals concluded either with Liszt's glittering *Grand Galop chromatique* or his transcription of Schubert's *Erlkönig*; these pieces made exciting finales to virtuoso programs.

Even programs like these, however, may have been influenced by circumstances. We saw in Chapter III that German crowds often called for encores, and Liszt generally obliged them with exciting performances of favorite works. Furthermore, he was sometimes influenced by national or patriotic choices in choosing program selections. On 26 November 1846, for example, he presented a recital in Transylvania which concluded with several selections from his own *Ungarische Nationalmelodien*—in this instance, identified on a contemporary advertising poster as the *Magyar dalok*.[30] In Hungary, works like the *Nationalmelodien* would have been ideal concert cappers. In Germany, on the other hand, the *Réminiscences de Don Juan* would probably have been better received. Nevertheless, Liszt also played "Hungarian" pieces in Germany, and he performed many "German" pieces throughout Europe.

During his early tours, Liszt seems to have introduced somewhat more variety into his programs than he did later on. In 1841-1842, for example, he performed virtually all of the works that made up his solo German repertory. And in Berlin between December 1841 and March 1842 he played more different works than during any other phase of his virtuoso career. It was then, for example, that he gave his only performance (albeit fragmentary) of Beethoven's massive "Hammerklavier," and one of only two Bach "Chromatic Fantasy and Fugue" performances. It was also only in Berlin that Liszt played selections from his *Album d'un voyager*, and only in Berlin and Leipzig that he performed his "Mazeppa" etude.[31]

---

[30] See Walker, p. 436. NB: The poster in question gives "Magyar dalok" and "Mélodies hongroises" as alternate titles for the same work.

[31] Whether this last work was performed as published in the *24* [sic] *Grandes etudes* of 1838, or in the revised 1847 editions of Haslinger and Schlesinger, cannot be determined. With regard to these various editions, see {R. 2a, 2c}.

After 1842 Liszt performed fewer different solo works. Most of the recitals he gave during the autumn of 1843, for example, featured one of two set "programs." The first consisted of the overture to *Guillaume Tell*, the "Andante finale" from *Lucia di Lammermoor*, the "Don Juan" fantasy, transcriptions of Schubert songs (especially *Ständchen* and *Erlkönig*), and the *Galop chromatique*. The second program (presented when an orchestra was available and, apparently, only when Liszt dallied long enough in one place to perform twice in public) consisted of Weber's *Konzertstück*, the *Somnambula* fantasy, Weber's "Introduction to the Dance," and the *Hexameron* variations (with orchestra). Often Liszt varied these programs slightly. On 27 November 1843, for example, he played his "first" program in Karlsruhe, but with two changes: the addition of a Chopin mazurka, and the substitution of Schubert's *Ave Maria* for the *Ständchen*. In Heidelberg the following evening, he added Weber's *Aufforderung zum Tanz* to the original version of the same program. Liszt evidently liked both programs, because he repeated them regularly during 1844-1845. Indeed, he liked certain works so much that he played them with or without "assistance" (i.e., with or without the presence of an orchestra or chamber partners). When he could not play Weber's *Konzertstück* with a supporting ensemble, for instance, he played it alone. When he had to or wanted to, he played the Hummel Septet as a solo; otherwise, as we saw in Chapter III, he played it with either four or six other artists.

Liszt changed his virtuoso repertory gradually throughout his German tours. Perhaps the most substantial changes involved the more frequent appearances on post-1842 programs of the *Réminiscences de Don Juan*, and on post-1843 programs of Chopin's mazurkas. Other works gradually came to be performed less frequently: these included *Hexameron* for solo piano, the *Réminiscences de Robert le diable*, and Liszt's transcriptions of Schubert's *Ständchen* and *Ave Maria*. Other works disappeared entirely after 1842, among them the *Adelaïde* and "Pastoral" symphony transcriptions. To some extent these changes seem to have been interrelated. Liszt, for example, used Chopin's mazurkas to replace Schubert song transcrptions after c. 1843; and during his later Vormärz tours he used the "Don Juan" fantasy to replace other operatic para-phrases, including his paraphrase on Meyerbeer's *Robert*.

To what extent Liszt permitted his repertory to be deter-mined by his whims—or those of others—we cannot tell. Most of his performances of Beethoven sonatas took place in Berlin, Hamburg, and Munich, before sophisticated city audiences, but he also played sonatas in towns like Elberfeld, Krefeld, and Kiel. Again, the presence of singers may have influenced his decisions to present certain operatic fantasies. On 5 October 1841, for example, he accompanied Fanny Kemble and one Herr Schunk in several numbers from Bellini's *Norma* and played his own fantasies on *La Somnambula* and *Don Giovanni*. A week later at Aachen, when Kemble sang a "Cavatina" from *Somnambula*, Liszt played the overture to *Tell* instead of his *Somnambula* fantasy. On other occasions, how-ever, he seems to have presented individual operatic fantasies simply because he wanted to.

Certain questions about Liszt's German repertory con-tinue to tantalize students of his virtuoso travels, including the present author. Why, for instance, did he continue to play his *Réminiscences de Lucia di Lammermoor* so often, after he had completed his paraphrases on *Lucrezia Borgia* and *La Somnambula*? Why did so much of his adult repertory consist of compositions he first performed publically in childhood: works like the B-minor Hummel Concerto, for example, or the piano works of Weber?[32] Eyewitness accounts by excellent mu-sicians prove that Liszt was a superb sightreader and a voracious sampler of unfamiliar music, at least in the company of friends. Why, then, did he play so few "new" works in Germany after 1842? And why, when he performed his *Erlkönig* transcription so often—more often, in fact, than al-most any other work in his repertory—did he refuse on 21 January 1843 to play it as an encore? Perhaps he had grown tired of riding that particular warhorse. But on that occasion he mounted another instead: Weber's *Afforderung zum Tanz*.[33]

---

[32] Liszt played the Hummel Concerto in the 1820s in Vienna, and he played Weber's *Momento capriccioso* as early as 1823. See Walker, pp. 87-88 and 135. NB: Walker [pp. 372n-373n] accidentally omits Weber's works from his tabulation of Liszt's 1842 Berlin repertory.

[33] See BrPSZ No. 20 (24.1.1843), pp. 142-143.

The most powerful factor governing Liszt's repertory and programming strategy seems to have been showmanship. The overwhelming majority of the works he played repeatedly, at least in Germany, were operatic paraphrases, transcriptions, and showy "finales," especially the *Galop chromatique*. Between works like these he sandwiched more "delicate" compositions—as much for musical and emotional contrast, it would seem, as for the sake of the works themselves. True, we saw in Chapter III that some of his "heavy" programming selections, like his "Pastoral" symphony transcription, were mocked with some frequency by critics. Yet Liszt's preference for keyboard display is revealed most clearly not by the gradual elimination of certain "heavier" works from his primary repertory, but by the absence from that repertory of his own "heavier" (i.e., more imaginative) compositions. During the whole of his German tours, he almost never played any of the pieces which, when revised, became part of his *Années de pelèrinage*, nor did he play his *Apparitions* or his early Berlioz transcriptions. Furthermore, he never performed in Germany any of the early versions of his E-flat Major piano concerto or the original version of his *Harmonies poétiques et religieuses*. It is more for these works than for his *Galop chromatique* that Liszt is remembered today.[34] Yet the fact remains: none of the *Harmonies* or *Années* or *Apparitions* is "showy," at least not in the same way that the *Erlkönig* transcription is showy.

According to many sources, Liszt's motto was "Génie oblige!" Does—should—this motto suggest, though, that the artist "obliges" (i.e, gives in) to his audience, or that he has obligations *toward* his audience? And, if the latter, what obligations? The issue of "popularity" had an enormous impact not only on the reviews Liszt received in Germany, but on the reputation he established as a composer—a reputation which, remarkably, survives mostly unchanged to the present day. This reputation will be discussed in the following chapter.

---

[34] Whether the *Galop* represents Liszt better than pieces like the *Harmonies poétiques* is another matter—one, in fact, that is touched upon below in Chapter V.

CHAPTER V
Liszt and the German Critics

Die Weltgeschichte ist das Weltgericht.
Schiller

To a considerable extent Liszt's reputation has rested for more than a century on the opinions of nineteenth-century critics, especially German critics. We have seen that an enormous amount of criticism about Liszt was produced during the 1840s, much of it in response to his "transcendental" performances. We have seen too that, for the most part, this criticism—at least in Germany—was positive, even adulatory. As a pianist Liszt wrung from his reviewers a torrent of praise for his technique, touch, and interpretive abilities; and as a composer he was less often, but nevertheless quite often, complimented on his talent and accomplishments. The surprising thing is not, perhaps, that Liszt's reputation as a virtuoso has stuck with him to the present day, but that it continues to overshadow his reputation as one of nineteenth-century Europe's most important musical innovators. Or, as Charles Rosen has put it:

> The worst criticisms made during [his] lifetime . . . are still repeated by musicians today: Liszt is cheap and flashy . . . [his] melodies are banal, his harmonies tawdry, his large forms repetitious and uninteresting . . . The durability of the old criticisms is exceptional and suggests that [Liszt's] importance . . . is felt instinctively, but only imperfectly grasped, and that we have not yet learned a critical approach to [his] work, a way of elucidating what [he was] up to.[1]

Only recently, in fact, has Liszt's reputation as a composer begun to improve, mostly because he is at last winning recog-

---

[1] Quoted from the *New York Review of Books* 31/6 (12 April 1984), p. 17. These and other important remarks about Liszt appeared in Rosen's review of Walker's *Virtuoso Years* volume.

nition for such remarkable works as the B-minor Sonata, the *Faust* symphony, the *Via crucis*, and the late piano pieces. None of these compositions has anything directly to do with Liszt the "transcendental" virtuoso (except, perhaps, the keyboard writing of the B-minor Sonata), nor have his "transcendental" works (e.g., the *Huguenots, Lucia, Robert,* and "Don Juan" fantasies, the Schubert song transcriptions, the *Galop chromatique,* etc.) had much impact on his overall reputation as a composer. As a creative artist Liszt continues to be associated primarily with compositions like *Les préludes* and the first "Mephisto Waltz," pieces he wrote in the 1850s and 1860s. Yet many people speak of him even today as first and foremost a pianist, and only after that as a composer.

One reason for this may be that musicologists like Ernst Günther Heinemann continued into the 1980s to evaluate Liszt's music in terms of antithetical categories drawn from nineteenth-century criticism: "art" vs. "entertainment," "popularity" vs. "profundity," and "profundity" vs. "display." These antitheses, employed in dialectical arguments to reach synthetic conclusions, are part and parcel of the "Geschichtsphilosophie" German intellectuals have practiced since the early nineteenth century. In striving for new insights into Liszt's place in history, however, Heinemann and his ilk have succeeded only in conjuring up the "old" Liszt: that successful, flashy showman who also (even incidentally) was a creator of uneven, stylistically unconvincing potpourris masquerading as art works.[2] In doing this, they have emphasized important but isolated characteristics of their subject's work.[3] To quote Rosen a second time: "Only a view of Liszt that places [pieces like] the Second Hungarian Rhapsody"—or the

---

[2] See Ernst Günther Heinemann, *Franz Liszts Auseinandersetzung mit der giestlichen Musik* (Munich 1978).

[3] Especially aspects of his late style. See, for example, Lájos Bárdos, "Ferenc Liszt the Innovator," *Studia Musicologica* 17 (1975), pp. 3-38; Bengt Johnsson, "Modernities in Liszt's Works," *Svensk Tidskrift for Musikforsking* 46 (1964), pp. 83-117; and Paul Pisk, "Elements of Impressionism and Atonality in Liszt's Last Piano Pieces," *The Radford Review* 23 (1969), pp. 171-176. Liszt's early works have also been singled out for special study. See Dieter Torkewitz, *Harmonisches Denken im Frühwerk Franz Liszts* (Munich 1978). Other studies are identified in Saffle, *Franz Liszt: A Guide to Research.*

Réminiscences de Don Juan or even the *Grand Galop chromatique*—"in the center of his work will do him justice."[4]

In order better to understand Liszt's reputation, we must keep in mind several things. First, as we have already seen, the German press of the 1840s—especially the musical press, and especially in terms of magazines like the *Allgemeine musikalische Zeitung*, the *Neue Zeitschrift*, and the *Blätter für Musik und Literatur*—was the largest, best organized, and most authoritative of its day. Consequently, his German performances were advertised and reviewed in dozens of newspapers and magazines, and this does not include "greater German" periodicals published in places like Vienna and Prague.

Second, Liszt's German tours took place in the geographical and cultural heart of Europe. This would be a trivial observation, were it not for biographers who have overemphasized the colorful and exotic aspects of their subject's life.[5] During 1844-1845, for example, Liszt gave only a handful of concerts in Iberian cities and towns. The notices and reviews these concerts generated make fascinating reading today,[6] and the concerts themselves had a real impact, especially on later nineteenth-century Spanish music. But few people outside Portugal and Spain read about those concerts during the 1840s, and the impact of what *was* read on Liszt's European reputation was comparatively slight. By contrast, German periodicals like the *Augsburger allgemeine Zeitung* and the *Neue Zeitschrift* were read internationally, and their impact was enormous. So too, of course, was that of non-German "mainstream" music magazines like the *Revue et Gazette Musicale de Paris*. But periodicals like the *Revue* often reprinted reviews and notices that appeared originally in German publications; so did the *Gazetta Musicale di Milano*, the *Wiener allgemeine Musik-Zeitung*, and *Le Monde musicale* (to name

---

4   See the *New York Review of Books* 31/6 (12 April 1984), p. 20.

5   This has been especially true of Eastern European biographers since World War II. As one would expect, the "exotic" elements emphasized by these experts have been primarily proletarian and Russian ones. The importance of Hungary and even of Russia in Liszt's life should not be underestimated, but neither should that of Germany.

6   See Stevenson, "Liszt in the Iberian Peninsula." Also cited in Chapter I.

but three that referred to German musical events regularly). When Liszt appeared in Vormärz Germany, reports of his activities appeared in print everywhere. When, on the other hand, he appeared in Barcelona or Constantinople or Pécs or even St. Petersburg, his activities were often publicized locally, or not at all.

Liszt's "transcendental" reputation was and is interpenetrated by a host of elements, some of them difficult to evaluate today: his own personality, prejudices, and behavior; his penchant for comfortable living and a good time; his reputation as a ladies' man; his decorations and titles, especially that of "Doctor"; his noteworthy success with admiring students and "progressive" young people like Prince Lichnowsky; his complex approach to political issues—which extended, as we have seen, to the composition (as a foreigner, whether French or Hungarian) of "German" patriotic songs;[7] his enormous income, his charitable activities, and so on. Most of these topics cannot be addressed at length here. Moreover, it would seem that the assumptions upon which his reputation was built in Vormärz Germany—and upon which it rests even today—were three: 1) that Liszt was *primarily* a pianist, and only *secondarily* a composer or accompanist or conductor; 2) that he was *fundamentally a popular figure*; and 3) that his artistry could be evaluated adequately *in terms of technical pianism*, and his pianism *in terms of other composers' music*.

Let us consider these assumptions one by one: The first—that Liszt was primarily a pianist—can be justified to a considerable extent by how he presented himself to his public. When he performed, it was almost always as a pianist; throughout the 1840s he appeared as a conductor only infrequently. And, as we saw in Chapter IV, he rarely played what critics today would consider his most interesting pre-1845 works: early versions of the pieces that eventually comprised the first volume of the *Années de pèlerinage*, for instance, or early versions of the "Transcendental Etudes." Instead, he presented "original" pieces by other composers or played fan-

---

7 Liszt won renown for his transcriptions of Italian music as well as for his performances of the German classics: "Auch Liszt schürte die Flammen dieser italienischen Feuersbrunst, und hob den klassischen Eindruck, der er durch den Vortrag der Beethoven- und Weber'schen Konzerte hervorbrachte" [AmZ 43 (1841), col. 878].

tasies of his own based on the other composers' music. This does not mean that during the 1840s Liszt was ignored altogether as a composer. Some of his compositions were received enthusiastically in Germany and, as we saw in Chapter III, only the *Galop chromatique* was lampooned—perhaps because it had become so familiar and, therefore, so closely associated with its composer's brand of virtuosity. Uncommon, perhaps, but nevertheless real were observations like those that appeared in the *Kleine Musikzeitung* in 1845:

> [The Beethoven Festival Cantata] is an entirely effective work that contains some extraordinarily lovely passages and demonstrates that Liszt has learned much more about composition than he has demonstrated previously in his fantasies and transcriptions.[8]

Interestingly enough, Liszt's vocal compositions of the 1840s were generally mentioned in newspapers and magazines *only* when they were praised. The nationalistic character of some of these works may have inspired favorable reviews in the press. Or it may be that German audiences and critics may simply have enjoyed pieces we rarely hear today: songs like *Nonnenwerth* and male-choral numbers like *Das deutsche Vaterland*.

Nor was pianism despised by a majority of Liszt's critics. Occasional complaints appeared about the way he played certain compositions, or about the compositions he didn't play, and even his interpretive artistry was sometimes called into question. On one point, however, the critics were unanimous: Liszt was a staggering keyboard technician. Above all, he could play every kind of figure—diatonic and chromatic scales, parallel thirds and sixths, octaves, staccato passages, repeated notes, and so on and so forth—with amazing speed, clarity, and control. It was his masterful technique, not his repertory or subtleties of interpretation—that earned him such titles as "king of pianists," "prince of piano virtuosos," and "Piano God."[9] Vir-

---

8 "Die Cantata von Liszt ist ein ganz tüchtiges Werk, enthält außerordentlich viel Schönes und beweist, daß Liszt bei weitem mehr gelehrt hat, als er bisher in seinen Phantasien und Uebertragungen zeigte" [BML 6 (1845), p. 154]. See also Appendix D, quotation 19.

9 In her study of Clara Schumann's career, Joan Chissell cites an 1838 ar-

tuosity, in short, was admired by almost everyone. It was en-
joyable: Liszt's performances were fun, because brilliance,
power, and wit are fun. Or, to quote William Blake, "Energy is
Eternal Delight."

One of the most important articles about Liszt published
in the contemporary German press was a detailed analysis of
his keyboard technique that appeared in an 1843 issue of the
Frankfurter Konversationsblatt. (As we saw in Chapter II, Liszt
himself admired this analysis.) According to the anonymous
author of this article, three interrelated accomplishments made
Liszt master of his instrument: a secure, smooth, and elastic
attack or touch ("Anschlag"); carefully cultivated dexterity in
both hands and all ten fingers; and complete, controlled inde-
pendence for each finger. Taken together, these skills enabled
him to create almost unbelievable, never-before-heard keyboard
effects: dynamic shadings, melodic cantilenas, and so on. Liszt
also mastered the piano's pedals, used the instrument's lower
register in distinctive ways, and perfected octaves of
thunderous power. It was as a pianist, then, that he *proved*
himself; and it was in terms of performance and *only* performance that his genius was finally epitomized by his critics:

> What learning, what labor, what unbending will, what
> endurence, what renunciation and self-deprivation must have
> been necessary for [Liszt] to reach this never-before-achieved
> pinnacle of perfection! There have been so many outstanding
> pianists in the past and there are more than a few real
> virtuosos today, but . . . Liszt is incomparable [as a per-
> former].[10]

Liszt's contemporaries did not necessarily despise his
compositions, conducting, and chamber performances; we saw
in Chapter III that most of them respected these "other" activities and accomplishments and even praised them. But it was

---

ticle from the *Neue Zeitschrift* which compared her subject with Henselt,
Thalberg, and Liszt. According to this study, Liszt got top marks as an
improviser, a sight-reader, a "deep musician," and so on; there was no
category for "technique," though. (Interestingly, none of the four
pianists—not even Clara—was deemed worthy of a mark for "objectivity
in performance.") See Chissell, *Clara Schumann: A Dedicated Spirit*
(London 1983), p. 53.

[10] Translated from FKB No. 27 (27.1.1843), p. 108. See also Appendix D,
quotation 11.

his technique that "typed" Liszt as a virtuoso—all too often, as *only* a virtuoso. No one argued seriously during the 1840s that Liszt was the greatest living composer, or even one of the greatest; by the same token, no one disputed seriously that he was the greatest living pianist, probably the greatest pianist of all time.[11]

Second, German critics generally considered Liszt a "popular" phenomenon. There were two reasons for this: he was "fashionable," and the fashion itself—at least during bouts of "Lisztomania"—was perceived by many critics (Heine among them, at least to some extent) as little more than mindless adulation by the masses.[12] Sometimes, as we saw in Chapter III, even reputable Liszt criticism sometimes approached hagiography during the 1840s. If Liszt did great and good things, though, he was able to do them *because* of the influence and wealth he acquired through virtuosity. If he contributed money to charitable causes, it was *because* virtuosity enabled him to earn that money; little or none of it, apparently, came from sheet-music royalties or fees the *Revue et Gazette Musicale* must have paid him for his occasional but highly interesting essays. Popularity, therefore, was the result of virtuosity, and virtuosity itself—or at least, the results of virtuosity—was *good*, morally and often musically. It was in light of reasoning like this, therefore, that Schreiber portrayed Liszt rewarding the faithful with performances of fantasies and show-pieces: with virtuosity itself, that is, instead of money or favors.[13]

It is true that Liszt was popular: he was an almost universal favorite with German audiences (indeed, with audiences everywhere), and his livelihood depended on his popularity. It is also true that he specialized as a performer in "popular" pieces like operatic fantasies and arrangements of national melodies. But "popularity" has many definitions, and only a few

---

[11] Contrary views, like those expressed for time to time in *Signale*, seem to have been exceptions to a generally accepted rule. See, for example, Appendix D, quotation 16.

[12] For "masses," of course, read "the music-loving middle class." As we saw in Chapter I, most Vormärz Germans could no more have afforded to attend Liszt's performances than they could have hoped to win the extraordinary wealth the same performances brought him.

[13] See Appendix D, quotation 12.

of them fit Liszt. That he provided his audiences with "a series
of psychologically unfamiliar innovations" and with pleasure
"evoked through the formal recurrence of a standard repertory
of *clichés*, quotations, stylizations, etc., shared to the greatest
possible extent by author and public alike,"[14] for example, is
true only to a certain extent. Liszt certainly was a psychological
innovator in music, but much of his virtuoso keyboard writing
was anything but clichéd. Instead, his operatic fantasies and
reminiscences as well as his transcriptions of vocal and instrumental works often commented on or even *reconstructed* the
music of other composers, helping to make it more or, occasionally, more meaningful.[15] In Liszt's day, however, commen-
tary and reconstruction—what Renaissance artists would have
called "parody"—were not respected creative venues. Nor have
they been in our own century, at least for the most part. Picasso
may repaint Velasquez or Stravinsky recompose Pergolesi, but
Liszt (at least according to Busoni) should not have
"rewritten" *Don Giovanni*—even if the result has as little to do
directly with Mozart's opera as the *Damoiselles d'Avignon* with
African masks, or Mann's *Doktor Faustus* with the dramas of
Marlowe and Goethe.[16]

Third, German critics of the 1840s for the most part shied
away from discussing Liszt's compositions in and of themselves.
When they did, they often compared his works unfavorably
with compositions of very different kinds: Beethoven sonatas,
for example. This is like comparing apples and oranges—or,
more appropriately, David and Delacroix. Of course, most
Vormärz critics were "mere" journalists interested in Liszt primarily as a "newsworthy" figure. During 1840 and 1841, how-

---

14 Quoted from Giovanni Morelli, "Forms of Popularization of Music in the
    19th Century and Up to World War I," *Acta Musicologica* 59/1
    ["Supplement"] (1987), p. 13.

15 See Morelli, p. 16.

16 "The *Don-Juan* fantasy treats sacred themes [i.e., Mozart's music] in al-
    together too worldly a fashion" [Ferruccio Busoni, *The Essence of Music*
    (London 1957), p. 92].
       Robert Hughes, in *The Shock of the New* (New York 1988), observes
    of Picasso's *Damoiselles* that it "is still a disturbing painting after three
    quarters of a century, a refutation of the idea that the surprise of *art*, like
    the surprise of *fashion* [*vide* Liszt; italics added], must necessarily wear
    off" [Hughes, p. 21].

ever, these journalists were more inclined to investigate his music than pass it by. Prior to the outbreak of "Lisztomania" in Berlin, the critics had not yet decided what Liszt was and, like Wiest, they were willing to discuss him as a composer (someone involved with French Romanticism, perhaps), and to write about his operatic paraphrases as if they were "real" compositions.[17] In fact, no less a critic than François-Joseph Fétis published an article in 1841—and in German—about Liszt as the culmination of a new school of piano *composers*.[18]

After 1842, however, Liszt became more and more frequently "typed" as a virtuoso entertainer, albeit one of the highest calibre. From then on his keyboard compositions were usually evaluated by contemporary critics primarily in terms of his spectacular technique.[19] Besides, there was little need to listen to Liszt's music when one could listen to Liszt himself play it—or *not* listen, as the case may be, but attend his fashionable performances, worship, sneer, or (at the very least) see and be seen. The occasion of a Liszt concert, therefore— and to a considerable extent—turned attention away from the very music the concert presented. Critics of Liszt's German performances often relied upon circumstances or their own preoccupations to describe the social, rather than musical, events they witnessed.[20] Thus the most fulsome account of his German music-making appeared in 1842 in Berlin's *Gesellschafter* as a

---

17 See Appendix D, quotation 2.
    The decision that Liszt's music can be divided into "original" works (read: "better") vs. "transcriptions" and "arrangements" (read: "worse") has influenced even the arrangement of catalogs of his compositions. This situation may at last be set to rights in one or both of the two new Liszt catalogs identified above in Chapter IV.

18 See François-Joseph Fétis, "Liszt und die Claviercomponisten der Neuzeit," BML 2 (1841), pp. 117-121. Fétis's opinion of Liszt's music was not uniformly high, but the very existence of his article testifies to his conviction about the importance of its topic: Liszt as composer rather than performer.

19 To quote but one review of the *Réminiscences de Robert le diable*, which echoes negative German attitudes but appeared in 1842 in London's *Musical World*: "We can conceive no other utility in the publication of this piece, than as a diagram in black and white of M. Liszt's extraordinary digital dexterity" [World 17 (1842), p. 75]. See also HZCor No. 152 (29.6.1843) for a similar evaluation of Liszt's technique and musical output.

20 See, for example, Appendix D, quotation 13. There can be no doubt that

description of a concert *as a social affair*, a description devoted primarily to the chit-chat of audience members between and even during the musical numbers themselves.[21] Even Schumann, for reasons of his own, all but ignored *what* Liszt played (unless it had been written by another composer) and concentrated on *how* he played it.[22]

In short, then, Liszt, then, was perceived to a considerable extent during the 1840s as a delightful entertainer[23] who sometimes performed great works but more often merely paltry ones, a competent if somewhat uneven arranger of pleasant "popular" melodies, and a composer of limited scope and ability. His refusal for whatever reason to present himself as a different, possibly more "German" kind of composer during his "transcendental" tours helped transform the perceptions of his critics into "facts." Furthermore, his occasional lapses in performances of German masterpieces contributed to his reputation as an overimaginative or even vulgar technician. Perhaps Liszt was just what his opponents claimed he was; but probably not. We have already seen how difficult it can be to verify where, what, and when he played; how much more difficult, if not impossible it is today, to determine *how* he played. What is important, however, is not whether the critics were right about Liszt, but that their opinions have become the "truth." Thus Schiller's famous dictum: The history of the world *is* the world's judgment.

---

circumstances (in the case of this quotation, an abandoned nunnery) inspired descriptions of Liszt's playing in terms of "soul" and "spirit."

21 See F. Bellegne, "Ein Concert von Franz Liszt," BGes Nos. 34-36 (1842), pp. 161ff.

22 Plantinga puts the same thing into different words: "When Schumann became a critic he was convinced that the piano virtuosi operating out of Paris were responsible for most of the musical ills of Europe. . . . It is easy to understand that he should find Liszt more acceptable than many of the other virtuosi. Liszt, after all, sometimes played Chopin, Schumann, and later, Beethoven in addition to his *Valse di bravura*, *Galop chromatique*, and variations on Meyerbeer. . . . [Despite all this, however, Schumann's critical] writing about Liszt—especially Liszt the composer—remained cautious" [Plantinga, *Schumann as Critic*, p. 218].

23 Or a shoddy one, at least on occasion. See Appendix D, quotations 3, 5, 8, 16, and 18.

Plate 11

A page from Liszt's *Serenata et l'Orgia* fantasy
(Mainz: B. Schott & Sons, Plate 4724.1 [early version])

Plate 12

A page from Liszt's *Puritani* fantasy
(Mainz: B. Schott & Sons: Plate 4723)

Plate 13

A page from Liszt's finale to *Hexameron*
(Vienna: Tobias Haslinger: Plate T.H. 7700)

We do not *know* today that Liszt played surpassingly well; we can only surmise that he did, if not always as well as he could. But we *have* his compositions, and they testify to his greatness both as composer and performer. Indeed, they are our only "hard evidence" of his virtuosity. Because, during the 1830s and 1840s, no one else wrote anything like them, we have reason to believe that no one else could have played anything like them. Three very different passages composed by Liszt and performed by him during his virtuoso tours—the first a "mixed" passage containing cross-hands writing and a variety of textures from the "Serenata et l'Orgia" fantasy on Rossini's *Soirées*; the second a "delicate" passage from the *Puritani* fantasy; and the third a "brilliant" passage from the finale to the *Hexameron* variations—demonstrate the inadequacy of stereotyping him as nothing more than an entertainer. These passages speak for themselves, especially to anyone capable of performing them with confidence and skill. The passages themselves are reproduced as Plates 11, 12, and 13.

Finally, we should not forget that Liszt's compositions cannot easily be separated from their realization in performance. Put it another way: before (and even after) the appearance of composers like Liszt, criticism fostered respect for "abstract" or "absolute" music, and for formal and emotional coherence in instrumental composition and performance. According to advocates of musical absolutism, Bach and Beethoven can be studied profitably "in the leaf"—indeed, their music is often talked about as if it *exists* in written form (i.e., in some quasi-Platonically "perfect" realm); and as if poor performances are poor, at least for the most part, because they *differ from the score*. "Romantic" music, however, requires—but has only occasionally been judged by—fundamentally different standards. Liszt's pieces could have been (and probably were) played any way Liszt liked: he was, after all, the composer, and he created the music *as he played it* and *however he played it*. In his performances there was no "authority" other than himself. This is why the existence of so many editions of his early keyboard works is important: it suggests that he quite likely "made up" (or "remade up") even his "published" compositions as he performed them.

The works of composers like Beethoven make use of a "dialectic of form" compared with which the works of the Romantics could only be found wanting. But Liszt's work is predicated on a "dialectic of experience" that makes paraphrases and transcriptions like the *Réminiscences de Don Juan* and the "Rákóczy March"—whether in his own version as an Hungarian Rhapsody, or in Berlioz's version as part of the *Damnation of Faust*—valid, even elevated forms of expression. For Bach or Beethoven, the composition of variations upon a given tune brought timeless musical structures into existence. For Liszt, the creation of fantasies, on the printed page *and* in performance, created elusive Romantic musical *experiences* and made them immediate, personal, even unique. It is for this reason, if for no other, that fifty years ago Paul Bekker (himself a defender of Liszt) *underestimated*, if anything, the damage critics had done to his subject's overall reputation when he observed that "[Liszt] fell a victim to the virtuoso" throughout most of the nineteenth and twentieth centuries, and that his "spectacular triumphs [as a performer] . . . have provoked much mockery among shallow wits."[24]

---

[24] See Paul Bekker, "Liszt and his Critics," MQ 22 (1936), p. 277. See also Bekker, "Franz Liszt Reconsidered," MQ 28 (1942), pp. 186-189.

Periodical Sigla and Abbreviations

Nineteenth-Century Newspaper and Magazine Sigla:

Each nineteenth-century periodical mentioned in the present study is identified below by siglum and complete title. When possible, newspapers are identified by entry numbers {in curved brackets} used in Gert Hagelweide's *Deutsche Zeitungsbestände in Bibliotheken und Archiven* (Düsseldorf 1974). Places of publication [in square brackets] and archival locations are also given for some periodicals. Familiar sigla (e.g., "AmZ" for the *Allgemeine musikalische Zeitschrift*) have been used whenever possible. New sigla have been modelled on older ones, and most new newspaper sigla are preceded by a letter or letters referring to place of publication (e.g., "Mz" for Mainz). References to a few additional newspapers identified only by titles appear throughout Chapters I-V and in Appendix B.

AmZ	*Allgemeine musikalische Zeitung* [Leipzig].
APSZ	*Allgemeine Preußische Staats-Zeitung* [Berlin]. Universitätsbibliothek, Heidelberg.
AuMP	*Der musikalische Postillon* [Augsburg].
AuPZ	*Augsburger Post-Zeitung* {58}.
AuTb	*Augsburger Tageblatt* {67}.
AuZ	*Allgemeine Zeitung* [Augsburg] {63}.
BamZ	*Berliner allgemeine musikalische Zeitung.*
BauEr	*Erzähler an der Spree* [Bautzen]. Staatsarchiv, Dresden.
BauN	*Budinisser Nachrichten* [Bautzen]. Staatsarchiv, Dresden.
BdB	*Badesche Beobachter.* NB: Not to be confused with the "Beobachter" supplement of the modern *Badeblatt.*
BdWb	*Badener Wochenblatt* {81}.

BFig	*Berliner Figaro.* Deutsche Staatsbibliothek, Berlin (1842 and 1844 only).
BGes	*Der Gesellschafter, oder Blätter für Geist und Herz* [Berlin]. Stadt- und Universitätsbibliothek, Frankfurt a.M.
BgS	*Der Sammler* [Brieg]. Library of the University of Wroclaw, Poland
BML	*Blätter für Musik und Literatur.* After 1844, the *Kleine Musikzeitung.*
BnWb	*Bonner Wochenblatt* {271}.
BrB	*Breslauer Beobachter.* Library of the University of Wroclaw, Poland.
BrEr	*Breslauer Erzähler.* Library of the University of Wroclaw, Poland.
BrPSZ	*Privilegirte Schlesische Zeitung* [Breslau] {336}.
BrZ	*Breslauer Zeitung* {333}.
BsAn	*Braunschweigischer Anzeigen* {294}.
CAmtN	*Caecilia: Algemeen musikaal tijdscrift van Nederland* [Utrecht].
DmGHZ	*Großherzogliche Hessische Zeitung* [Darmstadt] {402}.
DoWb	*Wochenblatt für die Stadt und den Kreis Dortmund* {430}.
DrAn	*Dresdner Anzeiger* {461}.
DrWb	*Dresdner Wochenblatt für vaterländische Interessen.* Staatsarchiv, Dresden.
DüsKb	*Düsseldorfer Kreisblatt and Täglicher Anzeiger* {483}.
DüsZ	*Düsseldorfer Zeitung* {492}.
EfZ	*Elberfelder Zeitung* {1956}.
ElbAn	*Elbinger Anzeiger* {514}.
EmsLK	*27te Liste der Kurgäste* [Ems]. Stadtarchiv Ems.
ErAn	*Allgemeine Anzeiger* [Erfurt].
ErEut	*Euterpe: Ein musikalisches Monatsblatt für Deutschlands Volksschullehrer* [Erfurt].
ErSLb	*Erfurter Stadt- und Landbote* {524}.
ErZ	*Erfurter Zeitung* {530}.
FadOT	*Der Telegraph. Ein Unterhaltungsblatt* [Frankfurt a.d.O.]. Staatsbibliothek, Berlin.
FadOWb	*Frankfurter patriotisches Wochenblatt* [Frankfurt a.d.O.] {619}.

FbOb	*Der Oberländer. Ein volkstümliches Blatt für Jedermann* [Freiburg i.B.] {643}.
FbOZ	*Oberrheinische Zeitung* [Freiburg i.B.] {644}.
FbZ	*Freiburger Zeitung* {641}.
FDid	*Didaskalia. Blätter für Geist, Gemüth und Publizität* [Frankfurt a.M.].
FGCh	*Frankfurter Gemeinnüßige Chronik* [Frankfurt a.M.]. Stadtarchiv, Frankfurt a.M.
FJ	*Frankfurter Journal* [Frankfurt a.M.] {610}.
FKB	*Frankfurter Konversations-Blatt* [Frankfurt a.M.].
FM	*La France musicale*. Bibliothèque nationale, Paris.
FOPZ	*Frankfurter Ober-Post-Amt-Zeitung* [Frankfurt a.M.] {613}.
FürWb	*Fürstenwälder Wochenblatt.*
GMdM	*Gazetta Musicale di Milano.*
GötWb	*Göttingen Wochenblatt.*
GSLb	*Glogauer Stadt- und Landblatt*. Library of the University of Wroclaw, Poland.
HalC	*Der Courier* [Halle] {790}.
HanMZ	*Hannoversche Morgen-Zeitung*. Copy supplied by Geraldine Keeling.
HanP	*Die Posaune* [Hannover] {1225}.
HanVb	*Hannoverische Volksblatt.*
HanZ	*Hannoversche Zeitung* {854}.
HbIb	*Intelligenz-Blatt von Heilbronn* {920}.
HeJ	*Heidelberger Journal* {898}.
HFrs	*Der Freischütz* [Hamburg].
HNach	*Privilegirte wöchentliche Gemeinnützige Nachrichten* [Hamburg] {834}.
HNZ	*Hamburger Neue Zeitung* {816}.
HTfD	*Telegraph für Deutschland* [Hamburg].
HZCor	*Staats- und Gelehrte Zeitung der Hamburgischen unpartheyischen Correspondenten* {832}. Also known as the "Correspondent."
Iris	*Iris im Gebiete der Tonkunst* [Berlin].
IsWb	*Iserlohner Wochen-Blatt*. Cited in Autexier.
JdF	*Journal de Francfort. Politique et Littérature* [Frankfurt a.M.]. Stadtarchiv, Frankfurt a.M.

JdNVM	*Jahrbücher des Deutschen National-Vereins für Musik und Ihre Wissenschaft* [Karlsruhe; 1839-1842]. Not to be confused with ZfDMV below.
JeWb	*Privilegirte Jenaische Wochenblätter* {980}.
KasS	*Der Salon* [Kassel]. Stadt- und Universitätsbibliothek, Frankfurt a.M.
KasZ	*Kasselsche allgemeine Zeitung* {1036}.
KlCb	*Correspondenz-Blatt* [Kiel] {1072}.
KlWb	*Kieler Wochenblatt* {1084}.
KobAn	*Coblenzer Anzeiger.* Stadtarchiv, Koblenz.
KobRB	*Der rheinische Beobachter* [Koblenz].
KobZ	*Rhein und Moselzeitung* [Koblenz]. Stadtarchiv, Koblenz.
KönPZ	*Königlich Preußische Staat- Kriegs, und Friedens-Zeitung* [Königsberg] {1140}. Also known as the "Hartungsche Zeitung."
KrTb	*Karlsruher Tagblatt* {1022}.
KrZ	*Karlsruher Zeitung* {1017}.
KZ	*Kölnische Zeitung* {1108}.
LAZ	*Leipziger Allgemeine Zeitung* {1218}.
LIZ	*Illustrirte Zeitung* [Leipzig]. Library of Congress, Washington, D.C.
LnSb	*Liegnitzer Stadtblatt* {1236}.
LTb	*Leipziger Tageblatt* {1217}.
LudWb	*Ludwigsburger Wochenblatt* {1250}.
LZ	*Leipziger Zeitung* {1216}.
MbEr	*Der Magdeburger Erzähler* {1291}.
MbZ	*Magdeburgische Zeitung* {1293}.
MEx	*The Musical Examiner* [London]. Library of the Royal College of Music, London; and the University of Toronto Library.
MJm	*Le Ménestrel: Journal de musique* [Paris]. Bibliothèque Nationale, Paris.
MLb	*Der Bayerische Landbote* [Munich] {1391}.
MMb	*Münchener Morgenblatt* {1415}.
MnDP	*Deutscher Postillon* [Mannheim] {1319}.
MnJ	*Mannheimer Journal* {1324}.
MnMb	*Mannheimer Morgenblatt* {1317}.
Monde	*Le Monde musicale.*

MRm	*La Mélomanie: Revue musicale, littérature, théatres* [Paris]. After 1843 *L'Europe musicale et dramatique*. Bibliothèque Nationale, Paris.
MT	*The Musical Times* [London].
MTb	*Münchener Tageblatt* {1428}.
MünIb	*Münsterisches Intelligenzblatt.*
MünWM	*Westfälische Merkur* [Münster] {1441}.
MzGut	*Gutenberg. Unterhaltungsblatt für Stadt und Land* [Mainz].
MzRh	*Das Rheinland, wie es ernst und heiter ist* [Mainz].
MzT	*Das rheinische Telegraph* [Mainz]. Stadt- und Universitätsbibliothek, Frankfurt a.M.
MzUb	*Mainzer Unterhaltungsblatt.*
MzWb	*Mainzer Wochenblatt.*
MzZ	*Mainzer Zeitung* {1303}.
NürnK	*Nürnberger Kourier* {1511}.
NürnZ	*Nürnberger Zeitung* {1489}.
NZfM	*Neue Zeitschrift für Musik* [Leipzig].
OAdGR	*Offentliche Anzeigen der Grafschaft Ravensberg.*
ObBf	*Oberschlesischer Bürgerfreund* [?Neisse]. Library of the University of Wroclaw, Poland.
PfzB	*Der Beobachter* [Pforzheim] {1579}.
RDM	*Revue des Deux Mondes* [Paris].
RGMP	*Revue et Gazette Musicale de Paris.*
RMB	*Revue Musicale Belge.* New York Public Library.
RudWb	*Fürstl. Schwarzb. Rudolst. gnädigst privilegiertes Wochenblatt* [Rudolstadt] {1661}.
SAZ	*Stadt Aachener Zeitung* {12}.
SgB	*Beobachter* [Stuttgart] {1796}.
SgSM	*Schwäbischer Merkur* [Stuttgart] {1803}. NB: the "Chronik" was the second section of this paper.
SmW	*Signale für die musikalische Welt.*
SolKb	*Solinger Kreis-Intelligenzblatt.* Cited in Autexier.
StBNO	*Börsen-Nachrichten der Ostsee* [Stettin] {1756}.
StKPZ	*Königl. privil. Stettiner Zeitung* {1761}.
SZ	"Spenersche Zeitung" (i.e., the *Berlinersche Zeitung von Staats- und Gelehrter Sachen*) {143}.
TEM	*Das Echo am Memelufer* [Tilsit]. Deutsche Staatsbibliothek, Berlin.
Times	*The Times* [London].

VIb	*Vorordnungs- und Intelligenzblatt für die Furstenthum Hohenzollern-Hechingen* {886}. Copy supplied by Geraldine Keeling.
VZ	"Vossische Zeitung" (i.e., the *Königlich privilegirte Berlinische Zeitung von Staats- und gelehrten Sachen*) {115}.
WaMZ	*Wiener allegemeine Musik-Zeitung.*
WesNC	*Niederrheinische Correspondent* [Wesel 1841] {1089}.
World	*The Musical World* [London].
WpTA	*Täglicher Anzeiger* [Wuppertal] {1966}.
WrZ	*Weimarische Zeitung* {1879}.
WürzAb	*Würzburger Abendblatt* {1949}.
WürzM	*Mnemosyne* [Würzburg].
ZfDMV	*Zeitschrift für Deutschlands Musik-Vereins* [Karlsruhe; 1841-1845].
ZGP	*Zeitung des Großherzogthums Posen* {1598}.

Twentieth-Century Magazine Sigla:

A few, frequently cited, twentieth-century periodicals are identified in Chapters I-V by the following abbreviations:

JALS	*Journal of the American Liszt Society* (1977-).
LSae	*Liszt Saeculum* [Sweden] (1972-).
LSJ	*Liszt Society Journal* [Great Britain] (1975-).
MQ	*The Musical Quarterly* (1915-).
NHQ	*New Hungarian Quarterly* [Budapest] (1936-).

APPENDIX B
Frequently Cited Secondary Sources

A small number of secondary sources are cited frequently in Chapters I-V and throughout Appendix C according to the following abbreviations. Full bibliographic information for these and other secondary sources appears in the bibliography at the end of the present volume.

Andersen   Hans Christian Andersen, *A Poet's Bazaar* (New York 1871).

Autexier   Philippe A. Autexier, *Mozart & Liszt sub rosa* (Poitiers 1984).

Briefe   *Franz Liszt's Briefe*, 8 vols.; ed. La Mara (Leipzig 1893-1905).

BriefeHZ   *Briefe hervorrangender Zeitgenossen an Franz Liszt*, 3 vols.; ed. La Mara (Leipzig 1895-1902).

Burger   Ernst Burger, *Franz Liszt: A Chronicle of his Life in Pictures and Documents*, trans. Stewart Spencer (Princeton 1989).

Chorley   Henry Chorley, *Modern German Music*, 2 vols. (New York 1864).

Christern   J. W. Christern, *Franz Liszt. Nach seinem Leben und Werke aus authentischen Berichten dargestellt* (Hamburg 1841).

Gollmick   Carl Gollmick, *Feldzüge und Streifereien im Gebiete der Tonkunst* (Darmstadt 1846).

Homburg   Herfried Homburg, "Kassel zu Füßen von Franz Liszt," *Hessische Blätter* No. 16 (19 January 1962).

Huschke   Wolfram Huschke, *Musik im klassischen und nachklassischen Weimar, 1756-1861* (Weimar 1982).

Jacobs   Emil Jacobs, "Franz Liszt und die Gräfin Marie in Nonnenwerth, 1841-1842," *Die Musik* 11/1-2 (October 1911), pp. 34-45 and 93-112.

Liszt/Suttoni	Franz Liszt, *An Artist's Journey*, trans. Charles Suttoni (Chicago and New York 1989).
Little	William A. Little, "Mendelssohn and Liszt," *Mendelssohn Studies*, ed. R. Larry Todd (Cambridge and New York 1992), pp. 106-125.
Litzmann	Berthold Litzmann, *Clara Schumann: Ein Künstlerleben. Nach Tagebüchen und Briefen*, 3 vols. (Leipzig 1920, and other eds.).
Meyerbeer	*Giocomo Meyerbeer: Briefwechsel und Tagebücher*, ed. Heinz and Gudrun Becker; Vol. III (Berlin 1975).
Newman	Ernest Newman, *The Life of Richard Wagner*, 4 vols. (London: Alfred A. Knopf, 1933-1940).
Ollivier	*Correspondance de Liszt et de la Comtesse d'Agoult*, 2 vols.; ed. Daniel Ollivier (Paris 1933-1934).
Raabe	Peter Raabe, *Franz Liszt*, rev. Felix Raabe; 2 vols. (Tutzing: Hans Schneider, 1968).
Ramann	Lina Ramann, *Franz Liszt als Künstler und Mensch*, 3 vols. (Leipzig 1880-1894).
Rellstab	Ludwig Rellstab, *Franz Liszt. Beurteilungen — Berichte — Lebensskizze* (Berlin 1842). Reprinted in LSae 23-24, 27-28, and 32-34 (1978-1984).
Schreiber	F. J. A. Schreiber, *Franz Liszt und dessen Anwesenheit in Breslau* (Breslau 1843).
Suttoni	Charles Suttoni, "Liszt Correspondence in Print: An Expanded, Annotated Bibliography," JALS 25 (1989): entire issue.
Walker	Alan Walker, *Franz Liszt: The Virtuoso Years, 1811-1847*, rev. ed. (Cornell 1987; reprinted New York 1990).
Williams	Adrian Williams, *Portrait of Liszt by Himself and His Contemporaries* (Oxford and New York 1990).

APPENDIX C
Sources and Evidence for Individual Concerts

The catalog below identifies Liszt's documented German performances by city, date, place, program, and primary sources of information. Private, matinée, benefit, and "gratis" performances are identified as such, and each performance is numbered (in parentheses) for purposes of cross-reference. Secondary sources are cited below only when they contain important factual information, or when they reproduce documentary evidence through quotations or facsimile reproductions. NB: The programs below identify *only* works performed by Liszt or composed by him *and* presented on occasions on which he also performed (whether as solo pianist, chamber performer, vocal accompanist, or conductor).

The abbreviations used below and in Chapters II-V to identify frequently-performed compositions written or arranged by Liszt himself are explained at the beginning of the bibliography; as are the sigla for newspapers, magazines, and other primary sources of information. The titles and composers of works Liszt performed less frequently are identified below in context. Abbreviated dates are given in day-month-year order (e.g., 1.9.1841 for 1 September 1841). Archival sigla follow RISM conventions.

(1) DRESDEN ?14 March 1840: ?
private

PROGRAM: ?Sonata for violin and piano by Beethoven, with Karl Lipinski // ?Other numbers.
SOURCES: AmZ 42 (1840), col. 263. // LZ No. 65 (16.3.1840), p. 921. // AuZ (1840), p. 678. See also NZfM 12 (1840), p. 102.

(2) DRESDEN ?15 March 1840: ?
private

PROGRAM: unknown.
SOURCE: AmZ 42 (1840), col. 263.

(3)   DRESDEN   16 March 1840: Saal des Hotel de Saxe

PROGRAM: Huguenots // *Ständchen, Ave Maria,* and *Erlkönig* by
Schubert, with Wilhelmine Schroeder-Devrient // Lucia // Grand
Galop.
SOURCES: DrAn Nos. 75-76 (15-16.3.1840). // LZ Nos. 65 and 68 (16
and 19.3.1840), pp. 921 and 969. // AmZ 42 (1840), cols. 263-264. //
NZfM 12 (1840), pp. 102-103. Reprinted in part in Ramann II, pp.
61-62. // Iris 11 (1840), p. 52. // JdNVM 2 (1840), pp. 112 and 127-128.
// DrWb No. 23 (18.3.1840), p. 130. // AuZ (1840), p. 743. // Williams,
pp. 122-129. See also Briefe I, p. 35.

(4)   LEIPZIG   17 March 1840: Gewandhaus

PROGRAM: Pastoral // Niobe // Etude ("Harmonies du soir") //
Grand Galop // ?Vocal numbers, with Madame Schmidt // encore:
Valse di bravura.
SOURCES: LZ Nos. 66 and 68 (17 and 19.3.1840), pp. 948 and 969.
// LAZ Nos. 77-79 (17-19.3.1840), pp. 800, 812, and 816. // APSZ No.
81 (21.3.1840), p. 323. // AmZ 42 (1840), cols. 264-266. // NZfM 12
(1840), pp. 118-120. // Iris 11 (1840), p. 52. // JdNVM 2 (1840), pp.
112 and 127-128. // RGMP 7 (1840), p. 246. // ?BML 2 (1841), p. 68
[mentions Mazeppa]. // DrWb Nos. 24-25 (21 and 25.3.1840),
"Auberordentliche Beilage" and pp. 147-148. // DrAn No. 89
(29.3.1840); and Nos. 81-82, 85, 87, and 90 (21-22, 25, 27, and
30.3.1840): advertisements for a publication about Liszt in the
Leipzig-Dresden area. // DrAn No. 89 (27.3.1840): letter published
by Liszt to apologize for misunderstandings caused by the prices
charged for his Gewandhaus tickets. Reprinted in FKB No. 93
(2.4.1840), p. 372. // MzRh No. 54 (1840), p. 215. // Burger, p. 128:
poster facsimile; and p. 129: translations from the letters of Robert
Schumann and Clara Wieck. // Litzmann I, pp. 413 and 415.See also
Ramann II, pp. 62 and 65: quotations from the Leipzig *Tageblatt* and
MzRh.

(5)   LEIPZIG   20 March 1840: ?Schumann's home
                                                     private/matinée

PROGRAM: *Novelletten* by Schumann // ?"Fantasy" by Schumann
// ?Sonata by Schumann // ?Other numbers.
SOURCES: Litzmann I, p. 414. // Burger, p. 129. // D-WRgs Liszt
Kasten 364: hand-copied document headed "Leipzig, den 20. März
1840," about Clara Wieck. // ?Iris 1 (1840), p. 56: squib about private
performances in Leipzig. See also AmZ 42 (1840), col. 297. //
Wasielewski, p. 98.

(6)   LEIPZIG   22 March 1840: Raimund Härtel's home
                                                     private/matinée

PROGRAM: Chopin Etudes [?2] // Selection from the *Soirées
musicales* by Rossini-Liszt // Other numbers.
SOURCES: Litzmann I, p. 416 // Burger, p. 129. // ?Iris 1 (1840), p.
56: squib about private performances in Leipzig. See also AmZ 42
(1840), cols. 297 and 299.

(7)   LEIPZIG   23 March 1840: Gewandhaus
                                                                private

PROGRAM: Concerto in d minor for three keyboard instruments and orchestra by J. S. Bach, BWV 1063, with Mendelssohn, Hiller, and the Gewandhaus orchestra // Lucia // Erlkönig // ?Robert // ?Other numbers (including an encore).
SOURCES: LZ No. 74 (26.3.1840), p. 1061. // AmZ 42 (1840), cols. 299-300. // NZfM 12 (1840), p. 119. // Iris 11 (1840), p. 56. // *Felix Mendelssohns Briefe*, II, pp. 225-226: Mendelssohn to his mother, 30.3.1840. // Litzmann I, p. 416. // D-WRgs Liszt Kasten 173: a hand-copied concert program by Mendelssohn. [I was unable to examine this document in person; catalog entries date it as 24.3.1840.] // "Max Müller and Liszt," *Familienblatt* (Leipzig) No. 245 (20.10.1896), p. 980: reminiscences [contained in D-WRgs Liszt Kasten 281/17]. // Little, pp. 115-116.

(8)   LEIPZIG   24 March 1840: Gewandhaus

PROGRAM: Konzertstück, with orchestra // Huguenots // Ständchen and Ave Maria // encore: Erlkönig.
SOURCES: LZ Nos. 70, 72, and 74 (21, 24, and 26.3.1840), pp. 1000, 1032, and 1061. // LAZ Nos. 78, 81, 84, and 86 (18, 21, 24, and 26.3.1840), pp. 812, 844, 867, and 892. // LTb (?22-23.3.1840), pp. 867 and 872. // AmZ 42 (1840), cols. 266 and 297-298. // NZfM 12 (1840), p. 119. // Iris 11 (1840), pp. 52 and 56. // Burger, p. 129.

(9)   DRESDEN   ?26 March: Carl Krägen's home
                                                          private

PROGRAM: Concerto in d minor, Op. 40, by Mendelssohn (?piano part only). // ?Other numbers.
SOURCES: Briefe I, p. 33n. See also Little, p. 118.

(10)   DRESDEN   27 March 1840: Saal des Hotel de Saxe

PROGRAM: Sonata in F Major for violin and piano, Op. 47 ("Kreutzer"), by Beethoven, with Karl Lipinski // "Lieder," with Wilhelmine Schroeder-Devrient // Hexameron // Tarantelles napolitaines // Erlkönig.
SOURCES: DrAn Nos. 78-81, 83, and 86-87 (18-21, 23, and 26-27.3.1840). // LZ No. 77 (30.3.1840), p. 1109. // AuZ (1840), p. 743.

(11)   DRESDEN   29 March 1840: Saal des Hotel de Saxe
                                                          matinée/benefit

PROGRAM: unknown.
SOURCES: DresdnerA Nos. 88-89 (28-29.3.1840). No. 89 in Burger, p. 130; item 249. // LZ No. 77 (30.3.1840), p. 1109. // NZfM 12 (1840), p. 119. // Iris 11 (1840), p. 64.

(12)   LEIPZIG   30 March 1840: Gewandhaus
                                                          benefit

PROGRAM: Concerto in d minor, Op. 40, by Mendelssohn, with orchestra // Three Etudes by Hiller // Ten selections from *Carnaval*, Op. 9, by Schumann // Hexameron, with orchestra // encore: Grand Galop.
SOURCES: LZ Nos. 74, 76-77, and 79 (26, 28, 30.3. and 1.4.1840), pp. 1064, 1104, 1120, and 1146. // LAZ Nos. 86-88 (26-28.3 and 1.4.1840), pp. 892, 904, 916, and 955. // LTb (30.3.1840), p. 940. //

APSZ No. 93 (2.4.1840), p. 371. // AmZ 42 (1840), cols. 298-299. //
NZfM 12 (1840), pp. 107 and 119-120. Partial English translation in
Burger, p. 129. // Iris 11 (1840), p. 64. // Litzmann I, pp. 414 and
419-421. // Little, pp. 118-119: Mendelssohn to his mother, 30.3.1840.
// Briefe I, p. 33. See also Wasielewski, p. 98.

(13)   LEIPZIG   before 31 March 1840: ?
                                                          private

PROGRAM: Sonata in c minor for violin and piano, Op. 30, No. 3,
by Beethoven, with Ferdinand David // Two Chopin Etudes // Lucia.
SOURCE: AmZ 42 (1840), col. 299.

(14)   LEIPZIG   31 March 1840: Schumann's home
                                             private/matinée

PROGRAM: Erlkönig and Ave Maria // Etudes // ?Other numbers.
SOURCE: Litzmann I, pp. 420-421.

(15)   BADEN-BADEN   16 July 1840: Salle de Réunion

PROGRAM: Tell // Lucia // Ständchen and Ave Maria // Tarentelles
napolitaines // Grand Galop.
SOURCES: BdWb Nos. 61 and 65-69 (8 and 13-17.7.1840), pp.
668-759, 781, 792, 800, 824, and 833. // AmZ 42 (1840), col. 832. //
JdNVM 2 (1840), p. 256. // RGMP 7 (1840), p. 410. // AuZ (1840), pp.
1623, 1630, and 1757. // MRm No. 346 (26.7.1840). // Williams, p. 137.
// Ollivier II, pp. 9-10.

(16)   BADEN-BADEN   21 July 1840: Salle de Réunion

PROGRAM: Niobe // "Air" from *Lucia di Lammermoor* by Bellini,
and "Air" from *Robert le diable* by Meyerbeer; both with Varlerie de
Rupplin // Marche hongroise // Erlkönig (?as solo) // Hexameron.
SOURCES: BdWb Nos. 70-73 (18-21.7.1840), pp. 856, 871, 892, and
907. // AuZ (1843), p. 1757. // Iris 1 (1840), p. 124. // JdNVM 2 (1840),
p. 278. // RGMP 7 (1840), p. 410. // Ollivier II, p. 11. // Williams, p.
137.

(17)   MAINZ   23 July 1840: Saal des Hofes zum Gutenberg

PROGRAM: Puritani // "Air" from *Soirées musicales* by Rossini, and
"Grace" from *Robert le diable* by Meyerbeer; both with Mme Duflot-
Maillard // Ständchen and Ave Maria // Serenata-l'Orgia // Grand
Galop.
SOURCES: FJ Nos. 200 and 203-205 (18 and 21-23.7.1840). // FKB
No. 209 (26.7.1840), pp. 835-836. Reprinted in Gollmick, pp. 223-228.
// FOPZ Nos. 197-202 (18-23.7.1840), pp. 1640, 1651, 1655, 1664,
1672, and 1684. // MzWb No. 59 (22.7.1840), p. 933. // MzZ Nos.
199-202 (20-23.7.1840). // MzRh Nos. 89 and 91 (26 and 30.7.1840),
pp. 349-351 and 359. // MzT No. 60 (26.7.1840), p. 239. // JdNVM 2
(1840), p. 288. // RGMP 7 (1840), p. 410. // Two additional clippings
in F-Vm.

(18)   EMS   ?25 July 1840: Empress of Russia's apartments
                                                          private

PROGRAM: Mélodies hongroises // Ave Maria (and other "Lieder") // Huguenots // At least seven other numbers.
SOURCES: EmsLK (26-28.7.1840), entries 3250-3251. // RGMP 7 (1840), p. 435. See also Ramann II, pp. 84-86.

(19) **EMS**   ?27 July 1840: Kursaal
PROGRAM: unknown.
SOURCE: MzT No. 63 (5.8.1840), p. 251.

(20) **EMS**   28 July 1840: Empress of Russia's apartments
                                                           private
PROGRAM: unknown (at least ten numbers).
SOURCE: MzT No. 63 (5.8.1840), p. 251.

(21) **WIESBADEN**   30 July 1840: Theater
PROGRAM: Niobe // ?Tarantelles napolitaines // Hexameron, ?with orchestra // ?Other numbers.
SOURCES: FJ No. 210 (28.7.1840). // FOPZ No. 206 (28.7.1840), p. 1716. // MzZ Nos. 208-209 (29-30.7.1840). // FKB No. 252 (11.9.1840), p. 1008. // MzT No. 62 (2.8.1840), p. 248. // D-WRgs Liszt Kasten 240: Two advertising posters. See also AmZ 42 (1840), col. 832.

(22) **FRANKFURT a.M.**   5 August 1840: Theater
PROGRAM: Konzertstück // Ständchen // Tarantelles napolitaines // Lucia // Grand Galop.
SOURCES: FDid Nos. 216-218 and 223 (3-5 and 10.8.1840). // FKB Nos. 213-215 and 226-227 (3-5 and 16-17.8.1840), pp. 852, 856, 860, 904, and 908. Nos. 226-227, pp. 904 and 908, reprinted in Gollmick, pp. 229-235. // JdF No. 215 (5.8.1840). // MzZ No. 217 (7.8.1840). // JdNVM 2 (1840), p. 288. // AuZ (1840), p. 1781. // BnWb No. 96 (11.8.1840): article in French. Reprinted from the *Journal de Francfort* (otherwise unavailable). // *Tribunal für Musik, Literatur und Theater* No. 13 (1840): clipping. Contained in F-Vm; otherwise unavailable.

(23) **FRANKFURT a.M.**   7 August 1840: Theater
PROGRAM: Hummel Concerto, with orchestra // Erlkönig and Ave Maria // Hexameron, with orchestra.
SOURCES: FDid Nos. 220 and 223 (7 and 10.8.1840). // JdF No. 217 (7.8.1840). // FKB Nos. 217, 219, and 226-227 (7, 9, and 16-17.8.1840), pp. 868, 875-876, 904, and 908. // JdNVM 2 (1840), p. 288. // A French-language clipping in F-Vm.

(24) **MANNHEIM**   8 August 1840: Theater
PROGRAM: unknown.
SOURCES: MnJ Nos. 193-194 (7-8.8.1840), pp. 771 and 775. // MnMb Nos. 155-156 (8-9.8.1840), pp. 760 and 766. // AuMP No. 97 (14.8.1840), pp. 385-386.

(25)   FRANKFURT a.M.   10 August 1840: Theater
PROGRAM: Choral Fantasy // Hexameron, ?with orchestra //
Marche hongroise // Chopin Mazurka // Improvisation.
SOURCES: FDid Nos. 222-223 (9-10.8.1840). // FKB Nos. 219-220
and 226-227 (9-10 and 16-17.8.1840), pp. 876, 880, 904, and 908. //
JdF Nos. 219-220 (9-10.8.1840). // JdNVM 2 (1840), p. 288. // RGMP
7 (1840), p. 439. // AuZ (1840), p. 1815.

(26)   BONN   12 August 1840: Saale des Lesengesellschafts
                                                          benefit
PROGRAM: Pastoral // Moonlight // Niobe // Ständchen and
Erlkönig // Tarantelles napolitaines // Adelaïde // Grand Galop.
SOURCES: BnWb Nos. 92-93 and 95-96 (2, 4-5, 8, and 11.8.1840).
// KZ No. 216 (2.8.1840). // AmZ 42 (1840), col. 798. // NZfM 13 (1840),
pp. 72 and 120. // JdNVM 2 (1840), p. 376.

(27)   COLOGNE   13 August 1840: Großes Saal des Casino
PROGRAM: unknown.
SOURCE: KZ No. 227 (13.8.1840). See also Heinz Oepen, *Beiträge
zur Geschichte des Kölner Musiklebens, 1760-1840* (Cologne 1955),
p. 121.

(28)   HAMBURG   28 October 1840: Apollo-Saale
PROGRAM: Pastoral // Lucia // Ständchen and Ave Maria // "Duet"
for two pianos, with "Herr Herrmann" [pseud. Hermann Cohen],
?probably Hexameron // Grand Galop.
SOURCES: HNZ Nos. 251 and 254 (26 and 29.10.1840). // HNach
Nos. 255-256 and 258 (27-28 and 30.10.1840). // HZCor No. 254-255
and 257 (27-28 and 30.10.1840). // HFrs Nos. 44 (31.10.1840), cols.
701-702; and 48 (7.11.1840), cols. 718-719. // AmZ 42 (1840), col. 958.
// NZfM 13 (1840), p. 720. // BML 1 (1840), pp. 17-19 (reproduced in
facsimile in Burger, p. 131). // RGMP 7 (1840), pp. 501, 517, and 565.
// *Liszt in Hamburg* (Hamburg 1840). Copy in F-Vm. // Ollivier II,
pp. 37-47. // "Franz Liszt der Romantiker" from BML 1/4 (October
1840). Facsimile in Burger, p. 130. // Williams, pp. 144-147. // Josef
Sittard, *Geschichte der Musik- und Concertwesens in Hamburg*
(Leipzig 1890), pp. 236-239. Includes a lengthy quotation from
Thalia, otherwise unavailable.

(29)   HAMBURG   31 October 1840: Hotel zur alten Stadt London
PROGRAM: Hummel Septet (as quintet!), with local musicians //
Etudes by Moscheles and Chopin // Puritani // Adelaïde // Tell //
Moonlight // Ständchen // Hexameron.
SOURCES: HNZ Nos. 254-255 and 259 (29-30.10 and 4.11.1840). //
HZCor Nos. 257-258 and 260 (30-31.10 and 3.11.1840). // HNach Nos.
258-259 (30-31.10.1840). // HFrs No. 45 (7.11.1840), col. 719. // BML
1 (1840), pp. 19 and 24. // Christern, p. 36. // Andersen, pp. 34-36.
Translated in part in Williams, p. 146, which also quotes other doc-
uments related to this concert. // Additional clippings in F-Vm.

(30)   HAMBURG 2 November 1840: Hotel zur alten Stadt London
                                                          ?matinée

PROGRAM: Tell // Etudes by Chopin and Moscheles // Puritani // Adelaïde // ?"Lied(er)" by Schubert-Liszt // Hexameron.
SOURCES: HZCor No. 257 (30.10.1840). // HNZ No. 256 (31.10.1840). // HNach No. 262 (4.11.1840) NB: This review may refer to (28) above. // Ollivier II, pp. 47-50.

(31) **HAMBURG**   2 November 1840: ?

PROGRAM: Hexameron for two pianos, with "Herr Herrmann" [pseud. Hermann Cohen] // "Fantasy."
SOURCES: HNZ No. 256 (31.10.1840). // HNach No. 260 (2.11.1840). // HZCor Nos. 257 and 259 (30.10 and 2.11.1840). // HFrs No. 45 (7.11.1840), cols. 719-720.

(32) **HAMBURG** 6 November 1840: Hotel zur alten Stadt London

PROGRAM: Archduke, with local musicians // Lob der Thränen // Robert // Hummel Septet (as quintet!), with local musicians // Invitation // Ave Maria // Grand Galop // encore: Improvisation.
SOURCES: HZCor Nos. 261-263 and 272 (4-6 and 17.11.1840). // HNZ Nos. 258-259 (3-4.11.1840). // HNach Nos. 261-264 (3-6.11.1840). // HFrs No. 46 (14.11.1840), cols. 734-735. // BML 1 (1840), p. 28. // HNach No. 265 (7.11.1840): Liszt's relationship with the Stadttheater management.

(33) **HAMBURG**   10 November 1840: Theater
                                                            benefit

PROGRAM: Hummel Concerto // Hexameron, with orchestra // Konzertstück // Improvisation.
SOURCES: HZCor Nos. 265-266 and 272 (9-10 and 17.11.1840). // HNZ Nos. 262-263 (9-10.11.1840). // HNach Nos. 266-267 and 270 (9-10 and 13.11.1840). // HFrs No. 47 (21.11.1840), cols. 750-751. // BML 1 (1840), p. 28. // RGMP 7 (1840), pp. 565 and 630; and 8 (1841), p. 24. // BML 1 (1840), p. 35: Letter of thanks to Liszt from members of the Hamburg theater orchestra. // Ollivier II, p. 50. See also NZfM 14 (1841), p. 26.

(34) **HAMBURG**   7 July 1841: 3rd Norddeutsches Musikfest

PROGRAM: Choral Fantasy // Robert // Oberons Zauberhorn.
SOURCES: HZCor No. 160 (9.7.1841). // HNach No. 161 (9.7.1841). // HFrs No. 28 (10.7.1841), col. 446. // AmZ 43 (1841), cols. 576 and 656. // NZfM 15 (1841), pp. 15, 32, 41-42, and 51. // BML 2 (1841), "Festnummer," pp. 4 and 6; and 2 (1841), pp. 100 and 122. // Iris 12 (1841), p. 116. // MP No. 29 (17.7.1841), p. 118. // ZfDMV 1 (1841), pp. 368-370. // Franz Liszt, "Lettre d'un bachelier-és-musique: à M. Leon Kreutzer," RGMP 8 (1841), pp. 417-420. Reprinted in German in BML 2 (1841), pp. 160-165. Translated into English in Liszt/Suttoni, pp. 192-193. // RGMP 8 (1841), p. 484. // RMB 2 (1841), p. 72. // MJm No. 403 (5.9.1841). // Two additional clippings in F-Vm. // Ollivier II, pp. 164-167.

(35) **HAMBURG**   9 July 1841: Apollo-Saale
                                                            matinée

PROGRAM: Quintet for piano and winds, Op. 16, by Beethoven, with local musicians // Puritani-Polonaise // Robert // "Lieder" by

Beethoven and Schubert // Chopin Mazurka // Somnambula // God
Save the Queen.
SOURCES: HNZ Nos. 153-156 (3 and 5-7.7.1841). // HNach Nos.
156-161 (3-9.7.1841). // HZCor Nos. 151, 157-158, and 164 (1, 6-7, and
14.7.1841). // HFrs No. 29 (17.7.1841), cols. 462-463. // HTfD No. 121
(1841), p. 484. // BML 2 (1841), p. 128. // RGMP 8 (1841), p. 357. //
MJm Nos. 399-400 (8 and 15.8.1841). // HZCor No. 155 (4.7.1841). //
RMB No. 18 (1.8.1841), p. 72. // Ollivier II, pp. 170-171.

(36)   KIEL   ?12 July 1841: ?
PROGRAM: unknown.
SOURCES: KlCb No. 55 (10.7.1841), p. 227. // HTfD No. 121 (1841),
p. 484. // KlWb No. 58 (21.7.1841), pp. 235-236. // KlCb Nos. 55 and
57 (10 and 17.7.1841), pp. 227 and 236: other reports. See also NZfM
15 (1841), p. 32.

(37)   KIEL   27 July 1841: ?
PROGRAM: Moonlight // Hexameron // Marche hongroise //
Tarantelle // Chopin Mazurkas (?2) // Puritani-Polonaise // Erlkönig.
SOURCES: KlWb Nos. 58-59 and 61 (21, 24, and 31.7.1841), pp. 237,
241, and 247. // KlCb Nos. 60-61 (28 and 31.7.1841), pp. 248 and 252.
// Ollivier II, pp. 171-172.

(38)   HAMBURG   29 July 1841: Theater
PROGRAM: Oberons Zauberhorn // Ständchen // Huguenots // Fantasy (?Improvisation) on *God Save the Queen* and *Rule, Britannia*.
SOURCES: HNZ No. 175 (29.7.1841). // HNach No. 178 (29.7.1841).
// HFrs No. 32 (7.8.1841), cols. 510-511. // HTfD No. 105 (1841), p.
420. // RGMP 8 (1841), p. 357 [?false report; mentions Tell for this
program]. // Reminiscences by Emma Siegmund. Reprinted in part
in Kapp, *Franz Liszt* (Berlin 1909), pp. 141-142. Translated in part
in Williams, p. 167. // Ollivier II, pp. 171-174.

(39)   CUXHAVEN   30 July 1841: ?Theater
                                                          private

PROGRAM: Walzes and galops // ?Other numbers.
SOURCES: Unidentified clipping in F-Vm. // MzRh No. 104
(31.8.1841), p. 415. // "Lettre" reprinted in BML 2 (1841), pp.
164-165. Translated into English in Liszt/Suttoni, pp. 196-197. See
also Ollivier II, pp. 170-174.

(40)   NONNENWERTH   ?9 August 1841: Liszt's summer home
                                                          private

PROGRAM: unknown.
SOURCE: Jacobs, p. 36: the first in a series of letters addressed by
Marie von Czettritz to Isidore von Kitzing. Translated in part in
Williams, p. 168. // Burger, p. 138: several views of Nonnenwerth,
including a caricature of Liszt's children on the island. // See also
Liszt/Suttoni, pp. 197-199: Liszt's impressions of Nonnenwerth.

(41)   BONN   11 August 1841: ?

PROGRAM: unknown.
SOURCES: BnWb Nos. 95-96 (8 and 10.8.1841). // KZ Nos. 222-223
(10-11.8.1841). // Jacobs, p. 37. Translated in Williams, pp. 168-169.

(42)   NONNENWERTH   13 August 1841: Liszt's summer home
                                                private

PROGRAM: unknown.
SOURCE: Jacobs, p. 38. Translated in part in Williams, p. 169.

(43)   EMS   16 August 1841: Kursaal

PROGRAM: Lucia // Ständchen // Chopin Mazurka // Puritani-
Polonaise // Robert // Invitation // Grand Galop.
SOURCES: EmsLK (15-17.8.1841), p. 360. // RGMP 8 (1841), p. 533.
// Heinrich Wagner, "Unser Künstler und Künslerinnen im
Kursaal," *Emser Fremdenliste* (10.7.1926). // Jacobs, p. 38. Trans-
lated in Williams, p. 169.

(44)   NONNENWERTH   22 August 1841: Cloister
                                                private

PROGRAM: fantasy.
SOURCES: KZ No. 236 (24.8.1841). // DmGHZ No. 237 (27.8.1841),
p. 1129. // FKB No. 236 (27.8.1841), p. 940. // FJ No. 235 (26.8.1841).
// AmZ 43 (1841), col. 822. // BML 2 (1841), pp. 146-147. // Iris 12
(1841), p. 144. // RGMP 8 (1841), p. 407. // Christern, pp. 38-40. Reprinted in part in Kapp, pp. 143-144. See also Liszt/Suttoni, p. 199.

(45)   COLOGNE   23 August 1841: Saale des Casino
                                                benefit

PROGRAM: Tell // Tarantelle // Chopin Mazurka // Robert //
Puritani-Polonaise // Lucia-Andante // Erlkönig.
SOURCES: KZ No. 235-236 and 241 (23-24 and 29.8.1841). // MzUb
Nos. 235 and 242 (25.8 and 1.9.1841), pp. 939 and 968. // FKB No.
235 (26.8.1841), p. 940. // JdF No. 236 (27.8.1841). // MzRh No. 242
(1.9.1841), p. 968. // AmZ 43 (1841), col. 822. // NZfM 15 (1841), p.
80. // BML 2 (1841), pp. 146-147. // WaMZ No. 112 (18.9.1841), p. 468.
// RMB Nos. 21 and 24 (22.8 and 12.9.1841), pp. 83 and 96. // JdNVM
3 (1841), p. 288. // FM No. 37 (12.9.1841), p. 320. // MJm No. 401
(22.8.1841). // KZ No. 241 (29.8.1841): published concert receipts. //
Paul Ellmar. "Franz Liszt und der Kölner Dom," *Kölnische
Rundschau* 12 (20.1.1957), "Der Sonntag," p. 5. See also NZfM 15
(1842), p. 192.

(46)   KOBLENZ   25 August 1841: Saale des Jesuiten-Kollegiums

PROGRAM: Pastoral // Ständchen and Erlkönig // Robert // Adelaïde
// Invitation // Grand Galop.
SOURCES: KobAn Nos. 195-196 (24-25.8.1841). // KZ No. 236
(24.8.1841). // KobZ Nos. 229-230 (24-25.8.1841). // AmZ 43 (1841),
cols. 733-734. // F-Vm: unidentified newspaper clipping about this
concert. // Additional clipping in F-Vm.

(47)   NONNENWERTH   ?26 August 1841: Liszt's summer home
                                                    private

PROGRAM: unknown.
SOURCE: Jacobs, p. 42.

(48)   FRANKFURT a.M.   27 August 1841: Theater

PROGRAM: Emperor // Robert // Lucia-Andante // Grand Galop.
SOURCES: FKB Nos. 232-234, 236 and 242 (23-25 and 27.8; and
2.9.1841), pp. 928, 932, 936, 944, and 966-967. // FDid No. 243
(31.8.1841). // JdF No. 264 (24.9.1841). // MzUb Nos. 237 and 241 (27
and 31.8.1841), pp. 947 and 964. // AmZ 43 (1841), cols. 757 and 759.
// WaMZ No. 110 (14.9.1841), p. 460. // FM No. 37 (12.9.1841), p. 320.
// Williams, pp. 170-171, which also refers to concerts (47) and (54).

(49)   FRANKFURT a.M.   29 August 1841: Theater

PROGRAM: Konzertstück // Somnanbula // Hexameron, ?with orchestra // Grand Galop.
SOURCES: FKB Nos. 238 and 242 (29.8 and 2.9.1841), pp. 952 and
966-967. // JdF No. 264 (24.9.1841). // AmZ 43 (1841), cols. 757, 759,
and 817.

(50)   WIESBADEN   30 August 1841: Kursaal

PROGRAM: unknown.
SOURCES: MzZ No. 240 (30.8.1841). // MzT No. 74 (15.9.1841), p.
296.

(51)   MAINZ   1 September 1841: Hof zum Gutenberg

PROGRAM: Tell // Lucia-Marche et Cavatine // Ave Maria and
Ständchen // Robert // Puritani-Polonaise // Grand Galop.
SOURCES: FJ Nos. 238-240 (29-31.8.1841). // MzWb Nos. 69-70
(28.8 and 1.9.1841), pp. 1116 and 1130. // FOPZ Nos. 239 and 241
(30.8 and 1.9.1841), pp. 1964 and 1980. // JdF Nos. 239-240
(30-31.7.1841). // DmGHZ Nos. 237, 239, and 241 (23, 27, and
31.8.1841), pp. 1130, 1142, and 1150. //Fr. Wiest, "Ein Billet-doux,"
MzRh No. 104 (31.8.1841), p. 415; and No. 106 (5.9.1841), pp.
421-423. Reprinted in FKB No. 248 (8.1.1841), pp. 990-991; and in
BML 2 (1841), pp. 189-191 and 193-194. // MzZ Nos. 237, 239, and
241-242 (27, 29, and 31.8, and 1.9.1841). // MzUb No. 235 (25.8.1841),
p. 939. // MzT Nos. 69-70 (29.8 and 1.9.1841), pp. 276 and 280. //
RMB 2 (1841), p. 83. // FM No. 37 (12.9.1841), p. 320. // MzRh Nos.
106-107 (5 and 7.9.1841), pp. 423 and 427: separate notices. // Jacobs,
p. 94.

(52)   WIESBADEN   2 September 1841: ?

PROGRAM: unknown.
SOURCES: Monde (9.9.1841). // ?MzT No. 74 (15.9.1841), p. 296.

(53)   MAINZ   3 September 1841: Theater
                                                    ?benefit

PROGRAM: "I tuoi frequenti palpiti," from Niobe by Pacini, and
Adelaïde by Beethoven; both with Adelaide Kemble // Solo numbers.

SOURCES: MzZ Nos. 244 and 246 (3 and 5.9.1841). // MzRh No. 106 (5.9.1841), p. 423. // MzT No. 71 (5.9.1841), p. 284. // Jacobs, p. 92.

(54)   MAINZ   ?5 September 1841: Theater
                                               ?benefit

PROGRAM: unknown.
SOURCES: MzRh No. 106 (5.9.1841), pp. 423-424. // MzZ No. 246 (5.9.1841). // MzT No. 71 (5.9.1841), p. 284. // Jacobs, p. 94.

(55)   BADEN-BADEN
                 16 September 1841: Maison de Conversation

PROGRAM: Tell // Lucia-Andante // Robert // Tarantelle // Hexameron // Puritani-Polonaise // Grand Galop.
SOURCES: BdWb Nos. 136-139 (13-16.9.1841), pp. 1326, 1338, 1349, and 1361; and "Beobachter" [section] No. 138 (15.9.1841), p. 1346. // JdNVM 3 (1841), p. 327. // BdWb "Beobachter" [section] No. 138 (15.9.1841), p. 1334: separate notice. // Letter of Liszt dated 14.9.1841. Reprinted in *Magyar Zene* (1986), p. 31. See also Briefe VIII, pp. 26-28.

(56)   FRANKFURT a.M.   25 September 1841: Weidenbusch-Saal
                                                   benefit

PROGRAM: Hummel Septet, ?as piano solo // Ständchen and Ave Maria // Don Juan (from the ms.).
SOURCES: FDid Nos. 264 and 272 (21 and 29.9.1841). The second reprinted in part in MünWM "Beilage" No. 248 (9.11.1841) [incorrectly dated 22.9.1841]. // FJ Nos. 264-265 (24-25.9.1841). // FOPZ Nos. 264-265 (24-25.9.1841), pp. 2180 and 2188. // FGCh No. 9 (9.1841), p. 98. // FKB Nos. 262, 264, 273, and 277 (22 and 24.9; and 3 and 7.10.1841), pp. 1047-1048, 1055, 1092, and 1106-1007. // JdF No. 264 (24.9.1841). // AmZ 43 (1841), cols. 886 and 1073-1074. // NZfM 15 (1841), p. 132. // BML 2 (1841), p. 183. // Iris 12 (1841), p. 160. // JdNVM 3 (1841), p. 327. // RMB No. 28 (10.10.1841), p. 111. // AuMP No. 41 (9.10.1841). // Gollmick, "Die Mozart-Stiftung in Frankfurt am Main," in Gollmick, pp. 139-146. // Autexier, pp. 79ff. // ?RMB Nos. 26 and 33 (26.9 and 14.11.1841), pp. 103 and 130. // Two additional clippings in F-Vm. See also AmZ 44 (1842), col. 878. // FKB No. 269 (29.9.1841), p. 1075: letter from Liszt to Ludwig Heck.

(57)   NONNENWERTH
                 after 2 October 1841: Liszt's summer home
                                                   private

PROGRAM: unknown.
SOURCES: Jacobs, p. 95. // Clippings in F-Vm.

(58)   COLOGNE   5 October 1841: Theater

PROGRAM: Somnambula // "Aria" from *Norma* by Bellini, with Adelaide Kemble // Serenade and Orgy // "Duet" from *Norma* by Bellini, with Adelaide Kemble and A. Schunk // Don Juan // Invitation // Grand Galop // ?Other vocal numbers (as accompanist).
SOURCES: KZ Nos. 276, 278, and 280 (3, 5, and 7.10.1841). // SAZ Nos. 271 and 273 (3 and 5.10.1841). // FKB No. 290 (21.10.1841), p.

1159. // NZfM 15 (1841), p. 192. // RMB No. 24 (12.9.1841), p. 96. //
MJm No. 409 (17.10.1841). // Jacobs, p. 94. // Ollivier II, pp. 176-177.

(59)   **AACHEN**   12 October 1841: Theater
PROGRAM: Tell // "Aria" from *Norma* and "Cavatina" from
Somnambula (both by Bellini), with Adelaide Kemble // Ständchen
and Ave Maria // Robert // Grand Galop // ?accompaniments for vocal
numbers.
SOURCES: SAZ Nos. 275, 277-280, and 288 (7, 9-12, and
20.10.1841). // RMB No. 30 (24.10.1841), p. 119. // SAZ No. 288
(20.10.1841).

(60)   **NONNENWERTH**   22 October 1841: Liszt's summer home
                                                    private
PROGRAM: unknown.
SOURCE: Jacobs, p. 100. Reprinted in E. Fleckner, "Franz Liszt
feierte seinen 30. Geburtstag auf der Rheininsel Nonnenwerth,"
Mitteilungen der Arbeitsgemeinschaft für rheinische Musikgeschichte
38 (1972), pp. 142-144. // BML 2 (1841), p. 176 [gives "22
November" as date].

(61)   **NONNENWERTH**   c. 22 October 1841: Liszt's summer home
                                                    private
PROGRAM: Don Juan.
SOURCE: Jacobs, p. 99.

(62)   **ELBERFELD**   27 October 1841: Saale des Casino
PROGRAM: Tell // Lucia-Andante // Robert // Ave Maria and
Ständchen // Tarantelle // Puritani-Polonaise // Grand Galop.
SOURCES: EfZ Nos. 294, 297, and 299 (24, 27, and 29.10.1841). //
WpTA (26-27 and 29.10.1841). // BML (1841), p. 168.

(63)   **DÜSSELDORF**   28 October 1841: Gurten'schen Saal
PROGRAM: Pastoral // Ständchen and Erlkönig // Hexameron // *Auf
Flügel des Gesanges* by Mendelssohn-Liszt // Grand Galop.
SOURCES: DüsKb Nos. 293-294 (27-28.10.1841). // DüsZ Nos.
296-297 (27-28.10.1841). // RGMP 8 (1841), p. 484; MJm No. 413
(14.11.1841); and RMB No. 30 (24.10.1841), p. 119: references to
Düsseldorf, Gotha, Weimar, and other travel goals.

(64)   **BONN**   1 November 1841: Hotel Trierschen Hof
                                                    private
PROGRAM: *Das deutsche Vaterland* as piano solo (?improvisation).
SOURCES: Paul Kaufmann, "Franz Liszt am Rhein," *Die Musik* 26
(1933), pp. 119-20: excerpts from a letter written by Leopold
Kaufmann in ?November 1841. // Jacobs, p. 101. // RGMP 8 (1841),
p. 520. // D-WRgs Liszt Kasten 174: a printed copy of Dr.
Breidenstein's toast in Liszt's honor at a banquet given in Bonn on
31.10.1841. See also WaMZ No. 144 (2.12.1841), p. 603. // Kapp, p.
145: claims that Liszt performed at this event *and* for students at the
University of Bonn.

(65) DÜSSELDORF 2 November 1841: Theater

PROGRAM: unknown.
SOURCES: DüsKb Nos. 298 and 300 (1 and 4.11.1841). // DüsZ No.
301 (1.11.1841). // RGMP 8 (1841), p. 484.

(66) ELBERFELD 3 November 1841: Saale des Casino

PROGRAM: Moonlight // Hexameron // Huguenots // *Auf Flügel des Gesanges* by Mendelssohn-Liszt // Invitation // Serenade and Orgy.
SOURCES: EfZ Nos. 300-302 (31.10-3.11.1841). // WpTA (1 and
2-4.11.1841).

(67) KREFELD 4 November 1841: Rump'chen Saal

PROGRAM: Konzertstück (as solo piano) // "Variations" by
Thalberg! // Sonata in A Major, Op. 101, by Beethoven // "Lieder" by
Schubert-Liszt // Grand Galop.
SOURCES: Jacobs, p. 101. // Ollivier II, p. 177. // Carl Pieper,
"Meister der Tone in Krefeld," *Die Heimat* [Krefeld] 13 (1934), p. 217.
// Ernst Klusen et al., *Das Musikleben der Stadt Krefeld, 1780-1945*
(Cologne 1979); Vol. I, pp. 49-50.

(68) WESEL 7 November 1841: "Saale der ersten Societät"
benefit

PROGRAM: Tell // Lucia-Andante // Konzertstück (?as solo) //
Ständchen // Adelaide // "Chromatic fantasy" by Bach // Grand Galop.
SOURCES: WesNC Nos. 131-134 (2, 4, 6, and 9.11.1841). // Ollivier
II. p. 177.

(69) MÜNSTER 9 November 1841: Saale des Krameramthauses

PROGRAM: Tell // Lucia-Andante // Hexameron // ?Konzertstück //
Ave Maria and Ständchen // Grand Galop.
SOURCES: MünWM Nos. 268-269 (9. and 10.11.1841). // MünWM
No. 268 (9.11.1841): two additional notices. // Ollivier II, p. 177.

(70) MÜNSTER 11 November 1841: Schauspielhaus

PROGRAM: Don Juan // ?"Gesangstücke" // Tarantelle // Puritani-
Polonaise // Robert // Erlkönig // Grand Galop.
SOURCES: MünWM No. 270 (11.11.1841). // MünWM Nos. 272-273
(13-14.11.1841): poem and notice of departure. // Ollivier II, p. 178.

(71) OSNABRÜCK 12 November 1841: ?home
private/matinée

PROGRAM: unknown.
SOURCE: Niedersächsisches Staatsarchiv: Shelf number Erw A 12
Nr. 12 Bd. 18: Diary of Albrecht Pagenstecher (10-13.11.1841).

(72) OSNABRÜCK 12 November 1841: Großerklub

PROGRAM: Tell // Lucia // Don Juan // Adelaïde // ?Other numbers.
SOURCES: Pagenstecher diary. // Jacobs, p. 104. // Ollivier II, p.
178. // MünWM "Beilage" No. 268 (9.11.1841).

(73)   **BIELEFELD**   13 November 1841: ?
        PROGRAM: unknown.
        SOURCES: OAdGR (1841), p. 364 [dated 8.11.1841]. // Jacobs, p.
        104. // Ollivier II, pp. 177-178. // OAdGR (1846), pp. 175-176: review
        of a concert by Wilhelmine Schröder-Devrient which refers to
        Liszt's earlier appearance in Bielefeld. See also BML 2 (1841), p. 192.

(74)   **DETMOLD**   15 November 1841: Hoftheater
                                                           benefit
        PROGRAM: Don Juan // ?other numbers.
        SOURCES: AmZ 43 (1841), col. 1102. // RGMP 8 (1841), p. 533. //
        Ollivier II, p. 181. // Jacobs, p. 104. // Carl Ziegler, "Franz Liszt. Den
        16. November 1841." Reprinted in Ziegler, *Dramaturgische Blätter*
        (Lemgo 1861), pp. 13-14. // Williams, p. 191.

(75)   **KASSEL**   17 November 1841: Ludwig Spohr's home
                                                   private/matinée
        PROGRAM: Bach chorale harmonizations.
        SOURCE: Reminiscences of Friedrich Nebelthau. Reprinted in
        Homburg.

(76)   **KASSEL**   18 November 1841: Ludwig Spohr's home
                                                           private
        PROGRAM: Quintet in c minor for piano and strings by Spohr, with
        local musicians // Ständchen // ?Other Schubert transcriptions.
        SOURCE: KasS No. 36 (4.12.1841), pp. 322-323.

(77)   **KASSEL**   19 November 1841: Hoftheater
        PROGRAM: Konzertstück // Don Juan // Robert // ?"Lied" by
        Schubert, with Herr Biberhofer // Etude ("Andante") // Grand Galop.
        SOURCES: KasZ Nos. 312-315 and 319-321 (12-15 and
        18-20.11.1841), pp. 2194, 2202, 2206, 2210, 2234, 2242, and 2238;
        and "Beiblatt" No. 48 (29.12.1841). // KasS No. 35 (27.11.1841), p.
        316; No. 36 (4.12.1841), pp. 322-323; and No. 38 (18.12.1841), pp.
        338-339. // Iris 12 (1841), p. 192. // RGMP 8 (1841), p. 560. // RMB
        No. 38 (15.12.1841), p. 156. // Hessisches Staatsarchiv Bestand 300
        A 5/12 Bd., 1: Permission for Liszt to present his concert and pay
        nothing for lighting or heat. // Hessisches Staatsarchiv Bestand 159
        Nr. 15 Bd. II: receipts. // Ollivier II, p. 181.

(78)   **KASSEL**   21 November 1841: C. von der Maulsburg's home
                                                           private
        PROGRAM: Quintet in c minor for piano and strings by Spohr, with
        local musicians // Several pieces by Liszt himself // "Riesesonata" by
        Spohr [at sight] // Fantasy on the *Alchymist* by Spohr [at sight].
        SOURCES: Reminiscences by Frau Nebelthau. Reprinted in
        Homburg. // Spohr, *Autobiography* (New York 1864), Vol. II, p. 239.

(79) KASSEL   22 November 1841: Hoftheater

PROGRAM: Emperor // Ständchen, Ave Maria, and Erlkönig //
Hexameron, with orchestra // "Lieder," with Dr. Derska (vocalist) and
Herr Bander (clarinet) // Invitation.
SOURCES: KasZ Nos. 322-323 (21-2.11.1841), pp. 2254 and 2258;
and "Beiblatt" No. 48 (29.11.1841). // KasS Nos. 35-36 and 38 (27.11,
4.12, and 18.12.1841), pp. 316, 323, and 338-339. // RGMP 8 (1841),
p. 535. // WaMZ No. 148 (11.12.1841), p. 620. // RMB No. 39
(15.12.1841), p. 156 [gives date as 29.11.1841]. // Hessisches
Staatsarchive Bestand 159 Nr. 15 Bd. II: receipts. // Homburg: facsimile of an advertising poster. // Ollivier II, pp. 180-181. See also
NZfM 15 (1841), p. 152.

(80) GÖTTINGEN   24 November 1841: Universitätssaal

PROGRAM: Don Juan // ?Konzertstück // ?Emperor.
SOURCES: GötWb No. 48 (27.11.1841). // Reminiscences by
Christian Friedrich Lueder. Reprinted in Homburg. // KasZ No. 1
(8.1.1844): article by Dr. Heinroth, written in 1843, mentioning this
concert. // F. Hardege, "Große Musiker in Göttingen," *Göttinger
Jahrbuch* 2 (1953), p. 91. // D-WRgs Liszt Kasten 261/7: ?notice about
this concert from "Hannover"; mentions Hummel. // Reminiscences
of Kurt von Schlözer. Quoted in Williams, p. 172. // Ollivier II, pp.
181 and 183.

(81) WEIMAR   ?25 November 1841: Schloß
                                        private

PROGRAM: unknown.
SOURCES: Williams, p. 174. // Unidentified clipping in F-Vm. See
also AmZ 44 (1842), col. 161. // NZfM 15 (1841), p. 191.

(82) WEIMAR   26 November 1841: Schloß
                                        ?private

PROGRAM: unknown.
SOURCES: ?NZfM 15 (1841), p. 191 [gives no date]. // AuZ (1841),
p. 2734. // Unidentified clipping in F-Vm. See also Huschke, p. 103.
// AmZ 44 (1842), col. 161.

(83) WEIMAR   ?27 November 1841: Schloß
                                        private

PROGRAM: unknown.
SOURCES: Williams, p. 174. // Unidentified clipping in F-Vm. See
also AmZ 44 (1842), col. 161.

(84) WEIMAR   28 November 1841: Schloß
                                        ?private

PROGRAM: unknown.
SOURCES: ?NZfM 15 (1841), p. 191 [gives no date]; and 16 (1842),
p. 4. // AuZ (1841), p. 2734. // Unidentified clipping in F-Vm. See also
Huschke, p. 103. // AmZ 44 (1842), col. 161.

(85)   **WEIMAR**   29 November 1841: Hoftheater
                                                        benefit

PROGRAM: Don Juan // Invitation // Hexameron // Erlkönig //
Grand Galop // encore: Robert.
SOURCES: WrZ Nos. 95 ("Beiblatt") and 96 (27.11 and 1.12.1841).
// AmZ 44 (1842), col. 161. // NZfM 15 (1841), p. 191; and 16 (1842),
p. 4. // RGMP 8 (1841), p. 585. // JdNVM 3 (1841), p. 407. // BML 3
(1842), p. 7. // AuMP No. 51 (18.12.1841). See also D-WRgs Liszt
Kasten 130: diploma awarding Liszt the Order of the White Falcon.
// WaMZ No. 156 (30.12.1841), p. 652. // AmZ 43 (1841), col. 1102. //
RMB No. 46 (3.2.1842), p. 188 [dated 3.2.1842]. // World 16 (1841),
p. 413. // Burger, p. 139: facsimile of poster (Robert omitted from
program). // Reminiscences of Emil Genast. Quoted in Williams, pp.
172-173. // Three additional clippings in F-Vm. // Ollivier II, p. 182.
// Huschke, pp. 103-104 and 196: programs [omit Robert].

(86)   **JENA**   30 November 1841: ?
                                                        matinée

PROGRAM: unknown.
SOURCES: NZfM 16 (1842), p. 4. // AuZ (1841), p. 2734. // JdNVM
3 (1841), p. 407. // Three additional clippings in F-Vm.

(87)   **LEIPZIG**   1 December 1841: Schumann's home
                                                        private

PROGRAM: unknown.
SOURCE: Williams p. 174.

(88)   **LEIPZIG**   2 December 1841: Schumann's home
                                                        private

PROGRAM: unknown.
SOURCE: Williams, pp. 174-175.

(89)   **DRESDEN**   4 December 1841: Saale des Hotel de Saxe

PROGRAM: Tell // "Lieder" by Schubert, with Wilhelmine
Schroeder-Devrient and Herr Tichatschek // Don Juan // Lucia-
Andante // Robert.
SOURCES: DrAn Nos. 336-337 (2-3.12.1841). // NZfM 16 (1842), p.
4. // BML 3 (1842), p. 15.

(90)   **LEIPZIG**   6 December 1841: Gewandhaus

PROGRAM: Hexameron for two pianos, with Clara Schumann [who
also played Lucia on the same concert] // *Rheinweinlied* by Liszt
sung.
SOURCES: LZ Nos. 290 and 297 (4 and 13.12.1841), pp. 4492 and
4597. // LAZ Nos. 339-340 and 343 (5-6 and 9.12.1841), pp. 3992,
4009, and 4035-4036. // LTb Nos. 339-340 (5-6.11.1841), pp. 2828 and
2836. // AmZ 43 (1841), cols. 1070 and 1099-1100. // NZfM 15 (1841),
pp. 176 and 198-199; and 16 (1842), p. 4. // Litzmann II, p. 38. //
Williams, p. 175. // Three additional clippings in F-Vm. // Ollivier II,
pp. 181-184. See also BML 2 (1841), p. 192.

(91) DRESDEN 9 December 1841: Saale des Hotel de Saxe

PROGRAM: Archduke, with Lipinski and Kummer // "Aria," with Pantaleoni // Tarantelle // Chopin Mazurka // Puritani-Polonaise. **SOURCES:** DrAn Nos. 341 and 343 (7 and 9.12.1841). // NZfM 16 (1842), p. 4. // BML 3 (1842), p. 15.

(92) DRESDEN 11 December 1841: Home of Karl Lipinski
private

PROGRAM: unknown (?chamber works).
SOURCE: NZfM 16 (1842), p. 4. // BML 3 (1842), p. 15. // Ramann II, p. 145.

(93) LEIPZIG 12 December 1841: Schumann's home
private

PROGRAM: Hummel Septet, ?with local musicians.
SOURCE: Williams, p. 175.

(94) LEIPZIG 13 December 1841: Gewandhaus

PROGRAM: Hummel Septet (as piano solo) // Don Juan // Adelaïde // Erlkönig // Hexameron for two pianos, with Clara Schumann // ?"Italian aria," with Pantaleoni // *Rheinweinlied* and *Rattenlied* by Liszt sung.
SOURCES: LZ Nos. 294 and 297 (9 and 13.12.1841), p. 4556 and 4584. // LAZ Nos. 343 and 351 (9 and 17.12.1841), pp. 4044 and 4131. // LTb Nos. 343-344 and 346-347 (9-10 and 12-3.12.1841), pp. 2858, 2866, 2887, and 2895. // AmZ 44 (1842), cols. 16-18. // NZfM 15 (1841), pp. 199-200; and 16 (1842), p. 4. // Litzmann II, p. 39. // Williams, p. 175. See also Dörffel, p. 214.

(95) ALTENBURG 14 December 1841: ?

PROGRAM: unknown.
SOURCE: NZfM 16 (1842), p. 4.

(96) LEIPZIG 16 December 1841: Gewandhaus

PROGRAM: Emperor // Robert // *Das deutsche Vaterland* by Liszt sung // encore: Grand Galop.
SOURCES: LZ No. 299 (15.12.1841), p. 4648. // LAZ Nos. 349 and 351 (15 and 17.12.1841), pp. 4115 and 4131. // AmZ 44 (1842), cols. 16 and 18-20. // NZfM 16 (1842), p. 4. // D-WRgs Liszt Kasten 249/1: handwritten notes about this concert. // Williams, p. 175 [implies that Liszt performed a fantasy by "Robert" Schumann]. // Ollivier II, pp. 184-185.

(97) HALLE 18 December 1841: Saale des Kronprinzen Hotels

PROGRAM: unknown.
SOURCES: HalC Nos. 293 and 295-296 (16, 18, and 20.12.1841). // NZfM 16 (1842), p. 4. // Ollivier II, pp. 185-186.

(98)   HALLE   19 December 1841: ?
                                                            private

PROGRAM: unknown.
SOURCES: NZfM 16 (1842), p. 4. // Walter Serauky,
Musikgeschichte der Stadt Halle II (Halle 1942), p. 539 [cites documents unavailable today]. // Williams, p. 192. // Ollivier II, p. 185;
possibly also pp. 186-188.

(99)   BERLIN   27 December 1841: Saale der Singakademie

PROGRAM: Tell // Lucia-Andante // Robert // Adelaïde // Chromatic
Fantasy and Fugue in d minor (BWV 903) by Bach // Erlkönig //
Grand Galop.
SOURCES: VZ Nos. 301-302 and 304 (24, 27, and 29.12.1841). No.
304 reprinted in Rellstab, pp. 1-5. Translated into English in Burger,
p. 141; and Williams, pp. 177-178. Quoted in Kapp, *Franz Liszt*, pp.
154-155. Reprinted in part in Ramann II, p. 156. // SZ Nos. 301-302
and 304 (24, 27, and 29.12.1841). // KönPZ No. 9 (9.1.1842), pp.
34-35. // BFig Nos. 2-3 (4-5.1.1842), pp. 7-8 and 11-12. // AuZ (1842),
pp. 13-14. // AmZ 44 (1842), cols. 143-144, 162, and 186. // NZfM 16
(1842), pp. 12 and 16. // "Franz Liszt in Berlin," BML 3 (1842), pp.
9-12, 29-32, and 49-52. // JdNVM 4 (1842), pp. 15 and 54. // RGMP
9 (1842), pp. 15 and 47. // RMB No. 43 (12.1.1842), p. 176. // Monde
3 (1842), p. 15. // RDM 30 (1842), pp. 159-160. // BGes No. 2
(3.1.1842), p. 8. // World 17 (1842), p. 37. // D-WRgs Liszt Kasten 240:
two playbills; and 135: receipts for this and eight other Berlin concerts. // Varnhagen von Ense, *Tagebücher* (Leipzig 1861), Vol. I, p.
385: diary entry for 27.12.1841. Reprinted in Ramann II, p. 150.
Quoted in English in Williams, pp. 176-177. // AuZ (1842), p. 416. //
APSZ No. 9 (9.1.1842), pp. 34-35. // Ollivier II, pp. 188-190.
    Additional references to this and other 1842 Berlin concerts ap-
pear in the following sources: "A. Brennglass" [pseud. Adolf
Glassbrenner], *Franz Liszt in Berlin: eine Komödie*: a satirical sketch
about Liszt's Berlin triumphs. Reprinted in FKB No. 199 (21.7.1842),
pp. 794-795. // Albert Enssenhardt, *Das Lißt-ge Berlin*, 3 vols. (Berlin
?1842). // Additional illustrations and caricatures of Liszt in Berlin
appear in Burger, pp. 140 and 143-143. // See also Burger, p. 144:
poem from the *Zeitung für die elegante Welt* (otherwise
unavailable);[1] and Burger, pp. 143-145: other reports of Liszt in
Berlin. Finally, see World 17 (1842), p. 188.

(100)   BERLIN   1 January 1842: Saale der Singakademie

PROGRAM: Moonlight // Huguenots // Invitation // "Fugue" and
"Variations" in e minor by Handel // Tarantelle // Chopin Mazurka
// Puritani-Polonaise // Marche hongroise // encore: Erlkönig.
SOURCES: VZ Nos. 304-305 (29-30.12.1841); and 1 (3.1.1842). // SZ
Nos. 306 (31.12.1841); and 1 (3.1.1842). // BFig Nos. 2-3 (4-5.1.1842),
pp. 7-8 and 11-12. // APSZ No. 1 (1.1.1842), p. 4 [omits "Variations"
by Handel]. // AmZ 44 (1842), cols. 144-145. // NZfM 16 (1842), pp.

---

[1]   The present author has been able to locate only the 1833-1834 issues of
    this periodical, which were reprinted in 1971 by Athenaeum of Frankfurt
    a.M.

74-75. // JdNVM 4 (1842), p. 15. // Rellstab, pp. 5-10. // SZ No. 306
(31.12.1841): additional notice.

(101)   BERLIN   3 January 1842: ?
                                                            private
PROGRAM: unknown.
SOURCE: Reminiscences of Eduard Devrient. Quoted in Williams,
pp. 179-180.

(102)   BERLIN   5 January 1842: Saale der Singakademie
                                                            benefit
PROGRAM: Hummel Septet (as quintet!), with local musicians //
"Aria" from *Niobe*, with Pantaleoni // Ständchen and Ave Maria //
?"Pedalfuge" by Bach, possibly the Prelude and Fugue in e minor
(BWV 533). // Valse di bravura // *Rheinweinlied* by Liszt sung // encore: Robert.
SOURCES: VZ Nos. 2 and 5 (2 and 7.1.1842). // SZ Nos. 1-2 and 5
(3-4 and 7.1.1842). // BFig No. 5 (7.1.1842), pp. 19-20. // APSZ No. 5
(5.1.1842), p. 20. // AmZ 44 (1842), cols. 145-146. // NZfM 16 (1842),
pp. 74-75. // BGes No. 11 "Beilage" (19.1.1842), p. 53. // Rellstab, pp.
10-13. // F. Bellegne, "Ein Concert von Franz Liszt," BGes Nos. 34-36
(Feb 1842), pp. 161-162, 166-167, and 169-171: a very lengthy and
satirical review [mentions Ave and Robert, but also ?Beethoven]. The
first installment is mentioned in Jacobs, p. 108. // BFig No. 7
(10.1.1842), p. 27: discussion of Liszt's phenomenal musical memory.
// BFig Nos. 8-9 (11-12.1.1842), pp. 29-30 and 34: biography of Liszt
by Dr. Weyl. // Ollivier II, pp. 191ff., esp. p. 194.

(103)   POTSDAM   8 January 1842: Casino
                                                            matinée
PROGRAM: Tell // Invitation // Robert // Ave Maria and Erlkönig //
Grand Galop // Valse di bravura.
SOURCES: VZ No. 7 (10.1.1842). // AmZ 44 (1842), col. 194. // BFig
No. 8 (11.1.1842), pp. 31-32. // NZfM 16 (1842), pp. 60 and 74-75. //
Burger, p. 140, and Williams, p. 180: both give incorrect dates for
this concert (Burger two different dates!).

(104)   BERLIN   9 January 1842: Saale der Singakademie
                                                            benefit
PROGRAM: Quartet for piano and strings by Prince Louis
Ferdinand of Prussia, with the Brothers Ganz and "Herr Richter" //
Don Juan // *Momento capriccioso* by Weber // Etudes by Moscheles
and Chopin // Prelude and Fugue in a minor (BWV 543) by Bach //
Hexameron.
SOURCES: VZ Nos. 4 and 8 (6 and 11.1.1842). // SZ Nos. 5-6
(7-8.1.1842). // KönPZ No. 9 (9.1.1842), p. 35. // APSZ Nos. 8-9
(8-9.1.1842), pp. 32 and 35-36. // AmZ 44 (1842), cols. 146, 148, and
235. // NZfM 16 (1842), pp. 60 and 74-75. // BML 3 (1842), pp. 12 and
30. // BGes No. 11 "Beilage" (19.1.1842), p. 53. // Rellstab, pp. 13-17
[Rellstab, pp. 18-25, refers to other 1842 Berlin concerts]. // BGes
No. 11 "Beilage" (19.1.1842), pp. 53-54: a more general treatment of
Liszt's Berlin concerts. // BGes No. 53 (23.2.1842), p. 156. // Ollivier
II, p. 191.

(105) BERLIN   ?before 12 January 1842: ?
                                                        private
       PROGRAM: unknown.
       SOURCE: Williams, p. 180.

(106) BERLIN   12 January 1842: Hotel de Russie
                                                        benefit
       PROGRAM: Niobe // Quartet from *I Puritani* by Bellini, with
       vocalists // "I tuoi frequenti palpiti" from *Niobe* by Pacini, and *Der
       Mönch* by Meyerbeer; ?both with Pantaleoni // "Aria" from *Csar and
       Zimmerman* by Lortzing, ?with Pantaleoni // encores: Erlkönig, and
       fantasy on Invitation. // Grand Galop [billed as concluding number].
       SOURCES: VZ Nos. 9 and 11 (12 and 14.1.1842). // SZ Nos. 8-9 and
       11 (11-12 and 14.1.1842). // BFig No. 11 (14.1.1842), p. 44. // APSZ
       No. 12 (12.1.1842), p. 48. // NZfM 16 (1842), pp. 74-75. // Ollivier II,
       pp. 194-195.

(107) BERLIN   16 January 1842: Saale der Singakademie
                                                        matinée
       PROGRAM: Pastoral // Somnambula // Mazeppa (etude) // "Sonata"
       and "Katzenfuge" by Scarlatti // "Valse cappriccio" // Improvisation
       on God save the Queen.
       SOURCES: VZ Nos. 11 and 14 (14 and 18.1.1842). // SZ Nos. 10-11
       and 14 (13-14 and 18.1.1842). // APSZ Nos. 14 and 16 (14 and
       16.1.1842), pp. 56 and 64. // AmZ 44 (1842), col. 235 [gives "15.
       Januar" as date]. // NZfM 16 (1842), pp. 74-75. // JdNVM 4 (1842),
       p. 35. // Ollivier, p. 194.

(108) BERLIN   20 January 1842: "Englischen Hause"
                                                   matinée/?benefit
       PROGRAM: unknown.
       SOURCES: VZ Nos. 13-14 (17-18.1.1842) [No. 14 only: "Hr. Liszt
       wird zugegen sein"]. // ?AmZ 44 (1842), col. 235. // Enssenhardt, *Das
       Lißt-ge Berlin* III, pp. 24-32: skit about this concert.

(109) BERLIN   21 January 1842: Saale der Singakademie
       PROGRAM: Konzertstück, with orchestra // Lucia-Marche et
       Cavatine // Sonata in d minor, Op. 31, No. 3 ("Tempest"), by
       Beethoven // Lob der Thränen // *Capriccio* in f-sharp minor, Op. 5,
       by Mendelssohn // God Save the Queen // Grand Galop.
       SOURCES: VZ 14-16 and 19 (18-20 and 24.1.1842). // SZ Nos. 15-16
       and 19 (19-20 and 24.1.1842). // APSZ No. 19 (19.1.1842), p. 76. //
       AmZ 44 (1842), col. 235. // NZfM 16 (1842), pp. 74-75 and 130. //
       D-WRgs Liszt Kasten 240: playbill. // BriefeHZ I, pp. 33-35: Wilhelm
       Wieprecht to Liszt, 20.1.1842.

(110) BERLIN   23 January 1842: Saale der Singakademie
       PROGRAM: Don Juan // Ständchen, Ave Maria, and Erlkönig // In-
       vitation // Improvisation // Robert.
       SOURCES: VZ Nos. 18 and 20 (22 and 25.1.1842). // SZ Nos. 18 and
       20 (22 and 25.1.1842). // APSZ No. 23 (23.1.1842), p. 91. // AmZ 44

(1842), col. 235. // JdNVM 4 (1842), p. 39. // BGes No. 19 (2.2.1842), p. 92. // JdNVM 4 (1842), p. 54.

(111) BERLIN 24 January 1842: Saale der Singakademie
benefit

PROGRAM: An aria from *Lucia di Lammermoor* by Donizetti, with Marie Shaw.
SOURCES: VZ Nos. 17, 19, and 21 (21, 24, and 26.1.1842) [only No. 21 (26.1.1842) mentions Liszt]. // APSZ Nos. 20 and 22.1.1842), pp. 80 and 84 [neither mentions Liszt]. // AmZ 44 (1842), col. 237-238. // BML 3 (1842), p. 30. See also APSZ No. 38 (7.2.1842), p. 156. // WaMZ No. 21 (17.2.1842), p. 84. // AmZ 44 (1842), col. 237: Liszt presents a toast at a midday banquet the same day.

(112) BERLIN before 25 January 1842: "chez la Princesse"
matinée/private

PROGRAM: unknown.
SOURCES: Ollivier II, p. 197. // AuZ (1842), p. 416. See also BML 3 (1842), p. 29: claims that Liszt gave twenty private performances in Berlin in 1842.

(113) BERLIN before 25 January 1842: "chez la Princesse"
matinée/private

PROGRAM: unknown.
SOURCES: Ollivier II, p. 197. // AuZ (1842), p. 416.

(114) BERLIN before 25 January 1842: "chez la Princesse"
matinée/private

PROGRAM: unknown.
SOURCES: Ollivier II, p. 197. // AuZ (1842), p. 416.

(115) BERLIN before 25 January 1842: "chez la Princesse"
matinée/private

PROGRAM: unknown.
SOURCES: Ollivier II, p. 197. // AuZ (1842), p. 416.

(116) BERLIN 25 January 1842: Aula der Universität
benefit/matinée

PROGRAM: Tell // Erlkönig // Invitation // "Agatha-Aria" from *Der Freischütz* by Weber-Kullak // Grand Galop // *Rheinweinlied* [?as solo] and ?*Es war eine König in Thule*, both by Liszt; both sung by the "Hofsängerin."
SOURCES: VZ No. 21 (26.1.1842). // SZ Nos. 22 and 31 (27.1 and 7.2.1842). // BFig No. 24 (29.1.1842), pp. 95-96. // APSZ No. 38 (7.2.1842), p. 155. // KönPZ No. 38 (7.2.1842), p. 155. // AmZ 44 (1842), col. 235. // BML 3 (1842), pp. 21 and 30. // Rellstab, p. 30. // Ollivier II, pp. 197-202, esp. pp. 200-201. // Williams, p. 182. See also BML 3 (1842), p. 72: the Hungarian court contributes an additional 100 gold ducats for student charities.

(117) **BERLIN**   30 January 1842: Saale der Singakademie

PROGRAM: Puritani and Puritani-Polonaise [!] // Mélodies
hongroises // Sonata in f minor, Op. 57 ("Appassionata"), by
Beethoven // Campanella and Carnival of Venice // Prelude and
Fugue in c-sharp minor from WTC I by Bach // Serenata et l'Orgia
// encore: Erlkönig.
SOURCES: VZ Nos. 22 and 26 (27.1 and 1.2.1842). // SZ Nos. 22 and
26 (27.1 and 1.2.1842). // APSZ No. 28 (28.1.1842), p. 112. // AmZ 44
(1842), col. 236 [gives "Hotel de Russie" as location for this concert].

(118) **BERLIN**   1 February 1842: Aula der Universität
                                                    benefit/matinée

PROGRAM: Lucia-Andante // Robert // Erlkönig // Invitation //
Gaudeamus igitur [free fantasy] // Songs with Zchiesche and
Pantaleoni.
SOURCES: VZ Nos. 27-28 (2-3.2.1842). // SZ No. 31 (7.2.1842). //
KönPZ No. 38 (7.2.1842), p. 155. // APSZ No. 38 (7.2.1842), p. 155. //
AmZ 44 (1842), col. 235. // BML 3 (1842), pp. 21 and 30. // JdNVM 4
(1842), p. 63. // BGes No. 19 (2.2.1842), p. 92. // Rellstab, p. 30. //
Burger, p. 140 [incorrectly gives 4.2.1842 as the date of this concert].
// BriefeHZ I, p. 38: Mendelssohn to Liszt, 1.2.1842.

(119) **BERLIN**   2 February 1842: Saale der Singakademie

PROGRAM: Niobe // "Funeral March" from the "Eroica" symphony
by Beethoven-Liszt // Sonata in A-flat Major by Weber // Au bord and
Au lac // Norma// Improvisation.
SOURCES: VZ Nos. 25 and 29 (31.1 and 4.2.1842). // SZ Nos. 25 and
29 (31.1 and 4.2.1842). // BFig No. 27 (2.2.1842), p. 108. // APSZ No.
32 (2.1.1842), p. 130 [gives "A-dur" as Weber Sonata key]. // AmZ 44
(1842), cols. 186 and 238. // NZfM 16 (1842), pp. 130-131. // Burger,
p. 140, incorrectly gives 3.2.1842 as the date of this concert.

(120) **BERLIN**   ?4 February 1842: ?
                                                            private

PROGRAM: Selections from *Les Huguenots* by Meyerbeer, with the
Princess of Prussia and members of the ?Opera chorus and orchestra.
SOURCE: KönPZ No. 38 (7.2.1842), p. 156.

(121) **BERLIN**   6 February 1842: Saale der Singakademie

PROGRAM: Andante con variazione // Lucrezia Borgia //
Campanella and Carnival of Venice // Two movements from the
Sonata in B-flat Major, Op. 106 ("Hammerklavier"), by Beethoven //
Der Mönch by Meyerbeer, as piano solo // Don Juan.
SOURCES: VZ Nos. 29 and 32 (4 and 8.2.1842). // SZ Nos. 29 and
32 (4 and 8.2.1842). // BFig No. 30 (5.2.1842), p. 120. // APSZ No. 36
(5.2.1842), p. 148. // AmZ 44 (1842), cols. 234-235 and 291. // Rellstab,
p. 23. // Ollivier II, p. 263. See also APSZ No. 38 (7.2.1842), p. 156:
comprehensive review and list of pieces performed to date at thirteen
public events in Berlin. // VZ No. 32 (8.2.1842): poem.

(122) **BERLIN**   8 February 1842: Royal York Masonic Lodge
                                                            private

PROGRAM: Sonata in A-flat Major by Weber // ?other numbers. **SOURCES:** VZ Nos. 36-37 (12 and 14.2.1842). // AuZ (1842), p. 416. // BML 3 (1842), p. 50. // D-WRgs Liszt Überformate No. 120: membership certificate in the Loge zur Eintracht, Berlin, dated 22.2.1842. // Autexier, pp. 88ff. // Ollivier II, p. 262 [gives wrong date].

(123) BERLIN 9 February 1842: Hotel de Russie
matinée/benefit

PROGRAM: Tell // Don Juan // Robert // Invitation // Grand Galop. **SOURCES:** VZ No. 36 (12.2.1842). // SZ No. 35 (11.2.1842). // AmZ 44 (1842), col. 238. // Ollivier II, p. 264. See also Ramann II, p. 159.

(124) BERLIN 9 February 1842: "Beer-schen Hause"
private

PROGRAM: Robert // Invitation // accompanies Act IV of *Les Huguenots* // *Rheinweinlied* and *Die Loreley* by Liszt sung. **SOURCE:** AmZ 44 (1842), cols. 238-239.

(125) BERLIN 10 February 1842: Theater
benefit

PROGRAM: Norma // Erlkönig // Grand Galop // God Save the Queen. // *Rheinweinlied, Rattenlied,* and *Das deutsche Vaterland* by Liszt sung; Liszt conducts. **SOURCES:** VZ Nos. 34 and 36 (10 and 12.2.1842). // SZ No. 36 (12.2.1842). // KönPZ No. 38 (7.2.1842), p. 156. // BFig Nos. 35-36 (11-12.2.1842), pp. 140 and 143-144. // APSZ Nos. 38-39 (7-8.2.1842), pp. 156 and 160. // AmZ 44 (1842), col. 235. // BML 3 (1842), p. 40. See also SZ No. 36 (12.2.1842): account of post-concert dinner and poem. // Ollivier II, pp. 202-204 and 261-265, esp. p. 263. // VZ No. 35 (11.2.1842): another poem.

NB: VZ and SZ No. 29 (4.2.1842); and APSZ Nos. 36-37 (5-6.2.1842), pp. 148 and 152, give the original date of this concert as 7 February.

(126) BERLIN 16 February 1842: Opera
benefit

PROGRAM: Konzertstück // Hexameron, with orchestra // Don Juan // Lucia-Andante // Erlkönig // Grand Galop. **SOURCES:** VZ Nos. 37-38 and 41 (14-15 and 18.2.1842). // SZ No. 41 (18.2.1842). // APSZ Nos. 45-47 (14-16.2.1842), pp. 188, 192, and 196. // AmZ 44 (1842), col. 291. // NZfM 16 (1842), p. 130. // BML 3 (1842), pp. 29-32 and 40.

VZ Nos. 42-43 (19 and 21.2.1842): description of a banquet honoring Liszt's election to the Prussian Academie der Künste 18.2.1842, and text of a poem read at that banquet. The official announcement appeared in APSZ No. 52 (21.2.1842), p. 215.; and a guest list of those who attended the banquet is preserved in D-WRgs Liszt Kasten 165/1. // D-WRgs Überformate 121a: certificate of membership in the Academie, dated 21.2.1842. See also AuZ (1842), p. 447. // WaMZ Nos. 26 and 62 (1.3 and 24.5.1842), pp. 104 and 256. // Monde 3 (1842), p. 80. // MJm No. 431 (20.3.1842). // Rellstab, pp. 35-36. // Ollivier II, p. 262.

(127)   BERLIN   19 February 1842: Opera
                                                        benefit

PROGRAM: Emperor // ?Tell // Norma // Invitation (with appended
fantasy) // Choral Fantasy // God Save the Queen.
SOURCES: VZ Nos. 38, 40, and 43 (15, 17, and 21.2.1842). // SZ No.
43 (21.2.1842). // BFig No. 42 (19.2.1842), p. 168. // APSZ Nos. 48-50
(17-19.2.1842), pp. 200, 204, and 210. // AmZ 44 (1842), cols. 291-292.
// BML 3 (1842), p. 40. See also VZ No. 51 (2.3.42), and SZ No. 53
"Beilage" (5.3.1842): itemization of concert proceeds as they were divided among several charities.

(128)   BERLIN   23 February 1842: Opera

PROGRAM: Somnambula // Hexameron, with orchestra //
Ständchen // Robert // Choral Fantasy [performed by request].
SOURCES: VZ Nos. 43 and 45-47 (21 and 23-25.2.1842). // SZ No.
47 (25.2.1842). // BFig No. 45 (23.2.1842), p. 180. // APSZ Nos. 52-54
(21-23.2.1842), pp. 218, 222, and 226. // AmZ 44 (1842), col. 292. //
BML 3 (1842), p. 40. // AuZ (1842), p. 447.

(129)   BERLIN   25 February 1842: Hotel de Russie
                                                        matinée

PROGRAM: Grand Galop // ?An operatic number, with Nina Morra
// Der Mönch by Meyerbeer, with Herr Zchiesche // ?other numbers.
SOURCES: VZ Nos. 46-48 (24-26.2.1842). // APSZ No. 56
(25.2.1842), p. 234. // BML 3 (1842), p. 50.

(130)   BERLIN   27 February 1842: "Schloß"
                                                        ?private

PROGRAM: Act IV of Les Huguenots by Meyerbeer, with Miss
Unger-Sabatini // ?Die Loreley by Liszt, also with Unger-Sabatini.
SOURCES: AuZ (1842), p. 510. // Jacobs, p. 107. See also Ramann
II, p. 159.

(131)   BERLIN   28 February 1842: Theater
                                                        benefit

PROGRAM: Symphony in c minor by Beethoven, and Overture to
Olympia by Spontini; both with Liszt conducting // "Cavatina" from
I Briganti by Mercadante, with Mlle Tuczek // Der Mönch by
Meyerbeer, with Herr Zschiesche // ?Other vocal numbers [final vocal
number was accompanied by a different pianist; Liszt fell during the
concert].
SOURCES: VZ Nos. 46, 48 and 51 (24 and 26.2, and 2.3.1842). // SZ
Nos. 47-48 and 51 (25-26.2 and 2.3.1842). // BFig Nos. 49 and 52 (28.2
and 3.3.1842), pp. 196 and 208. // APSZ Nos. 55, 57, and 59 (24, 26,
and 28.2.1842), pp. 230, 238, and 246. // AmZ 44 (1842), col. 293. //
NZfM 16 (1842), p. 130 [also mentions other concerts]. // VZ No. 54
(6.3.1842); and SZ No. 54 (6.3.1842): additional notices. See also
BML 3 (1842), pp. 43, 50, and 52. // VZ No. 54 (5.3.1842): a review
of Liszt's conducting.

(132) BERLIN   2 March 1842: Opera

PROGRAM: Concerto in c minor, Op. 37, by Beethoven, with orchestra // Oberons Zauberhorn, with orchestra [?!] // Don Juan // Ave Maria and Erlkönig // encore: Grand Galop.
SOURCES: VZ Nos. 51 and 53 (2 and 4.2.1842). // SZ No. 53 (4.3.1842). // APSZ Nos. 60-61 (1-2.3.1842), pp. 250 and 254. // AmZ 44 (1842), cols. 292-293. // BML 3 (1842), pp. 49-52. // AuZ (1842), p. 527. // Rellstab, p. 27.

(133) BERLIN   3 March 1842: Hotel de Russie
                                           matinée/benefit
PROGRAM: unknown.
SOURCES: VZ Nos. 53-54 (4-5.3.1842). // SZ Nos. 53-54 (4-5.3.1842). // AmZ 44 (1842), col. 377. // NZfM 16 (1842), p. 130. // BML 3 (1842), pp. 25-28 and 50. // RGMP 9 (1842), p. 110. // Rellstab, pp. 37-39. // See also VZ No. 53 (4.3.1842); and SZ No. 53 (4.3.1842): letter by Liszt upon his departure from Berlin. [See Briefe I, pp. 44-45]. // AuZ (1842), pp. 527 and 535: descriptions of Liszt's departure from Berlin. // KönPZ No. 57 (9.3.1842), p. 453. // RDM 30 (1842), p. 160. // Jacobs, p. 105. // FM 5 (1842), p. 119: ridicule following Liszt's departure. // BGes No. 41 (9.3.1842), pp. 195-196. // "Ein Sendschreiben Liszt's aus Berlin an den Redacteur der 'Rheinland'," MzRh No. 18 (10.2.1842), pp. 69-71: a counterfeit Liszt letter ridiculing Berlin musical life. Reprinted in BFig Nos. 54-55 (5 and 7.3.1842), pp. 214-215 and 218-219. Denounced by Liszt as a forgery in: BFig No. 68 (22.3.1842), p. 272. See also Ramann II, p. 167. // BGes No. 45 (16.3.1842), p. 216. // BFig Nos. 56-58 (8-10.3.1842), pp. 223-224, 228, and 231-232. // BML 3 (1842), p. 60. // D-WRgs Überformate No. 121: certificate of honorary directorship of the Academy for Men's Choral Music, dated 7.12.1842. // Williams, p. 184. See also VZ No. 53 (4.3.1842): correction of previous announcements for this concert, and Liszt's letter of 1 March 1842 apologizing for problems with arrangements.

(134) MARIENBURG   8 March 1842: Schloß
                                           private/?matinée
PROGRAM: unknown.
SOURCES: VZ Nos. 61 and 71 (13 and 26.3.1842).

(135) ELBING   8 March 1842: Saale des Gymnasiums.
PROGRAM: Lucia // Erlkönig // Invitation // Robert // Don Juan (?improvisation).
SOURCES: ElbAn No. 20 (12.3.1842). // KönPZ No. 62 (15.3.1842), p. 493. // VZ No. 61 (13.3.1842). // See also ElbAn Nos. 19 and 21 (9 and 16.3.1842): biographical sketch, "Lisztiana," and "Die Liszt-Periode in Berlin." // Erwin Kroll, *Musikstadt Königsberg* (Freiburg 1966), p. 149. // Ollivier II, pp. 204-205.

(136) KÖNIGSBERG   10 March 1842: Theater
PROGRAM: Tell // Robert // Ständchen and Erlkönig // Lucia-Andante // Grand Galop.
SOURCES: KönPZ Nos. 57, 60, and 62 (9, 12, and 15.3.1842), pp. 453, 477-478, and 493. // VZ No. 64 (17.3.1842). // NZfM 16 (1842),

p. 112. // BML 3 (1842), p. 60. // *Geschichte des Philharmonischen Vereins zu Königsberg*, p. 24.

(137) KÖNIGSBERG 11 March 1842: Theater

PROGRAM: Don Juan // Prelude and Fugue in c-sharp minor from WTC I by Bach // God Save the Queen // Fantasy on Invitation // Norma.
SOURCES: KönPZ No. 61 (14.3.1842), pp. 484-485. // ElbAn No. 21 (16.3.1842): "Lisztiana." // VZ No. 64 (17.3.1842). See also KönPZ Nos. 62-63 (15-15.3.1842), pp. 493 and 501: on Liszt's interpretation of Bach fugues. // L. Passarge, *Ein Ostpreußisches Jugendleben* (Leigzig 1906), p. 139: reminiscences.

(138) KÖNIGSBERG
13 March 1842: "Kniephosischen Junkerhofes" matinée

PROGRAM: unknown [?Galop].
SOURCES: KönPZ Nos. 60 and 62 (12 and 15.3.1842), pp. 478 and 493.

(139) KÖNIGSBERG 13 March 1842: Theater

PROGRAM: unknown [Galop].
SOURCES: KönPZ Nos. 60 and 62 (12 and 15.3.1842), pp. 478, 480, and 493. // ?VZ No. 64 (17.3.1842): mentions third Königsberg concert as last.

(140) KÖNIGSBERG before 14 March 1842: ?
private

PROGRAM: Erlkönig // ?other numbers.
SOURCES: Passarge, p. 140. // Reminiscences of Fanny Leward. Quoted in Williams, pp. 185-186.

(141) KÖNIGSBERG before 14 March 1842: ?
private

PROGRAM: Two songs (?one Erlkönig) by Schubert-Liszt.
SOURCES: Passarge, p. 140. // Fanny Lewald, *Meine Lebensgeschichte* (Berlin 1861-??). Quoted in Williams, pp. 185-186.

(142) KÖNIGSBERG 14 March 1842: University
matinée

PROGRAM: ?fantasy.
SOURCES: KönPZ No. 62 (15.3.1842), p. 493. // ElbAn No. 22 (19.3.1842). // VZ No. 65 (18.3.1842). // APSZ No. 79 (20.3.1842), p. 331. // AmZ 44 (1842), col. 406. // NZfM 16 (1842), p. 112. // BML 3 (1842), p. 60. // GMdM 1 (1842), pp. 36 and 100. See also D-WRgs Liszt-Sammlung: several copies of Liszt's doctoral diploma and associated documents. // K. Lehrs, "Franz Liszt. Ehrendoctor der philosophischen Facultät der Universität zu Königsberg," *Wissenschafliche Monats-Blätter* [Königsberg] 4 (1876), pp. 175-176: speech by K. G. Jacobs. Reprinted in English in Williams, p. 185. Liszt's reply was published in VZ No. 72 (29.3.1842). // BFig No. 74 (31.3.1842), p. 296: letter of thanks from Liszt to the University of

Königsberg, dated "Königsberg, 14. März 1842." See also Williams, p. 185; and Briefe I, pp. 45-46 [dated Mittau, 18.3.1842]. // Ollivier II, p. 207. See also WaMZ No. 42 (7.4.1842), p. 175 [this page was erroneously numbered "174"].

(143) KÖNIGSBERG 14 March 1842: Theater

PROGRAM: Don Juan // Erlkönig.
SOURCES: KönPZ No. 63 (16.3.1842), p. 501. // BFig No. 67 (21.3.1842), p. 268. // VZ No. 66 (19.3.1842): two notices. // TEM No. 22 (17.3.1842), pp. 124-125.

(144) TILSIT 15 March 1842: Hotel de Russie

PROGRAM: Robert // Ständchen, Ave Maria, and Erlkönig // Lucia-Andante // Tarantelle // Chopin Mazurka // Grand Galop // ?Other numbers.
SOURCES: TEM Nos. 22-23 (17 and 21.3.1842), pp. 174-175 and 181-182. // KönPZ No. 63 (16.3.1842), p. 501.

(145) TILSIT 16 March 1842: "Mittagsgellschaft" matinée

PROGRAM: unknown.
SOURCE: TEM No. 23 (21.3.1842), p. 183. // TEM No. 23 (21.3.1842), pp. 181-182: "Zur Erinnerung an Franz Liszt." // KönPZ No. 69 (23.3.1842), p. 565. // Ollivier II, pp. 205-206.

(146) MEMEL after 16 March 1842: ?

PROGRAM: unknown.
SOURCE: Clipping provided by the Library of the University of Wroclaw, Poland.

(147) LÜBECK before 3 June 1842: ? private

PROGRAM: "I tuoi frequenti palpiti" from Niobe by Pacini, with Pantaleoni // Improvisation and "fantasies."
SOURCE: BML 3 (1842), p. 85.

(148) LÜBECK 3 June 1842: "Liebhaberkonzert" series benefit

PROGRAM: Tell // Barcarolle by Pantaleoni [arr. by Liszt], with Pantaleoni // Don Juan // Erlkönig // Grand Galop.
SOURCES: BML 3 (1842), pp. 85-86. // RGMP 9 (1842), p. 245. // ?MRm No. 46 (30.6.1842), p. 4. // Johann Hennigs and Wilhelm Stahl, Musikgeschichte Lübeck I (Kassel 1951), p. 159. // Ollivier II, p. 215. See also NZfM 16 (1842), p. 200. // BML 3 (1842), p. 88: thanks for Liszt's contributions to victims of the 1842 Hamburg fire.

(149) BRÜHL 10 September 1842: Schloß private

PROGRAM: "Ungarische Nationalmarsch."
SOURCES: KZ No. 244/245 (11.9.1842). // APSZ Nos. 255-256 (14-15.9.1842), pp. 1090 and 1092. // AuZ (1842), p. 2070. // ?WaMZ

Nos. 114-115 (22 and 24.9.1842), pp. 462 and 468. // Ollivier II, p.
220. // Williams, p. 190. See also Klaus Körner *Das Musikleben in
Köln um die Mitte des 19. Jahrhunderts* (Cologne 1969), p. 85. // FJ
No. 252 (12.9.1842). // VZ No. 214 (14.9.1842). // FOPZ No. 253
(13.9.1842), p. 2173.

(150)   COLOGNE   12 September 1842: Agrippina-Loge
                                                          private

PROGRAM: unknown.
SOURCES: SolKb No. 75 (17.9.1842). // KZ No. 249 (15.9.1842). //
Autexier, pp. 115ff.

(151)   COLOGNE   13 September 1842: Haus zu "Rheingasse"
                                                  matinée/benefit

PROGRAM: Two movements from the Konzertstück (?as solo) // God
Save the Queen // *Angiolin dal biondo crin* by Liszt, with Pantaleoni
// *Kennst Du das Land?* by Liszt, with Sophie Schloß // ?Other vocal
accompaniments // Robert.
SOURCES: KZ Nos. 245-247 (11-13.9.1842). // FOPZ No. 255
(15.9.1842), p. 2194. // NZfM 17 (1842), pp. 161 and 165-166. // BML
3 (1842), p. 203. // RGMP 9 (1842), p. 391. // Monde No. 38
(22.9.1842), pp. 151-152. // MRm Nos. 68 and 71 (18 and 29.9.1842).
// RMB No. 21 (29.9.1842), p. 91. // D-WRgs Überformate 140: hon-
orary membership, Kuntvereins [dated 28.8.1842]. // Paul Ellmar,
"Franz Liszt und der Kölner Dom," *Kölnische Rundschau*, "Der
Sonntag" (20.1.1957). See also APSZ No. 259 (18.9.1842), p. 2005
[ignores Liszt, but mentions that 2,000 thalers were raised for the
Cathedral fund].

(152)   AACHEN   17 September 1842: Salle de la Redoute

PROGRAM: Don Juan // Norma // ?Accompaniments for vocal
numbers.
SOURCES: SAZ Nos. 253, 255, and 259 (12, 17, and 30.9.1842). //
Ollivier II, pp. 222-223. See also Meyerbeer III, p. 416.

(153)   WEIMAR   23 October 1842: Schloß

PROGRAM: Somnambula // Chopin Mazurka // Puritani-Polonaise
// "Aria " by Mozart, "Aria" from Rossini's *Stabat mater*, *Adelaïde* by
Beethoven, and two "Arias" by Donizetti; all with Rubini // Erlkönig.
SOURCES: WrZ No. 86 (29.10.1842). // ErZ No. 140 (29.10.1842). //
APSZ No. 297 (26.10.1842), p. 2164. // AmZ 45 (1843), cols. 72-74. //
NZfM 17 (1842), pp. 122 and 154; and 18 (1843), p. 4. // RGMP 9
(1842), p. 424. // MRm No. 2 (22.10.1842), p. 14. // Ollivier II, pp.
223-225. See also Meyerbeer III, p. 415. // Briefe I, p. 46.

(154)   JENA   26 October 1842: Saale der Rose
                                                         benefit

PROGRAM: ?"Sie sollen ihn nicht haben," conducted by Liszt //
?Other numbers.
SOURCES: JeWb Nos. 83 and 85 (26.10 and 1.11.42), pp. 341 and
350. // WrZ "Beilage" No. 85 (26.10.1842), p. 382. // NZfM 17 (1842),

p. 154. // D-WRgs Überformate 131: certificate of honorary citizenship, Jena [dated 27.10.1842]. // Ollivier II, pp. 225-226.

(155) ERFURT 28 October 1842: Gasthaus Zum Schlehendorn
benefit
PROGRAM: Lucia-Andante // "Duo" from *Robert le diable* by Meyerbeer, with Ostergaard and Rubini // "Arias" from *Niobe* by Pacini, and from *Robert le diable* by Meyerbeer; both with Pantaleoni // "Aria," with Rubini // "Romance," with Ostergaard // *Der Erlkönig* by Schubert, with Madame Pabst // Grand Galop.
SOURCES: ErZ Nos. 138-142 (25.10 — 3.11.1842). // AmZ 45 (1843), col. 253. // NZfM 20 (1844!), p. 87. // BML 3 (1842), pp. 185-186.

(156) WEIMAR before 29 October 1842: ?Schloß
private
PROGRAM: ?Vocal numbers, with Rubini // ?other numbers.
SOURCES: AmZ 45 (1843), col. 74. // Huschke, p. 104 [apparently drawn from information not available to other researchers]. See also NZfM 17 (1842), p. 122. // BML 3 (1842), p. 164.

(157) WEIMAR before 29 October 1842: ?Schloß
private
PROGRAM: unknown.
SOURCES: AmZ 45 (1843), col. 74. // Huschke, p. 104.

(158) WEIMAR 29 October 1842: Hoftheater
benefit
PROGRAM: Somnambula // Chopin Mazurka // Puritani-Polonaise // "Aria" by Mozart, "Aria" from Rossini's *Stabat Mater*, and *Adelaïde* by Beethoven; all with Rubini // Erlkönig.
SOURCES: WrZ "Beilage" No. 86 (29.10.1842); and No. 87 (2.11.1842). // APSZ No. 306 (4.11.1842), p. 2207. // AmZ 44 (1842), col. 1013; and 45 (1843), col. 74. // NZfM 17 (1842), p. 186; and 18 (1843), p. 4. // AuZ (1842), p. 2502. // RGMP 9 (1842), p. 461. // GMdM No. 49 (4.12.1842), p. 412; and No. 7 (12.2.1843), p. 29. // WaMZ No. 138 (17.11.1842), p. 556; and No. 13 (31.1.1843), p. 56. // Monde No. 48 (1.12.1842), p. 192. // D-WRgs Liszt Kasten 130: Hofkapellmeister appointment certificate. Reproduced in Huschke, plate 26. // BML 3 (1842), p. 188. // RMB No. 28 (17.11.1842), p. 111. // Ollivier II, esp. p. 233.

(159) ERFURT 31 October 1842: Schauspielhaus
PROGRAM: ?Don Juan // ?God Save the Queen.
SOURCES: ErZ No. 141 (31.10.1842). // AmZ 45 (1843), col. 253. // ErZ No. 149 (17.11.1842): letter of thanks from Liszt, written in Gotha on 8.11.1842.

(160) COBURG 1 November 1842: Am Hof
PROGRAM: Lucia-Andante // Tell // Robert // Grand Galop // ?accompaniments for vocal numbers.
SOURCES: ErZ No. 139 (27.10.1842). // BML 3 (1842), p. 186. // RGMP 9 (1842), p. 461. // GMdM No. 49 (4.12.1842), p. 214. // MJm

No. 466 (20.11.1842). // World 18 (1843), p. 43. // Ollivier II, pp.
227-228. // Ebart, *Hundert Jahre Coburgische Theatergeschichte*
(Coburg 1927), p. 20. See also AmZ 44 (1842), col. 1013.

(161)   COBURG   4 November 1842: ?Am Hof
                                                        benefit

PROGRAM: Norma // Invitation // Erlkönig // ?accompaniments for
vocal numbers.
SOURCES: APSZ No. 317 (15.11.1842), p. 2256. // NZfM 17 (1842),
p. 178. // Ebart, p. 20. // Monde No. 46 (17.11.1842), p. 183.

(162)   GOTHA   9 November 1842: Theater

PROGRAM: unknown.
SOURCES: FDid No. 314 (14.11.1842). // *Gothaische Zeitung* [una-
vailable]. Cited by Friedrich Schnapp in his preface to Franz Liszt,
Die Gräberinsel der Fürsten zu Gotha (Budapest 1983; Plate Z
12786). // D-WRgs Liszt Kasten 128: diploma of the Ernestinischen-
Hausorden, dated 7.12.1842. // See also Ollivier II, p. 226-228. // BML
4 (1843), p. 6. // JALS 19 (1986), pp. 179-180: translation of
Schnapp's preface (mentioned above).

(163)   FRANKFURT a.M.   15 November 1842: Weidenbusch-Saal

PROGRAM: Don Juan // Etude // Marche hongroise // Prelude and
Fugue ("mit Pedal") by Bach // "Cavatina" from *Niobe* by Pacini, and
"Aria" from *Lucia di Lammermoor* by Donizetti; both with Rubini //
?accompaniments for other vocal numbers by Rubini and Ostergaard
// Norma.
SOURCES: FJ Nos. 313 and 315 (13 and 15.11.1842). // FOPZ No.
315 (15.11.1842), pp. 2711-2712. // JdF No. 313-315 and 318 (13-15
and 18.11.1842). // AuZ (1842), p. 2582. // AmZ 44 (1842), col. 1013;
and 45 (1843), col. 90. // NZfM 18 (1843), p. 93. // BML 3 (1842), p.
206. // WaMZ No. 148 (10.12.1842), p. 595. // RMB No. 29
(24.22.1842), p. 116. // Williams, pp. 190-191. // Ollivier II, p. 230.

(164)   COLOGNE   ?18 November 1842: Hotel Royale
                                                        matinée

PROGRAM: Norma // Lob der Thränen // Erlkönig //
?accompaniments for vocal numbers by Rubini and Ostergaard // Don
Juan.
SOURCES: KZ Nos. 322 and 327 (18 and 23.11.1842). // BML 3
(1842), p. 193.

(165)   MÜNSTER   26 December 1842: Gerbanletschen Saale

PROGRAM: Norma // "Lieder" by Schubert, ?with Rubini //
?accompaniments for other vocal numbers by Rubini and Ostergaard
// Don Juan.
SOURCES: WM No. 308 (25.12.1842). // MünIb Nos. 190-191 (25
and 26.12.1842), pp. 1216 and 1217. // Ollivier II, pp. 246-247.

(166)   WEIMAR   29 December 1842: ?Schloß
                                                        private

PROGRAM: unknown.

SOURCE: NZfM 18 (1843), p. 4 [dated 29.12.1842].

(167) BERLIN 31 December 1842: ?
private

PROGRAM: Don Juan // Figaro.
SOURCE: Rellstab's letter to Liszt of 2 January 1844. Reprinted in BriefeHZ I, p. 62.

(168) BERLIN 5 January 1843: ?Theater

PROGRAM: vocal works as guest conductor of the Berlin Männergesangverein.
SOURCE: VZ No. 6 (7.1.1843).

(169) BERLIN 8 January 1843: Saale der Singakademie

PROGRAM: Archduke, with the Brothers Ganz // Fugue in a minor by Bach // Somnambula // Huguenots // Tarantelle // Chopin Mazurka // "Etude" (*La Chasse*) by Heller // Hexameron for two pianos, with Döhler.
SOURCES: VZ Nos. 4-5 and 8 (4-5 and 10.1.1842). // APSZ No. 6 (7.1.1843), p. 24. // AmZ 45 (1843), cols. 136 and 178-179. // NZfM 18 (1843), p. 20. // RGMP 10 (1843), pp. 15 and 42. // WaMZ No. 13 (31.1.1843), p. 56. // GMdM No. 7 (12.2.1843), p. 29. // MRm No. 14 (15.1.1843), p. 112. // BGes No. 18 "Beiblatt" (2.2.1843), p. 90; and "Kunst und Gewerbe Beiblatt" No. 1 (1843), p. 50. // Ollivier II, pp. 249-251. See also WaMZ No. 18 (11.2.1843), p. 76: comparison of Liszt and Döhler.

(170) BERLIN 11 January 1843: Theater

PROGRAM: Hummel Septet, with local musicians // "Aria" from *Anna Bolena* by Donizetti, and "Aria" from *Niobi* by Pacini; both with Rubini // ?accompaniments for other vocal numbers by Rubini and Ostergaard // Figaro // Mélodies hongroises // Marche hongroise // encore: fantasy.
SOURCES: VZ No. 8 (10.1.1843), and "Beilage" Nos. 9 and 11 (11 and 13.1.1843). // APSZ No. 11 (11.1.1843), p. 44. // AmZ 45 (1843), cols. 179-180. // BML 4 (1843), pp. 22-24. // WaMZ No. 10 (21.1.1843), p. 44; and No. 24 (25.2.1843), p. 100. // RMB No. 38 (26.1.1843), p. 143.

(171) BERLIN 12 January 1843: "Am Hof"
private

PROGRAM: Don Juan // Puritani // ?other numbers.
SOURCES: VZ No. 12 (14.1.1843). // FOPZ No. 17 "Beiblatt" (17.1.1843), p. 138. // SmW 1 (1843), p. 24. // RGMP 10 (1843), p. 33. // Meyerbeer III, p. 424. See also VZ No. 12 (14.1.1843): poem.

(172) BERLIN 15 January 1843: Saale der Singakademie

PROGRAM: Sonata for four hands by Moscheles, with Döhler // Hexameron for two pianos, with Döhler.
SOURCES: VZ Nos. 8, 10, 12, and 14 (10, 12, 14, and 17.1.1843). // APSZ No. 15 (15.1.1843), p. 60. // AmZ 45 (1843), cols. 136 and 178. // SmW 1 (1843), p. 24. // WaMZ No. 24 (25.2.1843), p. 100. // BML

4 (1843), p. 44. // GMdM No. 11 (12.3.1843), p. 47. // BGes No. 18 "Beiblatt" (2.2.1843), p. 90. See also GMdM No. 9 (26.2.1843: comparison of Liszt and Döhler.

(173) BERLIN   18 January 1843: Schauspielhaus
                                                          benefit

PROGRAM: Konzertstück // ?accompaniments for vocal numbers by Rubini and other singers // Chopin, *Mazurkas*, Op. 50 // Don Juan. SOURCES: VZ Nos. 13-14, and 17 ["Beilage"] (16-17 and 20.1.1843). // APSZ Nos. 17-18 (17-18.1.1843), pp. 68 and 72. // FKB No. 27 (27.1.1842), pp. 107-108. // AmZ 45 (1843), col. 180. // BML 4 (1843), pp. 22-24. // SmW 1 (1843), p. 24. // WaMZ No. 24 (25.2.1843), p. 100. // Monde No. 2 (12.1.1843), p. 8. // BGes No. 20 (4.2.1843), p. 100. See also APSZ No. 19 (19.1.1843), p. 75: letter from Liszt about the Bonn Beethoven project.

(174) FRANKFURT a.d.O.   19 January 1843: Schauspielhaus

PROGRAM: Tell // Lucia-Andante // Robert // Ave Maria and Erlkönig // Grand Galop // encore: Invitation. SOURCES: FadOWb Nos. 5 and 7 (18 and 25.1.1843), pp. 61 and 77-79. // FadOT Nos. 8-10 (19, 21, and 23.1.1843), pp. 32, 35-36, and 38-39. // BrZ No. 19 (23.1.1843), p. 133. See also FadOWb No. 14 (18.2.1843), p. 156: poem.

(175) BRESLAU   21 January 1843: Musiksaal der Universität

PROGRAM: Tell // Lucia-Andante // Don Juan // Serenade and Orgy // Grand Galop. SOURCES: BrZ Nos. 16-20 (19-21 and 23-24.1.1843), pp. 113, 119, 126, 132, and 140-141. // BrPSZ No. 16 (19.1.1843), p. 114. // VZ No. 22 (26.1.1843). // AmZ 45 (1843), cols. 151-152, 178, 247, and 299. // SmW 1 (1843), p. 51. // RGMP 10 (1843), p. 42. // SmW 1 (1843), pp. 51 and 95. // GMdM No. 7 (12.2.1843), p. 29. See also BrPSZ No. 20 (24.1.1843), pp. 142-143: biography of Liszt and review by H. Wutter. // D-WRgs Liszt Kasten 240: large concert poster. // Schreiber, pp. 8-9: review. // Ollivier II, pp. 253-255. // WaMZ No. 24 (25.2.1843), p. 100.

(176) BRESLAU   24 January 1843: Musiksaal der Universität

PROGRAM: Konzertstück, with orchestra // Ständchen // Robert // Andante con variazione // Etude and Chopin Mazurka // Erlkönig. SOURCES: BrZ Nos. 19 and 23 (23 and 27.1.1843), pp. 134 and 161-162. // BrPSZ Nos. 19-20 and 25 (23-24 and 30.1.1843), pp. 136, 142-143, and 177. // BrZ No. 21 (25.1.1843), p. 149: poem in English! // D-WRgs Liszt Kasten 240: large concert poster.

(177) BRESLAU   26 January 1843: Aula Leopoldina

PROGRAM: Gaudeamus igitur // Robert // *Rheinweinlied* by Liszt sung // Grand Galop. SOURCES: BrZ Nos. 21-22 and 24 (25-26 and 28.1.1843), pp. 151, 157, and 169. // BrPSZ Nos. 21 and 25 (25 and 30.1.1843), pp. 149 and 177. // ?SmW 1 (1843), pp. 51-52. See also D-WRgs Überformate 124: certificate of Honorary Directorship in the Breslau Musik-Verein. // Schreiber, p. 10 [includes program].

(178) **BRESLAU** 27 January 1843: Saale des Königs von Ungarn

PROGRAM: Puritani // Erlkönig // "Prière di Brigandi" from *I Brigandi* by Mercadante, "Aria" from *Robert le diable* by Meyerbeer, and "Aria" from *Niobe* by Pacini; all with Pantaleoni // Grand Galop.
SOURCES: BrZ Nos. 21-24 (25-28.1.1843), pp. 150, 157, 163, and 169. // BrPSZ Nos. 21-23 and 25 (25-27 and 30.1.1843), pp. 148, 156, 163, and 177.

(179) **BRESLAU** 29 January 1843: Aula Leopoldina

PROGRAM: Moonlight // Somnambula // Lucia-Marche et Cavatine // Romanesca // Marche hongroise // Tarantelle // Chopin Mazurka // Puritani-Polonaise.
SOURCES: BrZ Nos. 23-24 (27-28.1.1843), pp. 163, 169, and 170. // BrPSZ Nos. 23 and 30 (27.1 and 4.2.1843), pp. 163 and 210. // BrPSZ No. 31 (6.2.1843), p. 221: on pianos Liszt played in Breslau.

(180) **BRESLAU** 31 January 1843: Theater

PROGRAM: Emperor (1st movement only) // Ave Maria // Norma // Lucia-Andante // Mélodies hongroises and Marche hongroise.
SOURCES: BrZ Nos. 25-26 and 28 (30-31.1 and 2.2.1843), pp. 177, 184, and 196-197. // BrPSZ Nos. 26 and 30 (31.1 and 4.2.1843), pp. 184 and 210. // BrB No. 13 (31.1.1843), p. 48.

(181) **BRESLAU** 1 February 1843: Theater

PROGRAM: *Die Zauberflöte* by Mozart, conducted by Liszt.
SOURCES: BrZ Nos. 25 and 29 ["Beilage"] (30.1 and 3.2.1843), pp. 177 and 205. // BrEr No. 14 (1.2.1843), p. 56. // BrPSZ Nos. 27 and 30 (1 and 4.1843), pp. 190 and 210. // Ollivier II, p. 256.

(182) **BRESLAU** 2 February 1843: Theater

PROGRAM: Konzertstück, with orchestra // ?"Song" by Schubert-Liszt // Niobe // Invitation // Hexameron, with orchestra.
SOURCES: BrZ Nos. 27-28 (1-2.2.1843), pp. 191 and 198. // BrPSZ No. 27 (1.2.1843), p. 190. // BrBNo. 15 (4.2.1843), p. 59: note on Liszt's Breslau success. // D-WRgs Liszt Kasten 240: large concert poster. // Burger, p. 148: facsimile of concert poster.

(183) **BRESLAU** 3 February 1843: "Schullehrer-Seminar"
private/matinée

PROGRAM: Three "concert pieces."
SOURCES: BrZ Nos. 32 and 35 (7 and 10.2.1843), pp. 234 and 254. // Schreiber, pp. 11-12.

(184) **BRESLAU** 4 February 1843: Theater

PROGRAM: Hummel Septet, with local musicians // Somnambula // Campanella and Carnival of Venice // Robert.
SOURCES: BrZ Nos. 29 and 32 (3 and 7.2.1843), pp. 206 and 232. // BrPSZ No. 30 (4.2.1843), p. 211. // BrPSZ No. 31 (6.2.1843), p. 221: more on Liszt pianos.

(185) BRESLAU   before 6 February 1843: ?Liszt's hotel
                                                          private
PROGRAM: unknown.
SOURCE: Schreiber, pp. 12-13. See also SmW 1 (1843), p. 95. // VZ
No. 37 (13.2.1843).

(186) BRESLAU   before 6 February 1843: ?Liszt's hotel
                                                          private
PROGRAM: unknown.
SOURCE: Schreiber, p. 13. See also SmW 1 (1843), p. 95. // VZ No.
37 (13.2.1843).

(187) LIEGNITZ   6 February 1843: Theater
PROGRAM: Tell // Don Juan // Erlkönig // Grand Galop.
SOURCES: LnSb Nos. 5-6 (31.1 and 7.2.1843), pp. 37 and 44. // BrZ
No. 30 (4.2.1843), p. 214. // AmZ 45 (1843), col. 299. // Schreiber, p.
11.

(188) BRESLAU   7 February 1843: Theater
PROGRAM: Concerto in c minor, Op. 37, by Beethoven, with or-
chestra // Chopin Mazurka // ?Fiancée // Figaro.
SOURCES: BreslauerZ Nos. 31-32 (6-7.2.1843), pp. 222 and 233. //
BrPSZ No. 31 (6.2.1843), p. 222. // BrZ No. 33 (8.2.1843), p. 239:
poem. // BrZ No. 32 (7.2.1843), p. 234: on Liszt's generosity. // Ollivier
II, pp. 256-260 and ?262.

(189) BRIEG   8 February 1843: Theater
PROGRAM: Huguenots // Invitation // Ave Maria and Erlkönig //
Chopin Mazurkas (?2) // Grand Galop.
SOURCES: BrZ Nos. 24, 27-28, 30, and 36 (28.1, 1-2.2, 4.2, and
11.2.1843), pp. 169, 191, 199, 214, and 263. // BrPSZ Nos. 27-28. 30,
and 36 (1, 4, 6, and 11.2.1843), pp. 190, 197, 211, 222, and 252. // BgS
Nos. 5 and 7 (2.2 and 16.2.1843), pp. 18 and 56. // AmZ 45 (1843), col.
299. // Schreiber, p. 11. // BrPSZ No. 36 (11.2.1843), pp. 252-253:
satire about Liszt excursions in the Breslau area. // Nanni Stern,
"Ein Liszt-Konzert in Brieg," *Briegische Heimatblätter* (1927), p. 34.

(190) BRESLAU   9 February 1843: Theater
PROGRAM: Tell // Somnambula // Erlkönig // Invitation // Don Juan
// Grand Galop.
SOURCES: BrZ Nos. 33-36 (8-11.2.1843), pp. 241, 248. 254, and
263. // BrPSZ No. 36 (11.2.1843), p. 253 [with program information
for all previous Breslau performances]. // BrPSZ Nos. 31 and 34 (6
and 9.2.1843), pp. 221 and 241: letters from Belloni and from "a
friend of truth" about the Alexander piano used in Liszt's Breslau
concerts; and No. 39 (15.2.1843), p. 278: reply. // D-WRgs Liszt
Kasten 240: handwritten program [differs from published program].
// Ollivier II, pp. 260 and 263-264.

(191) BERLIN 12 February 1843: "Schloß"
private

PROGRAM: Ave Maria and Erlkönig // Hexameron for two pianos, with Döhler.
SOURCES: VZ No. 38 (14.2.1843) [gives wrong date]. // Meyerbeer III, pp. 424 and 429-430. // MJm No. 477 (26.2.1843). // D-WRgs Liszt Kasten 240: program. // Ollivier II, p. 254. // ?BriefeHZ I, pp. 55-56: Meyerbeer to Liszt, 6.2.1843.

(192) LIEGNITZ 13 February 1843: ?Theater
PROGRAM: unknown.
SOURCES: LnSb (7.2.1843). // AmZ 45 (1843), col. 299.

(193) BERLIN 16 February 1843: Schauspielhaus
benefit

PROGRAM: Overtures to *Coriolan* by Beethoven, and to *Oberon* by Weber, both conducted by Liszt // Concerto in d minor by Mendelssohn, with orchestra // Don Juan // *Das deutsche Vaterland, Rattenlied,* and *Reiterlied* by Liszt; sung by the Berlin Männergesang // ?Other vocal numbers conducted by Liszt.
SOURCES: VZ Nos. 39-40 and 42 (15-16 and 18.2.1843). // APSZ No. 47 (16.2.1843), p. 196. // AmZ 45 (1843), col. 249. // SmW 1 (1843), pp. 67-68. // RGMP 10 (1843), pp. 73 and 88. // Ollivier II, p. 254. See also VZ No. 42 (18.2.1843): advertisement for a "Bal paré, masqué et travesti" to be held on 25.2.1843 in Berlin, and to feature a "Polonaise-Galopp" by Liszt on themes from Meyerbeer's operas! // Meyerbeer III, p. 430.

(194) POTSDAM 18 February 1843: Casino
private

PROGRAM: Huguenots // Erlkönig and another song transcription by Schubert-Liszt // Chopin Mazurka // Puritani-Polonaise // Don Juan // Ungarischer Sturmmarsch // Invitation.
SOURCES: VZ No. 44 "Beilage" (21.2.1843). // AmZ 45 (1843), col. 248. // Williams, p. 195 [gives Breslau as the location of this concert]. // Ollivier II, p. 254.

(195) FÜRSTENWALDE 19 February 1843: ?
matinée/gratis

PROGRAM: Niobe // Erlkönig // Transcription from *Der Freischütz* by Weber-Kullak // Robert // Invitation // Ungarischer Sturmmarsch // At least one work for euphonium and piano, with Herr Sommer // Grand Galop.
SOURCES: FürWb Nos. 14-15 (18 and 22.2.1843), pp. 56 and 58. // VZ No. 44 "Beilage" (21.2.1843). // AmZ 45 (1843), col. 248. // SmW 1 (1843), p. 68. // D-WRgs Liszt Kasten 240: playbill. // D-WRgs Kasten 261/1: note from Magistrat of Fürstenwalde thanking Liszt for concert, dated 20.2.1843. See also VZ Nos. 19 (23.1.1843) and 42 (18.2.1843). // WaMZ No. 34 (21.3.1843), p. 140.

(196)   POSEN   21 February 1843: Hotel de Bazar
PROGRAM: Lucia-Andante // Don Juan // Etude and Chopin
Mazurka // Erlkönig // Grand Galop.
SOURCES: ZGP Nos. 44-45 (21-22.2.1843), pp. 375 and 383. // AuZ
(1843), p. 543. // AmZ 45 (1843), col. 196. // RGMP 10 (1843), pp. 88
and 137. // GMdM No. 13 (26.3.1843), p. 56. // RMB No. 47
(30.3.1843), p. 188. // ZGP Nos. 44-46 (21-23.2.1843), pp. 375, 383,
and 393: poems. // D-WRgs Liszt Kasten 240: playbill. // See also
Donath, "Franz Liszt und Polen," *Liszt-Studien* 1 (1977), p. 55.

(197)   POSEN   22 February 1843: Hotel de Bazar
PROGRAM: Tell // Marche hongroise // Tarantelle // Invitation //
Robert.
SOURCES: ZGP No. 47 (24.2.1843), p. 403. // AuZ (1843), p. 543. //
D-WRgs Kasten 240: playbill.

(198)   POSEN   24 February 1843: Hotel de Bazar
PROGRAM: Konzertstück (as solo) // Ständchen and Ave Maria //
Chopin Mazurkas (?2) // Puritani-Polonaise // Somnambula.
SOURCES: ZGP Nos. 46, 48-49, and "Beilage" (23, 25, and
27.2.1843), p. 393, 396, 410-411, and 422-423. // AuZ (1843), p. 543.
// D-WRgs Liszt Kasten 240: program. [A second, undated program
in Liszt's hand, marked "Posen," evidently refers to a program Liszt
heard in that city.]

(199)   POSEN   27 February 1843: Stadttheater
PROGRAM: unknown.
SOURCES: ZGP Nos. 48-49 and 51 (25 and 27.2, and 1.3.1843), pp.
411, 423, and 437-438. // AuZ (1843), p. 543. // GMdM No. 18
(30.4.1843), p. 76. // ZGP No. 51 (1.3.1843), p. 437: poem.

(200)   GLOGAU   1 March 1843: Stadttheater
PROGRAM: Tell // Erlkönig // Don Juan // Invitation // Somnambula
// Grand Galop.
SOURCES: GSLb No. 26 (1.3.1843), "Beilage," // BrPSZ Nos. 54 and
57 (4 and 8.3.1843), pp. 393-394 and 423. // AmZ 45 (1843), col. 299.
// GSLb No. 29 (8.3.1843), pp. 115-116: biography of Liszt. // D-WRgs
Liszt Kasten 240: handwritten program.

(201)   GLOGAU   3 March 1843: Theater
PROGRAM: unknown.
SOURCES: GSLb Nos. 27 and 29 (3 and 8.3.1843), "Beilage" and pp.
115-116. // BrPSZ No. 57 (8.3.1843), p. 423. // Ollivier II, p. 267.

(202)   GLOGAU   3 March 1843: Gasthaus
                                                              gratis
PROGRAM: unknown.
SOURCE: BrPSZ No. 57 (8.3.1843), p. 427.

(203) LIEGNITZ   4 March 1843: Hotel
PROGRAM: Fantasy // Chopin Etude // ?Chopin Mazurka // other
numbers.
SOURCES: LnSb No. 10 (7.3.1843), p. 77. // AmZ 45 (1843), col. 299.
See also LnSb No. 10 (7.3.1843), p. 80: ad for "Liszt cigars"! //
Meyerbeer III, p. 495.

(204) BRESLAU   7 March 1843: Aula Leopoldina
PROGRAM: *Weihe des Hauses* overture by Beethoven, and *Jubel-
Overture* by Weber; both conducted by Liszt // Tell // Somnambula //
Four-part chorus by Liszt sung // God save the Queen // encores: Don
Juan and Erlkönig.
SOURCES: BrZ No. 55 (6.3.1843), p. 406. // BrPSZ Nos. 55-56 and
58 (6-7 and 9.3.1843), pp. 409, 417, and 430. // D-WRgs Liszt Kasten
240: copy of ?*Breslauer Figaro* article about this concert [undated].
// BrB No. 28 (7.3.1843), p. 111: poem.

(205) NEISSE   9 March 1843: Resourcen-Saale
                                                              matinée
PROGRAM: Somnambula // Don Juan // ?other works.
SOURCES: ObBf No. 22 (18.3.1843), pp. 87-88. // BrZ No. 61
(13.3.1843), p. 455. // AmZ 45 (1843), col. 299.

(206) HAMBURG   26 June 1843: Stadttheater
PROGRAM: Don Juan // *Il bravo* and *Il Giuramento* by Mercadante,
and "Cavatina" from *Lucrezia Borgia* by Donizetti; all with Ciabatta
// Chopin Etude // *Marche héroique* by Wallweiler // Somnambula.
SOURCES: HZCor No. 152 (29.6.1843). // HFrs No. 19 (1.7.1843),
p. 208. // AmZ 45 (1843), col. 617. // SmW 1 (1843), p. 222. // D-WRgs
Liszt Kasten 124: honorary membership, Norddeutsches
Musikverein [dated 22.1.1842!]. // D-WRgs Überformate 129: letter
of thanks to Liszt from Hamburg, dated 1.11.1843; a second letter is
dated 15.11.1844. // Ollivier II, p. 283. See also NZfM 19 (1843), p.
8.

(207) SOLINGEN   11 August 1843: Casino
                                                    matinée/benefit
PROGRAM: unknown.
SOURCES: SolKb Nos. 63-64 and 69-70 (5, 9, 26, and 30.8.1843). //
APSZ No. 47 (16.8.1843), p. 308. Quoted in Autexier, p. 119. //
Ollivier II, p. 284-285. See also Julius Lippa, *Die Geschichte des
Solinger Musiklebens im 19. Jahrhundert*, pp. 20-21. // NZfM 19
(1843), pp. 40 and 64.

(208) BONN   18 August 1843: Leopold Kaufmann's home
                                                              private
PROGRAM: unknown.
SOURCES: Kaufmann, p. 120. See also Kaufmann, "Franz Liszt am
Rhein," *Das schaffende Rhein* 7 (1931), p. 49 [different article con-
taining some of the same information]. // RGMP 10 (1843), p. 252. //
Monde No. 29 (20.7.1843), p. 116. // MJm No. 503 (3.9.1843).

(209) DORTMUND   24 August 1843: Casino
                                                        benefit

PROGRAM: Don Juan // "Schubert Lieder" (including Erlkönig) //
?other numbers.
SOURCES: DoWb No. 35 (2.9.1843), p. 292. // APSZ No. 63
(1.9.1843), p. 407. // *Gymnasio Tremoniensi . . . p. XXIV. M. Aug. A.
MDCCCXLIII* [commemorating the 300th anniversary of the
Dortmund Gymnasium, held 24.8.1843] (Hamm 1844): program
[does not mention Liszt] and p. 21. // W. Lübke, *Lebenserinnerungen*
(Berlin 1893), pp. 73-75. See also "Franz Liszt in Dortmund," *Die
Heimat* [Dortmund] ("Beilage" to the newspaper *Tremonia*;
1924-1930), p. 16.

(210) COLOGNE   12 September 1843: Saal des Neuen Kuhberg
PROGRAM: "Duo" for two pianos by Pixis, with Mortier de Fontaine
// ?accompaniments for vocal numbers.
SOURCES: KZ for 12. and 19.9.1843. Cited in Körner, *Das
Musikleben in Köln*, p. 206n. // RGMP 10 (1843), p. 373.

(211) ISERLOHN   23 September 1843: Loge Trois-Globes
                                                        benefit

PROGRAM: unknown.
SOURCES: IsWb No. 38 (23.9.1843). Quoted in Autexier, p. 128. //
APSZ No. 102 (10.10.1843), p. 629 [gives 24.9.1843 as date].

(212) FRANKFURT a.M.   4 October 1843: Wilhelm Speyer's home
                                                  private/matinée

PROGRAM: "Polkas, Mazurkas, and Hungarian Dances" // *Retraite*
and *Drei Liebchen* by Speyer; both with Pichel.
SOURCES: FKB Nos. 304 and 306 (4 and 6.11.1843), pp. 1213-1214
and 1218-1219. Reprinted in Gollmick, pp. 240-247. // MzGut No. 161
(10.10.1843), p. 739. // AmZ 45 (1843), col. 837. // SmW 1 (1843), p.
332. // NZfM 19 (1843), p. 208: Liszt reported ill in Frankfurt a.M. //
Ollivier II, pp. 285-287. See also AmZ 44 (1842), cols. 627-628: review
of Speyer's songs.

(213) FRANKFURT a.M.   c. 4 October 1843: ?
                                                        private

PROGRAM: unknown.
SOURCE: MzGut No. 161 (10.10.1843), p. 738.

(214) WÜRZBURG   7 October 1843: Theater
PROGRAM: Tell // Lucia-Andante // Don Juan // Ständchen and
Erlkönig // Grand Galop.
SOURCES: WürzAb Nos. 276 and 279 (5 and 8.10.1843). // WürzM
Nos. 122-123 (10 and 12.10.1843). // SmW 1 (1843), p. 332. // Leo
Günther, *Würzburger Chronik: Personen und Ereignisse von
1802-1848* (Würzburg 1925), Vol. III, p. 823n. // World 18 (1843), p.
416. // Ollivier II, pp. 287-288.

(215) NUREMBERG   11 October 1843: Rathhaussaale
                                                        matinée

PROGRAM: Tell // Lucia-Andante // Don Juan // Ständchen and Erlkönig // Grand Galop. // Ungarischer Sturmmarsch.
SOURCES: NürnZ Nos. 282-283 (9-10.10.1843). // NürnK Nos. 282-283 and 286 (9-10 and 13.10.1843). // FbOb No. 124 (16.10.1843), p. 496. // NZfM 19 (1843), pp. 132 and 148. // SmW 1 (1843), p. 332. // WaMZ No. 135 (11.11.1843), p. 572. // NürnZ No. 287 (13.10.1843): two poems. // D-WRgs Überformate No. 150: another poem. // D-WRgs Liszt Kasten 261/4: "Liszt in Nürnberg," *Der Korrespondent von und für Deutschland* No. 286 (13.10.1843), pp. 1777-1779: review and two poems [clipping]. // Ollivier II, pp. 288-291.

(216)   NUREMBERG   13 October 1843: Theater matinée

PROGRAM: Don Juan // ?other pieces.
SOURCES: NürnK No. 286 (13.10.1843). // SmW 1 (1843), p. 332. // NürnZ No. 288 (15.10.1843): two poems and notice of an award. // D-WRgs Überformaten 151-152: diplomas of the Albrecht-Dürer-Verein and the Mozart-Verein [dated, respectively, 13 and 14.10.1843]. // Ollivier II, pp. 291-292.

(217)   MUNICH   18 October 1843: Odéons-Saale

PROGRAM: Tell // Lucia-Andante // Don Juan // Ständchen and Erlkönig // Grand Galop.
SOURCES: MTb Nos. 288 and 290 (18 and 20.10.1843), pp. 1387 and 1395. // MLb Nos. 290, 294, and 303 (17, 21, and 30.10.1843), pp. 1196, 1212, and 1251. // MMb No. 86 (28.10.1843), p. 341. // AuZ (1843), p. 2340. // PfzB No. 88 (4.11.1843), p. 358. // APSZ No. 117 (25.10.1843), p. 721. // AmZ 45 (1843), cols. 804, 837, and 853. // NZfM 19 (1843), p. 132. // RGMP 10 (1843), p. 373. // SmW 1 (1843), p. 343. // WaMZ No. 137 (16.11.1843), p. 580. // GMdM No. 44 (29.10.1843), p. 188. // Monde No. 43 (26.10.1843), p. 168. // Burger, p. 150: poster facsimiles; p. 148: portrait of Liszt painted in Munich; and p. 151: Odéon illustration. // Ollivier II, pp. 293-296.

(218)   AUGSBURG   19 October 1843: Saal des Goldenen Traube

PROGRAM: Tell // Lucia-Andante // Don Juan // Ständchen and Erlkönig // Grand Galop.
SOURCES: AuTb Nos. 286-287 and 289 (18-19 and 21.10.1843), pp. 1229, 1232, 1236, and 1241-1242. // NürnK No. 293 (20.10.1843), p. 1237. // AuZ (1843), p. 2359. // AmZ 45 (1843), col. 804. // WaMZ No. 137 (16.11.1843), p. 580. // AuTb No. 288 (20.10.1843), p. 1237.

(219)   MUNICH   after 19 October 1843: ?Liszt's hotel private

PROGRAM: unknown (included songs sung by Armgart).
SOURCE: Reminiscences of Max von Arnim. Quoted in Williams, p. 202.

(220)   MUNICH   after 19 October 1843: ?Liszt's hotel private

PROGRAM: unknown (included songs sung by Armgart).
SOURCE: Williams, p. 202.

(221)   MUNICH   21 October 1843: Odéons-Saale

PROGRAM: Sonata in c minor, Op. 13 ("Pathétique"), by Beethoven; 1st movement only // Somnambula // Tarantelle // Chopin Mazurka // Puritani-Polonaise // Fugue in e-flat minor by Bach // Invitation. **SOURCES:** MLb Nos. 293-294 and 303 (20-21 and 30.10.1843), pp. 1208, 1213, and 1251. // MTb Nos. 291 and 294 (21 and 24.10.1843), p. 1400 and 1413. // MMb No. 86 (28.10.1843), p. 341. // PfzB No. 88 (4.11.1843), p. 358. // AmZ 45 (1843), cols. 804 and 853. // NZfM 19 (1843), p. 148. // GMdM No. 44 (29.10.1843), p. 188. // Burger, p. 150: facsimile of concert poster [gives c-sharp minor as the key for the Bach fugue].

(222)   MUNICH   25 October 1843: Hof- und Nationaltheater
                                                               benefit

PROGRAM: Invitation, with orchestra // ?Hexameron // Don Juan // Grand Galop // ?Accompaniments for vocal numbers // encore: Invitation, ?with orchestra. **SOURCES:** MMb No. 85 (25.10.1843), p. 340. // MLb Nos. 303 and 307 (30.10 and 3.11.1843), pp. 1251 and 1267. // PfzB No. 88 (4.11.1843), p. 358. // FbOb No. 133 (6.11.1843), p. 529. // AuZ (1843), p. 2397. // AmZ 45 (1843), cols. 804 and 853; and 46 (1844), col. 198. // NZfM 19 (1843), p. 148. // GMdM No. 45 (5.11.1843), p. 192. // MLb No. 304 (31.10.1843), p. 1253: poem. // Burger, p. 150: facsimile of concert poster; and p. 151: Hof- und Nationaltheater illustration. // Ollivier II, p. 296. See also APSZ No. 38 (7.2.1844), p. 237.

(223)   MUNICH   30 October 1843: Hof- und Nationaltheater
                                                               benefit

PROGRAM: Emperor // Somnambula // Fantasy. **SOURCES:** MTb Nos. 300 and 303 (30.10 and 2.11.1843), pp. 1437, 1438, and 1449. // MMb No. 87 (1.11.1843), p. 345. // MLb No. 307 (3.11.1843), p. 1267. // AuZ (1843), pp. 2411-2412, 2421, and 2437. // DmGHZ No. 304 (2.11.1843), p. 1507. // AmZ 45 (1843), cols. 804 and 853. // NZfM 19 (1843), p. 148. // WaMZ No. 147 (9.12.1843), p. 624. // SmW 1 (1843), p. 366. // GMdM Nos. 45, 47, and 49 (5 and 19.11 and 3.12.1843), pp. 192, 200, and 208. See also MLb No. 307 (3.11.1843), p. 1267: poem. // Burger, p. 150: facsimile of concert poster. // AmZ 46 (1844), col. 80.

(224)   AUGSBURG   1 November 1843: Theater

PROGRAM: ?vocal accompaniments // ?God Save the Queen. **SOURCES:** AuTb Nos. 299-300 and 302 (31.10, 1.11, and 3.11.1843), pp. 1286, 1290, and 1295-1296. // AuPZ Nos. 304-305 (31.10 and 1.11.1843), pp. 548 and 552. // AuZ (1843), p. 2359. // AmZ 45 (1843), col. 804. See also AuTb No. 300 (1.11.1843), p. 1287: poem. // MnMb Nos. 285-286 (5-6.12.1843), pp. 1140 and 1144: satiric sketch about Liszt.

(225)   AUGSBURG   4 November 1843: Theater
                                                               benefit

PROGRAM: unknown.

SOURCES: AuTb No. 303 (4.11.1843), pp. 1301 and 1304. // AuPZ No. 308 (4.11.1843), p. 564. // AuZ (1843), p. 2452. // AmZ 45 (1843), col. 804.

(226) STUTTGART ?6 November 1843: Hof
private

PROGRAM: unknown.
SOURCES: MzUb No. 312 (10.11.1843), pp. 1247-1248. // KrZ No. 307 (10.11.1843), p. 1112. // SgSM "Chronik" (7.11.1843), p. 1213. // BML 5 (1844), p. 12. // ?KrZ No. 314 (17.11.1843), p. 1648: refers to a private performance by Liszt in Stuttgart.

(227) STUTTGART 7 November 1843: Redoutensaal
benefit

PROGRAM: Tell // Lucia-Andante // Don Juan // Ständchen and Erlkönig // Grand Galop.
SOURCES: SB No. 221 (10.11.1843), pp. 882-883. // DmGHZ No. 318 (16.11.1843), p. 1597. // SgSM (1843), pp. 1206, 1214, 1221. // APSZ No. 135 (12.11.1843), p. 818. // AuZ (1843), pp. 2620-2621. // SmW 1 (1843), p. 373. // RGMP 10 (1843), p. 405. // GMdM No. 48 (26.11.1843), p. 204. // BML 5 (1844), p. 43. See also SB Nos. 229 (21.11.1843), p. 916: poem; and No. 327 (2.12.1843), pp. 947-948. // World 18 (1843), p. 424. // D-WRgs Überformate 166: certificate of honorary membership in the Gesellschaft des Glocke, dated 10.11.1843. // Ollivier II, pp. 298-301. // AmZ 46 (1844), col. 16.

(228) TÜBINGEN 11 November 1843: ?
PROGRAM: unknown.
SOURCES: SgSM "Chronik" No. 316 (19.11.1843), pp. 1261-1262. // KrZ No. 325 (29.11.1843), p. 1708.

(229) STUTTGART before 12 November 1843: Hof
private/?matinée

PROGRAM: unknown.
SOURCE: KrZ No. 314 (17.11.1843), p. 1648.

(230) STUTTGART
12 November 1843: Saale des Bürger-Gesellschaft
matinée/benefit

PROGRAM: Moonlight // Don Juan // Invitation // ?"Lieder" by Schubert-Liszt.
SOURCES: SgSM "Chronik" Nos. 307 and 309 (10 and 12.11.1843), pp. 1226 and 1234. // DmGHZ No. 328 (26.11.1843), p. 1627. // SgSM (1843), p. 1261. // SB Nos. 220-221 (8 and 10.11.1843), pp. 880 and 884. // AuZ (1843), pp. 2620-2621. // APSZ Nos. 152 and 154 (29.11 and 1.12.1843), pp. 915 and 931. // KrZ No. 324 (28.11.1843), pp. 1701-1702. // ?WaMZ No. 13 (30.1.1844), p. 52.

(231) STUTTGART 14 November 1843: Theater
PROGRAM: Konzertstück // Somnambula // Hexameron, with orchestra.

SOURCES: SgSM "Chronik" Nos. 309-311 (12-14.11.1843), pp. 1228, 1234, and 1242.

(232)   HEILBRONN   15 November 1843: Gasthof zum Falken

PROGRAM: Tell // Lucia-Andante // Don Juan // Ständchen and Erlkönig // Grand Galop.
SOURCES: HbIb Nos. 265-266 and 268 (11-12 and 15.11.1843), pp. 1302, 1310, and 1320. // KrZ No. 325 (29.11.1843), p. 1708. // *Heilbronner Tagblatt* (21.11.1843). Quoted (with other sources) in Hans Krämer, "Ein denkwürdiges Konzert in Ludwigsburg," *Ludwigsburger Geschichtsblätter* 40 (1987), pp. 195-196. // *Justinus Kerners Briefwechsel mit seiner Freunden*, ed. Theobald Kerner (1897), pp. 233-234: letter from Kerner to Sophie Schwab, announcing Liszt's anticipated arrival in Heilbronn. // Letter from D. F. Strauß to Herr Rabb, dated 16.11.1843. Reprinted in *Ausgewählte Briefe von David Friedrich Strauß* (Bonn 1895), pp. 154-156.

(233)   STUTTGART   16 November 1843: Theater

PROGRAM: "I tuoi frequenti palpiti" from *Niobe* by Pacini, with Pantaleoni // Robert // Fantasy on *Les Huguenots* for piano four-hands, with Wilhelm Krüger // Hexameron, with orchestra // ?accompaniments for vocal numbers.
SOURCES: KrZ Nos. 320 and 325 (23 and 29.11.1843), pp. 1682 and 1708. // VIb No. 48 (2.12.1843), p. 322. // SgSM (1843), p. 1261.

(234)   LUDWIGSBURG   17 November 1843: Saal des Waldhorns

PROGRAM: Don Juan // Invitation // "Variations" (?Hexameron) // ?other numbers.
SOURCES: LudWb Nos. 136-137 and 139 (14, 16, and 21.11.1843). // SgSM "Chronik" No. 316 (19.11.1843), pp. 1261-1262. // KrZ No. 325 (29.11.1843), p. 1708. See also Krämer, "Franz Liszt in Ludwigsburg," *Ludwigsburger Kreiszeitung* No. 173 (31.7.1987): mentions otherwise undocumented concert in Ulm.

(235)   HECHINGEN   18 November 1843: ?

PROGRAM: unknown.
SOURCES: SgSM "Chronik" No. 316 (19.11.1843), pp. 1261-1262. // VIb No. 48 (2.12.1843), // KrZ No. 325 (29.11.1843), p. 1708. // APSZ No. 164 (11.12.1843), p. 989. // RGMP 10 (1843), p. 445. See also PfzB No. 97 (6.12.1843), p. 393: announcement of Liszt's elevation to "Hofrat" by the Prince of Hohenzollern-Hechingen. // FbOb No. 153 (22.12.1843), p. 612. // MnMb No. 228 (8.12.1843), p. 1153. // ErEut 4 (1844), p. 80. // WaMZ No. 148 (12.12.1843), p. 628. // GMdM No. 52 (24.12.1843), p. 221. // D-WRgs Liszt Kasten 124: certificate of Haus-Orden award.

(236)   STUTTGART   21 November 1843: Hoftheater
                                                        benefit

PROGRAM: unknown.
SOURCES: SgSM "Chronik" Nos. 316-318 and 320 (19-21 and 23.11.1843), pp. 1264, 1266, 1270, and 1277. // DmGHZ No. 328 (26.11.1843), p. 1629. // APSZ Nos. 152 and 154 (29.11 and 1.12.1843), pp. 915 and 931. // AuZ (1843), pp. 2620-2621 and 2629.

// KrZ Nos. 320 and 324 (23 and 28.11.1843), pp. 1682 and 1701-1702.
// FbOb No. 144 (1.12.1843), p. 576. See also D-WRgs Liszt Kasten
132: materials concerning an award [?Order of the King of
Württemberg], dated 21.11.1843.

(237) DONAUESCHINGEN   before 25 November 1843: ?Theater

PROGRAM: unknown [may have included orchestral numbers conducted by Liszt].
SOURCES: *Das Fürstlich Fürstenbergische Hoftheater zu
Donaueschingen, 1775-1850* (Donaueschingen 1914), p. 101 [courtesy
of the Fürstlich Fürstenbergische Hofbibliothek]. NB: An advertisement for ?this concert evidently appeared in an issue of the
Donaueschinger Wochenblatt. This advertisement could not be located by the present author. // Max Rieple, *Musik in Donaueschingen*
(Donaueschingen 1959), p. 12. See also Ollivier II, p. 304 [dated
26.11.1843].

(238) DONAUESCHINGEN   before 27 November 1843: "Schloß"
private

PROGRAM: Erlkönig // "Ländler" // ?other numbers.
SOURCES: *Das Fürstlich Fürstenbergische Hoftheater zu
Donaueschingen, 1775-1850,* p. 101. // Rieple, p. 12. See also Michael
Kienzle, "Ein Liszt-Autograph in Donaueschingen," *Liszt information*
12 (1982), pp. 10-12 [on the "Ländler" Liszt composed for the
Princess Elise of Hohenzollern-Hechingen]. // Ollivier II, p. 304.

(239) DONAUESCHINGEN   before 27 November 1843: "Schloß"
private

PROGRAM: Ave Maria // ?other numbers.
SOURCES: *Das Fürstlich Fürstenbergische Hoftheater zu
Donaueschingen, 1775-1850,* p. 101. // Rieple, p. 12. See also Ollivier
II, p. 304.

(240) KARLSRUHE   27 November 1843: Große Saal des Museums

PROGRAM: Tell // Lucia-Andante // Don Juan // Chopin Mazurka
// Ave Maria and Erlkönig // Grand Galop.
SOURCES: KrZ Nos. 320-321, 323, 325, and 329 (23-24, 26, and
29.11, and 3.12.1843), pp. 1682, 1688, 1692, 1709, and 1735-1736. //
KrTb Nos. 324 and 326-327 (24 and 26-27.11.1843), pp. 1395, 1404,
and 1407. // MnJ Nos. 329 and 336 (2 and 9.12.1843), pp. 1314 and
1342. // GMdM No. 52 (24.12.1843), p. 221. // Ollivier II, p. 305.

(241) HEIDELBERG   28 November 1843: Saale des Museums

PROGRAM: Tell // Lucia-Andante // Don Juan // Chopin Mazurka
// Ständchen, Ave Maria, and Erlkönig // Invitation.
SOURCES: HeJ Nos. 323-326 and 328 (25-28 and 30.11.1843), pp.
1333, 1338, 1342, 1346, and 1353. // KrZ No. 328 (2.12.1843), p. 1728.
// MnJ No. 329 (2.12.1843), p. 1314. // GMdM No. 52 (24.12.1843), p.
221. See also HeJ No. 331 (3.12.1843), p. 1366: wish-list for a second
concert. // K. G. von Leonhard, *Aus unserer Zeit in meinem Leben*
(Stuttgart 1854-1856), Vol. II, pp. 259-261: reminiscences.

(242)   HEIDELBERG   28 November 1843: K. G. Leonhard's home
                                                                    private
PROGRAM: Dance numbers.
SOURCE: Leonhard, Vol. II, pp. 260-261: reminiscences and a letter
from Liszt to Leonhard accepting an invitation to play a Heidelberg
soirée.

(243)   KARLSRUHE   29 November 1843: Rezidenzschloß
                                                                    private
PROGRAM: unknown.
SOURCES: KrZ No. 329 (3.12.1843), pp. 1735-1736. // MnJ Nos. 329
and 336 (2 and 9.12.1843), pp. 1314 and 1342.

(244)   KARLSRUHE   1 December 1843: Hoftheater
                                                                    benefit
PROGRAM: Konzertstück, ?with orchestra // Somnambula // Invi-
tation // Hexameron, with orchestra.
SOURCES: KrTb No. 331 (1.12.1843), p. 1423. // KrZ Nos. 326-327
and 329 (30.11, 1.12, and 3.12.1843), pp. 1713, 1722, and 1735-1736.
// MnJ Nos. 329 and 336 (2 and 9.12.1843), pp. 1314 and 1342. //
KrTb No. 331 (1.12.1843), p. 1424: biography of Liszt; and No. 333
(3.12.1843), p. 1432: poem.

(245)   MANNHEIM   3 December 1843: Aula-Saale
                                                                    matiné
PROGRAM: Huguenots // Etude and Chopin Mazurka // Don Juan
// Lob der Thränen and Erlkönig // Grand Galop.
SOURCES: MnJ No. 330 (3.12.1843), p. 1319. // Ollivier II, pp.
306-308 [?letter actually dated 8.12.43].// "List für Liszt," MnMb Nos.
285-286 (5-6.12.1843), pp. 1140-1141 and 1144: a satiric sketch.

(246)   KARLSRUHE   4 December 1843: ?
                                                                    benefit
PROGRAM: unknown.
SOURCES: KrZ Nos. 329-330 (3-4.12.1843). // KrTb No. 333
(3.12.1843). // ?MnJ No. 336 (9.12.1843), p. 1342.

(247)   MANNHEIM   6 December 1843: Aula-Saale
                                                                    matinée
PROGRAM: Konzertstück, ?with orchestra // Somnambula //
Tarantelle // Chopin Mazurka // Puritani-Polonaise // Robert.
SOURCES: MnJ Nos. 332 and 336 (5 and 9.12.1843), pp. 1327 and
1342. // RGMP 10 (1843), p. 445.

(248)   WEIMAR   7 January 1844: Hoftheater
PROGRAM: Symphony in c minor by Beethoven, conducted by Liszt
// Hummel Concerto // ?accompaniments for vocal numbers // Don
Juan.
SOURCES: WrZ Nos. 1 and 3 (3 and 10.1.1844), pp. 4 and 11. // AmZ
46 (1844), cols. 160, 163-165, 243-246, 290, and 292-294. Quoted in
part in Williams, p. 203; and in Huschke, pp. 105-106. // NZfM 20

(1844), p. 72. // RGMP 10 (1843), p. 445; and 11 (1844), pp. 39. // WaMZ Nos. 94 (8.8.1843), p. 396; and 5 and 7 (11 and 16.1.1844), pp. 20 and 28. // GMdM No. 2 (14.1.1844), p. 8. See also SmW 2 (1844), p. 29: on Liszt in Weimar. // Ollivier II, pp. 312-313. // Huschke, pp. 196-197: program. // APSZ No. 43 (12.2.1844), p. 271. // NZfM 19 (1843), pp. 148 and 208.

(249) GOTHA   18 January 1844: Hoftheater

PROGRAM: Symphony in F Major ("Pastoral") by Beethoven, conducted by Liszt // Konzertstück, with orchestra // Fantasy on *Les Huguenots* for 'cello and piano, with Herr Prüm // Somnambula.
SOURCES: AmZ 46 (1844), col. 293. // Ebart, p. 24. // Ollivier II, p. 316.

(250) WEIMAR   21 January 1844: ?Hoftheater

PROGRAM: Symphony in E-flat Major ("Eroica") and Incidental Music to *Egmont*, both by Beethoven; both conducted by Liszt. // Konzertstück, with orchestra // ?Accompaniments for vocal numbers.
SOURCES: WrZ Nos. 6 ["Beilage"] and 7 (20 and 24.1.1844), pp. 24 and 27. // JeWb No. 6 (20.1.1844), p. 21. // AmZ 46 (1844), cols. 161-165, 290, and 292-294. // NZfM 20 (1844), p. 72. // WaMZ Nos. 23 and 28 (22.2 and 5.3.1844), pp. 92 and 112. // RGMP 11 (1844), p. 39. // D-WRgs Liszt Kasten 261/7: unidentified clipping about this concert. // Ollivier II, pp. 320-323.

(251) RUDOLSTADT   27 January 1844: Gasthaus "Zum Ritter"
                                                                    benefit

PROGRAM: Lucia // "Cavatina" from *Niobe* by Pacini, and "Preghiera di Brigandi" from *I Brigandi* by Mercadante; both with Pantaleoni // Erlkönig // Grand Galop.
SOURCES: AmZ 46 (1844), col. 293. // Erich Jäcksch, "Franz Liszt in Rudolstadt," *Rudolstädter Heimathefte* 7 (1961), pp. 271-274. // RudWb No. 4 (27.1.1844), p. 17: poem. // Peter Gülge, *Musik und Musiker in Rudolstadt* (Rudolstadt 1963), pp. 52-53 [includes facsimile of Liszt's Rudolstadt program].

(252) WEIMAR   4 February 1844: Hoftheater

PROGRAM: Symphony in A Major and Concerto in c minor, Op. 37, both by Beethoven, and *Jubel-Overture* by Weber; all conducted by Liszt, with Wilhelm Krüger // Tarantelle // ?Chopin Mazurka // "Polonaise" (?Puritani-Polonaise) // *Nonnenwerth* by Liszt, with Götze // ?accompaniments for other vocal numbers.
SOURCES: WrZ Nos. 10-11 (3 and 7.2.1844), pp. 40 and 44. // AmZ 46 (1844), cols. 164-165 and 292-294. // NZfM 20 (1844), p. 72. // RGMP 11 (1844), p. 39. // Ollivier II, pp. 323-327. See also Huschke, p. 197: program.

(253) JENA   c. 5 February 1844: ?
                                                                    private

PROGRAM: Improvisations to readings from Goethe's *Faust*.
SOURCES: NZfM 20 (1844), p. 76. // Ramann II, pp. 226-227.

(254)   JENA   5 February 1844: ?

PROGRAM: unknown.
SOURCES: WrZ No. 11 (7.2.1844), p. 44. // JeWb No. 10 (3.2.1844),
p. 38. // AmZ 46 (1844), col. 293.

(255)   ERFURT   17 February 1844: Theatersaale

PROGRAM: Overtures to *Fidelio* by Beethoven and *Oberon* by
Weber, ?both conducted by Liszt // Konzertstück, with orchestra //
"Lieder" by Schubert-Liszt // Norma // *Nonnenwerth* by Liszt, with
Götze // ?accompaniments for other vocal and instrumental numbers.
SOURCES: ErZ (12, 15, and 17.2.1844). // ErSLb No. 8 (10.2.1844).
// ErAn No. 44 (14.2.1844), p. 562. // WrZ No. 13 "Beilage"
(14.2.1844), p. 52. // AmZ 46 (1844), col. 293. // NZfM 20 (1844), p.
72. //
Ollivier II, p. 331.

(256)   WEIMAR   before 18 February 1844: Hof
                                                           private

PROGRAM: unknown.
SOURCE: AmZ 46 (1844), col. 290.

(257)   WEIMAR   before 18 February 1844: Hof
                                                           private

PROGRAM: unknown.
SOURCE: AmZ 46 (1844), col. 290.

(258)   WEIMAR   before 18 February 1844: Hof
                                                           private

PROGRAM: unknown.
SOURCE: AmZ 46 (1844), col. 290.

(259)   WEIMAR   before 18 February 1844: Hof
                                                           private

PROGRAM: unknown.
SOURCE: AmZ 46 (1844), col. 290.

(260)   WEIMAR   18 February 1844: Hoftheater

PROGRAM: Symphonic movement by Schubert, *King Lear* overture
by Berlioz, and *Fest-Overture* by Lambert, all conducted by Liszt //
Fantasy on *Les Huguenots* for violin and piano by Thalberg, with
Stör // *Angiolin dal biondo crin* by Liszt, with Götze //
?accompaniments for other vocal numbers // Hexameron (?as solo).
SOURCES: WrZ Nos. 13-14 "Beilage" (17-18.2.1844), pp. 52 and 58.
// AuZ (1844), pp. 564-565. // AmZ 46 (1844), cols. 292-294. // NZfM
20 (1844), p. 72. // GMdM Nos. 7-8 (18 and 25.2.1844), 30 and 34
[incorrect information!]. // Ollivier II, pp. 331-332. See also Huschke,
p. 197: program.

(261)   DRESDEN   21 February 1844: Theater
                                                           benefit

PROGRAM: Konzertstück // Don Juan // ?other works.

SOURCES: LTb No. 64 (4.3.1844), p. 483. // AuZ (1844), pp. 558-559. // AmZ 46 (1844), col. 264. // NZfM 20 (1844), pp. 68 and 88. // SmW 2 (1844), pp. 68-69. // BamZ No. 7 (9.3.1844). // GMdM No. 13 (31.3.1844), p. 53. // FM No. 14 (7.4.1844). // BFig No. 56 (6.3.1844), p. 223. // WaMZ Nos. 32 (14.3.1844), p. 128.

(262) DESSAU   24 February 1844: ?

PROGRAM: unknown.
SOURCE: Ollivier II, pp. 332-334.

(263) DRESDEN   27 February 1844: Hoftheater

PROGRAM: Emperor // ?other numbers.
SOURCES: DrAn No. 56 (25.2.1844). // LZ No. 49 (26.2.1844), p. 709. // NZfM 20 (1844), pp. 68 and 88. // SmW 2 (1844), p. 69. // DrAn No. 59 (28.2.1844). See also VZ No. 58 (8.3.1844): mentions all three 1844 Dresden performances and Liszt's visit to Stettin.

(264) BAUTZEN   ?before 1 March 1844: ?

?PROGRAM: Don Juan // Robert // "Lieder" by Schubert-Liszt // Ungarischer Sturmmarsch // Valse de bravure // Grand Galop.
SOURCES: SmW 2 (1844), p. 93. // WaMZ No. 42 (6.4.1844), p. 168. See also BFig No. 54 (4.3.1844), p. 216: "wish list" for concert. // BauEr No. 11 (15.3.1844), p. 84: Liszt cancels concert at Zittau.

(265) DRESDEN   1 March 1844: Hotel de Saxe
                                                     benefit

PROGRAM: Lucia-Andante // Canzone // Tarantelle // Chopin Mazurka // "Prayer" from *I Brigandi* by Mercadante, "Aria" from *Robert le diable* by Meyerbeer, and an "Aria" from Rossini's *Stabat Mater*; all with Pantaleoni // Norma.
SOURCES: DrAn Nos. 60-62 (29.2, and 1 and 2.1844). // NZfM 20 (1844), p. 88. // BamZ No. 8 (16.3.1844). // FM No. 14 (7.4.1844). See also Ramann II, p. 229ff.

(266) BERNBURG   before 5 March 1844: ?

PROGRAM: unknown.
SOURCE: WaMZ No. 53 (2.5.1844), p. 212.

(267) BERNBURG   before 5 March 1844: ?hotel
                                                            private

PROGRAM: improvisation.
SOURCES: WaMZ No. 53 (2.5.1844), p. 212. // Ramann II, p. 231. See also Briefe I, pp. 47-48: ?Liszt in Berlin by 4.3.1844. // APSZ Nos. 68 and 72 (8 and 12.3.1844), pp. 410 and 434.

(268) STETTIN   7 March 1844: Saal des Hotel de Bavière

PROGRAM: Norma // Vocal numbers, with Ciabatta // Sonata in f minor, Op. 57 ("Appassionata"), by Beethoven // Somnambula // Erlkönig // Grand Galop // encore: Erlkönig.

SOURCES: StKPZ No. 32 (13.3.1844). // StBNO No. 20 "Zweite Beilage" (8.3.1844), p. 346. // WaMZ No. 38 (28.3.1844), p. 152. // BFig No. 58 (8.3.1844), p. 232.

(269)   STETTIN   8 March 1844: ?Saal des Hotel de Bavière

PROGRAM: unknown.
SOURCES: StKPZ No. 32 (13.3.1844). // WaMZ Nos. 38 and 42 (28.3 and 6.4.1844), pp. 152 and 168.

(270)   MAGDEBURG   14 March 1844: Saale der Stadt London

PROGRAM: Lucia // Don Juan // "Sonata" [?] by Beethoven // Erlkönig // Grand Galop.
SOURCES: MbZ Nos. 62-63 and 65 (13-14 and 16.3.1844). // BFig No. 64 (15.3.1844), p. 254. // SmW 2 (1844), pp. 99-100 and 110. // MbZ No. 65 (16.3.1844): poem.

(271)   MAGDEBURG   15 March 1844: Theater

PROGRAM: Huguenots // Two "Romances," with Ciabatta // "Sonata" [?] by Beethoven // Somnambula // Invitation.
SOURCES: MbZ Nos. 63-64 and 66 (14-15 and 18.3.1844). // BFig No. 64 (15.3.1844), p. 254. // SmW 2 (1844), p. 110. // MbZ No. 65 (16.3.1844): poem.

(272)   MAGDEBURG   17 March 1844: Theater

PROGRAM: Robert // Mélodies hongroises // Puritani-Polonaise // Two vocal numbers, with Ciabatta // Norma.
SOURCES: MbZ Nos. 65-66 (16 and 18.3.1844). // MbEr No. 11 (16.3.1844), p. 88. // BFig No. 69 (21.3.1844), p. 273. // SmW 2 (1844), p. 110. // BFig No. 72 (25.3.1844), p. 288.

(273)   MAGDEBURG   18 March 1844: ?
                                                    private

PROGRAM: Sonata for violin and piano, Op. 47 ("Kreutzer"), by Beethoven, with Franz Fesca.
SOURCE: Inscriptions on copies of the sonata (Paris: Simrock, c. 1805; Plate 422) owned by the Pierpont Morgan Library, New York City. NB: Liszt's signature appears on both the piano and violin parts.

(274)   BRAUNSCHWEIG   22 March 1844: Medicinisches Saal

PROGRAM: unknown.
SOURCES: BsAn Nos. 70-71 (21-22.3.1844), pp. 1667 and 1693. // BFig No. 77 (30.3.1844), p. 308. // Ollivier II, p. 335.

(275)   BRAUNSCHWEIG   25 March 1844: Theater

PROGRAM: unknown.
SOURCES: BsAn No. 73 (25.3.1844), p. 1844. // BFig No. 77 (30.3.1844), p. 308. See also NZfM 20 (1844), p. 139.

(276) HANNOVER   28 March 1844: Ballhofsaale

PROGRAM: Lucia // Improvisation // "Sonata" [?] by Beethoven // Puritani-Polonaise // Tarantelle // Erlkönig // Grand Galop.
SOURCES: HanZ (26-27.3.1844), pp. 430 and 445. // HanVb No. 52 (5.4.1844), p. 208. // HanP No. 39 (31.3.1844), pp. 154-155. // NZfM 20 (1844), p. 139. // SmW 2 (1844), p. 117: on Hannover caricatures of Liszt.

(277) HANNOVER   31 March 1844: Theater

PROGRAM: Tell // Don Juan // Ave Maria and Erlkönig // Invitation.
SOURCES: HanZ (29-30.3.1844), pp. 457 and 469. // HanVb No. 56 (12.4.1844), p. 224. // NZfM 20 (1844), pp. 139-140. // BML No. 12 (13.4.1844): Liszt to G. Perau, dated 1.4.1844.

(278) HANNOVER   31 March 1844: Hotel
                                                        gratis

PROGRAM: Dance numbers and other pieces.
SOURCE: NZfM 20 (1844), p. 120.

(279) BONN   7 August 1845: Reitbahn
                                                    open rehearsal

PROGRAM: Liszt's *Festkantata*.
SOURCES: BnWb (15.8.1845). // HanMZ (31.8.1845), p. 556 [gives wrong date]. // AuZ (1845), p. 1727. // H. K. Breidenstein, *Zur Jahresfeier der Inauguration des Beethoven-Monuments* (Bonn 1846), p. 10. See also AmZ 47 (1845), col. 573. // RGMP 12 (1845), pp. 256 and 272.

(280) BONN   ?9 August 1845: ?Beethovenhalle
                                                    open rehearsal

PROGRAM: unknown.
SOURCE: AmZ 47 (1843), col. 573.

(281) BONN   10 August 1845: ?Beethovenhalle
                                                    open rehearsal

PROGRAM: ?Pieces performed on (273-274).
SOURCE: FKB No. 223 (14.8.1845), pp. 890-891. // Times No. 19,001 (13.8.1845), p. 5. //Breidenstein, *Zur Jahresfeier*, p. 10. // *Leaves from the Journals of Sir George Smart* (London 1907), p. 305.

(282) BONN   12 August 1845: Beethovenhalle
                                                        matinée

PROGRAM: Emperor // Symphony in c minor, and Canon and Finale to Act II of *Fidelio*, all by Beethoven; all conducted by Liszt.
SOURCES: BnWb Nos. 223-224 (14-15.8.1845). // KZ Nos. 225-227 (13-15.8.1845). // AuZ (1845), pp. 1807-1808, 1814, 1822-1823, and 1845-1846. // FKB Nos. 223 and 232-233 (14 and 23-24.8.1845), pp. 890-891, 927, and 930-391. // LIZ No. 116 (20.9.1845), pp. 195-197. // AmZ 47 (1845), cols. 525-526, 572-575, and 590-592. // NZfM 22 (1845), p. 28. // BML 6 (1845), pp. 113-114, 129-130, and 149-155. // BamZ Nos. 34 and 36 (23.8 and 6.9.1845). // RGMP 12 (1845), pp. 247

and 267-268. // WaMZ Nos. 95, 99, and 101 (9.8, 19.8, and 23.8.1845),
pp. 380, 396, and 404; and esp. Nos. 100-102 (21, 23, and 26.8.1845),
pp. 397-398, 401-404, and 405-406. Quoted in part in Ramann II, pp.
257ff. // ZfDMV 5 (1845), pp. 75-81. // Monde No. 34 (21.8.1845). //
GMdM Nos. 30, 32, and 34 (27.7, 10.8, and 24.8.1845), pp. 130,
137-138, and 144-145. // World 20 (1845), p. 469. // RDM 14 [Nouvelle
serié] (1845), pp. 744-746. // CAmtN 2 (1845), pp. 156, 166, and
190-194. // Times No. 19,004 (16.8.1845), p. 5. // Chorley II, pp.
289-290. // Karl Schorn, *Lebenserinnerungen* (Bonn 1898), Vol. I, pp.
193-216. // Breidenstein, *Festgabe zur der am 12ten August 1845
Stattfindenden Inauguration des Beethoven-Monuments* (Bonn 1845),
passim. // Breidenstein, *Zur Jahresfeier*, passim. // Theodor Anton
Henssler, *Das musikalische Bonn im 19. Jahrhundert* (Bonn 1959),
esp. pp. 169ff. // Spohr II, pp. 271-272. // Burger, p. 157: picture of
the monument itself. // Reminiscences of Karl Schorn and Ignaz
Moscheles. Quoted in Williams, pp. 214-221. See also other accounts
of the Festival as a whole.

(283)　BONN　　　　　　　　　　　13 August 1845: Beethovenhalle
　　　　　　　　　　　　　　　　　　　　　　　　　　　　　morning

PROGRAM: *Festkantata* by Liszt, conducted by Liszt // *Adelaïde* by
Beethoven, with Kratky.
SOURCES: KZ Nos. 225-227 (13-14.8.1845). // AuZ (1845), pp.
1839-1840 and 1845-1846. // AmZ 47 (1845), cols. 525-526, 572-576,
and 592-594. // NZfM 23 (1845), p. 28. // RGMP 12 (1845), pp. 247
and 268. // SmW 3 (1845), p. 248. // ZfDMV 5 (1845), pp. 75-79 and
391-392. // FM No. 33 (17.8.1845), pp. 261-262. // MRm No. 25
(22.6.1845). // ErEut 5 (1845), pp. 161-163. // CAmtN 2 (1845), p. 194.
// World 20 (1845), pp. 409ff. // Times No. 19,005 (18.8.1845), p. 5. //
Breidenstein, *Festgabe* and *Zur Jahresfeier*, both passim. // BriefeHZ
I, pp. 75-77: O. L. B. Wolff to Liszt on 11.7.1845, asking about the
possibility of reprinting the *Festkantata* in LIZ. // See also Meyerbeer
III, p. 616. // AmZ 47 (1845), col. 647. // Williams, pp. 214-221.

(284)　BRÜHL　　　　　　　　　　　　13 August 1845: Schloß
　　　　　　　　　　　　　　　　　　　　　　　　　　　　　private

PROGRAM: Norma // "Spanish Fantasy" // ?accompaniments for
vocal numbers.
SOURCES: BnWb No. 225 (16.8.1845). // FOPZ Nos. 226 "Beilage"
(17.8.1845), pp. 2223-2224; and 229 (20.8.1845), p. 2250. // AmZ 47
(1845), col. 766. // RGMP 12 (1845), pp. 269 and 278. // BamZ No. 34
(23.8.1845). // WaMZ No. 101 (23.8.1845), p. 404. // World 20 (1845),
p. 496. // LIZ No. 117 (27.9.1845), p. 197. // AuZ (1845), p. 1840 [does
not mention Liszt]. // Hans Bellinghausen, *Alt-Koblenz: Eine
Sammlung heimatkundlicher Abhandlungen* (Koblenz 1932), p. 283.
See also Meyerbeer III, p. 603: Meyerbeer to Friedrich Wilhelm IV
of Prussia, 7.7.1845.

(285)　COLOGNE　　　　　　　　　　　　　14 August 1845: ?
PROGRAM: unknown.
SOURCES: BrB No. 227 (15.8.1845). // AuZ (1845), p. 1840. // GMdM
No. 35 (31.8.1845), p. 151.

(286) STOLZENFELS 16 August 1845: with Queen Victoria
private

PROGRAM: unknown.
SOURCES: BnWb No. 225 (16.8.1845). // FOPZ Nos. 227 "Beilage"
(18.8.1845), p. 2234; and 229 "Beilage" (20.8.1845), p. 2254. // GMdM
No. 36 (7.9.1845), p. 156. // Bellinghausen, p. 285. // Briefe VIII, pp.
42-44: Liszt to Theodor von Bacharacht, 17.7.1845. // *Chronik der
Stadt Koblenz* by J. J. Lucas [handwritten], No. 997, p. 430 [property
of the Koblenz Stadtarchiv]. See also RGMP 12 (1845), p. 269: gives
date and place as "15, à Coblentz."

(287) KLEVE 18 August 1845: "Treasury"
?benefit

PROGRAM: Andante con variazione // ?Other numbers.
SOURCE: CAtmN 2 (1845), p. 194 // AmZ 47 (1845), col. 766. //
World 20 (1845), p. 459. See also Ramann II, p. 267.

(288) BADEN-BADEN before 26 August 1845: ?
private

PROGRAM: Tarantelle // Mélodies hongroises // ?Chopin Mazurka
// Robert.
SOURCES: NZfM 23 (1845), p. 148. // WaMZ No. 126 (21.10.1845),
p. 504. // RGMP 12 (1845), pp. 292-293 [issue of 7.9.1845]. // World
20 (1845), p. 473.

(289) BADEN-BADEN ?after 26 August 1845: ?
private

PROGRAM: unknown.
SOURCES: NZfM 23 (1845), p. 148. // WaMZ No. 126 (21.10.1845),
p. 504.

(290) BADEN-BADEN 21 September 1845: ?Kursaal
PROGRAM: unknown.
SOURCES: BdWb Nos. 144, 152, and 187 (12, 19, and 25.9.1845),
pp. 1570, 1668, and 1786. // BdB (14 and 21.9.1845), pp. 1597-1598
and 1683. // BML 6 (1845), p. 163. // GMdM No. 38 (21.9.1845).

(291) STUTTGART 29 September 1845: Redoutensaal
PROGRAM: Lucia-Andante // "Aria" from *Robert le diable* by
Meyerbeer, "Aria" from *Linda von Chamounix*, and *Die junge Nonne*
by ?Schubert; all with Jenny Lutzer // Norma // "Fantasie à
capriccio" // "Fête villageoise" and "Mélodies hongroises."
SOURCES: SgSM (1845), pp. 1010, 1050, 1055, 1059, and 1069. //
BamZ No. 46 (15.11.1845). // RGMP 12 (1845), p. 347. // GMdM No.
43 (26.10.1845), p. 184. // WaMZ No. 124 (16.10.1845), p. 496. See
also Hermann Haering and Otto Hohenstatt, *Schwäbische
Lebensbilder* (Stuttgart 1941), Vol. II, p. 103: Franz von
Dingelstedt's marriage to Jenny Lutzer.

(292) DARMSTADT
8 October 1845: Saale der vereinigten Gesellschaft

PROGRAM: Tell // Lucia-Andante // Norma // Tarantelle // Chopin
Mazurka // Puritani-Polonaise // Grand Galop.
SOURCES: DmGHZ Nos. 278 and 281-282 (7 and 10-11.10.1845),
pp. 1503, 1515, and "Beilage." Reproduced in partial facsimile in
Burger, p. 158. // NZfM 23 (1845), p. 167. // Philipp Schweitzer,
Darmstädter Musikleben im 19. Jahrhundert (Darmstadt 1975), pp.
155-156.

(293)   STUTTGART   10 October 1845: ?
PROGRAM: unknown.
SOURCES: WaMZ No. 124 (16.10.1845), p. 496. // RGMP 12 (1845),
p. 347. // World 20 (1845), p. 513. // Monde No. 43 (23.10.1845). See
also Liszt's letter to Dingelstedt, 13.10.1845. Reprinted in LSae 24
(1979), p. 28.

(294)   ?STUTTGART   ?after 10 October 1845: ?
                            private (for the "King of Bavaria")
PROGRAM: unknown.
SOURCES: RGMP 12 (1845), p. 347. // World 20 (1845), p. 513. //
MRm No. 43 (26.10.1845). // BriefeHZ I, pp. 78-80: Franz Dingelstedt
by Liszt, 27.10.1845. See also Liszt to Dingelstedt, 13.10.1845. Pub-
lished in LSae No. 24 (1979), p. 28.

(295)   DARMSTADT   c. 12 October 1845: ?
                                                      private

PROGRAM: Archduke, with local musicians.
SOURCE: NZfM 23 (1845), p. 167.

(296)   DARMSTADT   12 October 1845: Hoftheater
PROGRAM: Konzertstück, with orchestra // Robert // *Ständchen*
and *Erlkönig* by Schubert, with Agnes Pirscher // Somnambula.
SOURCES: Poster facsimile [courtesy of Geraldine Keeling]. //
Schweitzer, pp. 156-157.

(297)   HEIDELBERG   15 October 1845: Museums-Saale
                                         ?private/?benefit
PROGRAM: unknown [presented with Pantaleoni].
SOURCES: HeJ Nos. 281-282 (14-15.10.1845) [photocopies courtesy
of the Heidelberg Stadtarchiv]. // MnJ No. 282 (15.10.1845), p. 1129.

(298)   FREIBURG i.B.   17 October 1845: Kaufhaus-Saale
PROGRAM: Tell // Lucia-Andante // Don Juan // Andante con
variazione // Erlkönig // Puritani-Polonaise // Grand Galop.
SOURCES: FbOZ Nos. 287-290 and 293 (15-17 and 20.10.1845), pp.
1203, 1208, 1215, and 1225-1226. // FbZ Nos. 288 and 293 (14 and
19.10.1845), pp. 1658 and 1689-1690. // RGMP 12 (1845), p. 355. See
also Monde No. 43 (23.10.1845).

Longer Quotations from Contemporary Foreign-language Sources

The following quotations are arranged in chronological order according to the date(s) of the event(s) they describe. Five of them—quotations 1, 4, 10, 12, and 17—are reprinted complete in the original German. The rest are excerpts from French- and German-language newspapers and magazines; these excerpts are not complete, but their contents are in correct order.

Quotation 1: From the *Leipziger Zeitung* No. 74 (26 March 1840), p. 1061.

Leipzig, 25. März. Gestern gab Herr Franz Liszt im Saale des Gewandhauses sein zweites und zu unserm Bedauern sein letztes*) Concert, mit Begleitung unsres trefflichen Orchesters. Er trug das Concertstück von C. M. v. Weber (Op. 79) vor; dann nach seiner Composition eine Fantasie und zwei Lieder von Franz Schubert (Ave Maria und das Ständchen). Ueber die reiche und großartige Entfaltung seiner außerordentlichen Kunstkraft könnten wir nur das wiederholen, was in unsern und andern Blättern bereits über sein geniales Spiel gesagt worden ist. Nur Liszt versteht es, sein Instrument so in der höchsten Potenz zu beherrschen und den von ihm aufgeregten Sturm der Tonmassen so zu besänftigen. Ein ungewöhnlicher und anhaltender Beifallsruf erfüllte den Saal. Nach dem Schlusse überreichte die Sängerin Fräulein Schlegel dem Meister unter Jubelruf einen Blumenkranz, und der Gefeierte dankte der Versammlung, indem er an das Pianoforte zurückkehrte und den "Erlkönig" vortrug. — Am 23. d. Abends hatte unser berühmter Musikdirector Dr. Mendelssohn-Bartholdy dem europäischen Gaste zu Ehren ein großes musikalisches Fest im Saale des Gewandhauses gegeben, wo u. a. ein Concert von Sebast. Bach an drei Flügeln von Liszt, Mendelssohn-Bartholdy und Ferd. Hiller, unter Quartettbegleitung, u. a. m. gespielt wurde.
*) So eben erfahren wir, daß Herr Franz Liszt *zum Besten des Institutfonds für alte und kranke Musiker* Montag den 30. d. noch ein Concert geben wird. (Redaction).

Quotation 2: From *Das Rheinland* No. 59 (26 July 1840),
   pp. 349-350:

Liszt hat in Mainz gespielt, und der Dom steht noch unverrückt an
jener Stelle, wo er von jeher gestanden! Alle die merkwürdigen
Vorgänge und geschichtlichen Weltbegebenheiten, die Liszts Spiel an
andern Orten hervorgerufen, sind in Mainz weggeblieben! Es sind
keine Ohnmächtigen aus dem Saale geschleppt worden, es wären
eher noch Zuhörer hineinzuschleppen gewesen, der Wahnsinn des
Entzückens brach nicht in den abgespielten Gefühlstonleitern der Ah!
Oh! Ih! und Uh! durch; die weiblichen Wesen streckten zwar auch die
Tauben- und Schwanenhälse aus, um etwas von Liszts Spiel
abzulernen, aber sie verrenkten sich dabei nicht, wie in andern
deutschen Städten, mit dem Halse zugleich den ganzen Kopf, man
verfiel nicht, wie anderswo, während Liszt spielte, in Jubeldelirien,
wenn er die langen Locken von der einen Seite des Kopfes zur andern
warf . . .
   Meiner Ansicht nach muß dem vollendeten Clavier-*Virtuosen*
Liszt, dem kühnen Bezwinger der Technik, der Künstler Liszt, der
poetisch-schaffende Liszt, der geistige Erfasser des Instruments
untergeordnet werden. Diese *geistige* Richtung, in welcher sich Liszt
fortbewegt, und in welche er durch mannichfache äußere
Lebensverhältnisse geschleudert wurde, mag unangetastet
hingehen. . . . Seine Compositionen, wenn mann ausgesponnene
Inspirationen des Augenblicks so nennen darf, sind phantastische
Rhapsodien, immer umdämmert vom mystischen Zwielicht der
sogenannten Neu-Romantik. Eine urkräftig-schöpferische
Geistesmacht für sein Instrument ist Liszt keineswegs. Seine
Nachbildungen, seine Uebertragungen, z. B. der Schubert'schen
Lieder, müssen Meisterstücke der Uebersetzungskunst genannt
werden, aber eine poetisch-schaffende Natur würde solche Lieder
ohne Worte aus der eignen Innerlichkeit herausgebildet haben. . . .
   Liszt selbst bohrte in Mainz nicht einmal durch sein Spiel an
Einem Abend [sic] ein halbes Dutzend Claviere in Grund und
Boden. . . . Darum auch verdiente Ehrung und Anerkennung dem
herrlichen Clavier-Virtuosen Liszt, aber keine blinde Vergötterung,
kein sich selber als Zugthier einspannen vor den Triumphwagen
solcher Kunstcelebritäten! Das ist die Affen-Schande des
Jahrhunderts, das heute einem Wohlthäter des Menschengeschlechts
Monumente setzt, und morgen die Menschenwürde erniedrigt, indem
es um das Schnupftuch einer Primadonna, um den Schuh einer
Tänzerin, um die Haarlocke vom Haupte eines Clavierspielers buhlt.

Quotation 3: From *Der Freischütz* No. 29 (17 July 1841), col.
   462:

[D]as Beethoven'sche Quintett [Op. 16] beginnt. Brillant, höchst
brillant, mein Herr Liszt, das nenne ich Fertigkeit, Präcision; aber
mit den Tempis springen's doch halt a Bissel zu willkührlich um. Der

alte Vetter ist gar nit so ein Perückenstock, der mit gewaltiger grüner
Brille die Nase ins Notenbüchel steckt, und nun bei jeder kleinen
Licenz sich ein gewaltiges Monitum macht, und der Bettler weiß
auch, daß einem Künstler wie Liszt sehr, sehr vieles freisteht, wobei
man der lieben Kunst-Schuljugend gewaltig auf die Hände klopfen
würde; aber zu viel kann der gute Meister Beethoven selbst von so
einem seiner Schoßkinder, wie Franz Liszt es ist, nit vertragen.

Quotation 4: From an unidentified clipping in the "Second
   Scrapbook" of the Comtesse d'Agoult [F-Vm]:

(Brieflich.) Am Freitage bleibt Sturmes halber das holländ.
Dampfschiff in Cuxhaven. Fünf Herren steigen ans Land, und
langweilen sich über alle Maßen, da der Regen keine Sekunde
aufhört; endlich gegen Abend, lassen sie den Schauspieldirektor der
Truppe, die jetzt dort spielt, holen, und erkundigen sich was am
Abend gegeben wird? — Es ist kein Theatertag! — Ob der Direktor
wohl geneigt sey, für eine bestimmte Summe einige Lustspiele zu
geben? — Er zeigt sich bereit, und außer den fünf Herren, finden sich
zwar nicht sehr viele Zuschauer ein, doch darunter einige hübsche
junge Damen, aus dem Lande Hadeln [sic] und Wursten. Die Herren
sind heiter und galant und wissen ein Gespräch anzuknüpfen; die
Damen beklagen sich, daß in den Zwischen-akten Musik fehle. Einer
der Herren ruft: "[illegible] ein Clavier, so spiele ich, ich bin der
Musikus Liszt." Liszt?! Ist es Scherz, ist es Ernst? nein, es ist Ernst,
er ist es wirklich! und spielt auf dem schnell herbeigeholten Clavier,
wiewohl dies wahrhäftig kein Erard'scher Flügel war. Nach dem
Theater schlug er den Damen vor, ihnen nun auch zum Tanz zu
spielen; doch darein willigen diese nicht; dagegen möchten sie mit
ihm tanzen, daß wollten sie sich gerne rühmen können. Auch dazu
zeigte er sich bereit. Schnell wird Musik besorgt, und ein Duzend [il-
legible] aus Rißebüttel und der Marsch, beten Liszt der Reihe nach
zum Tanz. Das [illegible] seiner Anwesenheit verbreitet sich schnell;
vor dem Wirthshause, worin er wohnt, erschallen Musik und
"Vivats", während er drinnen fröhlich ißt und trinkt, und sich seines
Triumphes in diesem Erdenwinkel freut.

Quotation 5: From the *Blätter für Musik und Literatur* 2 (1841),
   p. 146:

Nach Beendigung des Mahles ging es nach Nonnenwerth zurück, wo
sich eine zahlreiche Menge Menschen aus der Umgegend versammelt
hatte. Liszt fühlte sich durch den allgemeinen Wunsch, ihn zu hören,
veranlaßt, einen Flügel in die Kapelle bringen zu lassen und sein,
durch kein Wort zu bezeichnendes Talent, der versammelten,
horchenden, hingerissenen Menge zu zeigen. Die verödeten Hallen
der Kapelle hatten nun auf einmal wieder Seele und Geist
bekommen; ja schwerlich haben die Nonnen, die ehemals ihre Gebete

von hier aus zum Himmel sandten, mit größerer Wahrheit das
Göttliche empfunden, als diese etwas weltliche Versammlung durch
Liszt's electrisirendes Spiel.

Quotation 6: From the *Allgemeine musikalische Zeitung* 43
(1841), col. 759:

Franz Liszt hat vor acht Tagen in Frankfurt zwei Konzerte im Theater gegeben, und imponirte wie immer, obgleich das zweite Konzert
nur schwach besetzt war. Das Urtheil über diesen Virtuosen stellt
sich nach und nach bei der Majorität einer unbefangenen Jury fest.
Diese sagt, um es kurz zu fassen, dass Liszt — sein feuriges Talent,
die geniale Auffaussung klassischer Kompositionen und eine
fabelhafte Technik, die mit dem Schwierigsten tändelt, wie der
Gigante mit einem Kinde, in Ehren gehalten — doch mehr verblendet
als Licht gibt, mehr Staunen als Wohlthum erregt, mehr nach
Vergötterung der Menge ringt, als nach dem stilleren aber innigeren
Kennerbeifall.

Quotation 7: From Paul Kaufmann, "Franz Liszt am Rhein,"
Die Musik 26 (1933), p. 119:

Der Saal war prächtig ausgeziert, Liszts Büste mit einem Lorbeer
versehen. Das Publikum war etwas gemischt, indem die ganze
Bürgerschaft daran teilnahm. . . . Toaste drängten sich, den besten
sprach unstreitig Professor Breidenstein Liszt zu Ehren. Sehr
interessant war es, wie Liszt anwortete. Das Deutsche wurde ihm
ziemlich schwer, so daß er nur immer gebrochen sprach und sich
damit entschuldigte, er tue alles aus dem Stegreif, auch in der Musik.
Sein Toast galt der Stadt Bonn, die an sich klein und unbedeutend,
durch Beethoven groß und berühmt geworden sei. Der Champagner
floß wahrhaftig und bald merkte man ihn in der lebhaftesten
Stimmung.

Quotation 8: From the *Neue Zeitschrift für Musik* 15 (1841), p.
191:

Aber — wir haben nicht gefühlt. Es ist mehr Geist als Herz in
Liszt's Schöpfungen. Das Feuer seiner Leidenschaft ist kein
erwärmendes, belebendes, sondern ein vulkanisches, prachtvoll
glänzend, aber zerstörend. Seine Poesie ist durchaus die moderne
Zerissenheitspoesie. Ihr Referent kann, mit vielen Gleichgesinnten,
dieses häufige Zerreißen alles rhythmischen Ebenmaßes nie schön
finden, und hat ihm in dieser Hinsicht der Vortrag von Weber's
Aufforderung zum Tanze und des Erlkönigs am wenigsten, am
meisten der des Hexameron gefallen.

Quotation 9: From the *Vossische Zeitung* No. 11 (14 January 1842):

Nun der Concertgeber *en masque*, Hr. Liszt. . . . — Zum Schluß war uns nur noch der Galopp chromatique versprochen. Hr. Liszt trat auf die Orchestra, man wurde aufmerksam, still; er fing nicht an zu spielen, sondern an zu sprechen, doch seine Worte waren, wie uns dünkt, dem Publikum noch angenehmer als seine Töne gewesen wären, denn er sagte: "Man hat gewünscht, ich möchte vor dem Galopp noch ein Musikstück spielen; da die Wahl ganz unbestimmt ist, so ersuche ich Sie, zu entscheiden, ob ich den Erlkönig oder die Aufforderung zum Tanze . . . Denn schallten die Worte Erlkönig und Aufforderung zum Tanz, so wie sie gesprochen waren hundertfältig zurück. Der Rechner Dase, der im Saal gewesen sein soll, und dessen Ueberblick im raschen Ueberzählen vieler Einzelnheiten bekannt ist, hatte *allein* die Voten gezählt und 351 Stimmen für die Aufforderung zum Tanz, 350 für den Erlkönig verisiert. . . . Hr. Liszt erklärte jedoch die Abstimmung für zweifelhaft, und da zum Serutinium nicht wohl Zeit war, stellte er der Kammer die Frage: "Ob sie ihm erlauben wolle *erst* den Erlkönig, dann die Aufforderung zum Tanz und zum Schluß den Galopp zu spielen?" Daß dieser Antrag von 701 Stimmen, durch *mehr* als Acclamation angenommen wurde, dafür glaubt der Berichterstatter eine unbedingte Bürgschaft stellen zu können. . . . Endlich, da er so lange zum Tanz aufgefordert hatte, mußte dieser selbst auch erfolgen, und im wilden phantastischen Galopp jagte der verwegene Reiter bis ans Ende des Concerts.

Quotation 10: From Frankfurt's *Didaskalia* No. 314 (14 November 1842):

Gotha, 9. Nov.
    Gestern trafen Liszt und Rubini hier ein. Noch denselben Abend gaben sie ein Konzert im herzogl. Hoftheater, wo, ohngeachtet der erhöhten Preise, das Haus gedrängt voll war. Es bedarf wohl kaum der Erwähnung, daß auch hier die Leistungen dieser Heroen der Kunst die glänzendste Anerkennung fanden und auch hier die Begeisterung erregten, zu welcher ihr Erscheinen allgemein hinreißen muß. Nach dem Konzert hatte sich ein dichter [sic] Kreis im Gasthause zum "deutschen Hof" versammelt, und bei dem fröhlichen Abendessen fehlte es nicht an ehrenden und heiteren Trinksprüchen. Insbesondere wurde Liszt's liebenswürdige Persönlichkeit von Allen, die ihm nahten, erkannt und gepriesen.

Quotation 11: From the *Frankfurter Konversationsblatt* No. 27 (27 January 1843), pp. 107-108:

Aus Berlin. // (19. Januar) // — // Franz Liszt. (Eine Analyse.)
    Ueberall, wo Liszt bis jetzt sich hören ließ, hat er den außerordentlichsten Erfolg gehabt, einen glänzenderen, als je ein

anderer Virtuos auf dem Pianoforte. Seine Bewunderer haben ihn in
Gedichten besungen, und die Kritiker in lobpreisenden Artikeln ohne
Zahl seine höchste Meisterschaft anerkannt. Allein nirgends findet
sich eine Analyse seiner Kunst, noch keinem ist gelungen, dem Leser,
der ihn nicht gehört, in *Worten zu verdeutlichen, worin die Wunder
seines Spiels bestehen*, und durch welche Mittel er sich zum
Koryphäen aller Virtuosen auf dem Pianoforte
emporgeschwungen. . . . In so weit man unter Virtuosität zunächst
den höchsten Grad technischer Fertigkeit auf deiem musikalischen
Instrument, bei vollkommener Einsicht in den Geist desselben,
versteht, treten im Allgemeinen folgende Eigenthümlichkeiten bei
Franz Liszt hervor: 1) ein unfehlbar sicherer, bewunderungswürdig
gleicher und elastischer Anschlag. 2) Eine durchaus gleichmäßige
Ausbildung der Beweglichkeit und Fertigkeit beider Hände und jedes
einzelnen Fingers, so wie daraus hervorgehende vollkommene
Beherrschung jeder denkbaren Schwierigkeit der Applikatur und, 3)
eine feste, durch sein Gedächtniß unterstützte Willenskraft in
Beziehung auf eine gleichzeitige, jedoch ganz verschiedenartige
Anwendung der einzelnen Finger. Mit diesen Vorzügen ausgerüstet,
ruft er unglaubliche, nie gehörte Effecte ins Leben. Im Adagio
entzückt er durch das Hervorziehen eines glockenartigen Tons und
durch ein wunderbares Tragen der Cantilene, wie man es bei keinem
andern Meister wiederfindet, so wie durch überraschende
Anwendung der graziösesten Fiorituren. Welch' ein *cresdendo* ferner
und *decrescendo*, welch' ein *pianissimo* und *fortissimo*! . . . In seinem
Spiel wird, mit einem Worte, den bis zur höchsten Potenz
gesteigerten Anforderungen entsprochen. Welche Studien, welcher
Fleiß, welcher eiserner Wille, welche Ausdauer, welche Entsagungen
und Entbehrungen müssen dazu reichen! Es hat schon so manchen
ausgezeichneten Pianisten gegeben; auch die Gegenwart zählt
vortreffliche Virtuosen auf dem Fortepiano; allein d e r Grad der
Vollkommenheit, welcher ihnen eigen war und ist, kann durch
Beharrlichkeit von Allen erreicht werde; L i s z t dagegen ist
unerreichbar, gerade wie P a g a n i n i, der, wiewohl er Nachahmer
in Menge gefunden hat, dennoch für alle Zeit einzig in seiner Kunst
dastehen wird.

Quotation 12: From F. J. A. Schreiber, *Dr. Franz Liszt
    und dessen Anwesenheit in Breslau* (Breslau 1843), p. 13:

D e r   K a n t o r. Ein armer Kantor aus einer eine Tagereise von
Breslau entfernten Stadt, als er vernommen, daß Herr Liszt in
Breslau angekommen, nimmt sein erspartes Geld und macht sich auf
zur Reise nach der Hauptstadt, um einen Inbegriff von der
weltberühmten Kunst dieses gefeierten Mannes sich zu verschaffen.
Seine Ersparnisse reichten grade [sic] aus, um die Hin- und Rückreise
zu Fuß und hierselbst sich ein Entréebillet zum Concert zu
verschaffen. Aber zu seinem Leidwesen vernimmt er bei der Ankunft,
daß kein Billet mehr zu haben sei. Was sollte er thun? Noch einen

Tag länger hier zu weilen, dazu reichte seine Baarschaft [?] nicht aus;
er geht daher mit sich zu Rathe und faßt sich ein Herz, den Künstler
aufzusuchen. Aengstlich tritt er bei diesem ein, und so sehr er auch
vorher über der Reder studirt, mit welcher er den großen Gönner
begrüßen wollte, so stotterte er jetzt doch nur unzusammenhängende
Worte — Staunen und Ehrfurcht hielten seine Sinne besangen. Nach
vieler Mühe gelingt es ihm entlich, sich verständlich zu machen, daß
er, um ihr zu hören, eine so weite Reise gemacht, und nun kein Billet
mehr erhalten könnte; noch einige Tage in Breslau zu verweilen,
wär' er außer Stande, und dennoch möchte er ihn so gern einmal
spielen hören. Der Künstler eröffnet ihm, daß auch er ihm unter den
obwaltenden Umständen zu keinem Billet verhelfen könne, forscht
dabei den Alten näher aus, und erfreut über seine zunehmende
Redseligkeit nimmt er sich vor, dem Fremdling eine stille Freude zu
bereiten. Er läßt ihm ein Frühstück bereiten, nöthigt ihm zum Essen,
setzt sich dann an das Fortepiano und trägt dem Ueberraschten
einige Fantasie-Stücke vor. Wie dem Kantor zu Muthe sein mochte,
läßt sich leicht denken; daß er vor Ueberraschung und Entzücken das
Essen vergaß, ist gewiß. Die Freudenthräne seines Auges zeichte von
der Würdigung dessen, was er sah und hörte. Man hätte in seinen
Augen die Worte lesen können; nun möchte ich vergnügt sterben,
denn ich gab ihn ja, den größten Künstler der Welt gehört! Mit
tausendsachem Danke nahm er Abschied, versehen mit einem
Geschenk um die Rückreise nicht mahr zu Fuß machen zu dürfen,
sondern um behaglich in einem Wagen sich in den seligsten
Rückerinnerungen wiegen zu können.

Quotation 13: From the *Oberschlesischer Bürgerfreund* No. 22 (18 March 1843), pp. 87-88:

F. Liszt. // (Verspätet) // Wer kennt die Völker, nennt die Namen, //
Die gastlich hier zusammen kamen?
Wer in den Nachmittagsstunden des 9. März als Fremder unserer
freundlichen Stadt einen Besuch abgestatter und anbekannt mit der
Veranlassung das Treiben beobachtet hätte, was sich in den
mannigfaltigsten mitunter recht komischen Bildern entwickelte,
würde schwerlich den Grund dafür selbst aufzufinden gewußt haben.
Alle Gasthöfe ersten und zweiten Ranges waren förmlich wie mit
einer Wagenburg umlagert, unaufhörlich rollten Reiseequipagen im
buntesten Gemisch am Ringe herauf, man las auf allen Gesichtern,
"daß etwas Ungewöhnliches, Seltenes der Beweggrund zu dieser
aufgeregten Stimmung sein müsse. Und was war es, was diese
ungewöhnliche Lebendigkeit, diese überall stattfindende einstimmige
Conversation hervorreif? — L i s z t! — Sein Name war der Magnet,
der aus Nah und Fern Neugierige herbeizog; seine Kunstfertigkeit
der Talisman, vermöge welchem er die Zwei- und Einthalerstücke auf
die solideste Weise aus unsern Taschen escamotirte, und die
eleganten Räume des Resourcen-Saales mit Hör- und Schaulustigen
zu füllen vermochte. . . . Bereits von 6 Uhr war der Concert-Saal

mit einer meist gewählten Gesellschaft gefüllt. Die
verschiedenartigsten Gerüchte hatten einen nicht zu billigenden
Umstand hervorgerufen, der für das zwar später, aber immer noch
zur rechten Zeit ankommende Publikum, besonders in Betreff der
Damen höchst unangenehm und lästig wurde. Ein jeder hatte sich
mit seinem Entree das Recht des möglich besten Platzes erworben,
was Wunder also, wenn mitunter nöthige Rücksichten bei Seite
gesetzt und störende Collisionen veranlaßt wurden. Alles dieses
jedoch schwand bei dem Gedanken an das zu Erwartende. Liszt war
der Name, der auf Aller Lippen schwebte, lächelnd wurden Rippen-
und Degenstöße hingenommen (ein Phantasie über Thema's aus der
Somnambule entschädigt ja für alle diese unfansten Berührungen)
und mit dem besten Humor von der Welt amüsirte man sich an den
angestrengten komischen Bemühungen Einzelner, sich durch die auf
beiden Seiten des Saales befindlichen dichten Knäule von Hörern
durchzuarbeiten. . . .
    Daß nach beendigung des Conzertes die vielen auswärtigen und
namentlich Gräfenberger Herrschaften die Conditoreien, besonders
die Schminder'sche sehr zahlreich besuchten, gegen 150 derselben
daselbst dinirten und ein dort angebrachter geschmackvoller Transparent mit den Worten: "A l l e s mit L i s z t" vielen Beifall fand,
verdient ebenfalls einige Erwähnung.

Quotation 14: From the *Bayerische Landbote* No. 303 (30 October 1843), p. 1251:

Bevor wir endlich zu den Vorträgen des Concertgebers selbst
übergehen, müssen wir mit wenigen Worten seiner Erscheinung und
seiner Leistungen im Allgemeinen gedenken. Herr Liszt pflegt zu
kommen, zu spielen und zu siegen. Auch unter uns war dies in seinem
Concerte vom 18. Oktober der Fall. Sein *Grand Galoppe*
chromatique, sein Andante aus Lucie von Lammermoor, seine
Schubert'schen Lieder, vor allen andern Nummern aber seine
Ouvertüre aus Wilhelm Tell und seine Reminiscenzen aus Don Juan,
steigerten den Beifall von Stufe zu Stufe bis zur vollsten
Bewunderung der ganzen Eigenthümlichkeit seines Spieles und der
Unvergleichlichkeit seines Vortrags. Die Wahl der Gegenstände für
das Concert vom 21. Okt. war im Ganzen keineswegs geeignet dem
gefeierten Künstler bei unserm Publikum neue Triumphe zu bereiten,
im Gegentheil, die *Sonate pathétique* (erster Satz) von Beethoven, ließ
dasselbe fast mehr als kalt. Gleichwohl bedurfte es nur der
außerordentlichen Zugabe des "Heil unserm König Heit" am Schlusse
des Concertes, um den Triumphator seinen raschen Sieg vom 18. neu
zu sichern. So fehlte denn gerade nur dieses dritte Concert, um ihn
wirklich als den Unwiderstehbaren erscheinen zu lassen, wie man ihn
wohl vorzugsweise genannt hat, als den Meister der Meister auf dem
Piano.

Quotation 15: From the *Allgemeine musikalische Zeitung* 46 (1844), cols. 243-244:

Wir hatten früher öfter gehört und gelesen, dass unser als Claviervirtuos so hoch gefeierten Liszt beim Dirigiren ein gar hitziger Herr, und, in einem gewissen Sinne, ein recht schlimmer Marschall Vorwärts sei; allein bei Aufführung der C moll-Symphonie bemerkten wir davon, abgesehen vom zweiten Satze derselben, welcher nach unserer Ueberzeugung etwas zu rasch genommen und dadurch aus seinen poetischen Schwerpuncten herausgehoben wurde, nicht die geringste Spur. Sein Feuergeist dämpfte sich vielmehr dabei zu ächt künstlerischer Ruhe und Besonnenheit, ohne an Kraft und Lebendigkeit zu verlieren. Wenn Herr Fr. Liszt diese Ruhe und Sicherheit auch in der Oper bewährt und sie mit jener Geduld und Ausdauer verbindet, welche zum Einstudiren neuer Werke erforderlich ist (wir möchten wohl einmal die neunte in Weimar noch nie gegebene Symphonie Beethoven's unter seiner Direction hören!), so können wir uns nur darauf freuen, ihn öfter an der Spitze einer Capelle zu sehen, welche freilich Meister in sich begreift, die auch gar tüchtig den Commandostab zu führen verstehen.

Quotation 16: From *Signale für die musikalische Welt* 2 (1844), p. 68:

Liszt spielte am 21. Februar in dem Concert für die Naumannstiftung im Theater Weber's Concertstück und seine Don Juan-Fantasie. Nein — er spielte nicht, sondern verzerrte, karrikirte beide Stücke auf so unnatürliche, verkehrte, unmusikalische und widerliche Weise, daß selbst ein Theil des Publikums stutzte und sich indignirt, wenigstens kopfschüttelnd zeigte. Dr. Liszt hatte nie wahren und schönen Clavierton, denn seine Hände schweben meist in der Luft und die Finger stechen von oben hinunter, oft in gerader Richtung, aber diesmal spielte er noch tonloser und ruschelicher als früher, obgleich mit seiner besondern staunenswerthen Rapidität, woraus man zwei schöne, gesunde, wahre Clavierspieler machen könnte. — Er schwang noch immer die Hände ein bis zwei Ellen über die Claviatur, spielte nicht vier Takte im Takt, macht keine Passage ohne Eilen oder Anhalten, brachte endlose Bandwürmer von Verzierungen an, kokettirte mit hohlem, unwahrem, bodenlos affektirtem Vortrag und — unsere talentlose Clavierjugend wird nun wieder mit erneueten Kräften dem großen Muster nachreiten, nachjagen, nachdreschen ec. . . .

Quotation 17: From the *Magdeburgische Zeitung* No. 66 (18 March 1844):

Wir haben Herrn Hof-Kapellmeister Dr. Liszt nun in zwey Concerten gehört. Gewiß ein Genius so außerordentlicher Art, daß er uns bisher nur einmal in Paganini so erschienen ist. Nicht nur, daß uns hier eine

Virtuosität des Spiels entgegen tritt, die über die äußersten Grenzen, die man sich hier zu denken hat, hinausgeht, der Geist, der Genius, der in ihm waltet, ist es zugleich mit, der uns so wunderbar ergreift, daß wir, ihm ganz hingegeben, uns von einem Extrem zum anderen fortgerissen fühlen. Wenn wir uns mächtig in den Zauberkreis seiner eigenen Fantasien hineingezogen fühlen, so regt er ebenso in innerster Seele uns auf, wenn er in den ewig unvergänglichen Schöpfungen Beethovens sich ergeht. Die Beethoven'schen Sonaten von ihm gehört zu haben, gehört zu dem Schönsten, was uns der Art je geworden ist.

Quotation 18: From *Der Posaune* No. 39 (31 March 1844), p. 155:

Das Programm verkündete 7 Vorträge des Concertgebers ohne Zuziehung irgend einer anderseitigen Unterstützung. . . . Diese 7 Piecen bestanden nun nicht etwa in Meisterwerken, sondern waren mit Ausnahme einer Beethovenschen Composition größtentheils Arrangements beliebter Opernmelodien. Nur die Fantasie über Bellinis Nachtwandlerin zeichnete sich durch Compositionswerth aus und verdunkelte die erste über Motive aus Lucia, die man nur ein einfaches Arrangement nennen kann, ganz und gar. . . . Über L[iszt]'s Spiel ist schon so viel gesagt und geschrieben, daß es schwierig ist, etwas Neues hinzuzufügen. Seine Technik ist vollendet und steht jedenfalls jetzt einzig da. . . . [Aber] sein Vortrag ist nicht immer schön, zuweilen unnatürlich und zu sessellos. So bricht er oft mitten in einer Melodie ab, was auf uns den Eindruck machte, den vielleicht ein durch Schnitte zersetztes Bild hervorbringen würde. Von diesen Mängeln belieb selbst Beethovens Werk nicht verschont . . .

Quotation 19: From the *Zeitschrift für Deutschlands Musik-Vereine* 5 (1845), p. 79 [on Liszt's Beethoven Festival Cantata]:

Herr Liszt hat durch die Art, wie er diese Aufgabe gelöst, auf's Neue und Ueberraschendste Beweise seiner Vielseitigkeit und Genialität geliefert und alle Erwartungen um so mehr übertroffen, als dieselben eigentlich nicht sehr gross gewesen sind. Im Gegentheil! Nur Wenige trauten dem hochgefeierten Virtuosen, von dem bis jetzt nur kleinere Werke für sein Instrument bekannt geworden sind, solche Compositionsgabe zu; man erwartete eine tändelnde Modearbeit, allerdings nicht ohne Effect, keineswegs aber das, was er bot! Verkennen wir auch nicht, dass — besonders wenn man die Partitur vor sich liegen hätte — immerhin manche Ausstellungen zu machen seyn könnten, so müssen wir dennoch die Arbeit eine würdige nennen; die zwar einige Seltsamkeiten in der Form, manches Bizarre und mehrere Längen, aber auch höchst wirkungsvolle und originelle

Schönheiten hat, unter welche namentlich die Instrumentation
mancher Stellen zu rechnen ist.

Quotation 20: From the *Revue et Gazette Musicale de Paris* 12 (1845), p. 292:

Quant à l'arrivée, elle n'a pas été moins agréable, car j'ai appris que
Liszt s'était décidé à donner concert ce jour-là; à cette nouvelle jugez
combien je me suis hâté! J'entre donc dans la salle. A pien ai-je eu le
temps d'en admirer les proportions élégantes, et l'éclairage splendide;
à peine ai-je pu jeter un regard sur toutes ces fraîches beautés qui
viennent demander aux naïades bienfaisantes une santé qu'elles
n'ont jamais perdue, que Liszt se présante et que le concert com-
mence. Il faut en convenir, jamais coquette ne mit plus de soin à
composer les plis de son vêtement et à disposer les fleurs de sa
chevelure, que Liszt n'en apporta ce soir-là à l'arrangement de son
programme: e'était d'abord la tarentelle de Rossini, les mélodies
hongroises, puis une improvisation pleine d'art et de caprice sur une
mazurka de Chopin, et enfin le formidable morceau de *Robert*. Vien
rarement, à ce qu'il m'a paru, le grand pianiste ne montra plus
deverve, de grâce et d'audace; peut-être le plaisir de nous trouver
dans une salle élégante, au milieu d'une assemblée choisie, et
d'assister, pour ainsi dire, à un concert intime, était-il pour quelque
chose dans notre enthousiasme.

Liszt Letters in Vormärz Periodicals

The six Liszt letters that follow are not the only ones published in German newspapers and magazines between 1840 and 1845. Other letters are identified in Suttoni's revised bibliography cited above and identified in Appendix B. References to Suttoni's work and to Burger's documentary biography appear below [in square brackets], as do statements identifying letters previously unknown to biographers and scholars.

Letter 1: From the *Frankfurter Konversationsblatt* No. 93 (2 April 1840), p. 372

[Suttoni: item 308
Reprinted from another source in Burger, p. 130]

Erklärung. // Ich habe mit eben so viel Befremden als Leidwesen vernommen, daß in einem Blatte ein Correspondenzartikel aus Leipzig abgedruckt war, worinnen mehre Beschuldigungen gegen mich ausgesprochen waren. Gewohnt, nur einer Beurtheilung meiner künstlerischen Leistungen entgegensehen zu dürfen, hätte ich wohl kaum erwarten können, daß man es mir zumVorwurf machen würde: 1) *durch die Annoncen meiner Concerte*, 2) *durch Verweigerung von Freibillets, gefehlt zu haben.* Was die Annoncen betrifft, so waren je die meisten noch vor meiner Ankunft eingerückt, keine aber weder von mir redigirt, noch mit meiner Namensunterschrift versehen. Eine Billets-Verweigerung hat niemals stattgefunden; da jedoch mein Concert wenige Stunden nach meiner Ankunft erfolgte, so ist es wohl möglich, daß in dieser kurzen Zwischenzeit übersehen ward, einigen [sic] von den Personen, welche gewöhnlich Freibillets zu empfangen pflegen, solche zuzustellen, was mir aufrichtig leid ist. Hat Herr Hofmeister gewiß das Arrangement des Ganzen mit eben so großer Bereitwilligkeit als Thätigkeit und Gefälligkeit übernommen, so sind doch jedenfalls die leidigen Mißverständnisse auch eine Folge der fraglichen Annoncen und Arrangements gewesen, und wenn ich gewiß der Letzte war, der davon Kenntniß erlangte, so haben sie mich deshalb nicht minder unangenehm berührt.

Um so erfreulicher war es mir, sowohl in Dresden als in Leipzig unaufgefoderte [sic; this should be "unaufgeforderte"] Vertheidiger unter den Gebildeten zu finden; reichlich entschädigte mich die so schmeichelhafte Anerkennung in beiden Städten, die liebenswürdige mir gewordene Auszeichnung des von mir hochverehrten Dr. Mendelssohn, unter Mitwirkung des ausgezeichneten Leipziger Orchesters und Chors, und ich ergreife mit wahrer Freude diesen Anlaß, um auszusprechen, daß ich von beiden Städten mit dem Gefühl tief empfundener Dankbarkeit und Achtung scheide.
Dresden, am 27. März 1840

> Franz Liszt

Letter 2: From the *Frankfurter Konversationsblatt* No. 269 (29 September 1841), p. 1075

> [Suttoni: item 313 (addressed to Ludwig Beck)]

Frankfurt, den 26. September 1841. Ich will Frankfurt nicht verlassen, mein lieber Beck, ohne Ihnen meinen aufrichtigsten Dank gesang zu haben. Das Pianoforte, welches mir zu lieben die Güte hatten und welches ich so oft gespielt habe (in einem Dutzend Conzerten, eingerechnet Mainz und Wiesbaden) ist ein Instrument *ohne Furcht und Tadel*. Jedermann war befriedigt, ja überrascht, und ich würde mich glücklich schätzen, wenn ich direkt oder indirekt Ihren Ruf als ausgezeichneten Instrumentenverfertiger, welchen Sie in jeder Hinsicht verdienen, gründen könnte. Viele herzliche Grüße von Ihrem ergebenen Franz Liszt.

Letter 3: From the *Vossische Zeitung* and *Spenersche Zeitung*, both No. 53 (4 March 1842)

> [previously uncataloged]

Mon cher Schlesinger,
    Les préparatifs et arrangements du *Concert de Jeudi* [i.e., the farewell matinée] ne me regardent en aucune manière — pas plus que la recette, qui est destinée à des actes de bienfaisance. L'annonce des journaux de ce matin n'a point été redigée par moi — je ne puis par conséquent en prendre la responsabilité. Je regrette *beaucoup*, qui nous ne nous soyons pas vu ce matin — deux mots auraient tout expliqué.
Ce 1 mars 1842

> Tout à Vous
> *F. Liszt*

Letter 4: From the *Berliner Figaro* No. 68 (22 March 1842),
    p. 272

[Suttoni: item 315]

Erklärung. // Tilsit, den 17. März 1842. // Ich erkläre hiermit, daß ich
an der Abfassung des und dem Journal "Rheinland" von Ihrem Blatte
abgedruckten Briefes mit meines Namenunterschrift nicht den
mindesten Antheil habe etc.

F. Liszt

(An L. W. Krause,
Redakteur der Berliner Figaro.)

Letter 5: From the *Erfurter Zeitung* No. 149 (17 November
    1842)

[previously uncataloged]

Um so mehr erfreut es mich, auch die Gelegenheit zu finden, Ihnen
noch einmal zu sagen, wie wahrhaft ich dem Erfurter Publikum
dankbar bin für die freundliche warme Aufnahme, welche mir
gestattet worden ist. Empfangen Sie noch insbesondere für Herrn
Kapellmeister Golde meinen persönlichen herzlichen Dank, und seyn
Sie versichert, daß die Erinnerung an die D-dur Symphonie, welche
derselbe so prächtig gesetzt und so vortrefflich aufgeführt hat, nie
erlöschen wird. Im Laufe des künftigen Jahres hoffe ich das
Vergnügen zu haben, Sie öfters von Weimar aus zu besuchen. En at-
tendant, lieber Freund! Behalten Sie mich in gutem Andenken, und
vertrauen Sie auf meine freundschaftliche Ergebenheit.

F. Liszt

Letter 6: From the *Allgemeine Preußische Staats-Zeitung*
    No. 19 (19 January 1843), p. 75

[previously uncataloged]

In Beziehung auf verschiedene Korrespondenz-Artikel aus Bonn, über
das Verfahren des Comité zur Errichtung des Denkmals für
Beethoven in Bonn finde ich mich zu nachstehenden Bemerkungen
veranlaßt.
    Die Korrespondenten scheinen nicht genau von der Sachlage
unterrichtet, da sie Herrn Professor A. W. von Schlegel noch als
Mitglied des Comité's bezeichnen, obwohl derselbe schon seit Jahren
ausgetreten und mithin jeder Verantwortlichkeit überhoben ist.
    Meinen Antheil an den Geschäften des Comité's habe ich aber
einzig und allein auf die musikalische Feier, die bei der Einweihung
des Denkmals beabsichtigt wird, beschränkt, für welche ich meine
Mitwirkung vorbehalte. In allen übrigen Beziehungen würde des

Vorsitzende des Comité's, Herr Professor B r e i d e n s t e i n in Bonn, unzweifelhaft als Vertreter zu betrachten seyn.

Berlin, den 17. Januar 1843.

Fr. Liszt.

APPENDIX F
Repertory Abbreviations and Information

Compositions or Transcriptions by Liszt:

Identified below in alphabetical order are the works written or arranged by Liszt *and* performed by him most frequently during his German concerts of 1840-1845. The title of each piece is abbreviated (e.g., "Tell" for Liszt's solo-piano arrangement of the overture to Rossini's *Guillaume Tell*). Each abbreviation is followed by a more complete title, the name of the composer other than Liszt on whose themes or music the work is based [in square brackets], publication information about early editions (in parentheses), and an entry number or numbers from Raabe's "Verzeichnis" {in curved brackets}. Only approximate dates are given for many works, because it is impossible today to determine which edition or editions Liszt used during his German tours, as we saw in Chapter IV. Titles of other works written or arranged by Liszt appear in italics (for formal titles) or quotation marks (for informal titles or abbreviations) throughout Chapters II-V and in Appendix C. Titles only are indexed at the end of this volume.

Adelaïde	Liszt's arrangement of Beethoven's song (Breitkopf & Härtel, 1840) {R. 121}. Not to be confused with Beethoven's song of the same name, which Liszt occasionally performed with vocalists (in italics throughout Appendix C).
Au bord	*Au bord d'une source* from Liszt's *Album d'un voyageur* (Haslinger and Schlesinger, 1842) {R. 8/2b}.
Au lac	*Au lac de Wallenstadt*; see "Au bord" above {R. 8/2a}.
Ave Maria	Liszt's arrangement of this Schubert song (Diabelli, c. 1838) {R. 243/12}.

Campanella	Difficult to identify. Either No. 3 of Liszt's "Paganini Etudes," first version (Haslinger, c. 1840) {R. 3a/3}; or his *Grande Fantaisie de bravoure sur la Clochette de Paganini* (?Mechetti; Hofmeister; etc., late 1830s) {R. 231}. ?Also referred to as "Carnival of Venice" in several reviews. See below.
Carnival of Venice	Possibly a cognomen for "Campanella" above. ?Also the unfinished piano piece preserved in D-WRgs Liszt Ms. J56 {R. 665}, or a related work.
Canzone	Liszt's *Canzone Napolitana* (Meser, 1843) {R. 92}.
Don Juan	Liszt's *Réminiscences de Don Juan* [Mozart] (Schlesinger, c. 1843) {R. 228}.
Erlkönig	Liszt's arrangement of this Schubert song (Diabelli, c. 1838) {R. 243/4}. Not to be confused with the song itself (identified by title *in italics* throughout Appendix C), which Liszt occasionally performed with vocalists.
Etude[s]	Probably refers to one or more of Liszt's *24 Grandes Etudes pour le Piano* (Schlesinger; Haslinger; Ricordi, 1838-1839) {R. 4a}. See also "Mazeppa" below. Etudes by Chopin and Moscheles are identified no more precisely in contemporary programs and reviews.
Fiancée	Liszt's *Grande Fantasie sur la Tyrolienne de l'opéra La Fiancée* [Auber] (Troupenas; Mechetti; etc., late 1830s) {R. 116}.
Figaro	Liszt's ?unfinished fantasy on themes from Mozart's *Le Nozze di Figaro* {see R. 660}.
Gaudeamus igitur	Liszt's concert paraphrase on this popular German student song (Breslau 1843) {R. 99}.
God Save the Queen	Liszt's paraphrase on this patriotic British tune (Schuberth; Mayaud;

etc., c. 1841) {R. 98}. Also known in Germany as "Heil dir im Siegenkranz."

Grand Galop

Liszt's *Grand Galop chromatique* (Hofmeister; etc., late 1830s) {R. 41}.

Hexameron

Hexameron. Morceau de Concert. Grandes Variations de Bravoure sur le Marche des Puritains for solo piano [Bellini] (Latte; Troupenas; Ricordi; etc., late 1830s) {R. 131}. Also performed by Liszt in Vormärz Germany in two-piano/four-hands and piano-orchestra arrangements.
     A joint effort, *Hexameron* was also composed in part by Chopin, Czerny, Herz, Pixis, and Thalberg.

Huguenots

Liszt's *Grand fantasie sur des thèmes de l'opéra Les Huguenots* [Meyerbeer] (Schlesinger; Hofmeister; etc., late 1830s) {R. 221}. Not to be confused with the opera itself, scenes from which Liszt accompanied at the piano in Berlin in 1842.

Lob der Thränen

Liszt's arrangement of this Schubert song (Haslinger, c. 1838) {R. 242}.

Lucia

Liszt's *Réminiscences de Lucia di Lammermoor* [Donizetti] (Hofmeister; Ricordi; etc., c. 1840) {R. 151}.

Lucia-Andante

Probably the simplified version of Liszt's *Réminiscences de Lucia* (Grus, 1840s) {see R. 151}. Also known as the "Andante finale." See above.

Lucia-Marche et Cavatine

Liszt's *Marche et Cavatine de Lucia di Lammermoor* [Donizetti] (Hofmeister; Schott; etc., c. 1841) {R. 152}. Intended as part of "Lucia" identified above; consequently, performances of the "Marche et Cavatine" are tabulated with those of "Lucia" in Chapter IV, Table 2.

Lucrezia Borgia	Liszt's *Réminiscences de Lucrezia Borgia* [Donizetti] (Schott c. 1841) {R. 154}.
Marche hongroise	Probably Liszt's *Heroischer Marsch im ungarischen Styl* (Cranz, 1840) {R. 53}.
Mazeppa	Possibly an early version of Liszt's *Mazeppa* (Schlesinger and Haslinger, c. 1847) {R. 2c}. See also "Etude[s]."
Mélodies hongroises	Possibly one or more of Liszt's arrangements of Schubert's *Mélodies hongroises* (Diabelli; etc., after 1840) {R. 250}. On at least some occasions, though, Liszt's *Ungarische Nationalmelodien* (Haslinger 1840) {R. 105d} or *Magyar dallok* and *Magyar rhapsodiák* {R. 105a-b}.
Niobe	Liszt's *Grande Fantasie sur des motifs de Niobe* [Pacini] (Latte; Cramer; etc., late 1830s) {R. 250}.
Norma	Liszt's *Réminiscences de Norma* [Bellini] (Schott; Latte; etc., early 1840s) {R. 133}.
Orgy	Probably Liszt's arrangement of the penultimate movement of Rossini's *Soirées musicales* {R. 236/11}. See also "Serenata-l'Orgia" below.
Pastoral	Liszt's arrangement of the 3rd, 4th, and 5th movements from Beethoven's Symphony in F Major {R. 128}. Not to be confused with the symphony itself, which Liszt conducted at least once in Germany during the 1840s.
Puritani	Liszt's *Réminiscences des Puritains* [Bellini] (Schott; Troupenas; etc., late 1830s) {R. 129}. May have been confused occasionally with the "Puritani-Polonaise" identified below.
Puritani-Polonaise	Liszt's *I Puritani. Introduction et Polonaise* [Bellini] (Schott; Troupenas; etc., early 1840s) {R. 130}.

Robert   Liszt's *Réminiscences de Robert le
                         Diable* [Meyerbeer] (Schlesinger
                         1841) {R. 222}. Also referred to as
                         the "Infernal Waltz" from that op-
                         era.

Romanesca   Liszt's *La Romanesca* (originally
                         published c. 1832; republished
                         Cranz, 1840) {R. 91}.

Serenade   Probably Liszt's arrangement of
                         the "Serenata" from Rossini's
                         Soirées musicales {R. 236/10{}. See
                         "Orgy" above.

Serenata-l'Orgia   Probably Liszt's *La Serenata et
                         l'Orgia. Grande Fantasie sur des
                         motifs des Soirées musicales*
                         [Rossini] (Schott; Troupenas; etc.,
                         late 1830s) {R. 234}. See also
                         "Serenade" and "Orgy" above.

Somnambula   Liszt's *Fantasie sur des motifs
                         favoris de l'opéra La Somnambula*
                         [Bellini] (Schuberth, 1842) {R.
                         132}.

Ständchen   Liszt's arrangement of this song
                         from Schubert's *Schwanengesang*
                         (Haslinger, c. 1840) {R. 245/7}.

Tarantelle   In many cases Liszt's transcription
                         of "La danza" from Rossini's
                         Soirées musicales {R. 236/9}. On
                         some occasions, however, possibly
                         an excerpt from the first version of
                         Venezia e Napoli (see below). Pos-
                         sibly even an early version of the
                         "Tarantelle" from *La Muette di
                         Portici* [Auber] (c. 1846) {R. 117}.

Tarantelles napolitaines Possibly Liszt's *Tarantelles
                         napolitaines* from the first version
                         of *Venezia e Napoli*, unpublished
                         during the 1840s {R. 10d/4}. See
                         also "Tarantelle" above.

Tell   Liszt's transcription of the
                         *Ouverture de l'opéra Guillaume
                         Tell* [Rossini] (Troupenas; Ricordi;
                         etc., c. 1835) {R. 237}.

Ungarischer Sturmmarsch Probably Liszt's *Seconde Marche
                         hongroise*, unpublished during the

	1840s {R. 54a}. Possibly also a lost or still-unpublished work.
Valse di bravura	Liszt's *Grande Valse di bravura* (Hofmeister; Schlesinger; etc., mid-1830s) {R. 32a}.

Frequently-Performed Works by Other Composers:

Keyboard works by other composers performed frequently by Liszt during his German concert tours are identified below by abbreviation, composer, and title, as well as by references to standard reference works like Schmieder's catalog of Bach's compositions (BWV) and Raabe's catalog of Liszt's works {in curved brackets}. Dates of compositions appear in parentheses, while subtitles and translations (e.g., "Moonlight," "Invitation to the Waltz") appear in quotation marks. Less frequently performed, non-Lisztian keyboard pieces are identified by composer and title throughout Chapters II-V and in Appendix C.

Andante con variazione	Beethoven's Sonata in A-flat Major, Op. 26 (1800-1801), or the first movement from that sonata.
Archduke	Beethoven's Trio for violin, 'cello, and piano in B-flat Major, Op. 97 (1812).
Choral Fantasy	Beethoven's Fantasy for piano, chorus, and orchestra, Op. 80 (1808-1809).
Chopin Etude(s)	One or more of Chopin's etudes, Opp. 10 and/or 25.
Chopin Mazurka(s)	One or more of Chopin's mazurkas, almost none of which is identified in any of Liszt's German concert programs or reviews.
Emperor	Beethoven's Concerto No. 5 in E-flat Major, Op. 73 (1809), known in the English-speaking world as the "Emperor" concerto.
Hummel Concerto	Hummel's Concerto in b minor for piano and orchestra, Op. 89 (c. 1821).
Hummel Septet	Hummel's Septet in d minor, Op. 74 (c. 1816). Arranged by Liszt for solo piano {R. 172} and sometimes performed by him in Vormärz

	Germany in a solo-piano arrangement, or in a reduced arrangement for five instrumentalists.
Invitation	Weber's popular *Aufforderung zum Tanze: Rondo brilliant* ("Invitation to the Waltz," 1819). Also employed by Liszt as a source of thematic material for improvisation.
Konzertstück	Weber's *Konzertstück* in f minor for piano and orchestra (1821). Sometimes performed by Liszt in a solo-piano version.
Moonlight	Beethoven's Sonata in c-sharp minor, Op. 27, No. 2 (the "Moonlight" sonata, 1801). Other Beethoven sonatas with nicknames performed by Liszt include the "Appassionata," "Tempest," and "Hammerklavier."
Oberons Zauberhorn	Hummel's fantasy of the same name, Op. 116 (1829). Apparently performed by Liszt in both solo-piano and piano-orchestra versions.
WTC	*Das wohltempirirte Clavier*, in two volumes, by Johann Sebastian Bach (1722, 1744). Apparently Liszt performed only preludes and fugues from Volume I of this work (BWV 846-869).

Bibliography

Aiton, John [pub. pseud. as "The Pedestrian"]. *Eight Weeks in Germany, comprising Narratives, Descriptions, and Directions for Economical Tourists.* Edinburgh: William Whyte, 1842.

Album d'un voyageur. F. Liszt Gedächtnisausstellung anlässlich der 170. Wiederkehr seines Geburtsjahres, ed. János Kárpáti and Peter Krajasich. Eisenstadt 1981.

Allsobrook, David Ian. *Liszt: My Travelling Circus Life.* Carbondale and Edwardsville: Southern Illinois University Press, 1991.

Altmann, Wilhelm. "Meyerbeer-Forschungen. Archivalische Beiträge aus der Registratur der Generalintendantur der Königlichen Schauspiele zu Berlin." *Sammelbände der internationalen Musikgesellschaft* 4 (1902-1903), pp. 519-534.

Andersen, Hans Christian. *A Visit to Germany, Italy and Malta, 1840-1841* ["A Poet's Bazaar I-II"], trans. Grace Thornton. London: Peter Owen, 1985.

_____. "Liszt." *Monthly Musical Record,* 1 April 1875.

Anonymous. *Allemagne et Pays-bas. Landscape Français.* Paris: Louis Janet, n.d. (1845).

_____. *150 Jahre Musik-Institut Koblenz, 1808-1958.* Koblenz: Musik-Institut, 1958.

_____. "Franz Liszt in Kassel." *Kasseler Post,* 12 November 1941.

_____. "Franz Liszt in Mainz am 23. Juli 1840. Der Bericht über ein Konzert des genialen Künstlers und Piano-Phänomens." *Mainzer Journal* No. 247 (24 October 1931).

_____. "Liszt und die Hechenger Hofkapelle." *Hochzollern Blätter* No. 170 (30 July 1906).

Arnold, Ben, and Michael Saffle. "Liszt in Ireland (and Belgium): Reports from a Concert Tour." *Journal of the American Liszt Society* 26 (1989), pp. 3-11.

Atkinson, George Francklin. *Pictures from the North, in Pen and Pencil: Sketched During a Summer Ramble.* London: John Ollivier, 1848.

Auman, Elizabeth H., et al. *The Music Manuscripts, First Editions, and Correspondence of Franz Liszt (1811-1886) in the Collections of the Music Division, Library of Congress.* Washington, D.C.: Library of Congress, 1991.

Autexier, Philippe A. *Mozart & Liszt sub rosa.* Poitiers: Philippe A. Autexier, 1984.

_____. "Musique sans frontières? Les choix des programmes de Liszt pour ses concerts de la période virtuose." *Revue musicale* 405-406-407 (1987), pp. 297-305.

_____. "'Sein Forte gleicht dem Donner in den Gebirgen.' Franz Liszts Konzertbesuche in Frankfurt." *Frankfurter allgemeine Zeitung* ["Rhein-Main-Blatt"] No. 168 (24 July 1986), p. 23.

Bailey, George. *Germans: Biography of an Obsession.* New York: Discus, 1972.

Ballstaedt, Andreas, and Tobias Widmaier. *Salonmusik. Zur Geschichte und Funktion einer bürgerlichen Musikpraxis.* Beihefte zum Archiv für Musikwissenschaft, 27. Stuttgart: Franz Steiner, 1989.

Bárdos, Lájos. "Ferenc Liszt the Innovator." *Studia Musicologica* 17 (1975), pp. 3-38.

Barraclough, Geoffrey. *The Origins of Modern Germany.* New York: G. P. Putnam's Sons, 1963.

Bartels, Adolf. *Chronik des Weimarischen Hoftheaters, 1817-1907.* Weimar: Hermann Böhlaus, 1908.

Baser, Friedrich. *Grosse Musiker in Baden-Baden.* Baden-Baden: T. H. Schneider, 1973.

_____. *Musikheimat Baden-Württemberg: Tausend Jahre Musikentwicklung.* Freiburg i.B.: Atlantis, 1963.

Beattie, Dr. William. *Journal of a Residence in Germany, Written During a Professional Attendance on their Royal Highnesses the Duke and Duchess of Clarence during their Visits to the Courts of that Country in 1822, 1825, and 1826.* 2 vols. London: Longman, Rees, Orme, Brown & Green, 1831.

Bekker, Paul. "Franz Liszt Reconsidered," trans. Arthur Mendel. *Musical Quarterly* 28 (1942), pp. 186-189.

_____. "Liszt and His Critics." *Musical Quarterly* 22 (1936), pp. 277-283.

Bellas, Jacqueline. "Janin et Liszt, ou le critique et l'amitié." *Jules Janin et son temps: un moment du Romantisme.* Paris: PUF, 1974; pp. 61-84.

_____. "La tumulteuse amitié de Franz Liszt et de Maurice Schlesinger. Autour d'une correspondance inédite." *Littératures* [Toulouse] 12 (1965), pp. 7-20.

Bellinghausen, Hans. *Alt-Koblenz: Eine Sammlung heimatkundlicher Abhandlungen.* Koblenz: Krabbensche Buchdruckerei, 1932.

Berl, Heinrich. *Baden-Baden im Zeitalter der Romantik: Die literarische und musikalische Romantik des neunzehnten Jahrhunderts.* Baden-Baden: Willy Schmidt, 1981.

Berlioz, Hector. *Memoirs of Hector Berlioz from 1803 to 1865, Comprising his Travels in Germany, Italy, Russia, and England,* trans. Rachel (Scott Russell) Holmes and Eleanor Holmes; rev. Ernest Newman. New York: Tudor, 1932.

_____. *Memoirs,* trans. David Cairns. New York: Alfred A. Knopf, 1969.

Bernhardi, Theodor von. *Unter Nikolaus I. und Friedrich Wilhelm IV. Briefe und Tagebuchblätter aus den Jahren 1834-1857.* Leipzig: Hirzel, 1893.

Beyer, R. von. "Le voyage de Liszt à Berlin, d'aprés de vieux papiers de familie," trans. J. Payraube. *Revue musicale* ["Numéro special"] (1 May 1928), pp. 71-75.

Bibliographie der Zeitschriften des deutschen Sprachgebietes bis 1900. Vol. II: "Die Zeitschriften des deutschen Sprachgebietes von 1831 bis 1870," ed. Joachim Kirchner. Stuttgart 1977.

Bing, Anton. *Rückblicke auf die Geschichte des Frankfurter Stadttheaters:* Vol. 1: Das Frankfurter Stadttheater unter die ersten Aktionär-Gesellschaft, 1792-1842. Frankfurt a.M. 1892.

Blaze de Bury, The Baroness. *Germania: Germany as it is, or Personal Experiences of its Courts, Camps, and People, in Austria, Prussia, Bavaria, Bohemia, Hungary, Croatia, Servia, Italy, etc. Including Numerous Unpublished Anecdotes and Exclusive Information,* 2nd ed.; 2 vols. London: Henry Colburn, 1851.

Böhme, Helmut. *An Introduction to the Social and Economic History of Germany: Politics and Economic Change in the Nineteenth and Twentieth Centuries,* trans. W. R. Lee. New York: St. Martin's, 1978.

Bösken, Edmund. "Melchior Bernard Veltmann und die Begründung der öffentlichen Musikpflege in Osnabrück." *Osnabrücker Mitteilungen* 62 (1947), pp. 167-211.

Brand, C. M., and Karl Gustav Fellerer. *Beiträge zur Musikgeschichte der Stadt Aachen.* Beiträge zur rheinischen Musikgeschichte, 6. Cologne: Staufen, 1954.

Breidenstein, H. K. *Festgabe zur der am 12ten August 1845 stattfindenden Inauguration des Beethoven-Monuments.* Bonn: T. Habicht, 1845.

_____. *Festival Gift for the Inauguration of the Beethoven-Monument*, trans. Joan Morgan. *Liszt Saeculum* No. 27 (1981), pp. 28-41.

_____. *For the Anniversary of the Inauguration of the Beethoven Monument*, trans. Hilary Casson. *Liszt Saeculum* No. 31 (1983), pp. 23-49.

_____. *Zur Jahresfeier der Inauguration des Beethoven-Monuments.* Bonn: T. Habicht, 1846.

Briefe aus den Jahren 1830-1847 von Felix Mendelssohn-Bartholdy, ed. Julius Reitz. Leipzig: Hermann Mendelssohn, 1899.

Briefe hervorragender Zeitgenossen an Franz Liszt, ed. "La Mara" [pseud. Marie Lipsius]. 2 vols. Leipzig: Breitkopf & Härtel, 1895 and 1904.

Brown, Clive. *Louis Spohr: A Critical Biography.* London and New York: Cambridge University Press, 1984.

Buchner, Alexander. *Franz Liszt in Bohemia*, trans. Roberta Samsour. London: Nevill, 1962.

Burger, Ernst. *Franz Liszt: A Chronicle of his Life in Pictures and Documents*, trans. Stewart Spencer. Princeton, New Jersey: Princeton University Press, 1989.

Busoni, Ferruccio. *The Essence of Music*, trans. Rosamond Ley. London: Rockliff, 1957.

Calvert, George H. *First Years in Europe.* Boston: William v. Spencer, 1866.

Carrières, Marcel. *Franz Liszt en Provence et en Languedoc en 1844.* Beziers 1981.

Chiappari, Luciano. *La cinquecentesca Villa Abitata da Liszt a Monte S. Quirico di Lucca.* Ospedaletto 1991.

Chissell, Joan. *Clara Schumann, A Dedicated Spirit: A Study of her Life and Work.* London: Hamish Hamilton, 1983.

Chorley, Henry. *Modern German Music: Recollections and Criticism.* 2 vols. London: Smith, Elder; 1854.

Christern, J. W. *Franz Liszt. Nach seinem Leben und Werke aus authentischen Berichten dargestellt.* Hamburg: Schuberth, 1841.

Conati, Marcello. "Saggio di critiche e cronache verdiane delle 'Allgemeine musikalische Zeitung' di Lipsia (1840-48)." *Il*

Melodramma italiano dell'Ottocento. Studi e ricerche per Massimo Mila. Torino 1977; pp. 13-43.

Correspondance de Liszt et da la Comtesse d'Agout, ed. Daniel Ollivier. 2 vols. Paris: Bernard Grasset, 1933-1934.

Correspondance de Liszt et da sa fille Madame Emile Ollivier, 1842-1862, ed. Daniel Ollivier. Paris: Bernard Grasset, 1936.

Csatkai, André. "Versuch einer Franz-Liszt-Ikonographie." *Burgenländische Heimatblätter* 5/2 (1936), pp. 34-67.

Dalmonte, Rossana. *Franz Liszt: La vita, l'opera, i texti musicali.* Milan: Giangiacomo Feltrinelli, 1983.

Danek, Victor. "Liszt (and his Contemporaries) on Stamps." *Journal of the American Liszt Society* 23 (1988), pp. 3-18.

Das Fürstlich Fürstenbergische Hoftheater zu Donaueschingen, 1775-1850. Donaueschingen 1914.

Deaville, James. "Die Mainzer Musikkritik im Vormärz." *Mitteilungen der Arbeitsgemeinschaft für mittelrheinische Musikgeschichte* 42 (April 1981), pp. 63-88.

_____. *The Music Criticisms of Peter Cornelius.* 4 vols. Dissertation: Northwestern University, 1986.

Desmond, Robert W. *The Information Process: World News Reporting to the Twentieth Century.* Iowa City, Iowa: University of Iowa Press, 1978.

Die deutsche Presse. Verzeichniss der im Deutschen Reiche erschienenden Zeitungen und Zeitschriften. Vol. 1: "Politische Zeitungen, Amts-, Local- und Anzeigeblätter." Forbach: Robert Hupfer, 1885.

Die Projekte der Liszt-Forschung. Bericht über das internationale Symposion in Eisenstadt, 19.-21. Oktober 1989, ed. Detlef Altenburg and Gerhard J. Winkler. Wissenschaftliche Arbeiten aus dem Burgenland, 87. Eisenstadt 1991.

Dömling, Wolfgang. *Franz Liszt und seine Zeit.* Laaber: Laaber-Verlag, 1985.

Dörffel, Alfred. *Geschichte der Gewandhausconcerte zu Leipzig vom 25. November 1781 bis 25. November 1881.* Leipzig 1884.

Donath, Adolf. "Franz Liszt und Polen." *Liszt-Studien* 1 (1977), pp. 53-64.

Early Letters of Robert Schumann, Originally Published by His Wife, trans. May Herbert. London: George Bell & Sons, 1888.

Ebart, Paul von. *Hundert Jahre Coburgische Theatergeschichte III (1827-1927)*. Coburger Heimatkunde und Heimatgeschichte, 2. Coburg 1927.

Eckhardt, Mária. "A New Thematic Catalog of Liszt's Compositions." *Journal of the American Liszt Society* 27 (1990), pp. 53-55.

_____. "The Liszt Thematic Catalogue in Preparation: Results and Problems." *Studia Musicologica* 34 (1992), pp. 221-230.

_____. "Une femme simple, mére d'un génie européen: 'Anna Liszt / Quelques aspects d'une correspondance'." *Revue musicale* 405-406-407 (1987), pp. 199-214.

Eduard von Simson: Erinnerungen aus seinem Leben, ed. Bernhard von Simson. Leipzig 1900.

"Elf ungedruckte Briefe Liszts an Schott," ed. Edgar Istel. *Die Musik* 5 (1905-1906), pp. 43-52.

Ellmar, Paul. "Eck & Lefebre: Pianofortefabrik und Musikverlag. Cöln, Cäcilienstraße 40." *Jahrbuch des Kölnischen Geschichtsvereins* 33 (1958), pp. 221-233.

_____. "Franz Liszt und der Kölner Dom." *Kölnische Rundschau*, No. 12 (20 January 1957), "Der Sonntag," p. 5.

Engel, Carl. "Views and Reviews." *Musical Quarterly* 22 (1936), pp. 354-361.

Engel, Hans. *Musik in Thüringen*. Cologne and Graz: Böhlau, 1966.

Enssenhardt, Albert. *Das Lißt-ge Berlin*. 3 vols. Berlin 1842.

Fambach, Oscar. *Kalendarium der Jahre 1700 bis 2080. Mit einem Vorwort und einer Beigabe: Kalendar von an I-XIV nebst den Monatstagen der gregorianischen Zeitrechnung*. Bonn: Ludwig Röhrscheid, 1982.

"'Fantastic Cavalcade': Liszt's British Tours of 1840 & 1841 from the Diaries of John Orlando Parry." *Liszt Society Journal* 6 (1981), pp. 2-16; and 7 (1982), pp. 16-26.

Faulkner, Sir Arthur Brooke. *Visit to Germany and the Low Countries in the Years 1829, 30, and 31*. 2 vols. London: Richard Bentley, 1833.

Federhofer-Königs, Renate. *Wilhelm Joseph von Wasielewski im Spiegel seiner Korrespondenz*. Tutzing: Hans Schneider, 1975.

Felix Mendelssohn Bartholdy: Briefe an Deutsche Verleger, ed. Rudolf Elvers. Felix Mendelssohns Briefe, 1. Berlin: Walter de Gruyter, 1968.

Felix Mendelssohn: Letters, ed. G. Selden-Goth. New York: Pantheon, 1945.

Fellinger, Imogen. *Verzeichnis der Musikzeitschriften des 19. Jahrhunderts.* Regensburg: Gustav Bosse, 1968.

Fétis, François-Joseph. "Liszt und die Claviercomponisten der Neuzeit." *Blätter für Musik und Literatur* 2 (1841), pp. 117-121.

Fleckner, E. "Franz Liszt feierte seinen 30. Geburtstag auf der Rheininsel Nonnenwerth. Ein Beitrag zum 160. Geburtstag." *Mitteilungen der Arbeitsgemeinschaft für rheinische Musikgeschichte* 38 (1972), pp. 142-144.

Franz Liszt: Briefe aus ungarischen Sammlungen, 1835-1886, ed. Margit Prahács. Kassel: Bärenreiter, 1966.

Franz Liszt: Gesammelte Schriften, ed. Lina Ramann. 6 vols. Leipzig: Breitkopf & Härtel, 1881-1899.

Franz Liszt in seinen Briefen, ed. Hans Rudolf Jung. Frankfurt a.M.: Athenaeum, 1989.

"Franz Liszt's Briefe an den Fürsten Felix Lichnowsky," ed. Hans von Wolzogen. *Bayreuther Blätter* 30 (1907), pp. 25-48.

Franz Liszts Briefe an seine Mutter, ed. "La Mara" [pseud. Marie Lipsius]. Leipzig: Breitkopf & Härtel, 1918.

Franz Liszts Briefe, ed. "La Mara" [pseud. Marie Lipsius]. 8 vols. Leipzig: Breitkopf & Härtel, 1893-1905.

Franz Liszt: Unbekannte Presse und Briefe aus Wien, 1822-1886, ed. Dezsö Legány. Wiener musikwissenschaftliche Beiträge, 13. Vienna and Graz: Hermann Böhlaus, 1984.

Frenzl, Heinrich. "Der deutsche Franz Liszt." *Zeitschrift für Musik* 101 (January 1934), pp. 23-27.

Gause, Fritz. *Die Geschichte der Stadt Königsberg in Preussen.* Vol. II: "Von der Königskronung bis zum Ausbruch des ersten Weltkrieges." Ostmitteleuropa in Vergangenheit und Gegenwart, 10/II. Cologne and Graz: Böhlau, 1968.

Gavoty, Bernard. *Liszt: le virtuose, 1811-1848.* Paris: Julliard, 1980.

The German Tourist, ed. O. L. B. Wolff and H. Doering; trans. H. E. Lloyd. London: D. Nutt, 1837.

Geschichte der deutschen Länder, Vol. II: "Die deutschen Länder vom Wiener Kongreß bis zur Gegenwart," ed. Georg Wilhelm Sante. Würzburg: A. G. Ploetz, 1971.

Geschichte des Philharmonischen Vereins zu Königsberg i. Pr. von 1838 bis 1888, zur Feier des 50järigen Bestehens des Vereins. Königsberg: Hartungsche Buchdruckerei, 1888.

Giacomo Meyerbeer: Briefwechsel und Tagebücher, ed. Heinz Becker and Gudrun Becker. 3 vols. Berlin: Walter de Gruyter, 1960-1975.

Gleig, G[eorge] R[obert]. *Germany, Bohemia, and Hungary, Visited in 1837.* 3 vols. London: John W. Parker, 1839.

Göllerich, August. *Franz Liszt.* Berlin: Marquardt, 1908.

Goldschmidt, Robert, et al. *Die Stadt Karlsruhe: Ihre Geschichte und ihre Verwaltung.* Karlsruhe: C. F. Müller, 1915.

Gollmick, Carl. *Feldzüge und Streifereien im Gebiete der Tonkunst.* Darmstadt: Jonghaus, 1846.

Graevenitz, G. *Musik in Freiburg: Eine Darstellung Freiburger Musiklebens aus alter und neuer Zeit.* Freiburg i.B.: Poppen & Ortmann, 1938.

Graßmann, Antjekathrin, and Werner Neugebauer. *800 Jahre Musik in Lübeck. Zur Ausstellung im Museum am Dom aus Anlaß des Lübecker Musikfestes 1982.* Lübeck: Senat der Hansestadt Lübeck, 1982.

Gülke, Peter. "Musik und Musiker in Rudolstadt." Sonderdruck des *Rudolstadter Heimathefte* 9 (1963).

Günther, Leo. *Würzburger Chronik.* 3 vols. Vol. III: "Personen und Ereignisse von 1802-1848." Würzburg: Bonitas-Bauer, 1925.

Gut, Serge. *Franz Liszt.* Artigues-pré-Bordeaux: Delmas, 1989.

_____. "Nationalisme et supranationalisme chez Franz Liszt." *Revue musicale* 405-406-407 (1987), pp. 277-286.

_____. "A 'Reply' to Alan Walker." *Journal of the American Liszt Society* 30 (1991), pp. 48-57.

Gymnasio Tremoniensi quartum saeculum auspicanti p. XXIV. M. Aug. A. MDCCCXLIII. Hammone: Typus Schulzianus, ?1844.

Haering, Hermann, and Otto Hohenstatt. *Schwäbische Lebensbilder,* 2 vols. Stuttgart 1941.

Hagelweide, Gert. *Deutsche Zeitungsgestände in Bibliotheken und Archiven.* Düsseldorf 1974.

Hamburger, Klára. *Liszt,* trans. Gyula Gulyás; rev. Paul Merrick. Budapest: Corvina, 1987.

Hamilton, Kenneth. "Liszt Fantasizes — Busoni Excises: The Liszt-Busoni 'Figaro Fantasy'." *Journal of the American Liszt Society* 30 (1991), pp. 21-27.

Hansen, Bernard. "'Nonnenwerth.' Ein Beitrag zu Franz Liszts Liedkomposition." *Neue Zeitschrift für Musik* 122 (1961), pp. 391-394.

Haraszti, Emile. "Liszt à Paris: Quelques documents inédits," *Revue musicale* 165 (1936), pp. 241-258; and 167 (1936), pp. 5-16.

Hardege, Frohwalt. "Große Musiker in Göttingen." *Göttinger Jahrbuch* 2 (1953), p. 91.

Hartmann, Fritz. *Sechs Bücher Braunschweigischer Theatergeschichte.* Wolfenbüttel: Julius Zwißler, 1905.

Harzen-Müller, A. Niko. "Liszt, Wagner und Bülow in ihren Beziehungen zu Georg Herwegh." *Die Musik* 3-4 (1903-1904), pp. 355-366 and 448-457.

Hattingberg, Magda von. *Franz Liszts deutsche Sendung.* Vienna and Leipzig: Adolf Luser, 1938.

Heine, Heinrich. *Historisch-kritische Gesamgausgabe der Werke,* ed. Manfred Windfuhr et al. Vols. 13/1-14/1 ("Lutetia"), ed. Volkmar Hansen. Hamburg: Hoffmann & Campe, 1988 and 1990.

Heinemann, Ernst Günther. *Franz Liszts Auseinandersetzung mit der geistlichen Musik. Zum Komflikt zwischen Kunst und Engagement.* Musikwissenschaftliche Schriften, 12. Munich and Salzburg: Emil Katzbichler, 1978.

Hennenberg, Fritz. "Musikgeschichte der Stadt Leipzig im 19. und 20. Jahrhundert: Studien zur Methologie und Konzeption." *Beiträge zur Musikwissenschaft* 33 (1991), pp. 225-249 and 259-289.

Hennings, Johann, and Wilhelm Stahl. *Musikgeschichte Lübeck.* 2 vols. Kassel: Bärenreiter, 1951.

Henssler, Theodor Anton. *Das musikalische Bonn im 19. Jahrhundert.* Bonner Geschichtsblätter, 13. Bonn: Universitäts-Verlag, 1959.

Hertz, Frederick. *The German Public Mind in the Nineteenth Century: A Social History of German Political Sentiments, Aspirations, and Ideas.* Totowa, New Jersey: Rowman & Littlefield, 1975.

_____. *Nationality in History and Politics: A Psychology and Sociology of National Sentiment and Nationalism.* New York: Humanities Press, ?1966.

Heyden, Otto. *Das Kölner Theaterwesen im 19. Jahrhundert,
1814-1872*. Cologne: H. & J. Lechte, 1939.

Hill, S. S. *Travels on the Shores of the Baltic, Extended to Moscow*.
London: Arthur Hall, Virtue & Co., 1854.

"Hitherto Unpublished Material from Private Collections." *Liszt
Saeculum* 45 (1990), pp. 34-37.

Höcker, Karla. *Hauskonzerte in Berlin*. Berlin: Rembrandt, 1970.

Höslinger, Clemens. *Musik-Index zur "Wiener Zeitschrift für Kunst,
Literatur, Theater und Mode," 1816-1848*. Munich: Emil
Katzbichler, 1980.

Hofmann, A., and N. Missir. "Sur la tournée de concerts de Ferenc
Liszt en 1846-47 dans le Banat, la Transylvanie et les Pays
Roumains." *Studia Musicologica* 5 (1963), pp. 107-124.

Homburg, Herfried. "Kassel zu Füßen von Franz Liszt." *Hessische
Blätter* No. 16 (19 January 1962).

Hübner, Johannes. *Bibliographie des Schlesischen Musik- und
Theaterwesens*. Schlesische Bibliographie, 6. Breslau: Wilhelm
Gottlieb Korn, 1934.

Hughes, Robert. *The Shock of the New*. New York: Alfred A. Knopf,
1988.

Huschke, Konrad. *Unsere Tonmeister unter Einander* [sic]. Vol. III:
"Robert Schumann's Beziehungen zu Felix Mendelssohn-
Bartholdy, Richard Wagner, und Franz Liszt." Pritzwalk: Adolf
Tienken, 1928.

Huschke, Wolfram. *Musik im klassischen und nachklassischen
Weimar, 1756-1861*. Weimar: Hermann Böhlaus, 1982.

Hysel, Franz Eduard. *Das Theater in Nürnberg von 1612 bis 1863*.
Nuremberg: Franz Eduard Hysel, 1863.

Ihle, Ernst. "Liszt-Besuche und Liszt-Konzerte in Baden-Baden."
Badeblatt mit amtlicher Hauptfremdenliste No. 140/1 (19 June
1926).

Irmen, Hans-Josef. "Franz Liszt in Bonn: oder, wie die erste
Beethovenhalle entstand." *Studien zur Bonner Musikgeschichte
des 18. und 19. Jahrhunderts*, ed. Marianne Bröcker and Günther
Massenkeil. Beiträge zur rheinischen Musikgeschichte, 116.
Cologne: Arno Volk, 1978; pp. 49-65.

Jacobs, Emil. "Franz Liszt und die Gräfin d'Agoult in Nonnenwerth,
1841-1842." *Die Musik* 11/1-2 (October 1911), pp. 34-45 and
93-112.

Jäcksch, E. "Franz Liszt in Rudolstadt." *Rudolstadter Heimathefte* 7 (1961), pp. 271-274.

Jagemann, Ludwig von. *Deutsche Städte und Deutsche Männer. Nebst Betrachtungen über Kunst, Leben und Wissenschaft. Reiseskizzen*, rev. ed.; 2 vols. Leipzig: S. Berger, 1846.

James, Harold. *A German Identity, 1770-1990.* New York: Routledge, 1989.

Jameson, [Mrs.] Anna Brownell Murphy. *Visits and Sketches at Home and Abroad.* 3rd ed.; 2 vols. London: Saunders & Otley, 1839.

"J. B." "Lisztiana. Liszt in Schlesien." *Neue Musikzeitung* 33 (1912), p. 462.

Johnsson, Bengt. "Liszt og Danmark." *Dansk Tidsskrift* 37 (1962), pp. 79-82; and 38 (1963), pp. 81-86.

_____. "Modernities in Liszt's Works." *Svensk Tidskrift for Musikforsking* 46 (1964), pp. 83-117.

Joss, Victor. *Der Musikpädagoge Friedrich Wieck und seine Familie.* Leipzig: Damm, 1902.

Kabisch, Thomas. *Liszt und Schubert.* Berliner musikwissenschaftliche Arbeiten, 23. Munich: Emil Katzbichler, 1984.

Kapp, Julius. *Franz Liszt.* Berlin: Schuster & Loeffler, 1909.

_____. "Franz Liszt und Robert Schumann." *Die Musik* 13/2 (November 1914), pp. 67-85.

Kárpáti, János. "Liszt the Traveller." *New Hungarian Quarterly* 27/103 (1986), pp. 108-118.

Kaufmann, Paul. "Franz Liszt am Rhein." *Die Musik* 26 (1933), pp. 118-121.

_____. "Franz Liszt am Rhein. Unter Benutzung ungedruckter Briefe." *Das schaffende Rhein* [Koblenz] 7 (1931), pp. 44-55.

Keeling, Geraldine. "Liszt and the Legion of Honor." *Liszt Society Journal* 10 (1985), p. 29.

_____. "Liszt Pianos: Années de pèlerinage." *Liszt Society Journal* 10 (1985), pp. 12-20.

_____. "The Liszt Pianos — Some Aspects of Preference and Technology." *New Hungarian Quarterly* 27/104 (Winter 1986), pp. 220-232.

_____. "Liszt's Appearances in Parisian Concerts: 1824-1844." *Liszt Society Journal* 11 (1986), pp. 22-34; and 12 (1987), pp. 8-22.

Keiler, Alan. "Liszt Research and Walker's Liszt." *Musical Quarterly* 70 (1984), pp. 374-403.

Kempe, Friedrich. *Franz Liszt. Richard Wagner. Aphoristiche Memoiren und biographische Rhapsodien.* Eisleben: F. Kuhnt, 1852.

Kerner, Justinus. *Briefwechsel mit seinen Freunden,* ed. Theobald Kerner. Stuttgart: Justinus Kerner, 1897.

Kienzle, Michael. "Ein Liszt-Autograph in Donaueschengen." *Liszt Information. Communication. European Liszt-Center* 12 (1982), pp. 10-12.

Klee, Wolfgang. *Preußische Eisenbahngeschichte.* Stuttgart: W. Kohlhammer, 1982.

Klusen, Ernst et al. *Das Musikleben der Stadt Krefeld, 1780-1840.* 2 vols. Together: Beiträge zur rheinischen Musikgeschichte, 124. Cologne: Arno Volk, 1979. [Vol. I was originally published in 1938.]

Kobschantzky, Hans. *Streckenatlas der deutschen Eisenbahnen, 1835-1892.* Düsseldorf: Alba Buchverlag, 1967.

Koch, Lajos. *Liszt Ferenc bibliográfiai kisérlet / Franz Liszt: ein bibliographischer Versuch.* Budapest: Stadtbibliothek, 1936.

Körner, Klaus. *Das Musikleben in Köln um die Mitte des 19. Jahrhunderts.* Beiträge zur rheinischen Musikgeschichte, 83. Cologne: Arno Volk, 1969.

Krämer, Hans Joachim. "Ein denkwürdiges Konzert im Ludwigsburg des vorigen Jahrhunderts. Franz Liszt spielte am 17. November 1843 im Ludwigsburger 'Waldhorn'." *Ludwigsburger Geschichtsblätter* 40 (1987), pp. 191-196.

_____. "Franz Liszt in Ludwigsburg." *Ludwigsburger Kreiszeitung* No. 173 (31 July 1987).

Krautz, Rudolf. *Das Stuttgarter Hoftheater von den ältesten Zeiten bis zur Gegenwart.* Stuttgart: J. B. Metzler, 1908.

Kroll, Erwin. *Musikstadt Königsberg. Geschichte und Erinnerungen.* Freiburg i.B.: Atlantis, 1966.

Kross, Siegfried. "Aus der Frühgeschichte von Robert Schumanns 'Neuen Zeitschrift für Musik'." *Die Musikforschung* 34 (1981), pp. 423-445.

Lee, Alan J. *The Origins of the Popular Press, 1855-1914.* London: Croom Helm, 1976.

Legge, J. G. *Rhyme and Revolution in Germany: A Study in German History, Life, Literature, and Character, 1813-1850.* London: Constable, 1919.

Lehrs, K. "Franz Liszt. Ehrendoctor der philosophischen Facultät der Universität zu Königsberg." *Wissenschaftliche Monats-Blätter* [Königsberg] 4 (1876), pp. 175-176.

Leonhard, K[arl] G[ustav] von. *Aus unserer Zeit in meinem Leben.* 2 vols. Stuttgart: C. Schweizerbart, 1854-1856.

Letters of Franz Liszt, ed. "La Mara" [pseud. Marie Lipsius]; trans. Constance Bache. 2 vols. New York; Charles Schribners Sons, 1894.

Lewald, Fanny. *Meine Lebensgeschichte,* several vols. Berlin: Otto Janke, 1861-?.

Liszt Ferenc válogatott levelei. Ifjúság —virtuóz évek — Weimar (1824-1861), ed. Mária Eckhardt. Budapest: Zenemükiádó, 1990.

Liszt, Franz. *An Artist's Journey: Lettres d'un bachelier ès musique,* trans. Charles Suttoni. Chicago and New York: University of Chicago Press, 1989.

_____. *Die Gräberinsel der Fürsten zu Gotha* for solo piano; ed. Friedrich Schnapp. Budapest: Editio Musica, 1983. Plate Z.12 786.

_____. *Kantata zur Inauguration des Beethoven-Monuments zu Bonn,* ed. Günther Massenkeil. Frankfurt a.M. and New York: C. F. Peters, 1986.

"Liszt's British Tours: Reviews and Letters." *Liszt Society Journal* 8 (1983), pp. 2-8.

Little, William A. "Mendelssohn and Liszt." *Mendelssohn Studies,* ed. R. Larry Todd. Cambridge and New York: Cambridge University Press, 1992; pp. 106-125.

Litzmann, Berthold. *Clara Schumann: Ein Künstlerleben. Nach Tagebüchen und Briefen.* 3 vols. Leipzig: Breitkopf & Härtel, 1920.

Lübke, Wilhelm. *Lebenserinnerungen.* Berlin 1893.

Luppa, Julius. *Die Geschichte des Solinger Musiklebens im 19. Jahrhundert.* Dissertation: Universität Münster, 1933.

Mallon, Otto. "Bettina von Arnim und Franz Liszt. Ungedruckte Briefe." *Kölnische Zeitung* No. 398b (23 July 1929).

Mann, Golo. *The History of Germany Since 1789,* trans. Marian Jackson. New York: Frederick A. Praeger, 1968.

Mann, Michael. *Heinrich Heines Musikkritiken.* Hoffmann und Campe: Heinrich Heine Verlag, 1971.

Mansfield, Robert Blackford. *The Log of the Water Lily (Thames Gig) during Two Cruises in the Summers of 1851-2 on the Rhine,*

Neckar, Main, Moselle, Danube, and other Streams of Germany,
2nd rev. ed. London: Nathaniel Cooke, 1854.

Marggraf, Wolfgang. *Franz Liszt in Weimar.* Weimar: Tradition und
Gegenwart, 23. Weimar: Buchdruckerei Weimar, 1972.

Martin, Peter. *Salon Europas: Baden-Baden im 19. Jahrhundert.*
Konstanz: Friedrich Stadler, 1983.

Marwinski, Felicitas. *Zeitungen und Wochenblätter* [in Weimar].
Weimar: Nationale Forschungs- und Gedenkstätten, 1968.
Typescript.

Massenkeil, Günther. "Die Bonner Beethoven-Kantata (1845) von
Franz Liszt." *Die Sprache der Musik: Festschrift Klaus Wolfgang
Niemöller zum 60. Geburtstag*, ed. Jobst Peter Fricke. Kölner
Beiträge zur Musikforschung, 165. Regensburg: Gustav Bosse,
1986; pp. 381-399.

Meidinger, Heinrich. *Frankfurt's gemeinnüßige Anstalten. Eine
historisch-statistische Darstellung* . . . Frankfurt a.M.: Heinrich
Ludwig Brönner, 1845.

Mericka, Václav. *Orders and Decorations.* London: Paul Hamlyn,
1967.

Michel, Paul. "Tuchtig und glanzend: Hundert-jährigen Jubiläum des
Musikhochschule 'Franz Liszt' in Weimar." *Musik und
Gesellschaft* 22 (1972), pp. 449-456.

Mirus, Adolf. *Das Liszt-Museum zu Weimar und seine Erinnerungen.*
3rd edition. Leipzig: Breitkopf & Härtel, 1892.

Mohr, Albert Richard. *Musikleben in Frankfurt am Main.* Frankfurt:
Waldemar Kramer, 1976.

Morazé, Charles. *The Triumph of the Middles Classes: A Political and
Social History of Europe in the Nineteenth Century.* Garden City,
New York: Anchor, 1968.

Morelli, Giovanni. "Forms of Popularization of Music in the 19th
Century and Up to World War I." *Acta Musicologica* 59/1 (1987),
pp. 16-25.

Müller-Dombois, Richard. *Die fürstlich Lippische Hofkapelle:
Kulturhistorische, finanzwirtschaftliche und soziologische
Untersuchung eines Orchesters im 19. Jahrhundert.* Regensburg:
Gustav Bosse, 1972.

Müller von Asow, E. H. "Hermann Cohen, ein Lieblingsschüler Franz
Liszts." *Österreichische Musikzeitschrift* 16 (1961), pp. 443-452.

Münzer, Georg. "Eine Liszt-Karikatur." *Die Musik* 5/3 (1905-1906),
pp. 53-55.

Musikalische Rheinromantik. Bericht über die Jahrestagung 1985, ed. Siegfried Kross. Beiträge zur rheinischen Musikgeschichte, 140. Berlin and Kassel: Merseburger, 1989.

Neumann, W. *Franz Liszt. Eine Biographie*. Kassel: Ernst Balde 1855.

Newman, Ernest. *The Life of Richard Wagner*. London and New York: Alfred A. Knopf, 1933-1940.

_____. *The Man Liszt: A Study of the Tragi-comedy of a Soul Divided Against Itself*. London: Cassell, 1934.

Newman, William S. "Liszt's Interpreting of Beethoven's Piano Sonatas." *Musical Quarterly* 58 (1972), pp. 185-209.

Noyes, P. H. *Organization and Revolution: Working-class Associations in the German Revolutions of 1848-1849*. Princeton, New Jersey: Princeton University Press, 1966.

Oberschelp, Jürgen. *Das offentliche Musikleben der Stadt Bielefeld im 19. Jahrhundert*. Kölner Beiträge zur Musikforschung, 66. Regensburg: Gustav Bosse, 1972.

Oepen, Heinz. *Beiträge zur Geschichte des Kölner Musiklebens, 1760-1840*. Beiträge zur rheinischen Musikgeschichte, 10. Cologne: Arno Volk, 1955.

Ott, Bertrand. *Lisztian Keyboard Energy: An Essay on the Pianism of Franz Liszt*, trans. Donald H. Windham. Lewiston, New York: Edwin Mellen, 1992.

Otto, Ulrich. *Die historisch-politischen Lieder und Karikaturen des Vormärz und der Revolution von 1848/1849*. Cologne: Pahl-Rugenstein, 1982.

Passarge, Ludwig. *Ein ostpreußisches Jugendleben: Erinnerungen und Kulturbilder*, 2nd rev. ed. Leipzig: B. Elischer, 1906.

Perényi, Eleanor. *Liszt: The Artist as Romantic Hero*. Boston: Little, Brown, 1974.

Peth, Jakob. *Geschichte des Theaters und der Musik zu Mainz: Ein Beitrag zur deutschen Theatergeschichte*. Mainz: H. Prickarts, 1879.

Pfeiffer, Harald. *Heidelberger Musikleben in der ersten Hälfte des 19. Jahrhunderts*. Heidelberg: Brigitte Guderjahn, 1989.

Pieper, Carl. "Meister der Töne in Krefeld." *Die Heimat* [Krefeld] 13 (1934), p. 217.

Pisk, Paul. "Elements of Impressionism and Atonality in Liszt's Last Piano Pieces." *Radford Review* 23 (1969), pp. 171-176.

Plantinga, Leon B. *Schumann as Critic*. New Haven, Connecticut: Yale University Press, 1967.

Plevka, Bohumil. *Liszt a Praha*. Prague: Sopraphon, 1986.

Porter, Cecilia Hopkins. "The 'Rheinlieder' Critics: A Case of Musical Nationalism." *Musical Quarterly* 63 (1977), pp. 74-98.

Prosky, M. von. *Das Herzogliche Hoftheater zu Dessau. In seinen Anfängen bis zur Gegenwart*, 2nd ed. Dessau: Paul Baumann, 1894.

Putnam, George Palmer. *A Pocket Memorandum Book During a Ten Weeks' Trip to Italy and Germany in 1847*. Privately printed in 20 copies.

Raabe, Peter. *Franz Liszt*, rev. Felix Raabe. 2 vols. Tutzing: Hans Schneider, 1968.

_____. *Großherzog Carl Alexander und Liszt*. Leipzig: Breitkopf & Härtel, 1918.

_____. "Liszts erste Begegnung mit Leipzig: Auch ein Kapitel Gewandhausgeschichte," *Leipziger Neue Nachrichten*, 16 December 1931.

Rabes, Lennart. "Franz Liszt — The Freemason." *Arts Quatuor Coronatorum: Transactions of Quatuor Coronati Lodge No. 2076* [Herfordshire] 96 (November 1984), pp. 140-145.

_____. "Franz Liszt the Freemason." *Liszt Saeculum* 32 (1983), pp. 22-57; and 33 (1984), pp. 10-22.

Ramann, Lina. *Franz Liszt als Künstler und Mensch*. 3 vols. [often bound as 2]. Leipzig: Breitkopf & Härtel, 1880-1894.

_____. *Lisztiana: Erinnerungen an Franz Liszt in Tagebuchblättern, Briefen und Dokumenten aus den Jahren 1873-1886/87*, ed. Arthur Seidl and Friedrich Schnapp. Mainz and New York: Schott, 1983.

Rand McNally Historical Atlas of the World. Chicago: Rand McNally, 1981.

Reges, B. *Geschichte der Loge zur Einigkeit zu Frankfurt a.M., 1742-1892*. Frankfurt a.M.: R. Mahlau, 1892.

Rehberg, Elfriede, et al. *Deutsche Eisenbahnen, 1835-1985*. Berlin: VEB Verlag für Verkehrswesen, 1985.

Rehm, Jürgen. *Zur Musikrezeption im vormärzlichen Berlin. Die Präsentation bürgerlichen Selbstverständnisses und biedermeierlicher Kunstanschauung in den Musikkritiken Ludwig Rellstabs*. Studien zur Musikwissenschaft, 2. Hildesheim: Georg Olms, 1983.

Reinecke, Carl. "Erinnerungen an Franz Liszt." *Neue Zeitschrift für Musik* 78 (1911), pp. 570-573.

Reis, Eduard. *Mainz wie es ist, oder neues und vollständiges Panorama von Mainz (Ein Führer für Fremde u[nd] Einheimische).* Mainz: S. Hellermann, 1844.

Rellstab, Ludwig. *Franz Liszt. Beurteilungen — Berichte — Lebensskizze.* Berlin: Trautwein, 1842.

_____. *Musikalische Beurteilungen.* Leipzig 1848.

Rieger, Eva. "So schlecht wie ihr Ruf? Die Liszt-Biographin Lina Ramann." *Neue Zeitschrift für Musik* 147/7-8 (July-August 1986), pp. 16-20.

Rieple, Max. *Musik in Donaueschingen.* Donaueschingen 1959.

Rodes, John E. *Germany: A History.* New York: Holt, Rinehart & Winston, 1964.

Rosen, Charles. Review. *New York Review of Books* 31/6 (12 April 1842), pp. 17-20.

Rosenthal, Albi. "Franz Liszt and his Publishers." *Liszt Saeculum* 38 (1986), pp. 3-40.

Rücker, Curt. *Daten zur Musikgeschichte der Stadt Weimar.* Weimar: Fritz Fink, 1935.

Saffle, Michael. *Franz Liszt: A Guide to Research.* Garland Composer Resource Manuals, 29. New York: Garland Publishing, 1991.

_____. "Liszt in Germany: Problems and Discoveries." *Mitteilungen der Alexander von Humboldt-Stiftung* 48 (December 1986), pp. 15-23.

_____. "Liszt Research Since 1936: A Bibliographic Survey." *Acta Musicologica* 58 (1986), pp. 231-281.

_____. "Liszt's Reputation: The Role of 'Rezeptionsästhetik'." *Atti del XIV Congresso della Società Internazionale di Musicologia: Trasmissione e recezione delle forme di cultura musicale,* ed. Lorenzo Bianconi et al. Bologna: EDT, 1989; Vol. III ["Free Papers"], pp. 805-810.

_____. "The 'Liszt-Year' 1986 and Recent Liszt Research." *Acta Musicologica* 59/3 (September-December 1987), pp. 271-299.

Salmon, Lucy Maynard. *The Newspaper and the Historian.* London and New York: Oxford University Press, 1923.

Sampson, Henry. *A History of Advertising from the Earliest Times.* London: Chatto & Windus, 1874.

Sanden, Katharina von. "Franz Liszt und Bettina von Arnim."
Vossische Zeitung (8 April 1933).

Schaal, Richard. *Das Schrifttum zur musikalischen Lokalgeschichts-
Forschung.* Kassel: Bärenreiter, 1947.

Schäfer, Adelheid. *Hessische Zeitungen. Bestandsnachweis für die bis
1950 im Gebeit des ehemaligen Großherzogtums und Volksstaats
Hessen erschienen Zeitungen.* Darmstädter Archivschriften, 4.
Darmstadt: Historische Verein für Hessen, 1978.

Schäfer, H. L. "Franz Liszt in Detmold. Ein Blick in die
Vergangenheit." *Lippische Blätter für Heimatkunde* No. 1 (1972).

Schiedermair, Ludwig. *Musik am Rheinstrom. Entwicklungen und
Wesenheiten, Gestalten und Schickale.* Cologne: Staufen, 1947.

Schilling, Gustav. *Franz Liszt: Sein Leben und Wirken aus nächster
Beschauung.* Stuttgart: A. Stoppani, 1844.

_____. *Für Freunde der Tonkunst. Kleine Schriften vermischten
Inhalte.* Kißingen: G. F. Köpplinger, 1845.

Schlözer, Kurd von. *Römische Briefe, 1864-1869,* 2nd ed. Stuttgart:
Deutsche Verlags-Anstalt, 1913.

Schmidt, Rolf Diedrich, and Hans-Peter Kosack. *Bibliographie der
Landesbeschreibungen und Regionalatlanten Deutschlands.*
Berichte zur deutschen Landeskunde, "Sonderheft 14." Bonn-Bad
Godesberg: Bundesforschunganstalt für Landeskunde und
Raumordnung, 1972.

Schmitt-Thomas, Reinhold. *Die Entwicklung der deutschen
Konzertkritik im Spiegel der Leipziger "Allgemeinen musikalischen
Zeitung" (1798-1848).* Frankfurt a.M. 1969.

Schnapp, Friedrich. "Unbekannte Briefe Franz Liszts. Zum 40.
Todestag des Meisters veröffentlicht." *Die Musik* 18 (1926), pp.
717-732.

_____. "Verschollene Kompositionen Franz Liszts." *Vom
deutscher Tonkunst: Festschrift zu Peter Raabes 70. Geburtstag,*
ed. Alfred Morgenroth. Leipzig: C. F. Peters, 1942; pp. 119-152.

Scholcz, Peter. "Liszts eerste concerten in Nederland, 1842." *EPTA
Piano Bulletin* [special Liszt number] (1986), pp. 20-29.

Schoor, Hans. *Dresden: Vierhundert Jahre deutsche Musikkultur.*
Dresden: Verlags-Gesellschaft, n.d.

Schorn, Karl. *Lebenserinnerungen. Ein Beitrag zur Geschichte des
Rheinlands im neunzehnten Jahrhundert.* 2 vols. Bonn: F.
Hanstein, 1898.

Schreiber, F. J. A. *Andenken. Dr. Franz Liszt und dessen Anweisenheit in Breslau.* Breslau: G. Günther, 1843.

Schrickel, Leonhard. *Geschichte des Weimarer Theaters.* Weimar: Panses, 1928.

Schünemann, Georg. *Die Singakademie zu Berlin, 1791-1941.* Regensburg: Gustav Bosse, 1941.

Schulz, Klaus. *Münchener Theaterzettel, 1807-1982.* Munich: K. G. Saur, 1982.

Schusteritsch, E. "Lieben Sie Liszt? Zum seinem 150. Geburtstag — Seinerzeit im Schwabenland begeistert aufgenommener Gast." *Stuttgarter Zeitung,* 20 October 1961.

Schweitzer, Philipp. *Darmstädter Musikleben im 19. Jahrhundert.* Darmstadt: Justus von Liebig, 1975.

Searle, Humphrey. *The Music of Liszt,* rev. ed. New York: Dover, 1966.

_____, and Sharon Winklhofer. Catalog of Liszt's Compositions. *Chopin, Schumann, Liszt.* The New Grove Early Romantic Masters, 1. New York and London: W. W. Norton, 1985; pp. 322-368.

Serauky, Walter. *Musikgeschichte der Stadt Halle II.* Beiträge zur Musikforschung, 8. Halle: Max Niemeyer, 1942.

Sheehan, James J. *German History, 1770-1866.* Oxford: Clarendon Press, 1989.

_____. *German Liberalism in the Nineteenth Century.* Chicago and London: University of Chicago Press, 1978.

Shelley, [Mrs.] Mary Wollstonecroft. *Rambles in Germany and Italy in 1840, 1842, and 1843.* 2 vols. London: Edward Moxon, 1844.

Sievers, Heinrich. *Hannoversche Musikgeschichte.* 2 vols. Tutzing: Hans Schneider, 1984.

_____, A. Trapp, and A. Schum. *250 Jahre Braunschweigisches Staatstheater.* Braunschweig 1941.

Sittard, Josef. *Geschichte des Musik- und Concertwesens in Hamburg vom 14. Jahrhundert bis auf die Gegenwart.* Leipzig: A. C. Reher, 1890.

Smart, Sir George. *Leaves from the Journals of Sir George Smart,* ed. H. Bertram Cox and C. L. E. Cox. London: Longmans, Green & Co., 1907.

Smith, Anthony. *The Newspaper: An International History.* London: Thames & Hudson, 1979.

Snigurowicz, Diane. *RIPM: The Musical Examiner, 1842-1844*. Ann Arbor: UMI Press, 1992.

Spencer, E. [pub. pseud. as "An Englishman residing in Germany"]. *Sketches of Germany and the Germans, with a Glance at Poland, Hungary, & Switzerland, in 1834, 1835, and 1836*. 2 vols. London: Whittaker, 1836.

Speyer, Edward. *Wilhelm Speyer der Liederkomponist, 1790-1870: Sein Leben und Verkehr mit seinem Zeitgenossen*. Munich: Drei Masken, 1925.

Spohr, Louis [Ludwig]. *Autobiography*. New York: Schuberth, c. 1864.

Sprunger-Menke Hand-Atlas für die Geschichte des Mittelalters und der neueren Zeit, 3rd ed. Gotha 1880.

Steinacker, D. *Abklang der Aufklärung und Widerall der Romantik in Braunschweig*. Braunschweig 1939.

Stern, Nanni. "Ein Liszt-Konzert in Brieg." *Briegische Heimatblätter* (1927), p. 34.

Stevenson, Robert. "Liszt in the Iberian Peninsula, 1844-1845." *Inter-American Music Review* 7/2 (Spring-Summer 1986), pp. 3-22.

Stockhammer, Robert. *Franz Liszt im Triumphzug durch Europa*. Vienna: Österreichischer Bundesverlag, 1986.

Strang, John. *Germany in MDCCCXXXI*. 2 vols. London: John Macrone, 1836.

Suttoni, Charles. *Liszt Correspondence in Print: An Expanded, Annotated Bibliography*. Entire issue of the *Journal of the American Liszt Society* 25 (1989).

Taylor, A. J. P. *The Course of German History: A Survey of the Development of Germany since 1815*. New York: Coward-McCann, 1946.

Tenbrock, Robert-Hermann. *A History of Germany*, trans. Paul J. Dine. Munich and Paderborn 1968.

Thackery, William Makepeace. *Vanity Fair*, ed. J. L. M. Stewart. London: Penguin Books, 1968.

Tierney, Tadgh. *The Story of Hermann Cohen: From Franz Liszt to John of the Cross*. Oxford: Teresian, n.d.

Torkewitz, Dieter. *Harmonisches Denken im Frühwerk Franz Liszts*. Freiburger Schriften zur Musikwissenschaft, 10. Munich: Emil Katzbichler, 1978.

Traini, Carlo. *Giovan Battista Rubini: Re dei tenori*. Milano: Cura del Comitato per la celebrazione centenaria, 1954.

Traub, Hans, et al. *Standortskatalog wichtiger Zeitungsbestände in deutschen Bibliotheken*. Leipzig 1933; rev. Stuttgart 1974.

Treitschke, Heinrich von. *History of Germany in the Nineteenth Century*, trans. Eden and Cedar Paul; ed. Gordon A. Craig. Chicago and London: University of Chicago Press, 1975.

Trollope, Mrs. [Frances (Milton)]. *Belgium and Western Germany in 1833, including Visits to Baden-Baden, Wiesbaden, Cassel, Hanover, the Harz Mountains, etc., etc.*. 2 vols. London: John Murray, 1834.

Ubbens, Wilbert. *Zeitungen und zeitungsähnliche Periodika. Original- und Mikrofilmbestäde: 1. Dezember 1982*. Materialien der Staats- und Universitätsbibliothek Bremen, 1. Bremen: Staats- und Universitätsbibliothek, 1982.

Valentin, Veit. *The German People: Their History and Civilization from the Holy Roman Empire to the Third Reich*. New York: Alfred A. Knopf, 1946.

Vander Linden, A. "Liszt en la Belgique." *Studia Musicologica* 11 (1969), pp. 281-290.

Vogler, Rudolf. *Die Musikzeitschrift "Signale für die musikalische Welt," 1843-1900*. Regensburg: Gustav Bosse, 1975.

Wagner, Heinrich. "Unter Künstler und Künstlerinnen im Kursaal." *Emser Fremdenliste*, 10 July 1926.

Wagner, Richard. *Mein Leben*. Munich: Paul List, 1963.

Walker, Alan. *Franz Liszt: The Virtuoso Years, 1811-1847*, rev. ed. Cornell: Cornell University Press, 1987; and New York: Alfred A. Knopf, 1990.

_____. *Franz Liszt: The Weimar Years, 1848-1861*. New York: Alfred A. Knopf, 1989.

_____. "Serge Gut's *Liszt*." *Journal of the American Liszt Society* 26 (1989), pp. 37-51.

_____. "Schumann, Liszt, and the C Major Fantasie, Op. 17: A Declining Relationship." *Music & Letters* 60 (1979), pp. 156-166.

Walter, Friedrich. *Mannheim in Vergangenheit und Gegenwart*. 2 vols. Mannheim 1907.

Watson, Derek. *Liszt*. New York: Schirmer, 1989.

Weber, Carl Julius. *Deutschland, oder Briefe eines in Deutschland reisenden Deutschen*. 4 vols. Stuttgart: Hallberger'sche Verlagshandlung, 1849.

Weckbach, Hubert. "Als Franz Liszt in Heilbronn spielte. Der groß Klaviervirtuoso gab 1843 im Gasthof 'Zum Falken' ein Konzert." *Die Heilbronner Stimme* ["Schwaben und Franken"] 29/3 (March 1983), pp. 1-3.

Wedne, Peter. *Radikalismus im Vormärz. Untersuchungen zur politischen Theorie der frühen deutschen Demokratie.* Frankfurter historische Abhandlungen, 11. Wiesbaden: Franz Steiner, 1975.

Weilguny, Hedwig. *Das Liszthaus in Weimar,* 6th ed. Weimar 1973.

Weissman, Adolf. *Berlin als Musikstadt: Geschichte der Oper und des Konzerts von 1740 bis 1911.* Berlin: Schuster & Loeffler, 1911.

Wiener allgemeine Musik-Zeitung, 1841-1848 [RIPM guide], ed. James Deaville, with Beverly J. Sing. Ann Arbor, Michigan: UMI Research Press, 1989.

Wilkey, Edward. *Wanderings in Germany; with Moonlight Walks on the Banks of the Elbe, the Danube, the Neckar, and the Rhine.* London: Ball, Arnold, 1839.

Williams, Adrian. *Portrait of Liszt by Himself and his Contemporaries.* Oxford: Clarendon Press, 1990.

Willis, N[athaniel] Parker. *Rural Letters and other Records of Thought at Leisure, written in the intervals of more Hurried Literary Labor.* Detroit: Kerr, Doughty & Lapham, 1853.

Wolff, G. L. B., and H. Doering. *The German Tourist,* trans. H. E. Lloyd. London: D. Nutt, 1837.

Wright, William. "New Letters of Liszt," *Journal of the American Liszt Society* 31 (1992), pp. 7-33.

Yerushalmi, Ophra. "A Liszt Letter to Alexandre Weill (Frankfurt 1842)." *Journal of the American Liszt Society* 30 (1991), pp. 71-73.

Zeitung und Bibliothek: Ein Wegweiser zur Sammlungen und Literatur, ed. Gert Hagelweide. Pullach bei Müchen: Verlag Dokumentation, 1974.

Zellner, Eduard. *Ausgewählte Briefe von David Friedrich Strauß.* Bonn: Eduard Strauß, 1895.

Ziegler, Karl. *Dramaturgische Blätter.* Lemgo 1861.

Index

Only Chapters I-V and Appendices B and F are indexed fully below. Appendix C is indexed *only* for place names, names of performers other than Liszt, and titles of compositions. Appendices D-E are indexed *only* for titles of periodical sources. Nothing but *abbreviated* titles of compositions—e.g., "Archduke" for Beethoven's Op. 97 Trio; "Don Juan" for Liszt's *Réminiscences de Don Juan*, and so on—are indexed for Appendix F. (Abbreviated titles are also employed throughout the index below.) With regard to Chapters I-V: authors and/or titles of secondary sources are indexed *only* when cited for the first time or evaluated as sources; many secondary sources are identified fully *only* in the bibliography. Frequently cited nineteenth-century newspaper and magazine sigla and titles are identified fully *only* in Appendix A.

Maps, plates, and musical examples in Chapters I-V are identified below by page number(s) in **bold** type. Cities and towns where Liszt performed (as cataloged in Table 1 and Appendix C), frequently-performed compositions (as cataloged in Table 2), and nineteenth-century source materials drawn upon in Appendices D-E are all identified below by page number(s) in *italic* type.